MATERIALS MANAGEMENT

Prof. K.K. Ahuja
BSc. B.E. (Hons) Mech.
P.G.D.M.M., P.G.D.P.M. & I.R., M.B.A.
MIB; D.L.L. Advance Course in Management; Oxford U.K.

CBS
CBS Publishers & Distributors Pvt. Ltd.
New Delhi • Bengaluru • Chennai • Kochi • Kolkata • Mumbai
Hyderabad • Uttarakhand • Nagpur • Patna • Pune • Jharkhand

ISBN: 81-239-0065-1

First Edition: 1992
Reprint: 1999, 2008, 2009, 2011, 2013, 2014, 2019

Published by **Satish Kumar Jain** and produced by **Varun Jain** for
CBS Publishers & Distributors Pvt. Ltd.,
4819/XI Prahlad Street, 24 Ansari Road, Daryaganj, New Delhi - 110002
delhi@cbspd.com, cbspubs@airtelmail.in • www.cbspd.com
Ph.: 23289259, 23266861, 23266867 • Fax: 011-23243014

Corporate Office: 204 FIE, Industrial Area, Patparganj, Delhi - 110 092
Ph: 49344934 • Fax: 011-49344935
E-mail: publishing@cbspd.com • publicity@cbspd.com

Branches:
- ***Bengaluru:*** 2975, 17th Cross, K.R. Road, Bansankari 2nd Stage, Bengaluru - 70 • Ph: +91-80-26771678/79 • Fax: +91-80-26771680 E-mail: cbsbng@gmail.com, bangalore@cbspd.com
- ***Chennai:*** No. 7, Subbaraya Street, Shenoy Nagar, Chennai - 600030 Ph: +91-44-26681266, 26680620 • Fax: +91-44-42032115 E-mail: chennai@cbspd.com
- ***Kochi:*** Ashana House, 39/1904, A.M. Thomas Road, Valanjambalam, Ernakulum, Kochi • Ph: +91-484-4059061-65 Fax: +91-484-4059065 • E-mail: cochin@cbspd.com
- ***Kolkata:*** 6-B, Ground Floor, Rameshwar Shaw Road, Kolkata - 700014 Ph: +91-33-22891126/7/8 • E-mail: kolkata@cbspd.com
- ***Mumbai:*** 83-C, Dr. E. Moses Road, Worli, Mumbai - 400018 Ph: +91-9833017933, 022-24902340/41 • E-mail: mumbai@cbspd.com

Representatives:
- Hyderabad: 0-9885175004
- Patna: 0-9334159340
- Jharkhand: 0-9811541605
- Nagpur: 0-9021734563
- Pune: 0-9623451994
- Uttarakhand: 0-9716462459

Printed at:
J.S. Offset Printers, Delhi (India)

PREFACE

Materials Management is common to every organisation. Materials Management is essential not only to manufacturing but also to service industries and it exists not only in profit making enterprises but also in private non-profit sectors of the economy. Materials Management process adds value by getting materials into the hands of manufacturing and other using departments. In Materials Management capital is employed and cost are incurred to purchase something of economic value.

Materials Management problems often are not identified by that name, instead of that Management tend to relate them as specialised Materials Management sub functions viz. *Purchasing, Inventory Control, Production Control, Traffic, Warehousing, Receiving, Shipping, Materials Handling and related activities*. The basic reason for this is that the formal Materials Management Organisation is much younger than all its components. The concept of Materials Management as an integrated activity is of recent origin. But now Materials Management has won many converts and it is now a conventional practice to group together organisational activities that are concerned with Purchase, Movement and Storage of Materials. The book "MATERIALS MANAGEMENT" deals with in-depth study of various sub functions of Materials Management viz. Materials Management Concepts; Purchase Management; Inventory Management; Warehouse Management; Operation Research. In fact all these areas continues to grow and change and to stay reasonably current as a discipline. The main thrust of the book is on *Integrated Materials Management* function suited to Indian conditions.

As reflection of extensive changes that are occurring in Materials Management, the book "Materials Management" contains 37 chapters covering all aspects of Materials Management viz. *Concepts of Materials Management; Organisation of Materials Management; Materials Planning and Analysis; Materials Research; Evaluation of Materials Management; Application of various Management Techniques like PERT; Electronic Data Processing; Value Analysis; Inventory Management; Productivity Improvement Techniques. The book also covers various aspects Material Communication System; Inventory Management; Purchasing Procedures; Selection of Sources of Supply; Determination of Price; Transportation and Traffic Management; Warehouse Management; Safety and Good House Keeping; Stores Planning and Stores Control and Organisation of Materials Control.*

The book "Materials Management" is a text book covering 5 papers out of six papers of Post Graduate Diploma in Materials Management viz. Purchasing Management; Inventory Management; Warehouse Management; Distribution Management. The book "Materials Management" is a comprehensive text book useful to students who are pursuing Diploma in Materials Management or Master of Business Administration or various Post Graduate Diplomas in Management with Materials Management as one of its paper. This book will be of value not only to the students of Management at the Post Graduate level in various Universities and

Institute of Management but also to the practising Materials Managers working in industries. The book has a logical built up to enable the readers to gain a clear insight of the Integrated Materials Management function. Most of the materials in this book is written from current and past practice. Scattered through the book are some ideas that have not yet gained the wide acceptance viz. Materials Management as profit Centre; Use of price index for Materials Manager performance; Materials communication system; Legal aspects of Purchasing and Productivity of Materials Management etc. The basic text is written not only to describe Materials Management as it actually is but what it should be in the author's view. The preface of the book would not be complete without grateful acknowledgement to hundreds of Executives and Professors who contributed directly or indirectly for this book through personal conversation and discussion with the author. The book MATERIALS MANAGEMENT is a comprehensive volume, up to date, systematic with subject matter arranged in coherent manner and convincing style and is equally useful to executives/managers working in Materials/Purchase/Stores departments beside a textbook for students of Post Graduate Diploma in Materials Management; M.B.A.; and other diplomas in management courses.

I am sure the book will stimulate the much needed thinking and discussions on the critical subject of MATERIALS MANAGEMENT and will help the readers to develop a conceptual know-how in the areas of Materials Management.

Prof. K.K. AHUJA

MATERIALS MANAGEMENT COVERS

Materials Management of all the functions of management has the weakest conceptual base and poorest technology. In today's environment no organisation can achieve its mission and objectives without caring for its materials resource. Materials Management is a textbook designed to meet the curriculum requirement of students pursuing diploma Materials Management. MBA or Post Graduate Diploma in Business Management with Materials Management as a subject. The author has studied the syllabuses of following universities/Institutes imparting managements education.

1. Punjabi University, Patiala.
2. DAV College of Management, Chandigarh.
3. Indian Institute of Management, Patna.
4. Poddar Institute of Management, Jaipur.
5. Department of Business Administration, Aligarh Muslim University Aligarh.
6. Director Management Education, Annamalai University, Madras.
7. Department of Business Management, South Gujarat University, Surat.
8. Department of Business and Commerce, Guru Nanak Dev University, Amritsar.
9. Govt. Institute of Management, Hissar.
10. Indira Gandhi National Open University, New Delhi.
11. Faculty of Commerce and Management, Kurukshetra University, Kurukshetra.
12. Department of Business Administration, Lucknow University, Lucknow.
13. Faculty of Management Studies, Delhi University, Delhi.
14. Indian Institute of Management, Bangalore.
15. Department of Business Management, University of Indore, Indore.
16. Department of Business Management, University of Cochin, Cochin.
17. M.M. Institute of Management, Villiage Parle, Bombay.
18. Department of Business Administration, Osmania University, Hyderabad.
19. Motilal Nehru Institute of Management, Allahabad.
20. Department of Business Management, Nagpur University, Nagpur.

Contents

Chapter 1

MATERIALS MANAGEMENT

Introduction

Materials Management problems are common to every organisation. Materials management problems are often identified by the specialised materials management sub-functions viz. Purchasing; Inventory Control; Production Control; Traffic Management; Warehousing; Materials Handling and other related activities. The basic reasons for this is that the formal materials management organisation is much younger than any of its sub-functions. Materials Management is a basic part of any organisation that produces a product or service of economic value.

Materials are important determinant of the total cost of production as it occupied 20% to 35% of the total cost which in certain cases may be 60%. The materials require serious attention in any work of production. Materials mean raw materials, components, sub-assemblies and finished products. Materials are classified as Direct; and Indirect. Direct materials goes directly into product and forms a part of the end product while Indirect materials are used in processing or packaging the direct materials. Materials management is a specialised, systematic and scientific function of a group of people for better procurements/storage and distribution of materials.

Scope of Materials Management

Materials Management covers all aspects of materials, costs, materials supply and utilisation. It covers the whole range of functions involved in converting raw materials and ancillary supplies into finished products. It is concerned with the planning and programming of materials and equipments, market research for purchase; pre-design value analysis, procurement of all materials including capital goods, raw materials, components and assemblies, finishing materials, packaging and packing materials, stores control and inventory control; transportation of raw material and material handling; value analysis, disposal of scrap, surplus and salvage and operation research for materials.

Materials Management is basically a most important functional affair for any organisation or undertaking to achieve the best results is so far as profitability is concerned. Materials Management covers a much wider field and deals with all aspects of materials supply and utilization as well as costs. It is concerned with the entire range of functions which affect the flow, conservation, utilization, quality and cost of materials. *It covers that aspect of Industrial Management which is concerned with the activities involved in the acquisition, storage and flow of all materials directly and indirectly employed in the production and marketing of finished goods.*

The term "*Materials Management*" has found wider acceptance covering all the inter-related functions mentioned earlier. Hence small changes in material costs can result in large sums of money saved or lost. Materials Management should therefore, be considered as a function of prime importance for our industrial economy.

Materiais management provides tools and techniques, most of which are very simple, to reduce material costs. In addition to reducing material costs, efficient materials management can also bring about:

(i) Reduction of foreign exchange requirements by getting the maximum value out of the available foreign exchange or by reducing the value of imports, thus contributing substantially towards narrowing the foreign exchange gap.

(ii) Reduction of cost of finished goods of high quality and maintaining the quality at reduced cost.

Industrial managers have been slow in appreciating the importance of materials management as they have been preoccupied with other matters, such as finding new markets, labour problems and so on. Material management bring about increased profits, results in increased productivity of capital by preventing large amount of capital being locked up for long periods in inventories. Increased productivity is the only answer for the peculiar problems of today's Indian Economy of shortages, stagnation and the threatening recession. Productivity can be increased in a variety of ways such as increased production with fixed quantities of raw materials or same quality of finished goods and services with less use of capital and resources. Modern materials management tries to accomplish increased productivity through optimum use of capital employed. One of the basic functions of the management is to employ capital resources as efficiently as to yield the maximum results. This can be done in either of two ways or by both :

(i) By maximising the margin of profit.

(ii) By maximising production with a given amount of capital.

This means that the management should try to make its capital work as hard as possible. Much time is devoted to make only labour work harder and in this process the capital turnover and hence the productivity of capital is often neglected.

Definition

"Materials Management is a body of knowledge which helps the manager to improve the productivity of capital by reducing material costs, preventing large amounts of capital being locked up for long periods and improving the capital turnover ratio". Materials manager must derive its objectives by understanding of local environments and at the same time, taking into consideration the human factors, their attitude, sense of responsibilities and their mental make up and approach to new ideas. These factors together with the prevalent methods with their good and bad points must be studied in depth before a new procedure is evolved and implimented.

It may be easy to convince the higher management about the efficiency of a sophisticated method but down the line with others who are connected with the work. If the implementations of Materials management is taken up with an open mind, it would be easier to achieve the results sooner or later. While the field of Materials management covers all aspects of material costs, supply and utilization, the opinion is divided as to what functions should be included in materials management.

Objectives of Materials Management

The objectives of Material Management as such should be supported in every way by:

(i) Maintaining continuity of productive operations by ensuring a uniform flow of materials.
(ii) Reducing materials costs by systematic use of scientific-techniques.
(iii) Releasing working capital for productive purpose by efficient control of inventories.
(iv) Increasing the competitiveness of end products by ensuring right quality at the right price, especially in foreign markets.
(v) Saving foreign exchange through economic use of foreign purchases and import substitution.
(vi) Establishing good buyer-seller-relations.
(vii) ensuring low departmental costs and high efficiency.
(viii) Setting high ethical standards. In this way it is clear that Materials management covers all aspects of materials, including, flow, of materials cost, quality, supply, conservation and utilization.

The prime objective is to supply the user department with the required quantity at a constant rate with uniform quality so that production or service rendered is not held up. At the same time materials manager has to ensure the optimum usage of facilities like capital, storage space and other aspects of materials management. Materials management offers a wide scope for reducing costs, saving the foreign exchange, conserving scarce materials, improving productivity and increasing profits. It is much easier to reduce materials costs than to reduce labour costs and as material costs predominate in the total cost of a product, the saving is substantial. *By careful financial analysis, it can be shown that a 5% reduction in materials costs will result in increased profits equivalent to a 36% increase in sales.* The Break-even chart shown in Fig. 1.1 that a substantial increase in profits can be obtained with a small decrease in material costs which reduce the variable cost appreciably. The chart also shows that profits starts coming of much easier if the Break-Even point is shifted backward with the same total production.

Increased production and sales are necessary to bring about the same increase in profits which result in reducing material costs or increasing production and sales to the extent of 30% to 40% which is not easy. Increased production may need increase in fixed assets and increasing sales to that extent, may need increase in fixed assets and increasing sales to that extent, may not always be possible without extra sales efforts like *Additional Advertising* which increases sales expenses. Further it depends more on external-environments over which the management has little control. The primary task of the modern materials management, with an integrated view is purchasing material of:

Right Quality, Right Material, At the Right Price, From Right source, At the Right Time, Using Right Mode of Transport

Storing the materials in the different warehouses with appropriate methods also forms an important aspect of materials management, since uncontrolled Inventory is "Industry Cancer." The Materials manager is also responsible for the right quantity of inventory norms, *i.e.*, for fixation of safety stock, re-order point, reorder quantity, etc.

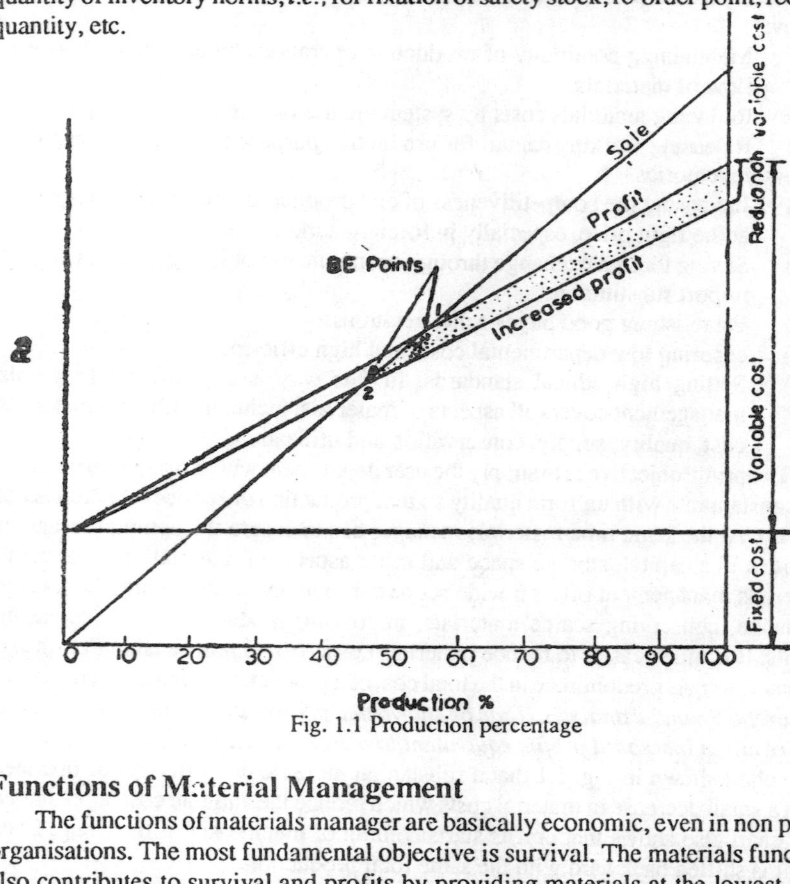

Fig. 1.1 Production percentage

Functions of Material Management

The functions of materials manager are basically economic, even in non profit organisations. The most fundamental objective is survival. The materials function also contributes to survival and profits by providing materials at the lowest total cost. The materials function also helps to achieve the objective when it boosts inventory turnover or gets material of superior quality. Following are some of the objectives of materials management which contribute to the achievement of some overall company objectives. If the contribution is made directly by the materials function we call it a *primary* objective. If it is indirect and results from the materials department's assistance to another department we call it a *secondary* objective.

Primary Materials Objectives. There are at least nine primary objectives of materials department. These are low prices, high inventory turnover, low cost of acquisition and possession, continuity of supply, consistency of quality, low pay roll costs, favourable relations with suppliers, development of personnel and maintenance of materials management records.

Secondary Materials Objectives. The secondary objectives of materials management are not so limited in scope and variety as primary objectives. Since they represent the materials department contribution to the achievement of the primary objective of some other departments, they can vary from industry to industry. Among the more common ones are economic make or buy decisions, promotion of standardisation, product improvement; effective interdepartmental relation etc.

Importance of Materials Management

The objectives not only vary in relative importance from industry to industry and even among companies within an industry, but objectives can vary within the same company. When sales are expanding the materials manager may concentrate on continuity of supply and consistency of quality. The manager is less interested in inventory turnover or low prices since the economic expansion should bring both higher sales and high prices and these objectives may be achieved automatically.

In a young company which is growing rapidly cash is perpetually short, all earnings and all borrowings are ploughed back into plant and equipment. In these situation materials manager is under considerable pressure to get along with as little stock as possible in order to make cash available for other purposes.

If an organisation does not identify its material management objective and develop a program to achieve them, it may be giving undue attention to some objectives and neglecting others. The efforts to achieve one primary objective almost necessarily involve relaxation of efforts to achieve some other objective. The materials manager who concentrate on inventory turnover pays higher prices and has higher costs of acquisition because he must buy more frequently in smaller quantities. The higher average inventories will inevitably raise costs of possession, although unit costs of acquisition will probably decline because of the greater average size of each shipment, continuity of supply and consistency of quality also may be affected. The materials manager will be tempted to go to cheap suppliers who cut prices and also cut corners on quality and fail to live up to their delivery promises. *Materials management objective should be balanced and responsibility for achievement should be delegated to a material manager who has authority to do the Job. The materials manager should always reevaluate the objective when business conditions change.*

The wrong objectives get undue emphasis when a purchasing manager is made subordinate to a marketing manager. Purchasing manager begins to take on marketing objective rather than those of materials management because every subordinate tries to please his boss.

INTEGRATED MATERIALS MANAGEMENT

Concepts

Materials Management as a function responsible for the co-ordination of planning, Sourcing, Purchasing; Moving; Storing and Controlling materials in an optimum manner so as to provide a pre-decided service to the customer at a minimum cost. If the above functions of Materials Management are separately handled a conflict of interests occurs and there is a need to balance the conflicting objective from a total organisation point of view so as to achieve optimum results for the organisation. The organisation which are following integrated Materials Management concept require the services of professional managers so that they can fulfill the requirements of an integrated materials management functions which demands an ability to bring together conflicting and yet inter-related functions.

Advantages

Following are some of the advantages of Integrated Materials Management:

Better Accountability: By effective centralisation of authority and responsibility for all aspects of materials function, a clear cut accountability is established. This helps in evaluating the performance of materials management in an objective manner.

Better Co-ordination: When the materials manager is responsible for all function it results in better support and co-operation in the accomplishment of the materials function. Better Co-ordination create an atmosphere of trust and better relation between the user departments and the materials management department.

Improved Performance: As all the inter-related functions are integrated organisationally, better performance and effectiveness is achieved. The need for materials is promptly brought to the notice by materials planning and Purchase department is fed with stock levels and orders status by stores department.

Adaptability to Computerisation: The Centralisation of materials functions has made it possible to design data processing systems. The integrated materials management facilitate the collection, process and analysis of data, leading to better decisions. Computerisation can be economically introduced under an integrated set-up.

Objectives of Integrated Material Mangement

The fundamental objectives of an integrated management approach can be viewed as:

(a) Procuring better value
(b) Obtaining better yield
(c) Reducing investments in stock through Inventory control and material flow.

In an integrated set-up the materials manager who is responsible for all such inter-related functions is in a position to exercise control and co-ordinate with an overview that ensures proper balance of the conflicting objective of the individual functions. Integration also helps in the rapid transfer of data, through effective and informal communication channels.

VALUE ADDED BY MATERIALS MANAGEMENT

Management have long been aware of the fact that manufacturing and marketing may be quite separate activities but now the management have realised the importance of third basic economic activity that is carried on daily in their organisation: Materials management. In materials management, as in the two better known activities, capital is employed and costs are incurred to produce something of economic value. Materials management is a perfectly obvious example of adding value by distribution. The management belief that they get something for nothing in materials management and assumes that purchased materials has a value at the stage where it is used that is equal to the original purchase price. Materials management adds value by distribution. The materials management process add value by getting material into the hands of manufacturing and other using departments; marketing takes material from manufacturing and gets it into the hands of a company customer. In non manufacturing organisations value added by the materials management process may he much greater. In hospitals or military organisation, there may be more than Rs. 1 of value added by materials management for each Rs. 1 of purchases.

In terms of basic value added to product, the materials manager is roughly but one fifth as important as the marketing manager and only one eighth as important as the manufacturing manager.

History of Materials Management

Organisations in which materials management plays its roles have rarely been created with a single stroke of the organisation builders. They have evolved gradually and in many cases have not yet matured. The scope of materials management in any particular industry is at-least as much a product of historical development as it is of economic logic. The evolution of materials management have followed the following pattern in phased manner.

First Phase : Executives who are primarily concerned with other functions have carried on almost unconsciously all materials management functions as sidelines.

Second Phase : The major materials management functions are recognised formally, but these activities report to variety of executives and are not centralised organisationally.

Third Phase : Materials management functions concerned with purchased materials are grouped together under a senior executive, who behaved like a line manager.

Fourth Phase : Materials management functions becomes a genuine value adding activity for purchased materials.

The studies have revealed that companies who claim to have reached the Fourth Phase of evolution have yet to achieved the performance. According to various surveys more than 75% of the manufacturing organisations have yet to approach the fourth phase of evolution.

Materials management is just as essential to the firm with 8 to 10 employees as it is to the large corporation with more than 50,000 employees. The large size corporations have full-time specialists in every phase of materials management. In a small firm the owner manager handles all the administrative Jobs but as small business grows the work load of the owner manager gets heavier. As profit grows he eventually feels prosperous but cannot afford the luxury of full-time staff specialists. As the organisation continues to expand, it becomes more complex. The Job is eventually dispersed among a number of executives working at different organisation levels, who report to executives interested in other functions particularly manufacturing and finance. Most companies enjoy unified materials management only in their infancy; unfortunately they are then still too small to enjoy the benefits of a specialist in the field. As the company continues to grow and reaches the stage where it has around hundred or more employees, the functional specialist becomes necessary and full time managers of finance, production, sales and engineering eventually appear. Finally a separate purchasing department is formed. At first it may be run by someone who holds another Job viz finance controller; company secretary; personnel manager or the like but eventually a full time purchasing agent is definitely a second string manager. As the organisation becomes progressive management realises that their purchasing, production control and traffic departments have Jobs so closely related that they can work together more effectively to achieve common objective if they are linked organisationally. With this integrated approach to materials management all the Jobs encompassed by these functions would be under the overall control of a materials manager.

THE FUTURE OF MATERIALS MANAGEMENT

The Need for Change

Materials management has become almost the need of the time. At least one leading company in every industry has an Integrated Materials Management set up.

In most cases the chief executive is probably be too preoccupied with other problems to worry about materials management unless there is pressure that encourage him to consider a change in organisation. Sometimes the pressures are the product of specific materials management problems. In many cases, they are at least partly contrived. Every real life organisation is a political entity in which change is far more likely is occur when some persons or group has a vested interest in that change. This is certainly true when a company creates an integrated materials management organisation. An executive who is trying to promote himself as materials manager is obviously a strong advocate of change. Most of the senior management team members are sensitive to the feelings of their subordinates-particularly if no overriding emergency forces them to get tough. The concept of "don't rock the boat" is tacitly accepted in almost every real-life organisation. Major changes often are postponed until they can be made smoothly. Eventually, every chief executive does make changes that be believes will strength his organisation. These are also for more rational reasons for the materials management from of organisation to gain wide acceptance and therefore number of companies are waiting to make the change when a strategic opportunity arises. The current political-economic change is working to make materials management and the supply function increasingly important.

The professional objectives of purchasing are buying the right quality, in right quantity, at the right price, from the right source and at the right time. The future of materials management will deal with identifying, and discussing these "rights". The centre of responsibility at present is on uninterrupted flow of materials and service that have been purchased wisely. The management objectives of purchasing: integration with other departments, development of competent personnel, etc. will continue to be the challenges for the future.

The ability of a purchasing department to accomplish its objectives is governed by the procurement functions assigned to it. In practice the purchasing departments of almost identical companies, even within the same industry, can be entirely different in composition and purpose. The current trend in business is toward consolidation of the functions of procurement. Consolidation frequently results in the establishment of a materials management department. In other situations, additional functions of procurement are assigned to the purchasing department with same result. Despite the increase in efficiency and profit in consolidation, the trend for centralisation has been relatively slow. The slowness of the concept of advancement can be explained by its newness, top management lack of knowledge concerning it, and by the tendency of business scholars to focus research and teaching efforts more intensely on the other areas of business.

But for the future more professionals are joining the materials management functions. The new entrants joining as trainees are mostly graduate in engineering with specialisation in materials management. These executives are going to apply the various management techniques to ensure continuity of materials supply at the right Price; Time; Source; Quantity and Quality. The impetus for advancement in materials management comes primarily from the business world itself. Materials management was not studied by the academic world to that extent as other areas of business. There are positive indications, however, that this situation is changing. Each year additional universities offer materials management. A marked increase in research activities has taken place recently in the field of materials management. The push for materials management has got started seriously and future will see faster acceptance of materials management in industry in general.

Profit Improvement Plans

The relationship between Man and Materials is indivisible. The condition of man is synonymous with Materials. Materials are the life blood of man's development. Materials acquired costs money. If not used and rotated to a desired degree, it could cause financial problems to organisations. As we know that the developing countries import materials for production and consumption and the import bill an materials is one of the major cause of the country's economic problems at the present time. The need of the hour is to make the material management functions contribute to the profit improvement plans of the organisation so that the gains are shared by owners, employees, customers, Government and society. The biggest challenge before the management is how to improve materials management functions to contribute to the Profit Improvement Plans of organisation at micro level. To implement Profit Improvement Plans a systematic attack on the areas of costs that have either by tradition largely been ignored in the past or that have not been recognised due to rapid changes in the cost composition of products.

It is therefore worth while to compute just how much of the materials brought into the company for manufacturing go out as finish products. The average cost on materials, industry wise is given as under:

S. No.	Industry	Average Materials Cost*
1.	Vehicles; Earth Moving Equipment, Fabrication	Above 65%
2.	Jute Wool, Cotton Yarn	Above 65%
3.	Cotton textiles, Bread	60-65%
4.	Engineering, Non ferrous	55-60%
5.	Ship Building, Machine tools	50-55%
6.	Chemicals, Tyres	50-55%
7.	Cement, Electricity	50-55%
8.	Pharmaceuticals	40-50%
9.	Steel, News paper fertilisers	40-45%

*These costs of materials relates to consumption costs derived financially while preparing the financial statements.

The other costs associated with materials are: Ordering Costs; Holding Costs; Stockout costs. The Ordering Costs varies from organisation to organisation depending upon the size; composition of costs, number of orders, purchase procedures and systems etc. In a multi-unit organisation the ordering cost would vary from unit to unit depending upon the above factors. By stream lining the purchase procedures and systems it would be possible to reduce the ordering costs thus contributing to the Profit Improvement Plans of the organisation. The Holding Costs incurred by organisation depends on the inventory levels as well as the sources of working capital for the organisation. If company's could hold flexible inventory levels, relating to cash outflows, production and sales plans, it would be possible to reduce the inventory levels thereby reducing the holding costs. These concepts would work where the stockout costs are lower than the holding costs but in situations where stockout costs are infinite these may not yield results. Companies could use the Ratio Analysis to good advantages to control costs incurred on materials. Some of the Ratios are:

$$\text{Material Cost Index} = \frac{\text{Material cost of the product}}{\text{Production cost of the product}}$$

$$\text{Material Cost to Sales} = \frac{\text{Material cost of each product}}{\text{Sales value of the product}}$$

$$\text{Lead Time} = \frac{\text{Average Lead Time during the current year}}{\text{Average Lead Time during the previous year}}$$

$$\text{Manpower Cost Index} = \frac{\text{Salary bill of the Materials Department}}{\text{Total salary bill of the Company}}$$

$$\text{Materials Planning Efficiency} = \frac{\text{Number of rush orders}}{\text{Total number of orders}}$$

$$\text{Material Price Variance} = \frac{\text{Standard Price} - \text{Actual Price}}{\text{Standard Price}}$$

$$\text{Material Usage Variance} = \frac{\text{Value of materials actually used}}{\text{Value of Standard material quantity}}$$

Materials Management Programme

In order to set a materials management programme successfully the following basic factors must be taken into consideration.

(a) **Intention Phase:** In this phase the management of the firm in a carefully worded statement should reveal the intentions of its backing to the Materials Management functions.

(b) **Preparation Phase:** In this phase the management prepare a programme of education at all levels in the enterprise to appraise the employees of the importance of the role of materials in man's life and the problems that surround it.

(c) **Diagnostic Phase:** In this phase management shall be concerned with gathering information and carrying out diagnostic studies of material usage, process, procurement, waste and other product cost and to identify areas that require detailed investigations, that promise substantial economy.

(d) **Programming Phase:** In this phase the priorities are fixed and a detailed programme with time targets of the work to be undertaken are drawn.

(e) **Objective Phase:** The main objective of this phase is one of cost reduction. Management in this phase, set the objectives for each of the programmed items and fix tentative; financial targets to be reached by the individuals undertaking various aspects of the work.

(f) **Action Plan Phase:** In this phase the management set the employees on their tasks with definite time plans tied to a reporting system. In this phase various management techniques will be used.

(g) **Implementation Phase:** In this phase the findings of the action phase would be implemented. At this step management must bear in mind the long term aspects of the enterprise by gearing the products to a much quicker cycle of change.

(h) **Follow up Phase:** In this phase the management takes the necessary steps to ensure that there is an organisation to constantly look at present materials management arrangements against the arrival on the scene of new improvements and new materials.

Once the organisation is set, the advantages of using the techniques and tools would accrue to the organisation by effectively managing of materials and contributing to Profit Improvement Plans.

Chapter 2

ORGANISATION STRUCTURE OF MATERIALS MANAGEMENT

Introduction

The concept of materials management was a part of the interdisciplinary systems approach of the 1950s but came into common usage and practice in business during 1990s. Its essential significance is that it highlighted for management the advantages of coordinating the related activities of production planning and scheduling, purchasing, shipping, storing, handling, and controlling of materials put into the manufacturing process. The co-ordination of all functional areas involved with moving materials into and through the plant are achieved under one oranisational head called materials manager. While the specific functional areas vary depending in the philosophy of the firm and the type of production process, the areas always included under the materials manager are purchasing, inventory control and traffic. As such materials management can be defined as an organisational approach that brings under one organisational component the responsibility for: (1) determining the production requirement (2) Scheduling the production process; and (3) procuring; storing and dispersing of materials, at minimum cost. The essential reasons for uniting materials department under a materials manager is to provide, improved co-ordination and control of the following issues involved.

(i) Utilising Management Tools. One reason for the growing use of Materials management is management's desire to employ the relatively new control tools such as operations research, electronic programming and profit centres.

(ii) Achieving Cost Reduction. Considerable cost reduction is possible by may of inventory reduction, transportation and purchasing as a result of improved co-ordination of these activities.

(iii) Reconciling Conflicting Objectives. Another important reason for the increasing acceptance of materials management is the realisation that materials departments often have conflicting objective that must be coordinated to optimise results.

(iv) Facilitating "Make and Hold" purchases. Effective utilisation of this service requires that supplier inventories be closely coordinated to developments in the buying company's materials departments such as production and inventory control.

Therefore, Materials management helps to co-ordinate supplier inventory management to the other internal materials operations. Materials management provide improved co-ordination and control of the materials sub-functions by centralising materials authority.

Reorganising For Materials Management

The majority of materials-related decisions have in the past been regarded as fairly low level decisions. The positioning of purchasing, production control, stock control and stores administration in the organisation structure has in consequence tended to be relatively law. One reason for the re organisation of materials-related activities into materials management departments has been to upgrade the organisational positioning of these interdependent activities which affect the flow of materials. There are ofcourse good reasons for the great variety of organisation structure which can be found in industry. There are differences in the type of the organisation considered appropriate for job production, batch production, mass production and process production. Production processes differ very considerably in complexity and in the technology employed and these differences lead to difference in organisation structure. Large firms are not organised along the same lines as small firms because there is limit to the number of people one manager can manage effectively. Consequently large firms need to introduce additional tiers of management between the top and bottom of the hierarchy. A hierarchy of managers implies a hierarchy of decisions. Short term decision which are quickly reversible are taken at lower levels in the hierarchy and long-term decisions which require major commitment of resources or determine the future direction of business are taken at higher levels. A typical materials management reorganisation is given in fig (2.2a). The materials-related activities of production control, stock control, purchasing and transport are brought together under a single materials manager.

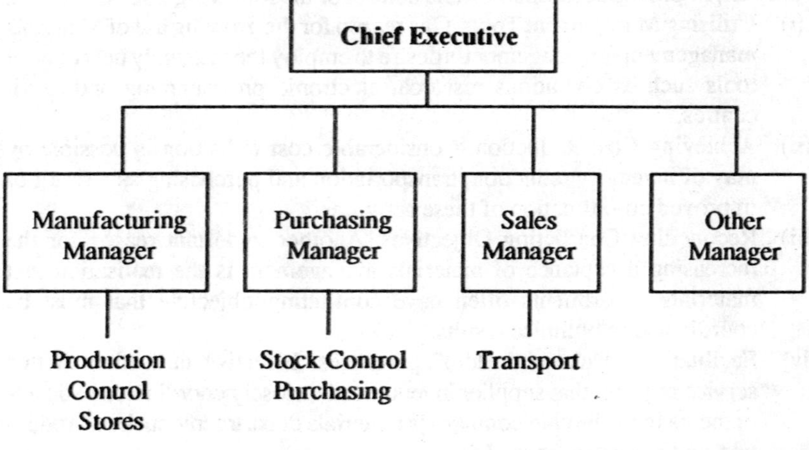

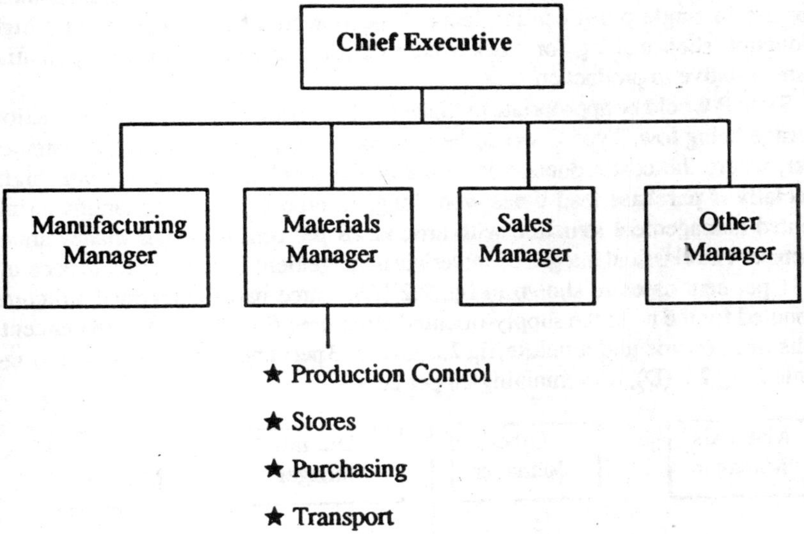

Fig. 2.1 Materials Manager, A Reorganisation

The Place of Purchasing In The Organisation

There are two views about the question of the materials manager's range of responsibility. In one, we add to purchasing a number of activities such as stores, stock control and transport, and perhaps Production Planning and Control. In other, we add to production a number of inter connected activities such as stores, stock control and transport.

Many purchasing experts do not look with favour on the incorporation of the purchasing function within a materials management structure. According to them Purchasing is about one thing and materials management is about something else. According to some experts Purchasing was about source marketing, and materials management about materials flow. The two functions require different kinds of expertise viz market knowledge, negotiating skills; and commercial flair on the one hand; technical skill in materials handling. Inventory control and shop scheduling on the other. In fact buyer should concentrate on developing skill significantly different from those already available in other functions.

One type of solution may be to split the purchasing function into two groups of activities : the source marketing part, which affects material flow only indirectly, and the ordering part which affects it directly. *The source marketing group might be located in corporate office which would deal with supplier appraisal and development, negotiation and contracts. The second group might be located in the plant as part of a material department, and would deal with timing and quantities of orders, delivery schedule and expediting.*

According to S.E Lauer Jr there are three types of materials management structure in single-profit centre plants. Type A would be appropriate in a high production shop making for stock where considerable cost reduction potential existed relative to product cost.

Type B would be appropriate to Make to Stock with purchasing cost reduction leverage being low. Type C would be appropriate in a plant making to customer order, where the cost reduction leverage of the purchase department was high, especially if purchase lead times were long. In type D which is manufacturing oriented management structure with around 28 per cent materials management structure. The classical integrated materials management structure, said to account for 31 per cent cases as shown in fig. 2.2 (A). Three partly integrated structure accounted for the rest : the supply-oriented structure ; fig 2.2 (B) ; for 18 per cent, the distribution oriented structure, fig 2.2 (C) for 23 per cent, and the manufacturing-oriented, fig 2.2 (D), for remaining 28 per cent.

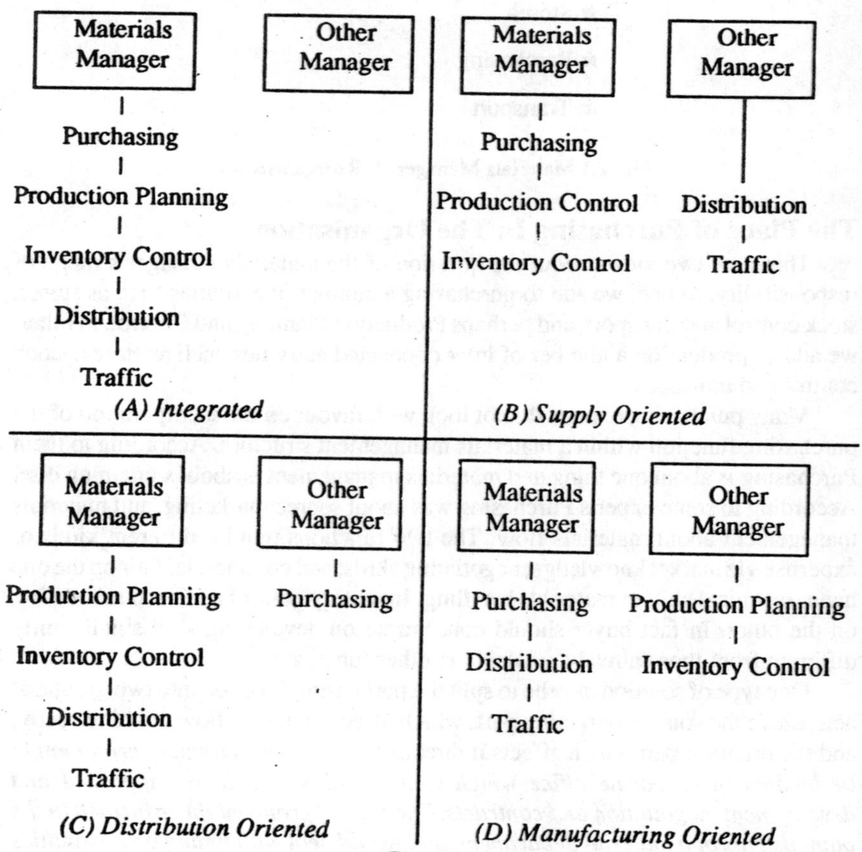

Fig. 2.2

Organisational Variations in Materials Management

The ultimate in materials management would have one organisational unit with the responsibility for buying and moving materials, parts and suppliers from outside sources ; Controlling them through the storage and processing stages ; and ware housing the finished product and supervising its movement to the customer. The various organisational charts of materials management organsation are given as under.

Non-M M Organisation

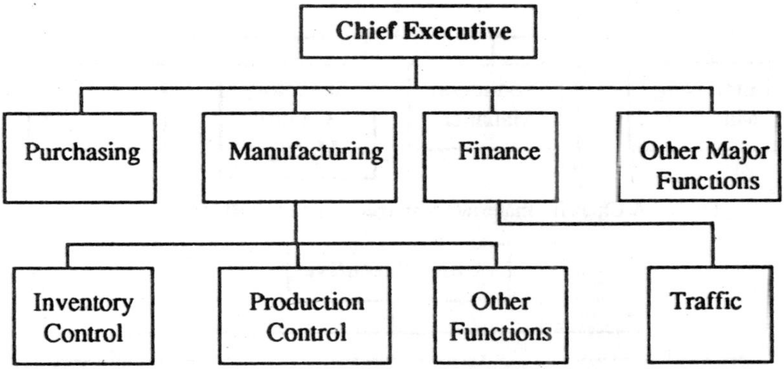

Fig. 2.3 Organisation Chart for the firm without conventional material management

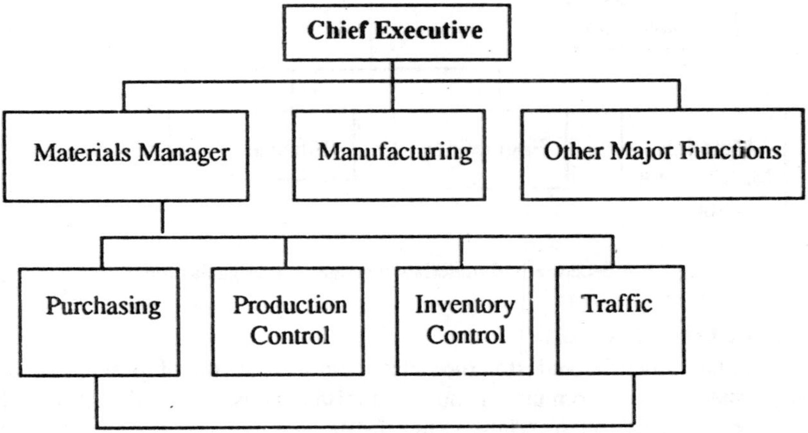

Fig 2.4 Organisational Chart for the firm with the materials management concept of management

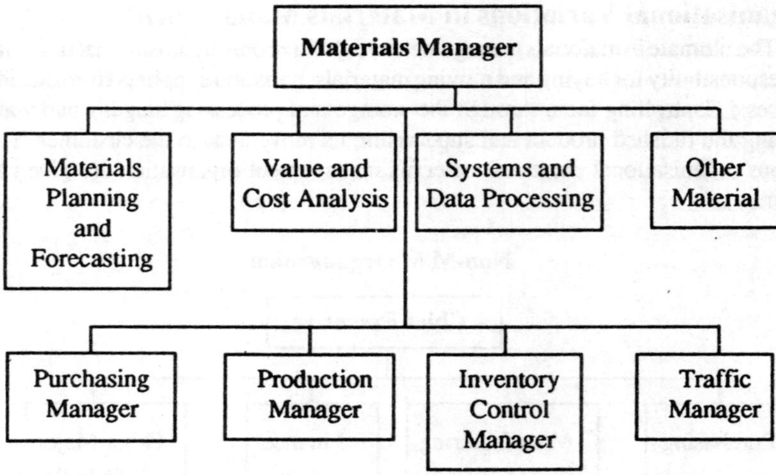

Fig 2.5 A Chart for materials management with staff functions added

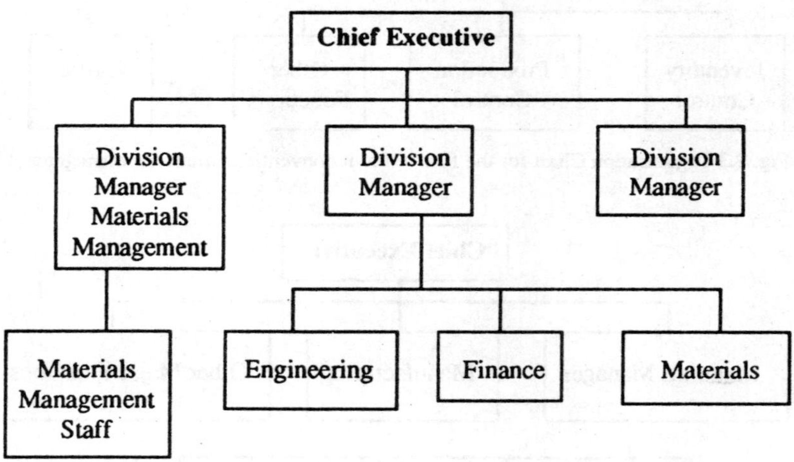

Fig 2.6 A decentralised materials management Organisational Chart

Sound Organisation

Sound organisational structure also permits a chain of promotion to be established. As a concomitant of sound organisation it is usual to find the development of job specifications. These in turn facilitate training of individuals for their own positions and for positions immediately above them. The existence of such a chain of promotion and systematic training for promotion greatly strengthens and improves morale within an organisation. Finally, a sound organisation will promote harmony among the component parts of the organisation. There is less possibility of jealousy and communication gaps if the organisational responsibility are clearly outlined. A sound organisation also defines authority so that each individual in the organisation knows to whom he reports and who reports to him. The benefit of sound organisation is the saving in time of executives. With proper assignment of responsibility and authority, most routine decisions can be handled by a subordinate and the executives can devote his time to broad procedural and policy matters. It should be recognised that these are distinct limitations to what can be achieved through organisation, and these are certain organisational weaknesses to be avoided in setting up a business organisation. The best principles of an organisation is placing right man for the right job if personnel responsible for a job is not capable of doing so, the best principles of organisation will be of little value. It has be recognised that most company organisation charts do not reflect the true lines of authority and responsibility which flow through men as well as their positions. The another limitation could be, the possibility of over organising. There are many organisations in which all duties and responsibility are so minutely defined that excessive "red tape" results. Over organisation leads to a slowing down of decision making because the channel to the decision making executive is too longer too devious. However there is a greater risk of poor performance through under organising than there is through over organising.

As seen earlier in purchasing there are two major organisational problems : (i) the place of the purchasing department in the overall company structure and (ii) Internal organisation of the purchasing department.

In any organisation there are two basic issues involved : (a) The desired degrees of centralisation of the purchasing function within the company and (b) the executive Level to which purchasing officer should be responsible.

Centralisation and Decentralisation

The materials management organisation can be flexible and can be adopted to suit the specialised needs of any profit or non profit institution. The various organisational forms can be expanded indefinitely to fit very large as well as smaller institutions. The expansion process can be achieved when each supervisor adds subordinates until the limits of span of control is achieved. Many small organisation have grown to grant organisations by following this process. Decentralisation has many advantages. It brings managers closer to the objectives of business, permits tighter control of costs and provides better environment for training future managers. It helps stimulate improvements in products and methods. Decentralisation : creates a major materials management problem of diluted buying power with decentralisation management faces a dilemma. Should it go only part way and continue to have a corporate office buying staff responsible for all major purchases? or should it completely decentralise the materials activities along with the rest of the organisation? With the former approach it preserves its buying power and with eater it dilutes its buying power. There is considerable variation among industrial companies in decentralising versus centralising of the firms. The better procedure would seem to be the centralisation of all policy matters and purchase of major raw material and equipment in corporate office. The various other units of the company would make all other purchases in accordance with policies established by the corporate office. Another reason for decentralisation is the better public relation that exist with the communities in which a firm has its plants. In a multi unit company in which each plant manufactures different products the case for decentralisation is more clear, since so many requirements will differ for each plant. Similarly there is difference in the local conditions or local laws and customs which may not be totally understood and appreciated by the staff of corporate office purchases department therefore purchased should be made in the light of local circumstances, and centralisation of purchasing in a multi-plant operation may not be able to cope with all the local conditions found in widely satteredplant locations.

Line And Staff Approach

Most of the major companies compromise and try to get the advantages of both centralisation and decentralisation. This they do with the so called "Line and Staff" approach.

Line activities, carryout its basic mission of adding value by distribution. Materials management must embrace all activities that are concerned with getting purchased material from suppliers up to the stage where value begins to be added by the manufacturer. The basic materials management activities would also be concerned with handling; storage; transportation of material prior to its incorporation into the manufacturing process. When the materials manager deals with purchased material, he is executing line functions and his role is comparable to that of manufacturing manager or marketing manager. In general, materials management is responsible as a line function for anything that is purchased, up to the point where value begins to be added by manufacturing. In addition materials management may also serve manufacturing in a staff capacity. In manufacturing as in materials management and marketing, material must be stored and moved physically from point to point. In fact manufacturing is often engaged in adding value by distribution as well as adding value by manufacturing. Similarly, if a partially finished product is temporarily stored, a cost is incurred that represents value added by distribution. The relation of materials manager to manufacturing is more varied and complex than it is to marketing, being strongly influenced by technology. In some cases, the relationship between materials management and production is quite well defined. In an electric utility, materials management delivers full to the generating station, and production uses the fuel in its boilers. A company may simultaneously purchase and make identical items, this may draw manufacturing and materials management closer together and makes it more difficult to determine where the responsibility of one ends and other begins.

The Marketing and Materials are virtually identical as regard responsibility for physical-distribution policy is concerned.

The marketing process embraces all activities necessary to get the product from the last manufacturing operation to the customer. This normally involved a great deal more than simply persuading the customer to buy the product. The product must be transported and stored, going through virtually the same process that is carried on when purchased material moves from the supplier to its point of use. This process of moving goods to the ultimate consumer is called physical distribution.

In any organization, at top of the materials management is a corporate staff often headed by Director (Materials) or G.M. (Material), or Materials manager. At this level division of responsibility is by function. With the staff and line organisation, most of the advantages of centralised buying are preserved. The corporate purchasing staff is able to consolidate purchased of all items used by a number of plants in order to get the lowest possible prices. The corporate materials manager in a big corporation does not supervise the plant materials manager directly, he usually has a small staff under his direct supervision. The staff provides specialised services to both the plant materials managers and top management. The various services provided as specialised services are Value Analysis; Administrative planning, economic analysis and electronic data processing.

Internal Departmental organisation

Purchasing departments are organised on line basis with purchasing agent or materials manager as incharge. The usual procedure is to assign a specific commodity or a group of commodities to buyer, and he is then holding responsibility for all purchasing activities in connection with those commodities. One of the more recent organisational developments is the assignment of purchasing responsibilities for a large and special type of project to a team, usually designated as a project group. This group has complete responsibility for whatever is needed for its project and consequently will overlap regular buying assignments. This type of organisation, therefore is appropriate only when a company wants to give a measure of priority to a major project or must meet stringent quality; cost or time requirements for such things as government or major construction projects. Organisationally the importance difference in the governmental and institutional purchasing departments and industrial purchasing is the multiple authority over the head of the purchasing department in governmental agencies and institutions. Internally the government and institutional purchasing departments and industrial purchasing depths are identically organised. A purchasing department exists to supply the needs of other departments in the company. The attitude and reactions of other departments towards purchasing department depends on the degree and kind of service the purchase department gives to other departments.

Grouping of Functions Into Organisational Structure

The organisation structure of any function determines the interaction of the personnel in this function with others within and outside their responsibility area.

The organisation structure thus plays a vital role in the effectiveness which the function can achieve and the essential contribution that it can make to the total organisation.

Taking Materials management as an example one organisation may consider the linkage between Materials Planning and Production Planning as more significant than another organisation which may give more weightage to the linkage between Materials Planning and Purchase. Therefore the problems arising out of an artificial division between the functions of Materials Planning and Purchase are considered more manageable than the problems arising out of a similar division between Materials Planning and Production Planning or vice-versa. The decision in this regard to organise these functions in certain groups will arise only from such consideration. Another factor which may determine the grouping of functions into organisational structures is the managerial convenience of evaluating, monitoring and controlling these functions. This would be dependent upon proper identification of the roles and responsibilities of these various departments. The growing specialised knowledge and experience of certain modern techniques may also influence the grouping of functions into various alternative structures in certain organisations. Depend on the need to promote specialisation in certain activities, emphasis in the form of separate departments may be given in such activities. Following are some of the alternatives which determining the grouping of functions into organisational structure:

Traditional Materials Management Structure

In most of the organisations, Materials Management is a centralised function reporting directly to the General Manager at a level equal to that of Personnel; Finance or Production. The traditional structure is given as under

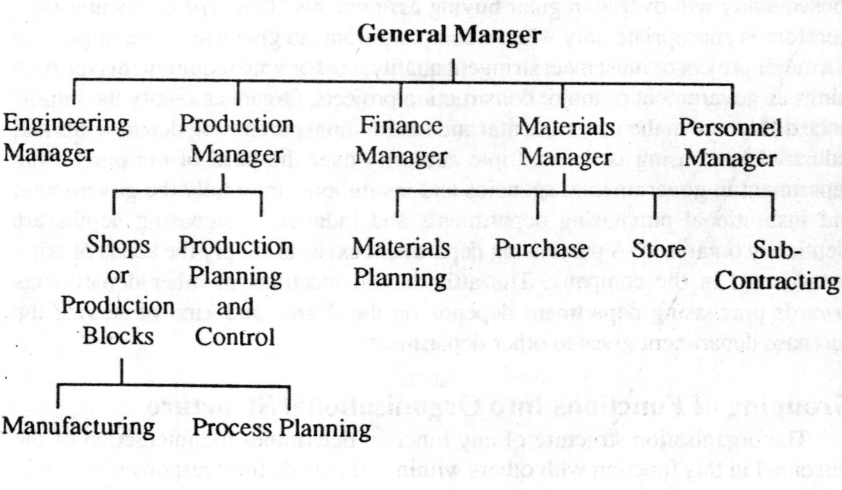

In such an organisation structure there is a tendency to exaggerate material non-availability by Production Planning and the conflicts between Materials Planning and Production Planning have to be sorted out only at the level of General Manger. The inadequate adaptation and adjustment of production plan to suit materials availability and vice verse may even result in non accommodation of the genuine problem of the Materials Planning function.

Controller of Purchase and Stores Structure

The structure visualises the centralisation of the planning function with respect to Production Programmes, material procurement plans and off-loading of items. In this structure the planning function reports to Production Manager and is isolated from the Purchase and Stores activities.

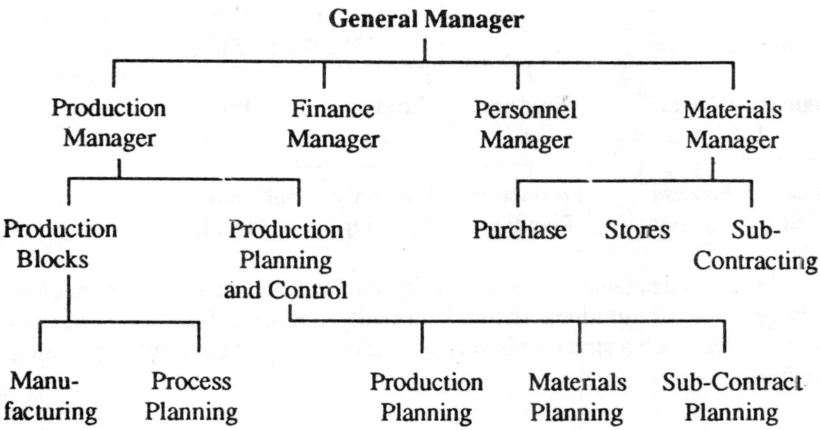

The advantage with this structure is the close and adaptive co-ordination between the Materials Planning and Production Planning functions. There would also be close co-operation between Production Planning and Manufacturing functions. the structure however may result in Inventory Management being considered a secondary function at the cost of ensuring uninterrupted production.

Operative Planning Structure-I

In order to overcome the deficiency noticed in controller of Purchase and Stores Structure Certain Organisations have dissociated the planning functions from the manufacturing activities. In operative planning structure it would be noticed that Production Blocks or Shop Floor, manufacturing activity and Process Planning reports to the General Manager directly and the operative planning Group comprising of both Production Planning and Materials Planning also reports independently to the General Manager. The Purchase, Stores and Subcontracting activities are a third independent entity at least equal to Manufacturing and operative activities. It would also be noticed that in this structure Production Planning and Materials Planning ties for different products to resolve interface problems as shown in the structure. In this structure Production Planning and Materials Planning activities for different product is carried out under the head of Operative Planning Manager who is reporting to General Manager.

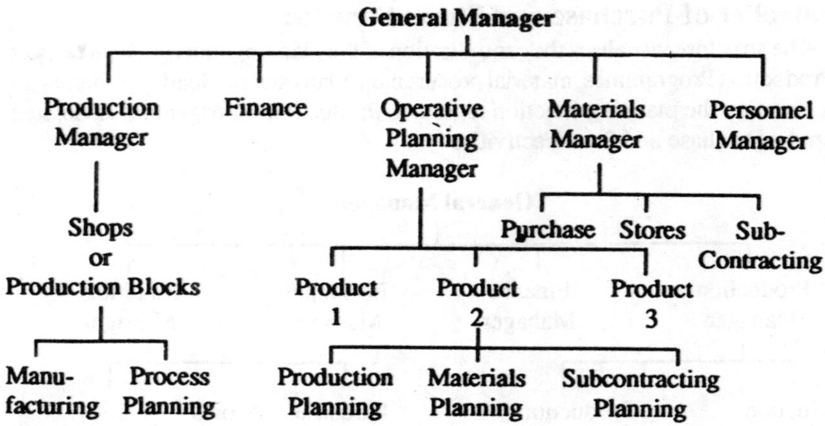

In this structure planning activities are given due share of their importance and are separated from the routine activities such as manufacturing, Purchase, stores and subcontracting. Such a structure is very conducive for effective product planning specialisation.

Operative Planning Structure Type II

The Operative planning structure Type II integrates the difficulties because of the decentralisation of the planning function product wise as highlighted in Operative Planning Structure Type I. This Type II structure is only a variant of Type I structure.

The Operative Planning functions of Production Planning, Materials Planning and Subcontract Planning have been integrated under a common individual who takes care of all the products. Thus this structure offers many advantages. The integration of Production and Materials Planning results in mutual adaptability and thus reduced inventories, since one executive is responsible for total inventory holdings. The production Manager does not have materials planning activities with him and thus the chances of deliberately planned over stocking is eliminated. Any conflicts arising of this set up is being resolved at the General Manger's level.

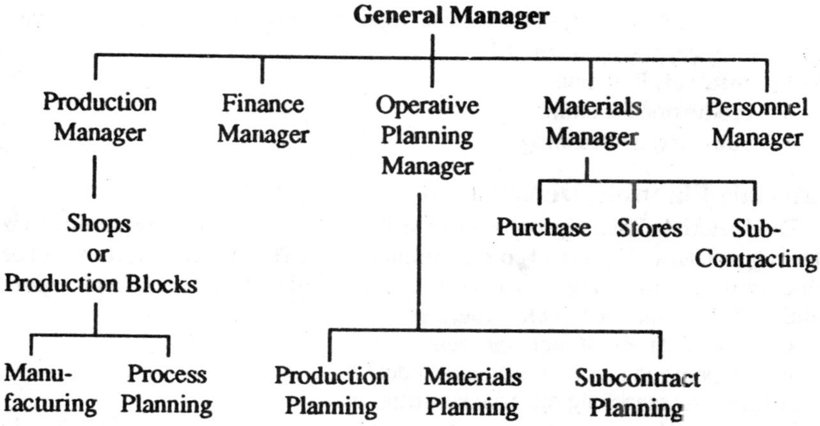

Integrated Materials Management Structure

The short comings of Operative Planning Type I and Operative Planning Type II structures have been overcome by Integrated Materials Management Structure by integrating Operative Planning activities and the Purchase, Stores and Sub contracting activities as given in the structure line diagram. This structure which incorporates the concept of "Integrated Materials Management" would have to be divided into two major groups viz:

(i) Operative Planning and
(ii) Purchase, Stores and Sub-Contracting.

The functions of various departments and sections in the area of Materials Management can be extended under this structure.

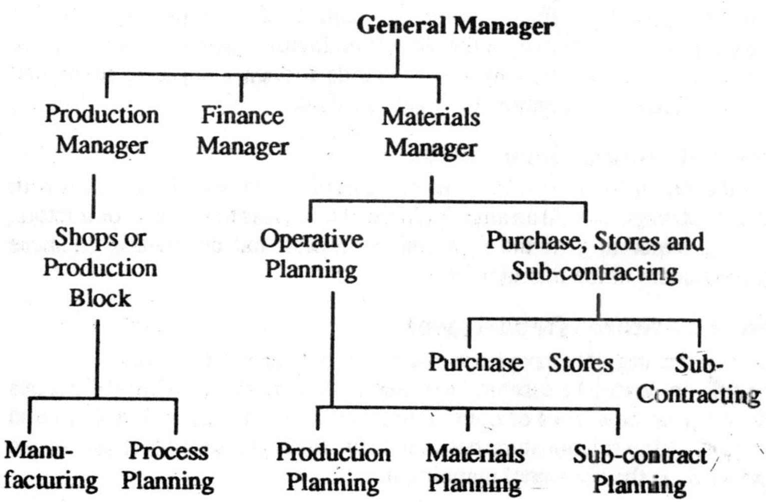

The head of Operating Planning who reports to Materials Manager will have the following departments with him:

★ Materials Planning
★ Production Planning
★ Sub-contract Planning

Materials Planning Department

The Materials Planning department will comprise of two major sections viz indenting section and issue and co-ordination section. The indenting section will be divided into material, category-wise/Product-wise cells. The functions and responsibilities of these indenting cells would be.

★ Consolidation of material requirement
★ Preparation and forwarding of indents.

Suggestions regarding material substitution.

The issue and co-ordination sections with materials planning would similarly be constituted product wise and would have the following functions and responsibilities:

★ Control on material issues
★ Preparation and forwarding of indents in the case of stock control materials.
★ Co-ordination for any transfer of materials.
★ Follow up section in the case of hold-up materials.

Production Planning Department

The production Planning and Control Manager would be responsible for ensuring that manufacturing shops have the necessary materials and components needed for meeting the overall production schedule.

Sub-Contract Planning Department

It would have the same functions for sub-contracted items as the production planning department would have for the shop manufactured items. It would also be issuing job orders and maintaining status records for sub-contracted items and ensuring timely deliveries to match the final schedules.

The Sub-contracting Department

This is the executive wing of the sub-contract planning department dealt with earlier. This department would arrange for issue of materials to the sub-contractors, follow up and expediting of the conversion process and accounting to these materials subsequent to the manufacture.

Purchase And Stores Department

These two departments have been discussed in details in this book.

In conclusion, it may be essential to reiterate that the structural modifications which may open up new lines of communication between various functions and offer the responsibility relationships between them, the organisational structure can only be effective as the personnel manning it.

Materials Management Organisation

The inter-related functions of materials management are normally looked after by individuals. As the materials functions expand, the functions of each individual becomes more and more specialized. The integrated materials management concept requires central co-ordination of all these related activities. Therefore the internal structuring of the various functions as well as the relationship of the materials management division with the other divisions—Engineering; Technical; Finance; Marketing in the overall organisation becomes critical. Therefore the materials function ought to be headed by a competent professional who must be a member of the senior management team as materials is a critical function. It the materials authority is dispersed among a number of departments in a company it gives an opportunity to the executive to a legitimate alibi. For example a purchasing manager reporting to a finance manager is in charge of buying parts and materials and a traffic manager reporting to sales manager buys transportation services and production control manager reporting to manufacturing manager schedules materials and controls inventories. Now suppose that one of the company's immediate objectives is to reduce materials cost by 5 percent. If the objective is achieved the purchase manager and traffic manager and their respective bosses, all can share the credit but who will be responsible if the objective is not achieved. Each will have legitimate alibi. The production control manager is not responsible for negotiating prices of materials and services. The purchasing manager buys in amounts determined by the material control department and his prices and bargaining power are determined by the quantity he buys. The traffic manager can't cut fright costs if purchasing insists on buying from suppliers of a particular place. The divided materials organisation not only makes it easy to pass the buck but it is wasteful. There is inevitably overlap of responsibility among materials functions; especially between production control and purchasing and consequent duplication of effort. If decisions reflect exclusively the view points of Personnel, Finance, Manufacturing, Sales and Engineering the best that can happen is that materials management is ignored.

Materials management position in the overall company organisation depends upon the company's operations and its environments. Once the relationship of materials management with regard to other departments in the overall organisational plan is finalised, the next phase is to finalise the internal structuring of the department. Some of the organisation charts of materials management department are discussed as under.

Organisation Based On Functions

Here the materials management department is structured on the basis of functions such as Stores; Transport; Receiving; Purchase; stock verification; Materials Control etc. Thus stores of different manufacturing division will be under one executive who will report to materials manager. The purchase activities will be under another executive who will report to materials manager. This system encourage specialisation and is being followed in many organisations.

Advantages. It is possible, in creating a materials organisation to divide work entirely by function. This would work well in small organisation, although these might be problems in a larger one. Following are the various advantages with this type of organisation:

(i) Efficient Operation: It is possible to become extremely adept at one particular job with functional specialisation.

(ii) More Flexible Organisation. An organisation with large number of functional specialisation can adjust more readily to changes in business volume. There is no need to have additional highly skilled people, who might not even be available in period of business expansion.

(iii) Encourage specialisation. With functional specialisation, Jobs can move readily by broken up into highly skilled and less skilled elements. Functional specialisation also makes it economic to hire specialists whom organisation could not other wise afford.

Disadvantages. The excessive application of the principle of functional specialisation can cause serious weaknesses in the organisation. Among them are the following.

(i) Employee dissatisfaction:—Executives get bored when their jobs become to specialised

(ii) Bureaucratisation:— If job becomes too specialised, everyone is liable to "pass the buck" and disclaim responsibility for solving a non-routine problem or for committing an error.

Organisation Based on Location

In case of a multi units organisation having several plants located in different parts of the country there are two alternatives. One is to have a centralised organisation located at the corporate office. The other is to have a decentralised materials management departments located in each units. When the materials organisation is by plant, materials personnel can work more closely with the other departments in that plant. They become more intimately familiar with the plant's problems. The major disadvantage of organisation by plant is that it tends to disperse the materials organisation. Some of the advantages of specialisation are lost and purchasing power is often diluted. On the other hand a centralised materials management department brings about a substantial reduction in procurement cost because of the bulk buying. In a centralised set up inter unit transfer of materials in emergency is possible. Surplus materials in one unit can be utilised in meeting the requirement of another unit. Since there is only one department dealing with various sources of supply, a high orders of skill can be expected.

A periodic reporting system should be established in the centralised materials management departments for multi-plant operations between the corporate office and the units. The corporate office may lay down common policies procedures and systems for all the plants.

Organisation Based on Product or Project

Each plant requires a materials organisation and at least part of the organisation must be physically located at the plant. Under this system of organisation, items are classified according to their nature as raw materials, bought out components, spares, imported items, finished goods and so an and they are assigned to executives. The advantages in such a system is that there is no wasteful duplication of efforts as each commodity is separately handled. The group of executives are intimately in touch with its respective commodity market and hence it becomes specialised. Since the materials organisation exist to help make some product or service more profitably, breaking up materials activities by product, process or project is logical when the overall materials organisation is broken up into a number of product groups, each member's job is more closely related to the profit objectives in a particular product line. The main disadvantage of organisation by product is that it tends to disperse the overall materials efforts.

Organisation By Stage of Manufacture

Organisation by stage of manufacture s consistent with the basic concept of materials management as the administration of the flow of materials to and from production equipment. Responsibility passes from department to department as the material or component moves from the idea stage to fabrication in the vendor's plant through the buyer's receiving and stores to the point where it is utilised in his manufacturing process. Each materials manager would be responsible for determining his own requirements, managing his own inventories, placing his own orders, and doing his own expediting. The fig (2.6) shows

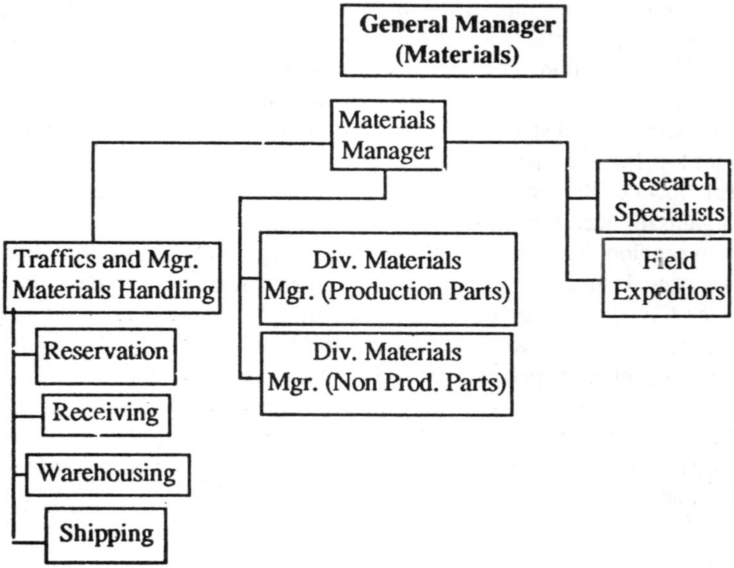

One or more specialists reporting to the plant materials manager could assist the materials managers with value analysis or economic analysis. Such specialist might also develop performance measurements so that the contribution of each materials manager to the achievement of overall objectives can be evaluated and reported.

Special Requirements

For organisations engaged in turn-key projects certain special aspects need to be considered. Erection of steel plants, commissioning of refineries, laying pipe-lines are some of the examples. In turn-key projects the project schedule will require timely procurement of materials and appropriate storage site where conventional stores management aspects are not relavent.

Span of Control

The five major ways in which to divide materials management work are:Organisation; location; product; stage of manufacturing and Special requirement, have been discussed Another fundamental principle of organising for material management is the concept of span of control which is concerned with how many division should be made. This does not mean it is desirable to have an organisation with many levels. On the contrary such an organisation has many disadvantages and there are many reasons why an organisation should be kept as 'flat' as possible. In a flat organisation the morale tends to be higher than in the deep organisation. The flat organisation is relatively democratic. To a great degree, everyone is his own boss and is forced to make his own decisions. Since people are on their own to a much greater degree, executive skill must be greater in the flat organisation and executives get much better training ground since they get a chance to make decisions at much earlier stage in their careers. The deep organisation also has advantages. Highly routine, unskilled job can easily be found for the inexperienced and relatively inept at the bottom of the pyramid, and the skills of the highly specialised and extra talented staff can be utilised to much greater degree in some position near the top. In the deep organisation fewer expects are needed since these is greater break down of the work by skill. The deep organisation also has some faults as the organisation tends to be bureaucratic and decisions are passed upward from echelon to echelon. Span of control in the ideal organisation is neither too broad nor too narrow. In such an organisation, the manager tries to get some of the initiative that the flat organisation of the deep structure. It is possible to build an effective organisation simply by applying the principles of division of work to each major job within the limits of span of control. The materials manager may want to have a certain executive reporting directly to him because he wishes to give particular attention to a certain area. The materials manager may want to have the buyer of the key material report directly to him, along with the purchasing agent, traffic manager and others.

Line And Staff Responsibilities

Line activities. To carry out its basic mission of adding value by distribution, materials management must embrace all activities that are concerned with getting purchased material from suppliers up to the stage where value begins to be added by manufacture. When the materials manager deals with purchased material, the materials manager is a line executive responsible for basic function of the business. Materials manager is also responsible for specialised service that logically fall under the control of either manufacturing or marketing. In general materials management is responsible as a line function for anything that is purchased up to the point where value begins to be added by manufacture. In addition materials management may also serve manufacturing in a staff capacity, Just as it does for marketing.

Distinction between line and staff

In modern business, the problems conforming the manager at all levels are so varied and complex that he cannot possibly master them all himself. The specialised assistance can be provided best by highly trained and experienced consultants or by agencies which have a staff relationship to the organisation as a whole. Line staff are those who can do the work in their respective discipline. A staff man cannot issue orders to a line officer. Staff prescribes the method, line follows the procedure.

Non-formal organisation. Existing within formal organisation is non-formal organisation that permits and sometimes encourages behaviour by members not intended or included in the formal organisation. This non-formal behaviour cannot only be desirable, which frequently it is, but it is also work oriented and contributes significantly to efficiency. Behavioural factors such as unnecessary socializing on the job, group values, and cultural likes and dislikes serve as bases for non-formal behaviour in formal organisation.

Non-formal organisation always exists along with formal organisation. It serves as an adjunct, is intangible, and takes on different degrees of importance depending upon the activity and the person involved. A manager should be aware of the presence and influence of non-formal organisation.

The informal organisation. It refers largely to what people do to their actions in terms of needs, emotions and attitude, not in terms of procedures and regulations. Organisation is nothing more than the informal systems of employers and employees groups which develop in any work environment for achieving explicit goals. In the informal organisation people work together because of their personal likes and dislikes. Informal groups may extend to other groups, as well as existing within the organisational unit. The effectiveness of this group depended upon the internal relations, the recognition of common goal, and desire to work together in accomplishing it. The formal organisation which fails to recognise and provide for the effective operation of such groups, loses its own effectiveness. The formal organisation can always be represented though line of authority and responsibility between superior and subordinates.

Changing concept of organisation requires distinction between the formal, defined and highly structured organisations and the informal organisation. The aim of the management should be to develop formal organisation of such scope as to encompass the varying, highly personal needs of the informal organisation. Organisation as described below, is extremely important to business enterprise. It facilitate administration, encourages sound, balanced growth and diversification, provides for the best use of human being and stimulate creativity for the overall growth.

Informal organisation is indefinite and rather structureless and has no definite subdivision. It may be regarded as a shapeless mass of quite varied densities. Informal organisation although comprising the processes of society which are cautious has two important classes of effects.

(a) It establishes certain attitudes, understandings, custom habits and institutions.

(b) It creates the condition under which formal organisation may arise.

Informal power attaches to a person, while formal authority attaches to a position. Informal power is personal, but formal authority is institutional. Informal organisations tend to remain smaller in order to keep within the limits of personal relationships.

Benefits of Informal Organisations

(a) The informal organisations blend with formal systems to make a workable system for getting the work done. Formal plans and policies cannot meet every problem in a dynamic situation because they are pre-established and partly inflexible.

(b) The informal organisation can lighten the work load of the formal manager.

(c) Informal organisation may act to fill in gaps in a manager's abilities.

(d) Informal organisation is that it can be a useful channel of employer communication.

(e) Informal organisation is like a safety valve for the frustrations and other emotional problems of group work.

Committee Organisation

Literally the word "committee" means those to whom some matter or charge is committed. It can be defined as: "A body of persons elected or appointed to meet on an organised basis for the discussion and dealing of matters brought before it".

Committees are common yet controversial in most organisations. They can and do exist at any organisational level, serve in various capacities and for different purposes, are known by many different names, and enjoy wide degrees of acceptance among management members. Extremely important work is accomplished via the committee route. Typically, educational enterprises are loaded with committees, and they are common in government and in business. In trade association and most professional societies, the major portion of the organisation structure is made up of committees.

The committee usually has a formally recognized and permanent place in the organisation structure. Its makeup, duties, membership, and decision-making power may be carefully spelled out. For example, some business enterprises have at the top level, a planning and policy committee, or a general management committee made up of selected company executives. The committee meets regularly-perhaps weekly-makes decisions, sees that they are enforced and participates in the management affairs of the company.

Reasons for the Widespread Use of Committees

(a) Expert and collective knowledge can be concentrated upon a specific problem. A wide range of experience can be tapped, exchange of ideas fostered, and effective give-and-take discussions are encouraged.

(b) **Coordination is assisted.** Different views can be unified and integrated, agreed prescribed courses of action established, and maximum understanding among committee participants achieved.

(c) Too much authority of one person is prevented. By its very nature, a committee tends to distribute its authority among the committee members, who can watch and check each other's actions.

(d) **Social values are provided.** Committee membership provided prestige, permits recognition as an equal with other members who have status, and tends to satisfy the human desire to belong and to do something worthwhile.

(e) **Encourages motivation.** Committee encourages, participation, cooperation is enhanced in the execution of a proposed action and is reasonably assured if the committee develops the plan. There is also knowledge acquired by the committee members and possibly pride of authorship gained by a member. Such characteristics have strong motivational value.

(f) **Education of members is promoted.** Each participant's viewpoint is broadened ; he gains an appreciation of the other unit's problems as well as those of the enterprise.

Social Organisation

It is apparent that in a democratic society, the ultimate authority of a business enterprise rests with public or society. The professional privileges are derived and controlled through laws and marketing process. Then beginning with the policies, a management system is organised to achieve the organisational objectives.

Chapter 3

ORGANISING MATERIALS MANAGEMENT DEPARTMENT

MATERIALS PERSONNEL MANAGEMENT

Introduction

The industrialisation has made the materials manager shoulder heavy responsibilities. The horizon of work of materials manager has been widening and he is expected to be in constant touch with supply sources, market trends and price levels. The materials manager regulates this flow of material in relation to changes in demand for finished products, actual or predicted prices of materials, supplier performance on quality and delivery availability of materials and other variables. He bases his decisions on information from other departments within his company suppliers and other sources, including news in business periodicals. Effective Materials Manager try to manage by exception. They try to organise their departments so that major problems requiring decisions are promptly called to their attention, while minor problems are automatically shunted to subordinates for solutions. The materials manager plays a vital role in make or buy decisions. Estimates of the variables of the market-place depend almost entirely upon his judgement. If he is wrong. The company may make a decision that will hurt its profits for years to come. The materials department is the company's prime contact with supply sources. The materials manager can bring know-how to bear on the company's technical problems. The professional materials managers often develop an expertise both from their educational back ground and from their association with suppliers. Professional materials specialists also should work closely with engineers engaged in manufacturing or production. The materials manager has a very important role in Production planning. The materials manager rarely is directly concerned with sales forecast but he is part of the group that translated the forecast into a master production schedule. The master production schedule influences the operation of every department in the company. It is normally the efforts of a committee to work for the final preparation and approval. The committee members are the materials manager; manufacturing manager and other key officials.

Materials Manager

Rapid changes in production technology have necessitated constant watch and re-evaluation of production techniques and raw material components. The advent of materials management as an organisational concept has emphasised the need for inter-functional co-operation in the materials area. These changes and many others have resulted in a new breed of materials management personnel. Gone are the days when the purchasing personnel were considered "schooled" if he spent years in the store house learning the parts used in production process. But today materials management personnel are professional and trained in management institutes with job skill similar to those of the company's executives. Personnel department has an important role in organising materials management department, Personnel management helps in the job of directing and coordinating the personnel of material management department with the objective of securing maximum production with minimum effort with clear objectives of caring for the individuals. *Some of the activities which need analysis are : Types of Position; Qualifications for purchasing; Sources of Materials management personnel; Selection of Purchasing personnel; Training; Compensation; Professionalism.*

The number of positions in a materials department varies from company to company and from industry to industry. The major factor that explain the variations are : the degree of centralisation; Variations in responsibilities, Size of the firm; differing production process. However with a centralised purchasing department the total number of man-hour spent on purchasing activities will tend to lie lower than in a company that decentralises its purchasing operations because centralised control leads to the efficiency that arises from specialisation. The nature of the production process also affects the size of the materials management department. In a company making a simple product on a high volume basis, material for a year's operation can be purchased on a few blanket type orders or systems contracts with delivery specified at regular intervals. On the other hand, a company making made-to-order units has to go through the entire buying routine for each unit, which requires many employees.

Duties And Responsibilities of Materials Manager

The number and kind of duties and responsibilities assigned to the materials manager depend to a considerable extent on the nature of his company's product and the level of management to which he belongs. The duties and responsibilities of materials manager generally include.

(i) Establishing and supervising materials management functions and procedures in line with company policies.

(ii) Internal organisation of materials management department so as to function efficiently in carrying out purchasing policies and procedures.

(iii) Organising and supervising departmental activities as the selection of Vendors, placing of orders, expediting, store-keeping and the approval of invoices for payment.

(iv) Development of sound supplier relationships.

(v) Co-ordination between materials department and other departments of the company. The head of the materials management department frequently serves on company's committees such as Product Development; Value Analysis; Budget committee and Quality assurance committees.

(vi) Preparing and analysing forecasts of supply conditions and price trends. The purchasing agent may also be responsible for establishing forward-buying policies in the light of these trends or he may serve as a member of a company committee that establishes these policies.

(vii) The auxiliary activities as disposal of scrap and surplus materials, inspection of incoming shipments, and traffic routing for incoming shipments are also frequently assigned to the materials manager.

(viii) Simplification, standardisation, and specification tasks in connection with materials and supplies that are purchased are sometimes the responsibility of materials manager.

(ix) Application of Electronic Data Processing; Computerisation and other Operations Research techniques for effective utilisation of various resources available to the materials manager.

The work of materials management department is broken down and assigned to other executives down in the hierarchy viz Assistant Materials manager; Senior Purchase Officer; Purchase Officer; Assistant Purchase Officer; Expediter; Production Coordinator; Materials Controller; Purchase Clerks etc.

Qualifications for Materials Management Department

The qualifications for various executives and other supervisory staff in materials management department may conveniently be grouped into three categories—Personal characteristics; Educational background, and business experience relevant to materials management functions.

The personal characteristics that promise success in purchasing are no different from those in any other field of business. The difference is likely to be in importance attached to some of the characteristics. It is unlikely that any experienced materials manager would agree precisely with the following personality traits:

(i) *Integrity:* Materials manager expend huge some of company money. They must be impervious to the financial temptations that accompany such a position of trust, whether in the form of an inordinate gift, or out right bribery. Personal integrity is also required to refrain from making unwarranted promises to potential suppliers in order to secure preferential treatment.

(ii) *Dependability:* The personality trait is important in purchasing personnel because frequently the continuity of operations of an industrial plant depends on the reliability of materials management department in following through on requisitions until goods are delivered according to specifications.

(iii) *Initiative:* Purchasing personnel are constantly faced with situations demanding initiative and imagination. The continual search for alternative sources of supply is one such area where initiative is importance.

(iv) *Tact:* Many materials managers consider tact the most important personal trait. The reason for this is the crucial importaince of maintaining sound and friendly vendor relations.

(v) *Industriousness:* Knowledge of materials and sources is acquired only after extended training and experience. The industriousness of materials management department is tested by the long hours they must work.

In addition to the above traits, the executives in materials management department should possess : Ability to learn; Ability to work on Details; Possess good human relations skills.

Education: Present educational trend is toward employing professionally qualified personnel as management trainee. Such trainees possess the post graduate qualification in management with specialisation in materials management. Most of trainees possess degree in engineering or science before completing their Business Administration qualification. Such trainees are provided one to two years training in various areas of materials management before being appointed as first level executives.

Business experience: Business experience is almost universally considered to be necessary for materials management in the higher-ranking position. Some of the large companies secure employees for positions in executive cadre by building up a pool of professionally qualified college graduate as trainees. These trainees are enrolled in an extended programme of indoctrination and work training, which rotates them through the major subdivisions of the company. During the training period those with an aptitude for and an interest in purchasing work can be selected out of the larger group and eventually assigned permanently to the purchasing department.

SELECTION PROCESS

The application blanks, tests and group discussion provide much valuable information about the candidate, yet they do not provide the complete set of information required of the applicant. Interview may be of great help in such cases. Interview may be taken to secure much information about a candidate in so far it enables the organisation to know about the applicant and vice versa. The main purposes of an employment interview are (a) to find out the suitability of the candidate, (b) to seek more information about the candidate and (c) to give the candidate an accurate picture of the job with details of terms and conditions and some idea of organisation policies and employer-employee relations. The factual data on the application blank may also be checked. The occasion i.e., personal meeting between the panel of interviewers and the candidate may also be used for testing the capabilities of the candidate. Thus an interview affords an opportunity to develop a clear total picture of the candidate.

Although personal interview is perhaps the most widely used method for selecting the employees, it has certain limitations also. Interview is an expensive device and sometimes, it is interpreted as having greater meaning and validity than is justified. Secondly, interview can test only the personality of the candidate and not his skill and ability for the job. Thirdly, interviewers may not be expert and may not be in a position to extract maximum information from the candidate. Fourthly, this device depends too much on the personnel judgement of the interviewers which may not always be accurate. Sometimes, there is a tendency to allow one prominent characteristic of the candidate to dominate appraisal of the entire personality and to colour the interviewer's judgement on the other traits. A good many psychologists take the view that interview is such an unreliable form of communication that it should be replaced by alternative methods wherever possible and that efforts devoted to training interviewers would much better be directed to developing, for instance, objective test of personality. It has been in big concerns that if after the interview a candidate is found to be satisfactory, he is sent to the department concerned to take the trade test. Scientifically designed tests are more objective than the interviews.

Interview Procedures and Techniques. Interview procedures and techniques vary from organisation to organisation and from individual to individual according to the purpose of the interview. The first point to hold an interview is the selection of candidates to called for the interview and preparing a schedule or plan for the interview. For this purpose the application forms filled by the candidates and the results of tests conducted by the personnel department may be used. Thus all pertinent information that can be gathered beforehand is assembled and an analysis is made to decide whether or not a particular applicant is worth interviewing. And if he is, the interview should be planned with him in the light of information supplied on the forms. This preparation saves time and mental efforts of the interviewers and enables them to sketch in advance at least a general picture of the interviewer. The selectors needs to match the facts supplied on the application form with the requirements of his job specifications—covering such obvious points as age, sex, materials status, essential qualifications and experience. He also needs to check the dates on the form to see that they provide a connected and coherent life history and he has to relate these dates to the applicant's age at the time to assess his suitability for the present job. In particular, the interviewer should match people to job by concentrating:

(i) The extent to which the applicant's previous work experience resembled the work in the post to be filled.
(ii) The applicant's social background, education and achievements.
(iii) The applicant's normal working tempo.
(iv) The applicant's initiative and decision making.
(v) The applicant's attitude towards authority and discipline.

While matching the people to the job, it is necessary that the interviewer must have the detailed knowledge of the requirements of the job and the qualities required to fulfil these requirements. For this purpose, he should go through very carefully the job description and the job specification drawn out by the personnel department.

This will help him in reconciling the requirements of the job and the qualities possessed by the individuals.

Setting for the Interview. The proper physical arrangements for the interview are of great importance. They enhance the reputation of the organisation in the eyes of the candidates. The interview should be conducted in a room free from disturbance, noise and interruptions, so that interview may be held confidentially and in a quiet environment. The main physical condition for successful interviewing is that the interviewer should look ready for the meeting and room look ready for a private discussion. Privacy and comfort are generally recognised as aids to free talk. People generally speak more freely and frankly when they are at ease and do not feel threatened.

Keeping to time is another important problem. The interviewers who keep to the appointed time are very few indeed. But a candidate who is called for an interview should not be expected to wait for too long. Waiting for an interview irritates many candidates more than any other single factor in the selection process. If unavoidable delays to develop, it is better to cut one interview short and risk injustice to one applicant than to fall further and further behind in schedule and risk injustice to many who have become nervous or annoyed. The applicants should be made to sit and wait in the waiting room only. Good organisations also offer cold or hot drinks to keep them fresh. Thus the candidates should not be made to feel that they are beggars who can wait anywhere and indefinitely. Since the interviewer who has a job to offer is in a who has come to present his life history to obtain it, the interviewer (employer) should try to create such conditions which are as convenient as possible.

Conducting the Interview. An important aid to conduct successful interview is that the candidate should be made to have a feeling of leisure. He will not be able to answer properly if he feels that he is being buried through the question—answer period. Under ideal conditions, a successful interview can be conducted from 20 to 30 minutes. But even then, an expert interviewer should manage to convey the impression that he has plenty of time. Leisure is a state of mind rather than a matter of minutes. Right at the start, the candidate should be given to understand that he is not taking an examination, but is being called in to give further information about himself, unless the candidate is put at ease, it is very difficult and doubtful whether a right assessment can be made of his capabilities. So the interviewers must try to create a harmonious atmosphere in which relevant information can be obtained by both the parties. No matter whether the candidate joins or not the interviewer must remember that he represents the organisation and the impression he gives is vitally important. The candidate's reactions to the interviewer will also deeply affect the value of the interviewers.

An interviewer cannot conduct an entirely useful interview if he has not prepared himself for that. He must have the knowledge of important points about the candidates, which can be had from the application form and other record supplied by the personnel department. On the basis of this knowledge of various facts he can chalk out the questions to be asked from the candidates. interviewers may sometimes find it helpful to put down a list of question to which they want specific answers. He should not do this with pencil poised over pad in the manner of a policeman, but use the list as a guide only. He should try to listen the candidate with intelligence and silence. The interviewer's attentive silence may be his best contribution to a successful interview.

Many interviewers are afraid to use the obvious device of taking notes because if unnecessarily irritates the interviewee. Notes should never be taken until after a satisfactory relationship has been established. At that time, note-taking may produce a favourable effect on the candidate since he is likely to think that his remarks are considered sufficiently important to be written down. If the candidate is not in a position to answer to a question, the interviewee should help to answer the question. At the end of the Interview, the Chairman of the Board should conclude the interview by thanking the candidate for giving more information about himself.

There are generally more than one candidate for any new position in the organisation, so it is important to make an assessment of the candidates as soon as possible. This may be committed to paper, recording his exceptional abilities and past experience, any training requirements he might have and an assessment of his potential. An interviewee assessment form may be used for this purpose.

After the interview is over, every interviewer should review his notes and consider what he has accomplished. The completed interview notes form an important part of a case record. They are valuable for all kinds of special reference, *e.g.*, to review before another interview with the same person. All the members of the interview committee or the Selection Board will deliberate on the matter and shall prepare a panel of candidates recommended for selection in order of preference.

Increasing interview effectiveness. In order to increase the effectiveness of employment interview proper attention should be given to the following factors :

1. Information about the applicant to be interviewed.
2. Information about the job.
3. Structure of the interview itself.
4. Interview skill.

Information about the applicant. Before a candidate is interviewed, all the relevant information about him is assembled and is passed on to the interviewer for his review. At this stage, the applicant's file will contain the application blank, reports of reference check, preliminary interviewer's notes and test scores. When the file is delivered to the employment interviewer, he review it and plans his interview accordingly. For this review of the applicant file, the interviewer shall determine:

(i) Does the applicant meet minimum standard set up for each hurdle in the selection process? Does the applicant fulfill the requirements of the job under consideration? Before beginning the interview, the interviewer must satisfy that the applicant possesses the minimum qualifications required for the job as revealed by the job specification and has passed all hurdles, the selection process. In the case of failure at one or more hurdles, the interview may be relatively brief ending in refection of the candidate.

(ii) What background factors and personal qualities must be explored? In the case of applicant who has passed all the hurdles successfully, the bulk of the interview time may be devoted to the giving of job and organisation information once the interviewer is satisfied that there are no obvious personal characteristics which would disqualify the applicant. But if the candidate is viewed as a borderline case, the task of interviewer will welcome more complex since he will have to search for evidence which can be used as a basis for recommendation for or against employment or to aid in placement on a job where specific limitations will not be a handicap.

Information about the job. What is the extent to which an interviewer should be familiar with job for which he interviews applicants? In fact, considerable information in the form of job specification and job description is necessary if the interviewer is both to give information and make valid judgments with respect to applicant abilities. Some people even believe that only individuals with work experience on specific jobs or related jobs are suitable for selecting other men for these jobs. But this may not be feasible always. It will do it the interviewer spends some time observing the jobs for which he is to interview to have the actual work experience. Undoubted this procedure and job specifications and job descriptions would do much to and to the interviewer's understanding of a specific kind of work. Some organisations even assign the employment interviewers to spend time with each foreman, observing the various plant operations add keeping abreast of changes in jobs as they are performed. This increase the knowledge of the interviewers and they are enabled to ask from the applicants the questions relating to the jobs for which they have applied. This also helps them not to repeat the errors resulting into faulty selection in the past.

The Interview Structure. Structure of the interview should be properly planned. Completely unstructured employment interview is little more than a casual or social conversation without direction, purpose, control or recognizable terminal point. Neither the applicant not the interviewer shall gain much in the way of relevant information from such a session. At the other extreme, the completely structured interview is inflexible and offers no opportunity to explore or probe the answers applicant may give. However, in order to avoid either extreme, the organisations should develop and use standardised interview.

Interviewer's Skill. *How should the Interview be Conducted?* Following are various points which an experienced interviewer should keep in mind while conducting the interview :

Job Knowledge. He should be thoroughly familiar with the specifications of the job for which the applicant has applied and should have the capacity to relate the job requirements to those qualifications of the applicant that can be judged in the interview.

Adequate background information about the applicant. The interviewer should know in advance the kind of information to be obtained in the interview so that no important areas are overlooked. For this purpose the interviewer should review the application blank, reference checks, preliminary interviewer's notes and test scores. He should not waste interview time by asking for information already available.

Schedule interviews to have enough time. Though neither the interviewer nor the interviewee can afford to spend unlimited time, the interviewer should ask the questions from the candidate in an unhurried atmosphere. He should avoid rapid fire questions. He should give the interviewee time to formulate his replies or to recall experiences so that full information may be gathered.

Holding interview in private. The interviewer should conduct the interview in a separate room meant for this purpose. He should avoid distractions and interruptions because of visitors, telephone calls or nay other reason, since they break the conversational flow and make it difficult for the applicant to give information in confidence.

Putting applicant at ease. The interviewer should establish a friendly and informal atmosphere at the start and should avoid impersonal approach by his interest in the applicant as an individual.

Listening the applicant. It should be recognised that the interview has been scheduled in order to obtain information about the applicant and if the interviewer goes on speaking, he will not be getting much information about the applicant. He should be a very good listener. While he guides and directs the interview as necessary to keep the topic of conversation on pertinent subjects, he should keep his own questions and comments as brief as possible in order to let the applicant express himself as fully as time allows.

Adjusting the level of the language to the ability of the respondent. While an interviewer always avoids any sign of talking down to applicant, he should also be on the alert for signs that his question is not understood.

Keeping control of the Interview. The interviewer should plan the interview beforehand so as to keep the interview from disgressing into areas not related to the purpose of the interview or which do not provide useful insights.

Bewaring of one's own prejudices. The interviewer should be particularly conscious of the dangers of allowing specific physical or cultural stereotypes to mark his accurate appraisal of the candidate. He should be careful to discount initial impressions whether favourable or unfavourable while evaluating specific traits and should avoid generalising form one trait to other traits.

Avoiding any suggestion of discrimination. The interviewer should be careful to guard against the introduction of subject matter that might be interpreted as evidence of discriminatory attitude on the part of the employer. Race, religion and political views are the topics which he should avoid.

Closing the Interview. It is necessary to learn how and when to close the interview. He should close the interview with the public relations objective in mind.

He should be courteous and friendly whether the applicant is qualified or not. Except in those instances in which he has been authorised to hire new personnel, he should give positive indication of company interest to the qualified applicant and arrange for final interview with the department. However, in case of panel interview, department head is present at the interview. Where the applicant is not qualified, this may be made known to him before the interview is concluded. Every candidate must be thanked for having shown interest in the organisation.

Recording the facts and observations. The interviewer should record the facts during the interview and impressions and judgments immediately thereafter. He should not trust the memory but record facts during the interview in an open and honest manner. He will strengthen the applicant's confidence that all important facts will be considered in the final judgement by making this record by doing so.

References. A referee is potentially an important source of information about a candidate's ability and personality if he holds a responsible position in some organisation or has been the boss or employer of the candidate. Prior to final selection, the prospective employer normally makes an investigation on the references supplied by the applicant and undertakes more or less a thorough search into the candidate's past employment, education, personal reputation, financial condition, police records etc. However, it is often difficult to persuade a referee to give his opinion frankly. The organisation may persuade him to do so by giving assurance that all information will be treated as strictly confidential. The referee may be encouraged to give precise and solvent information if he is sent a description of the job for which the applicant has applied and then asked specific questions about the applicant's abilities to perform the duties listed. He will find it easier to supply factual information than mere opinion. Reference method has its drawbacks also. The referee may not give accurate information about the candidate. He may give his good impression about him because of his relations with him or if he is his employer, he may give a good report to get rid of him. So this method cannot be relied upon completely.

Physical Examination. The pre-employment physical examination or medical test of a candidate is an important step in the selection procedure. Though in the suggested selection procedure, medical test is located near the end, but this sequence need not be rigid; an organisation may place the examination relatively early in the process so as to avoid time and expenditure to be incurred on the selection of medically unfit person. Some organisations either place the examination relatively early in the selection procedure or they advise the candidates to get themselves examined by a medical expert so as to avoid disappointment at the end. However, there are some good reasons for locating it last. Firstly, this step is time-consuming and expensive and secondly, the number of applicants who reach this stage are considerable less than the number who fill out application blanks. Finally, there may be an interval of time lapsing between initial screening by the personnel department and the actual entry into the organisation. Giving the medical test near the end ensures that employee is physically fit for the job at the time of actual entry.

Physical examination has at least three objectives:

(i) It serves to ascertain the applicant's physical capabilities to meet the job requirements;

(ii) It serves to protect the organisation against the unwarranted claims under worker's compensation laws or against law suits for damage; and

(iii) It helps to prevent communicable diseases entering the organisation. These objectives must not always become the grounds for the rejection of applicants, but may also be used discover what jobs they are qualified to fill in case of exceptional candidates.

TRAINING

After having selected the most suitable persons for various jobs in the organisation through the application of scientific techniques, the next function is to arrange for their training. No company has a choice of whether to provide training or not, the only choice is that of method. All types of jobs in the organisation usually require some type of training for their efficient performance. Employees talent are not fully productive without a systematic programme of training. Moreover, big organisations hire a large number of young people every year. Because the vast majority of these do not know how to perform jobs assigned to them in work organisations, they must be trained by their employers. Even those who have learnt a technical or professional field or work at some college or institution must receive some initial training in the form of orientation to the policies, practices and ways of their employing organisation. The need for a systematic training has increased because of rapid technological changes which create new jobs and eliminate old ones. New jobs require some sort of special skills which may be developed in old work-force only by giving them necessary training.

The employee tries to train himself by trial and error or by observing others if no formal training programme exists in the organisation. But it is an established fact that the absence of a systematic training programme will result in higher training costs. The employee will take a much longer time in learning the skills. He may not be able to learn the best operating methods. Thus adequate training is equally desirable for the organisation and the employee. Training is valuable to the employee in terms of better job security and greater opportunity for advancement. A skill acquired through training is an asset for the organisation and the employee can be taken away only by the complete elimination of the need for that skill because of rapid changes in technology. Therefore, whenever new persons are appointed, they must be trained for the efficient performance of their jobs. Even if a person is a skilled one, he requires some training because many jobs in the organisation consist of tasks which are unique and peculiar to it and many other jobs do not resemble exactly in work situations as found in the place of training.

Concepts. Training is the organised procedure for increasing the knowledge and skill of people for a definite purpose. The purpose of training is to achieve a change in the behaviour of those trained and to enable them to do particular job. In the industrial situations this means that the trainees will acquire new manipulative skills, technical knowledge, problems-solving ability or attitudes, etc. Any goods training programme lays down the procedure by which people gain knowledge and skill to perform their job effectively and efficiently.

Training And Education

Training must be distinguished from education. Training is concerned with increasing knowledge and skill in doing a particular job and the major burden of training falls upon the employer of the employee. But education is broader in scope. Its purpose is to develop individuals. It is concerned with increasing general knowledge and understanding of total environment. By education we generally mean formal instruction in a school or a college, whereas training is vocationally oriented an disimparted at the work-place. Training usually has a more immediate utilitarian purpose than education. Actually, the distinction between training and education is not precise because in many cases both training education occur at the same time. Some formal vocational school programmes are job-oriented only, whereas some employee development programmes in industry quite wider in scope and they may be viewed as education. Particularly, where the emphasis is being given on off-the-job training the objective of the industry is to increase the knowledge and understanding of the employees of the business and general environment. Thus business firms are also involved indirectly in the educational process when they are organising training for the development of their employees.

Need. Training is a vital tool of management, capable of making important contributions to the goals of the organisation. Starting with the identification of training needs and the requirements and problems of the organisation, training attempts to improve the performance of both by closing the distance between expectations and achievements. Training is a never ending process and an integral part of the business system, which aims at bringing about change in behaviour of people.

The effectiveness of an organisation's training programme depends upon the extent to which management is committed to support it, the proper assignment of responsibility to line managers and training incharge for the training effort, and the care and sill with which the training is planned, implemented and evaluated. Top management can greatly influence the quality of training in the organisation by the policies and practices it adopts and the extent to which it supports and participates in the training effort. Top management must provide a climate which is conducive to continued learning and growth.

Line managers have also a great responsibility for the training of their people. They must cooperate with the training specialists in determining the training needs and devising suitable training programme. They are also to help in conducting and evaluating the training activity. Lastly, their greatest contribution is to help the subordinates apply to their jobs what they have learnt from training.

Functions. Training enables the employees to get acquainted with jobs and also increase their aptitudes and skills and knowledge. It makes newly recruited employees fully productive in the minimum of time. Even for the old workers, it is necessary to refresh them and to enable them to keep up with new methods and techniques as well as new machines and equipments for doing the work. Thus training is not a 'one-step process', but it is a continuous or never ending process because it increases the knowledge and skill of new employees in performing their jobs and it serves as a refresher course for the old employees. Training job will never be finished as long as the organisation remains in business. At any given time the different phase of training programme will be found at practically every stage of progress. Men may be learning by their own experiences and by trial and error methods. Training does not disappear from any organisation merely because its presence is ignored.

Purpose of Training

The purpose of training is to bring about improvement in the performance of work. It includes the learning of such techniques as are required for the intelligence performance of definite tasks. It also comprehends the ability to think clearly about problems arising out of the job and its responsibilities and to exercise sound judgement in making decision affecting the work. Lastly, it includes those mental attitudes and habits of thought which are suggested under the general term 'morale'.

The basic logic of training can be described as consisting of following steps :

1. Identifying the training need or goals. This involves a clear concept of the knowledge, skills or attitudes which the trainee is supposed to acquire during his training period.
2. Selecting a group of trainees. This involves the section and preparation of employees who require training.
3. Designing the training programmes in terms of the appropriate learning theory, taking into account the nature of subject and capacity of trainees.
4. Selection of faculty and mode of training.
5. Evaluating the outcomes of training with a scientifically designed evaluation scheme. The evaluation programme should involve observation of the trainees back on the job at some period of time after training and should also determine whether changes observed are attributable to the training efforts.

Benefits. The major values of training are discussed below:

1. **Reduced learning time.** A systematic programme of training helps to reduce the learning time to reach the acceptable level of performance. The employees need not learn by trial and error or by observing others and waste at long time. The qualified instructors will help the new employees to acquire the skill and knowledge to do particular jobs within a short interval of time.

2. **Better Performance.** Well trained employees usually show a greater increase in and a higher quality of work output than an untrained group. Training increases the skill of employee in the performance of a particular job. An increase in skill usually helps in increase in both quantity an quality of output. Training is also of great help to the existing employees. It helps them to increase their level of performance of their present job assignment.
3. **Reduced Supervision.** If the employees are given proper training, the responsibility of supervision is lessened. Training does not eliminate the need for supervision, but it reduces the need for detailed and constant supervision.
4. **Standardisation.** With the help of training the best available methods of performing the work can be standardised and made available to all employees. Standardisation will make high levels of performance rule rather than the exception. Employees will work intelligently and make fewer mistakes when they possess the required know-how and have an understanding of their jobs and of the interdependence of one job on another.
5. **Economy.** Trained personnel will be able to make better and economical use of materials and equipments. Wastage will also be low. In addition, the rate of accidents and damage to machinery and equipment will be kept to the minimum by the well trained employees. These will lead to less cost of production per unit.
6. **Heightened Morale.** The morale of the employees is increased if they are given proper training. A common objective of organisation training programme will would employees attitudes to achieve support for organisation activities and to obtain better cooperation and greater loyalty. With the help of training dissatisfactions, complaints, absenteeism and turnovers can also be reduced among the employees. Thus training helps in building an efficient and co-operative work-force.
7. **Organisational stability and flexibility.** Training increases the stability and flexibility of the organisation. Creation of a reservoir of trained replacements will increase the stability of the organisation will be enabled to sustain its effectiveness despite the loss of key personnel. Training can also be used to help the employees to gain multiple skills to enable their transfer to job where the demand is higher, and thus organisation will be in a position to adjust to short run variations in the volume of work.
8. **Better Management.** A manager can make use of training to help him to manage in a better way. To him, training the employees can assist in improving his own planning, organising, and controlling abilities. For instance, maintaining higher standards of quality, building a satisfactory organisation structure, delegating authority and stimulating employees, are all assisted by effective training.

Under the umbrella of training, several useful functions of management can be performed. A manager can delegate authority and responsibility to his subordinates, who will not be reluctant to accept new assignments if they have been given the proper training. In addition, management can get better results and can put its plans into action surely with the help of trained work-force. Management can also increase the morale of employees and motivate them to work for the achievement of organisational goals by installing a suitable system of training.

Requisites of Training

Training is a continuous process which is aimed at increasing the skill and knowledge of new as well as old employees to enable them to perform their jobs well. The process of training is shown in the diagram. Training involves learning about the job by an employee. But sometimes, a manager decides to set up a training programme because it is the popular thing to do and because, other organisations are doing it. Such a tendency is not good in the long-run. Training programme should be set up only after having clear-cut objectives in mind. Training without objectives is useless and merely involves wastage of money.

Training programme should be established only when it is felt that they can aid in solving specific problems. The rational way of deciding what kind of training activity to undertake is to make an analysis of the job and the qualities of the employees to identify trouble spots where training may help.

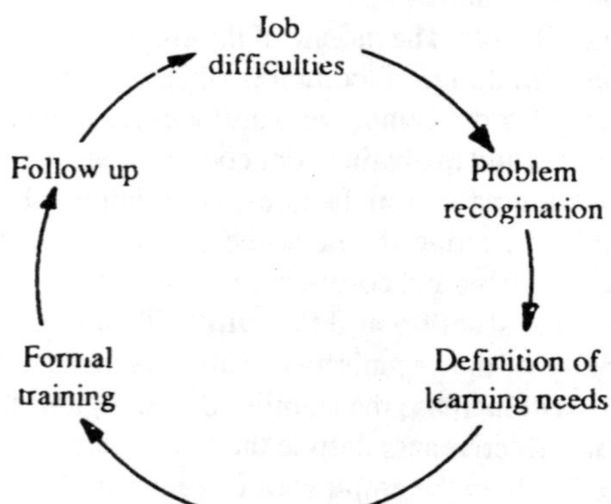

Fig. 3.1

Training is not the solution for all the troubles. For instance, if the employees' output is low this may be corrected by better skill training. But this problem may also be because of faulty material, process equipment or engineering design. If it appears that general caliber of the employees is low, this problem may be solved by training. But in other cases, the training will not be of much use. Following are the steps for discovering training needs :

1. *Analyzing jobs and men.* If the men are less capable to perform the particular jobs they can be given training to increase their skills.
2. *Identifying Managerial problems.* If there is low productivity, low productivity, poor quality, high costs, high rate of absenteeism and labour turnover and excessive grievances, indiscipline, these will indicate the need for training.
3. *Collecting employee and managerial opinions.* The training section may either by interviews or questionnaires obtain views of different people regarding necessary and desirable training programme.
4. *Aanticipating requirements of different jobs.* The line managers can forecast beforehand the requirements of manpower in the future on the basis of long-term plans regarding business expansion, new plants, new designs and new technology. Training may be given to the existing employees to enable them to meet the requirements of new jobs in the future.

When the training needs are found, it is advisable to lay down objectives of training on the basis of needs of circumstances of the case. The main objective of any training programme is to change the behaviour of the persons towards their jobs or to enable them to acquire skill and knowledge to do the jobs well. Training programmes must be chalked out with the aim to contribute towards the achievement of organisational objectives.

Chapter 4

MATERIALS MANAGEMENT PLANNING AND ANALYSIS

Introduction

Planning is a major part of every executive job. In most organisations, the materials manager can make significant contribution to the long range planning process. As other executives, the materials manager is also responsible for the professional development of his subordinates. While this effort may have almost no impact on current operations, it is vital to the achievement of broad long-range plans. Although materials manger can almost always make important contribution to long range,planning and materials manager is far more concerned with short term planning. The materials planning process always should be in terms of objectives. In his plan, the materials manager should indicate how he proposes to achieve each of his objectives. Some typical ways in which a materials manager might plan to achieve the objective of Low prices; High inventory turnover; Low-cost of acquisition and possession; Continuity of supply; Consistency of quality and favourable suppliers relations. In the context of materials management, planning has to be done for highly non-programmed decisions such as import policy, foreign exchange availability and credit squeeze. In a similar manner, planning has also to be done for highly programmed decisions such as hypothecating inventory for working capital, working out delivery schedules etc.

Materials Planning

Materials planning can be used to assess the firms requirement for different planning horizons. As the planning horizon exceed one year, the forecast becomes less reliable. Normally planning is done on a quarterly basis as materials planner at the beginning of every quarter will find that some materials are in short supply and some in excess, owing to errors in forecasting. Following are some of the guidelines which can be used for effective and reliable materials planning:

(i) In working out the horizon for planning purposes, the longest lead time that are anticipated must be taken into account so that they are adequately covered.

(ii) Operating environment of the firm must be carefully analysed.

(iii) When the planning horizon is short, if more plans are made in a year the materials plan will be more reliable.

(iv) Whenever possible, computerisation of materials planning process should be done. This is important because computers are ideally suited to handle fluctuations in demand and work out new and revised materials plan.

To understand Material Planning we must try to understand planning as a concept and the importance of planning in effective decision making. According to G.R. Terry, planning is a deliberate, concious research used to formulate the design and orderly sequence of actions through which it is expected to reach the objectives. Thus all planning involves anticipation of future course of events. Planning means deciding in advance what is to be done, how and where it is to be done, who will do it and how results are to be evaluated. In other words, planning is determination of a course of action to achieve the desired results. Planning therefore is necessary to ensure proper utilisation of human and material resources to achieve the objectives of the enterprise. Ideally the materials planning process should start at the bottom and work its way up. That is, the overall materials plan should represent a composite of the plans of the various sections that report to the materials manager. This plan would then be reviewed by the materials manager and other key subordinates. If it seems consistent with the overall plan, it would then be consolidated into a combined statement of objectives for materials department which the materials manager would submit to top management for approval.

The Nature of Planning

The nature of planning can be understood by four major aspects of planning: (i) contribution to objectives, (ii) primacy of planning, (iii) pervasiveness of planning and (iv) efficiency of plan.

(i) *Contribution to Objectives.* The purpose of any plan is to device certain predetermined objectives and purposes. Plans alone cannot make an enterprise successful. Planning seeks to achieve an objective through a consistent, coordinated efforts. It forecasts which actions will tend towards the ultimate objective and which tend away from it, which actions are likely to offset on an other and which are irrelevant.

(ii) *Pervasiveness of Planning.* Planning is a function of all managers in an enterprise irrespective of their position and authority. The channel and nature of planning may vary with the authority and responsibility of the manager depending upon the policies and the plans outlined by the superiors. Planning at various levels may vary in its importance but everyone in an organisation right from the Chairman to the Supervisor must plan. Planning at senior manager level may be more important and applicable to a larger portion of an enterprise.

(iii) *Efficiency of Plan.* The efficiency of a plan is measured by the amount it contributes to purpose and objectives as offset by the cost and other unsought consequences required to formulate and operate it. A plan which contributes to the attainment of objectives at too higher costs cannot be considered efficient. A plan can be regarded as efficient if when put into action it brings about the attainment of objectives with minimum efforts and with maximum positive gains, greater than the costs.

Types of Plan

Plans may also become inefficient in the attainment of objectives by jeopardizing group satisfaction. The failure to recognise the variety of plan results into difficulty in making planning effective. To build and equip a new factory is a plan but what is sometimes over looked is that a number of other cases of future actions are also plans thus we can see that plans are varied. They are also classified as (i) missions, (ii) objectives (iii) strategies, (iv) programmes and (v) budgets.

(i) *Missions.* Every kind of organised group operation has to be meaningful, a purpose or a mission. In every social system, an enterprise has to function in some environment of society. The purpose of business generally is the production and distribution of goods and services. The purpose of Public Works Department is to build public buildings. The purpose of courts is to administer law and so on. To achieve the missions one must have plans. It is sometimes thought that the missions of business is to make profit, it is true that every kind of business must have profits but this has to be achieved keeping in view the environment in which business exist and that is possible to accomplish by going in clear directions which needs proper planning.

(ii) *Objectives.* Objectives are the ends towards which an activity aims. They represent not only the end point of planning but the end towards which organising, directing and controlling are aimed. Thus, objective are plans and they involve the same planning process as any other type of planning. A sales goal for example cannot be guessed but it must be determined in the light of purpose and circumstances. Likewise a plan to accomplish a certain sales goal will have within it project or departmental goal.

(iii) *Strategies.* For years the military used strategies, or a grand plan, made in the light of what is believed an adversary might or might not do. While the term 'strategies' still usually has a competitive implications, it has been increasingly used to reflect broad overall concept of an enterprise operation. Strategies therefore, most often denote a general programme of action and deployment of emphasis and resources to attain comprehensive objective. Anthony defines them as resulting from "the process of deciding on objective of the organisation, on changes in these objectives, on the resources used to attain these objectives and on the policies that are to govern the acquisition used and disposition of these resources. Chandler defines, a strategy as the determination of the basic long-term goals and objectives of an enterprise, and the adoption of courses of action and the allocation of resources necessary to carry out the goals.

(iv) *Programmes.* Programmes are a complex of goals, policies, procedure, rules, task assignment, steps to be taken, resources to be employed, and other element to carry out a given course of action. They are ordinarily supported by necessary capital and operating budget. Programmes may be major or minor one. A primary programme may call for many derivative programmes. All the programmes necessitate coordination and timings, since the failure of any part of net work of derivative plans means delay for the major programme with consequent unnecessary cost and loss of revenue. Thus one seldom finds that a programme of any importance of an enterprise planning stand by itself. It is usually a part of complex of programmes depending upon some and effecting others. This interdependence of plan makes planning very difficult. The results of poor or inadequate planning are seldom isolated, for planning is only as strong as its weakest link. Even a seemingly unimportant procedure or rule, if badly conceived may wreck an important programme. Coordinated planning requires extra ordinarily managerial skill. It truly requires the most rigorous application of systems thinking and actions.

(v) *Budget.* A budget as a plan is a statement of expected results expressed in numerical terms. It may be referred to as a 'numbcrized' programme. As a matter of fact, the financial operating budget is often called a "profit plan". It may be expressed either in financial terms or in terms of man-hours, units of product, machine hours, any other numerically measurable term. It may deal with operations, as the expense budget does, it may reflect capital outlays as the capital expenditure budget does, or it may show flow of cash, as the cash budget does.

Steps in Planning

Although steps in planning are presented here in connection with major programmes but essentially the same steps could follow in any thorough planning process. As minor plans are usually simpler, earlier steps are more easily accomplished but practical steps are of general application. Obviously valuable time of top executives should not be wasted in making a decision of lesser consequence, but on the contrary it is also shocking if very little time is devoted to make a planning decision involving large investments.

(i) *Awareness of Opportunity.* Awareness of an opportunity is the real starting point for planning. It includes a preliminary look at possible future opportunities and the ability to see them clearly and completely a knowledge of where we stand in the light of our strengths and weaknesses. An understanding of why we wish to solve uncertainties, and a vision of what we expect to gain. Setting realistic objective depends of this awareness. Planning requires realistic diagnosis of the opportunity situation.

(ii) *Establishing Objectives.* The first step in planning itself is to establish planning objectives for the entire enterprise and then for each subordinate unit. Objectives specifying the results expected indicate the end points of what is to done, where the primary emphasis is to be placed, and what is to be accomplished by the network of strategies, policies, procedures, rules, budget and programmes.

Enterprise objectives should give direction to the nature of all major plans which, by reflecting these objectives, define the objectives of major departments. Major department objectives, in turn, control the objectives of subordinate departments, and so on down the line. The objectives of other departments will be better framed, however, if sub-division manager understand the overall enterprise objectives and the implied derivative goals and if they are given an opportunity to contribute their ideas to them and to the setting of their own goals.

(iii) *Premising*. A second logical step in planning is to establish and obtain agreement to utilise, and disseminate critical planning premises. These are forecast data of a factual nature, applicable to basic policies, and existing company plans. Premises, then are planning assumptions in other words, the expected environment of plans in operations. This step leads to one of the major principles of planning, the more individuals charged with planning understand and agree to utilize consistent planning premises, the more coordinated enterprise planning will be.

Forecasting is important in premising. Apart from forecasting the basic economical data forecasting of future, economic and social environments which may effect the project, is equally essential. A superior's plans effecting a subordinate manager's area of authority becomes premises for the latter's planning. Because the future environment of plans is so complex, it would not be profitable or realistic to make assumptions about every detail of the future to those which are critical, or strategic, to a plan, that is, those which influence its operation most.

Lack of planning coordination, through use by managers of different sets of premises, can be extremely costly. The use of consistent premises should therefore, be agreed upon. A single standard for the future is necessary for good planning, even though this standard includes several sets of premises with the instruction that different sets of plans be developed on each. Some companies, for example customarily develop plans in prospect of both peace and war so that, regardless of what occurs, the company will be ready. Obviously, only one set of premise if coordination of its element is to be achieved.

Since agreement to utilize a given set of premises is important to coordinated planning, it becomes a major responsibility of managers, starting with those at the top, to make sure that subordinate managers understand the premises upon which they are expected to plan. It is not unusual for chief executives in well-managed companies to force top managers with differing views, through group deliberation, to arrive at a set of major premises that all can accept. But whether they are acceptable to all or not, no chief executive can afford to change a situation where his lieutenants are planning their portions of the company's future on substantially different premises.

The importance of premising is illustrated by the case where a company president, believing that all departments should develop their own budget and to find that the budgets did not fit, and he had a complex of inconsistent plans of his hands. Had he been aware of the importance of premises, he would never have asked for budgets without first giving his department heads their guidelines.

(iv) *Determining Alternative Courses.* The third step in planning is to search for and examine alternatives courses of action. There is seldom a plan for which reasonable alternatives do not exist and quite often an alternative that is not obvious proves to be the best.

The more common problem is not finding alternatives, but reducing the number of alternatives so that the most promising may be analysed. Even with mathematical techniques and the computer, there is a limit to the number of alternatives that may be examined. It is, therefore, usually necessary for the planner to reduce by preliminary examination the number of alternatives to those promising the most fruitful possibilities or by mathematically eliminating, through the process of approximation, the least promising ones.

(v) *Evaluating Alternative Courses.* Having sought out alternative courses and examined their strong and weak points, the fourth step is to evaluate them by weighing the various factors in the light of premises and goals. One cours may appear to be the most profitable but require a large cash outlay and a slow pay back; another may be less profitable but involve less risk; still another may better suit the Company's long range objectives.

If the only objective were to maximize profits in a certain business, if the future were not uncertain, if cash position and capital availability were not a problem, and if most factors could be reduced to definite data, the evaluation should be relatively easy. But typical planning is replete with uncertainties, problems of capital shortage, and intangible factors, and so evaluation is usually very difficult, even with relatively simple problems. A company may wish to enter a new product line primarily for purposes of prestige; the forecast of expected results may show a clear financial loss, but the question is still open as to whether the losses is worth the gain.

Because the number of alternative courses in most situation are complex and the numerous variables and limitation are involved, evaluation can be also exceedingly complex. Due to these complexities, the newer methodologies and applications of operations research and analysis, are helpful. Indeed, it is at this step in the planning process that operations research and mathematical and computing techniques have their primary application to the field of management.

(vi) *Selecting a Course.* The fifth planning step, selecting the course of action, is the point at which the plan is adopted to the real point of decision making. Occasionally an analysis an devaluation of alternative courses will disclose that two or more are advisable, and the manager may decide to follow several courses rather than the best course.

Formulating Derivative Plans

At the point where a decision is made, planning is seldom complete, and a sixth step is indicated. There are almost invariably derivative plans required to support the basic plan.

Numberizing Plans by Budgeting

After decisions are made and plans are set the final step to give them meaning, as indicated in the discussion above on types of plans, is to numberize them by converting them to budgets. Each department or programme of a business or other enterprise can have its own budgets, usually of expenses and capital expenditure, which tie into the over-all budget. If done well, budgets become a means of adding together the various plans and also important standards against which planning progress can be measured.

Principles of Effective Plan

An effective plan should conform to the following principles.

(i) *The Principle of Limiting Factor.* A limiting factor is one which stands in the way of accomplishing a desired objective. If these factors are clearly recognized, the planners will confine their search for alternative which will overcome the limiting factors. In choosing from among alternatives, the more an individual can recognise and solve those factors which are limiting or critical to the attainment of desired goals, the more clearly he can select the most favourable alternatives. If we take any system or set of conditions or of circumstances existing at a given time, we recognise that it consists of element or parts or factors which together make up the whole system or set of conditions or circumstances. Now if approach this system or set of circumstance with a view to the accomplishments of a purpose, and only when we approach it the elements or parts become distinguished in two classes, those if absent or changed would accomplish the desired purpose, provided the others remain unchanged the first kind are called limiting factors, the second accomplishing factors.

(ii) *The Commitment Principle.* There should be some logic in selecting the right time range in planning. As planning and forecasting which underlies it are costly, one should therefore not blame for longer period than is economically justifiable yet it is equally risky to plan for too short periods.

The answer is to the right planning period, therefore lies in the 'commitment principle'. The logical planning period encompasses a period of time in the future, necessary to foresee through a series of actions.

The most correct application of this principle is the setting of a planning periods long enough to anticipate the recovery of cost sink in a course of actions. But since things other than cost can be committed for various lengths of time, and because a commitment to spend after precedes an expenditure and may be unchangeable as sink costs seen inadequate to refer to the recovery of cost alone what the commitment principle implies is that long range planning for future decisions but rather planning for the future impact of todays decisions. In other words decision is a commitment normally of funds, directions of action or reputation. And decision lies at the cost of planning.

(iii) *The Flexibility Principle*. The more the flexibility can be built into plans, the less the danger of losses incurred by unexpected events, but the cost of flexibility should be weighed against the risk involved in future commitments made. The flexibility principle applies to the building into plan an ability to change directions. The ability to change a plan without undue costs or friction, to keep moving towards a goal despite changes in environments or even failure of plan has great value. Flexibility is critical when the commitment is great and cannot be discharged in a short time. But flexibility is possible only within limits. In the first place a decision cannot always be put off long enough to assure its rightness. In the second place, built-in flexibility of plans may be so expensive that the benefit of hedging may not be worth the cost. A third major limit be building flexibility into plans is the fact that there are often cases where flexibility either cannot be built into plan at all or can be only with such difficulty as to impracticable.

(iv) *The Principle of Navigational Change*. The more planning decision commitment for the future, the more important it is to periodically check the events and results and redraw the plans as necessary to maintain a coarse towards the goals. Unlike the flexibility principle which applies to be adoptability built into plans themselves, this principle applies to the flexibility in the planning process. built in flexibility does not automatically revise plans, the planner, like the navigator must continually check his course and redraw plan to meet a desired goal.

(v) *Principle of Open System Approach*. It is essential for manager to take into account interactions with their total environment in every aspect of managing. Managing is not, nor could it be, a closed system approach to enterprise operation. This is nowhere more apparent than in theory and practice of planning. Objectives must obviously be set in the light of the economic technological, social, political and ethical elements of an enterprise environment. Planning premises represent a clear recognition that plans cannot be constructed, nor decisions made, in the vacuum of an internal system. The interfaces and interactions of plans with every element of the conditions and influences surrounding an enterprise are indeed many and complex. While certain authors criticize the closed system approach of operational management theory.

Objective of Planning

Without planning business decisions would become random or uncertain. Planning is carried out to attain the following objectives:

(i) *To offset change and uncertainty.* Business conditions are undergoing constant changes. Thus to meet the challenges of change and uncertainty, planning must be done.

(ii) *To focus attention on obligation.* Because all planning is directed towards achieving enterprise objectives, the very act of planning focuses attention on these objectives.

(iii) *To gain economical operation.* Planning minimises costs because of the emphasis on efficient operation and consistency.

(iv) *To facilitate control.* Planning also facilitates control. A manager can only check on his subordinates accomplishments if planned goals are there for making comparisons and assessments.

Advantages of Planning

Planning offers many advantages to an industrial company. These are :

(i) *Planning gives direction on objectives.* Activities of an organisation get a definite objective to move due to planning. Without planning everything may be haphazard and purposeless.

(ii) *Planning focuses attention on activities.* Planning helps to focus attention on objectives and in this way their importance gets highlighted. This helps in their proper persuit and fulfillment.

(iii) *Planning helps to offset change and uncertainty.* Since planning is done with the object of off-setting change and uncertainty, it helps to eliminate risk and avoid loss caused by changing factors.

(iv) *Planning facilities control.* Managerial controls are facilitated by planning because the actual performance can be compared with the planned performance.

(v) *Planning helps in the economical operations.* Planning lays down procedures, policies, objectives and operations. The staff gets a clear-cut idea about an operation, targets and goals.

(vi) *Planning accounts for growth.* Growth of a firm and expansion of its activities are greatly facilitated. This is so because the firm has a clear-cut idea about its future activities. It may therefore plan to grow. This means that the time and cost of growth are minimum.

(vii) *Planning helps to avoid bottlenecks in production.* Since everything is planned scientifically, bottlenecks are avoided and production goes on smoothly.

Short-range, Intermediate and Long-range Planning

Short-range planning normally covers a period of upto one year, though it can include eighteen months or two years. Intermediate planning extends over one to five years, with three years being the usual limit. Long range planning may be considered as any planning beyond three years. In technologically dynamic environments, it can extend as far into the future as twenty-five years. The length of time covered by planning relates to the type of organisation. A small retail outlet may have loose plans covering immediate seasonal operations. The single line manufacturing company may plan to meet this year's sales and to anticipate next year's sales and to anticipate next year's production. A multi-product organisation would plan for the short run and probably the intermediate range, perhaps projecting three to five years into the future. In practice, short range, intermediate and long range plans are not exclusive. Multiple programmes, projects and products will always be at different stage of planning and operational cycle.

The various levels of planning require different techniques since each operates within a unique time horizon. At the strategic level, long-range comprehensive plans seek to achieve the overall mission of the corporation. The objective of short-range planning is the creation of operating tactics and managerial planning is involved with translating strategy into tactics by developing procedure and policy and by uniting the total planning activity.

Planning and Control

Planning and control are so closely related that at times it is difficult to determine where one ends and other begins. A plan represents anticipated action; it is a passive concept and activity is actually initiated. At this point the control starts. For control to be established, standards of performance must be predetermined for use in measuring actual accomplishment. Control involves the correlations of functional activities in an integrated reporting system which is accurate, objective, fast and action-directed. A control system helps managers to improve performance; it permits them to initiate corrective action and make constructive recommendations. In its ideal setting, organisation for control can identify and group the work to be performed, define and delegate responsibility and authority, and establish relationships which enable people to work together most effectively to accomplish objectives. There are many types of control function in an organisation and they differ in important ways. Also there are several types of planning some of which are closely related to control and others not closely related. The planning and control activities can be classified as (i) strategic planning (ii) management control and (iii) operational control. These three planning and control activities are part of the information system of a company. The field of information system includes all activities having to do with the systematic flow of information within an organisation. Strategic planning sets the guidelines for management control and management control sets the guidelines for operational control. The complete management function involves an integration of all these processes and the process are complementary.

Forecasting

Characteristics of Production Planning and Production Control really starts when it is decided how many of each product to make. This requires forecasting. The forecasting function appears to be suspect; the methods are viewed as some form of applied black magic, partially at a result of bad experience many businessmen have had into the various statistical survey techniques, their assumptions and limitations, which are available to the present day professional business economist and market research staff. A forecast of demand of some type exists at least implicitly whenever the company management makes a decision in anticipation of future demand, whether this decision is to build a new plant or to manufacture another run of a particular item to restore inventory balances. Since the mid thirties more and more companies have come to recognise the need for formal forecasts of some type to set up formal methods for obtaining them. These methods may cover procedures for organisation and approval of forecast, methods or programmes for collecting data on which it will be based, or groups with technical facilities for analyzing the data as a basis for forecasting. These formal procedures in many cases, however, are restricted to rather broad company-wide or division-wide, forecasts covering periods from a quarter to a year. Forecasts can be classified at least by use or function, time span they cover, and method of generation. In this chapter we are considering forecasts used for production planning, inventory control and guidance to purchasing. The use to which forecast is to put determines or should determine, its form, content and details. It has been observed that business houses tend to make mistake in both directions in forecasting; they go into insufficient detail or they become too detailed. The difficulty with formal forecasts of this type is that they simply do not tell what the demands on the various operations are. The second tendency that of going into too much detail often follows as a reaction to the difficulties encountered from insufficiently detailed forecasts. The company then goes too far in attempting to detail the forecasts to make them useful to manufacturing, without carefully thinking out what type of detail is needed.

Forecast Reliability

The question of forecast reliability is one of the greatest sources of misunderstanding and frustration to forecasters in the construction of forecasts. A forecast is by nature an evaluation of incomplete evidence indicating what the future may look like. Thus no forecast can be expected to be entirely accurate. There is some evidence that business managers go through three phases of thinking about forecasts. During the first phase, a forecast, particularly if it is leased on any moderate amount of impressive statistical data, is viewed as fundamental truth of some sort. The second phase begins when the fact dawns that forecasts are usually wrong. This brings on a period of disillusionment and confusion probabily not too different from that experienced by some people in early period when the fact was brought home to them that the sun might not revolve around the earth. Finally the forecast user develops an appreciation of the forecast as an estimate or a guide tempered by the recognition that forecast will be in error to some degree and that plans must be made taking the magnitude of possible error in account.

Once it is recognized that forecasts are not merely desirable but logically necessary to a control system which is attempting to anticipate customer demand four basic steps must be taken. First comes the determination of what forecast are necessary? What are the functions of the control system with respect to each operating centre and inventory. Next comes the question How? Which forecasts should be made by the economist, if the company has one? Which can be made by statistical analyses of past sales or indicators of business activity. Thirdly there is a question of responsibility. Who will be responsible for making the procedures used and resulting accuracy? Finally the forecast must be controlled. Can control charts be set up? Can provision be made for periodic, possibly annual, review of routine detailed forecasts? Can charges for forecast errors be used as a basis for control.

Demand Forecast

Demand forecast has specific significance for the production department. Once the demand forecast for various products is known we can find the total demand for each time period and then the detailed production plans can be made. Demand forecast tells the production department what products will be required in what quantity and at what time. Knowing this, the production planning and control department can plan for the resources so as to meet the specified delivery dates. If a forecast is to be of use ot production department it must meet the following conditions:

1. The forecast must define expected demand in physical units.
2. The forecast should also include an indication of the probable variation around the expected demand, although admittedly such information is often very difficult to develop.
3. The forecast should be available in time to schedule all tasks required to achieve the necessary output.
4. The forecast must be made repeatedly during future periods to permit the necessary adjustments in materials and production requirement.
5. Finally, the forecast must be reliable because forecasting errors can cost considerable amount of money.

A forecast is essential to plan the production activities. A forecast is necessary to decide when to manufacture each item, how many to manufacture. Similarly a forecast is essential for purchasing new materials, parts or sub-assemblies to find out when to purchase, how much to purchase an item. The forecast is essential even for determining an economic lot size formula.

Sales forecasts are the first approximation in production planning They provide the base upon which plan may rest and adjustment may be made. For this accurate records sales showing the level and pattern must be known. Sales for each month, quarter and year must be estimated. In case of seasonal sales, analysis may show the need for new products to be sold in other seasons. Annual or monthly figures of production should not be the basis for forecasting sales. The actual sales figure should be employed and adjusted. The sales forecast will not yield accurate results during first few years.

Horizon of the Forecast

Horizon is determined by the lead time necessary to accomplish the purpose involved. In setting re-order points for inventory a probabilities forecasts will be needed. When the economic lot size is used to determine how much an item should be purchased, a forecast of demand will be needed which will hold as long as the proceeds of the lot will lost.

Forecast Overall Activity

Many production control decisions are based on the forecast of the overall level of activity. This include make or buy decisions, production smoothing etc. When one or a few types of end items are being produced in a given plant, the demand for sub-assemblies, parts and raw materials may be derived from the forecast of the end product. The requirements of various parts and components of a compressor can be worked out from the master schedule of an air-conditioning units.

Methods of Forecasting

The forecast may be based on the judgment of the experienced executives. An estimate may be obtained from the field salesman who are in close contact with the customers. The opinion of the traders in the market may also provide an estimate of the future sales. Although these methods are very simple, yet they may not be suitable because these are based on subjective estimates and may be biased. Therefore, it is essential to use some mathematical technique for forecasting.

Moving Averages. This is a very simple method which project the past into the future, if the forces determining the market demand will remain constant over time. A three month moving average is the average demand during the past three months *e.g.*, the demand in the month of April is an arithmetic mean of the demands in the months of January, February and March. Similarly, the demand in May is the average of the demands in February, March and April and so on. This is known as simple moving average. It may be desirable not to give equal weights to each of the preceding months. The most recent months may be given the highest weight. Then the weighted average may be the correct forecast. There is another way of weighting the demands and it is known as exponential smoothing.

Aggregate Forecast. The aggregate forecast is an important function of the business.It is of an asset to the marketing division as a basis for its planning and to the personnel division for hiring and training programmes. It forms the base for the annual budgets. The aggregate forecasts is not an activity of the production planning and control.

Forecast for Individual Component. To implement production planning and control for individual components, it is necessary to forecast these items. Unlike the aggregate forecasts, the individual forecasts are the responsibility of the individuals charged with production planning and control.

Derived Forecasts. It is always possible to derive forecasts for material from the overall forecast of demand for the individual end items. A bill of material lists, material required for each of end item produced. The forecast of demand for material on each bill of materials is obtained by multiplying the materials required per end item. The number of the end items to be manufactured.

The bill of materials also lists the specifications and the quantity required for each raw materials needed. The forecasts so obtained should be provided with an appropriate allowance for shrinkage, wastage, during the manufacturing process by applying yield and scrap factors. The final estimate need to be increased by the amount of spare parts required in addition to the number of assembly required. In certain products it is not possible to derive the forecast for individual items form the forecast of overall activities. This problem comes when the forecast of overall activity is not in end product but in monetary units or labour hours. When a series of end items of different specifications are produced it may be different to breakdown an aggregate forecast into end items. The problem of forecasting becomes still more complicated wher an item has multiple end item uses. It is true in case of raw materials such as copper or steel bars or angles or sheets of given specifications.

Statistical Forecast. When a manufacturing company makes a wide variety of end items these statistical techniques may be used to develop forecasts only of components but also of end items. Two important techniques of statistical forecasting are :

(i) Opinion forecast

(ii) Exponential smoothing.

In both these methods the forecasts are based on the record of past demand its level, trend and variation.

Opinion Forecast. The opinion forecast based on the judgement of the executive and the information obtained from the field salesman who are in direct touch with the customers. The opinion of the traders, distributors are also taken into consideration to estimate the future sales.

These methods are simple yet based on subjective estimate and biases of the various people involved, thus it is essential to involve mathematical techniques for forecasting. Following are the advantages and disadvantages of opinion forecast:

Advantages

(i) It is less elaborate and requires less technical skill.

(ii) It makes use of the knowledge of field personnel, *i.e.* gives first hand information.

(iii) The process of forecast passes through the review of number of people with various types of specific knowledge who can assess its accuracy.

Disadvantages

(i) It is a subjective approach.

(ii) It takes lot of time with the field and office personnel in making up the forecast.

(iii) Generally the final results depend far more on the opinions of a few influential or persuasive individuals.

Exponential Smoothing. In this case the demand for any period is based on two factors the old demand for this period and the actual demand during the previous period.

Regression or Correlation Analysis

It is likely that the sale of a certain product has some relationship with other products *e.g.* sales of gasoline is related with the sale of automobiles. The sale of a product may also be related with some other indices like material income, income per capita, size of population etc. For example, the time of population and the number of industrial units etc. will affect the demand of electricity in a town. The forecast will be good only if the said indices are coming from reliable sources. The variable which is to be forecasted may be called as the dependent variable and the other one as the independent variable.

In using this technique, first of all the relationship between the variables, is defined in the form of a curve. This is known as fitting the regression line, the line is then used to find the correlation between the variables. If the relationship between the two variables is linear then one can use simple linear correlation. The simplest form of a Regression line is given by the equation :

$$Y = a + b X$$

where, *Y* and *X* are the dependent and independent variables respectively we know the actual value *Y* for each value of *X*. Whereas the value of the dependent variable as obtained from the regression line is denoted by *Y*. The values of coefficients a and b are calculated so that the following conditions are satisfied:

$Y - y = 0.$

$(Y - y)^2 = \text{minimum}.$

When we have more than two variables we can use multiple co-relation.

Combination Methods

The combination of various approaches is used for forecasting. The statistical techniques and economic methods may be used together with the field forecasts of demand to provide a cross check. For example, an analysis of the trend in demand, together with fluctuations about the trend line may be used to obtain a preliminary estimate of demand, with a measure of estimated reliability.

Chapter 5

MATERIALS RESEARCH

Introduction

The increasing complexities in the procurement of industrial raw materials and components has given birth to new technique and method for increasing the system effectiveness. It depends to a greater extent on how effectively these techniques are utilised depending upon the availability of their own resources. All over the world large size organisations are spending a considerable amount on research in materials management. The research on availability should be attached more attention and importance. The availability research provides information concerning the availability of raw materials and components in national and International market at a right price.

Importance of Materials Research

Since the horizon of materials management has been widening and the materials manager is expected to be in constant touch with supply sources, market trends and price-levels therefore there is a need of continuous research in materials management. The materials manager today has to consider the implications of following factors :

(i) The company's long range requirements of material.

(ii) To develop alternative materials sources to reduce imports.

(iii) The likely sources of supply and their capacities over the next 10 years and anticipation of shortages in a particular industry.

(iv) The technological changes expected in the markets from which the materials are purchased.

(v) Appreciation of expected changes in the Government Policy in the related areas.

Some materials managers operate on the theory that since their orders help and support supplier research and development; they should see some of its tangible benefits. The purchasing agent's requests for substantiating evidence of supplier's R & D have not been particularly successful. Most suppliers are unable or unwilling to provide him with evidence of how R & D have helped him. Research and Development is being paid for by every suppliers customers, therefore buyers should be interested to find how successful supplier is in solving their own companies problems.

Definition

Materials Research can be defined as a systematic formal and continuous analysis of all factors affecting the materials management function. The aim of the research is to ensure optimal decisions, particularly for important items and key raw materials. *The scope of materials research activities is vast and some of the important factors which need analysis are :*

(i) **Economic Analysis:** The economic policies of the country influence the major decisions taken by various organisations. Factors such as growth rate; inflation; channelisation and other factors can seriously affect the availability of materials and consequently the price levels.

(ii) **Market Analysis.** The markets should be analysed for supply trends, technological innovations substitutes, evolution of new materials and materials specifications and standards.

(iii) **Supplier Analysis.** A continuous study regarding the present and future suppliers financial condition; their expansion plans and additions to their product lines should be available for better decision making. Study should highlight areas where new sources have to be developed. On a continuous basis the facilities of the suppliers should be inspected and initially evaluated.

(iv) **Transportation Analysis.** Transportation cost amounts to 25% to 30% of the cost of the material purchased in any organisation. The recent oil crises has further affected the cost of transportation, making it necessary to take fresh look at the transportation mix, proportion of goods moved by Trucks, Railways, Ships and Aeroplanes. Study should be made of new systems introduced for transportation such as Container Service, Quick Transit Service, Freight Forwarder Scheme, Mobile Booking Service, Parcel Express, Quick Mail service etc., as it pays to the organisation to avail of such facilities wherever suitable. Operations Research Techniques can be used to minimize transportation costs.

(v) **Price Analysis.** A regular study should be made available to analyse price increases made by suppliers on regular basis and their impact should be related to the cost of finished products.

(vi) **Purchase Analysis.** Cost benefit analysis must be done in vertical integration of critical raw materials and components.

Materials Research Executive

The organisation for Materials Research needs to be fully independent and should be directly responsible to Materials Manager. The suppliers analyst must be a technical competent executive who can ascertain the facilities of equipment and processes of the supplier, while price research executive must be well versed in analytical and forecasting techniques. The materials research team has an important role to play and should have freedom to develop and execute new research projects. The executive responsible to availability research should have the following attributes:

(a) Should be well aware of the organisation's objectives and its products.

(b) Should be well aware of the market trends and price variations.

(c) Should be a matured man who could withstand criticism.

(d) Should encourage communication and should be creative.

Purchasing Research

Purchasing research has as its objectives the continuous development and refinement of purchasing techniques designed to contribute profit to the firm. As such, research can be conducted as an adjust to the regular assignments of the members of a purchasing department who are usually called purchasing analysts. Although cost consideration will influence the form of the organisation, the consensus is that purchasing research can be carried out by executives who do not have primary responsibility for buying Purchasing research designed to increase profits by improving and refining purchasing planning and procedures may be classified into four groups:

(a) Procedural analyses (b) Vendor and Commodity research
(c) Economic projection (d) Special projects

Procedural Analysis

The classification involves study of the internal structure and flow of work within the purchasing department and between purchasing and other departments. Similarly other typical research subjects of a procedural nature include determination of job descriptions and specifications, personnel evaluation procedures, wage payment plans and receiving invoice procedures. Following are some of the areas of procedural research:

(a) Study of the feasibility of contract purchasing.
(b) More effective use of the blanket orders to minimise repetitive ordering.
(c) Investigation of forms generated and processed by purchasing to minimise the number and optimise their use.
(d) Development of purchasing manual.

Vendor and Commodity Research

This involves commodity studies including availability and price trends and include:

(i) Development of information helpful in locating and evaluating sources of supply.
(ii) Elimination of single sources of supply to stimulate competition.
(iii) Development of vender evaluation techniques.
(iv) Studies of terms and discounts from vendors with a view to obtaining the lowest net cost.

Economic Projections

This includes analysis of probable price changes and availability of purchased commodities and is an extension of vendor and commodity research.

Special Projects

This includes any type of research involving the purchasing function. This includes studies to determine economic order quantities, lease or buy decisions, quality control techniques and value analysis.

Chapter 6

PRODUCTIVITY AND MATERIALS MANAGEMENT

Introduction

There is no evidence to the fact that Man has managed his materials with efficiency in the past. We have yet to recognise that the way in which materials are managed will determine his very existence in future. There is a need to use new methods and management techniques, if we recognise the fact that all materials are finite. Productivity has been defined as the ability to produce goods and services efficiently and economically. The productivity as defined by the output obtained for resources expended must not only take into account diverse resources employed in the productive processes which are fairly measurable and brought together through the common media of "money costs", but must also take into account intangible factors as management supervision and control etc. Cost can furnish, if only with some difficulty, a dependable index of comparison of the common medium of bringing together such diverse inputs like men, machines and materials as well as capital. Reduction in cost has, therefore been recognised as an effective measure of productivity analysis for both inter-firm and intra-firm comparisons.

Materials Productivity

With the growth of modern system of production, organisation problems have come to the fore in determining the relative productivity of different units. Managements of today have to perform a wide range of functions. important among these are: efficient planning and procurement, control of quantity and cost of materials, effective flow of materials through production processes down to final distributions. In order to optimise production and reduce cost, management plays the key role. The elements are again bound by a common thread of coordination and control of many functions that is what constitutes Materials Management of Today. Productivity has many facets. *The main facets of Productivity could be grouped as : Productivity of technology ,Productivity of national objectives and policies, Productivity of Administration, Productivity of Management and Productivity of operations and programmes.* It has been observed that the effectiveness aspect of Productivity is far more vital than the efficiency aspect. To distinguish between effectiveness and efficiency, there are two distinct components: the conceptual part (objectives, plans, organisation and resources allocation) and the operational part (optimum use of resources, methods and procedures, efficiency of performance, communications and achievement as measured against targets). The former relates to the decision-making function of the administrators and latter to the implementation function of the task force. The former determines the level of effectiveness and the latter the measure of efficiency. In the real life situation effectiveness aspect of productivity is far more vital than efficiency aspect.

Productivity is affected not only by management's attitude and resourcefulness but also by day-to-day operation of productive organisation as well as its supervision and control. Management must not only keep abreast of the latest development and new improvements in the productive processes but also must consistently strive to improve methods and procedures in relation to materials. In order to understand Productivity and Materials Management let us study various aspects of Productivity.

Definition

Productivity is often confused with production. Productivity is simply the ratio of output to productive operations. Output can be translated into services and inputs cover all forms of resources such as man-power, materials, machines, money etc. With a given extra in-put of resources, if production increases, the productivity, has increased. Production remaining the same, if the output of resources is reduced, then also productivity can be deemed to increase. Even when the output and input remaining steady, but the quality of the 'output' is improved, even then the productivity has increased, as the intrinsic value of the output will be more in this case. The productivity in terms is mathematical concept is described as under:—

$$\text{Productivity} = \frac{\text{Output}}{\text{Input}}$$

Productivity refers to Relationship of Results and Means. Productivity refers to the relationship between the results and the means employed, or, between the product and the factors used for obtaining it. It is not merely volume of output, but output in relation to the resources employed. It will be maximum when highest output is obtained with minimum expense of resources. It will be the lowest when the resources are not used in the most economical manner. Peter Drucker, defines productivity as "the balance between all factors of production that will give the greatest output for the smallest effort".

Productivity stands for the elimination of waste in all forms. Waste of resources like materials, equipment, space and buildings. The waste of human morale through frustration and dissatisfaction to be eliminated. The application of productivity concepts and techniques is spread over three broad fields: human relations; industrial management and industrial engineering. The primary concern of productivity is with the most precious resource—the human. Thus productivity deals with human behaviour patterns in industrial environments. It studies the factors that motivate men, individually and in groups, to work and to work happily. The concept of productivity deals with industrial management. Management development programmes designed to serve right from top executive to shop supervisors, aim at giving management a better understanding of the different functional areas of the management like purchasing, marketing, cost and budgetary control, administrative etc. A service to efficient management is industrial engineering. Industrial engineering covers a number of scientific techniques like Work Study, Operation Research, PERT, Inventory Control,Production Planning and Control, Materials Handling, Engineering Economics, Organisation and methods, Plant layout, Preventive maintenance, Fuel efficiency, Quality control etc. The analysis of a work system through industrial engineering techniques help in correct decisions being arrived at for the optimum utilisation of resources towards the achievement of specified goals.

Productivity science has a vital means of promoting efficiency, effectiveness and efficiency of performance in every field of human endeavour. Productivity science must continuously make a significant contribution to the raising of standard of living and to the satisfaction of every growing material and social need of community as a whole. Productive science is a broad field and it is intra-disciplinary in nature. It is a science dedicated to task of building effectiveness and excellence in modern organisations. Productivity is a relationship between inputs and outputs. The inputs may be land, labour, capital, etc. Productivity can be improved if with a relatively smaller addition of inputs you get a proportionately larger output. It is this relationship between inputs and outputs which determines productivity. The productivity can be improved by better technology, by better management, by more efficient use of raw materials, by the avoidance of waste etc. The improvement of productivity is that the total cost per unit of output should be reduced to the minimum and not merely the labour cost.

Productivity Techniques

For proper acceptance of productivity techniques in the industry, the climate should be created so that there si positive attitude in workers and supervisors for improving the productivity of organisation. Unless the attitude and atmosphere in the organisation are proper, no amount of technical expertise of industrial engineer is going to be accepted and implemented in the organisation. Unless the ideas are accepted and implemented, productive drive cannot be successful. We often confuse labour productivity with total productivity, that is surely because ultimately it is the human factors which govern and organize all other factors, capital and technology. It is the human element which has to organize, control and utilize the plant and machinery or the raw materials or the better technology.

According to Prof. Gunnar Myrdal, it is not so much the deficiencies in the supply of capital as the attitudes to work and institutions that keep the under-developed countries poor and retard their progress. The emphasis has, therefore, to be given to the improvement of quality of the human material and its proper motivation—whether workers, managers or trade unionists. Low productivity generate low standards of health and education, which are bound to result in low productivity. The problem of productivity need to improve the quality of the human capital and its attitudes. This has to be done by raising the improvement of productivity to the level of a national purpose, and not leave it as a concern of the specialists alone. Thus, the crux of the matter lies in :

(a) Improving the quality of management and

(b) Improving the motivation of workers.

The concept of productivity, although it must have existed as long the existence of production process itself become extremely relevant in context of factory system of production.

Factors Affecting Productivity

Following are the factors which are effecting productivity and can be classified into two category:

1. External Factors 2. Internal Factors.

1. External Factors. The external factors include the infra-structure, availability of funds, power, water, transportation means, raw materials, government policies, political, social and economic conditions. All these factors influence productivity of a factory in a varying degrees but the individual factory alone cannot help much about them. The management of the factory is to increase the productivity within the limitation of these factors.

2. Internal Factors. Such as Products, Technology, Plant and Equipment, Raw Materials, Men Work Methods, Organisation and Management Practices etc.

(i) **Product.** The main concern of a factory is to produce the best product for the country. The product productivity can be improved by better product design and specification through R and D and through product development efforts. For example production of Antibiotics through high yield strains.

(ii) **Technological Factors.** The productivity can be increased through improvements in technology. Technological development and innovation, constitute the single most important basis for higher productivity. Although it is difficult to measure quantitatively, the degree of relationship between technical change and productivity. Long term gains in productivity stem mainly from the advancement in science and technology.

(iii) **Plant and Equipment.** Plant and Equipment play a significant role for higher productivity. The higher productivity is achieved by introduction of following factors:

(a) The industrial units in the under-developed countries are mostly wasteful of effort and time. The upkeep of equipments is usually poor and down time due to breakdown is more.

(b) Valuable machines remain idle for want of raw materials, timely availability of spare parts, non-availability of trained staff both operational and maintenance.

(c) Improving the availability and reliability of equipment for production by preventive maintenance and reducing frequency of breakdowns by systematic diagnosis of causes taking corrective measures and making improvements in life of parts through better materials of construction, design changes etc.

(iv) **Work Study.** Work study may be defined as a modern industrial discipline comprising, several scientific techniques which carry out a systematic, objective and critical analysis of all the facts of any work system in order to increase productivity.

(v) **Materials.** Materials constitute the most vital resources where productivity is of paramount importance, materials include raw materials, indirect materials such as process, chemicals, lubricants, fuels, spare parts, engineering materials, packing materials etc. Productivity of materials has several aspects such as—

(a) Utilisation and control of process waste.

(b) Upgrading of materials by initial processing to improve utilisation in actual process.

(c) Use of lower grade and cheaper materials.

(d) Import substitution.

(e) Improving inventory turn over ratio to made the funds locked in inventories more productive.

(f) Improved inventory management to avoid costly stock outs.

(vi) **Men.** The productive capacity of a unit is the result of many factors, series of inventions and innovations in machines and materials, development of assembly line techniques, standardisation interchangeable parts, division of labour etc., have vastly increased productive capacities. Yet all these factors are translated into productivity only when the human element is introduced. Workers can increase or decrease their productivity as they choose. This human, quality gives rise to one of managements greatest problems.

People differ not only in their "ability to do" but in their "will to do." The 'will to do" in our conditions does not appear to be strong enough. Motivation result in increased profits, through reducing direct labour costs per unit and reducing overhead costs per unit. For example as employee productivity increases, the fixed amount of overhead is spread over larger amount of production units and this results in lower costs per units.

(vii) **Management Practices.** The style of management and management practices have a profound effect on the productivity of the enterprise. Never in the history of industrial development was there a greater need of energetic enterprising, far sighted managerial talent imbued with the spirit of adventure, imagination and vigilance as it is today since the industrial units are likely to come up or go down with managers. The management must have organising capacity, imagination, judgement and willingness to assume risks.

In our particular socio-economic condition a high-task-high relations "type of management" could be more effective in most situations. The managers must set high targets and standards of achievement, demand high exertion and input effort on the one hand and on the other hand be deeply concerned with welfare, growth and advancement of the men.

Productivity of Executive Time

It is the time which an executive has at his disposal, to spend according to his own judgement on matters that are truly important. The higher up in the organization an executive has, the larger share of his time which is not under his control and is not spent productivity. Much of the working day of every executive, says Mr. Drucker. According to Peter larger part is inevitably wasted. He is under constant pressure to use his time in unproductive ways and these pressure increase with the size of the organization.

The first step is for the executive to make sure that he knows from a written record how his time is actually used. According to Drucker the managers must be concerned, in addition with time-wasting that results from poor management and deficient organization. Their first task is to identify time wasters which follow from lack of system of foresight. The symptom to look for is the recurrent "crisis". Such a crisis can be prevented or reduce to routine which clerks can manage. A third common managerial time is mal-organization. Its symptom is an excess of meetings. Organization will always require meetings because the knowledge and experience needed in specific situations are never available in one head; but wherever people find themselves in meetings a quarter of the time or more the system needs to be corrected.

The executive who has recorded and analysed all his time and attempted to prune time wasters can then turn to his discretionary time. The effective executive, however, knows that as little as one quarter of the day, if consolidated in large time units, is usually enough to get the important things done. There are a good many ways of consolidating time. Some people, usually very senior men work at home one day a week on this method.

Drucker observed that executives are for ever being exhorted to plan their work. Those executives who really get things done don't start with their work. They start with their time. Executives should also try to acquire new skills, to learn new things from mathematics to art appreciation and to work on developing themselves, their knowledge and their methods. Time management takes perseverance and self-discipline. But no other investment on the market pays higher dividends in terms of achievement and performance.

Raising the Productivity of an Enterprise

The productivity rise is achieved by efficient utilisation of the inputs for improving the level and the quality of the output. This can be achieved by two ways:

1. by elimination of wastes in utilising various resources and
2. by ensuring that maximum values are extracted from these and are added to the product
3. both the above objectives are achieved by managerial and technological improvements.

1. Management Improvement. Management improvement must necessarily be the starting point in raising the productivity of an enterprise. No matter what technology is followed, no matter what type of product is produced, management improvement is universally needed to achieve a higher level of productivity.

Even though management improvement is not altogether unrelated to technological development, yet by itself, it is mainly concerned with systems. It requires of people of training for planning, operating, controlling, motivating people all the time to reduce costs and add values to the products.

In most of the developing countries hardly 15 per cent of the costs incurred is on labour, while in a developed countries it is as high as 50 percent. In most developing countries nearly 80 to 90 percent of the working capital is deployed on materials. In most developing countries, plant, machinery equipment, spare parts and a substantial quality of raw material and components are imported from abroad. Repairs, replacement of material inputs are subjected to long delays. Any dislocation in these leads to ideal hours and other serious repercussions on the productivity of the enterprise. In addition to this certain specific techno-managerial areas such as Preventive Maintenance, Tool Engineering, Design and Value Engineering, Standardisation, Quality Control and Fuel Efficiency contribute a lot in eliminating wastes and enhancing the values of the product, thereby improving the productivity of an enterprise.

2. Technological Improvements. With rapid progress in the field of technology, the developed countries are going ahead at an amazingly fast rate and the developing countries are lagging behind, thus widening the gap between two. No doubt, a number of developed countries are giving a helping hand towards the economic development of the latter. Still the amount of assistance that is forthcoming is only a small fraction on the total requirement.

It must be realised that if self-reliance at the core and a satisfactory rate of growth are to be the ultimate goals of economic development, then these could only become realities adopting such technologies which will generate the requisite surpluses, for providing the capital to set into motion other productive activities, which in turn will provide more employment. If traditional technologies did not generate such surpluses, and at the same time absorbed major portions of economic activities, then these naturally would not have the requisite growth potentials.

Whenever more advanced technologies are adopted often a good deal of resistance to such changes are offered, by some of the trade unions which may not have all the facts at their disposal. In deciding whether to switch over to a higher technology or not, the main consideration is always the rise in productivity. In developing countries where there is a large number of people unemployed, expansion of production is always justifiable, provided it generated the requisite surplus of the output over the input sufficient to attract and motive people on a practical plane. It is necessary to encourage and sustain a continuous trend of adoption of progressive technologies.

Productivity Measurement

Usually productivity will be defined in ratios, for example, the exercise on productivity measurement for a machine shop is usually worked out in terms of productivity of individual factors contributing to the total productivity. Output from a machine shop basically is in the form of Physical measures like number of pieces produced. There are some advantages if the output is measured in terms of physical units or quantity. If the units of input are measured in the form of man-hours spent, the output can be converted to Rupees.

Measurement of Labour Input

Input measuring units are also of two types—(1) Time units (2) Labour force. The time units are the hours of work and labour force unit as number of persons employed. The time units are the hours of work of the operator. Labour force unit is in terms of number of persons engaged on the machine.

Factors Affecting Labour Productivity

In any production department, there are two types of factors affecting the labour productivity: One is **physical factor** and the other is **Psychological factor.**

1. Physical factors like large break downs of equipment, material waiting time low piece rates, no proper incentives etc.
2. Psychological factors like unwillingness and indifferences of production workman. The unwillingness may be due to feelings like
   (i) Management cannot take any action against us.
   (ii) Our supervisors are dishonest, then why should we work for them.

Many manufacturing units over emphasis the effect of physical factors of production, ignoring altogether the impact of psychological factors. This may be because of the difficulty in measuring psychological factors while physical factors can be immediately measured. The effect of various factors on labour productivity varies upto some extent from industry. In consumer goods industries the effects will be sell ability and profitability and in continuous process plants the effects will be break-down.

MATERIALS MANAGEMENT CONTRIBUTING TO PRODUCTIVITY

An Integrative Approach

The management of materials function which has grown into complexity under the present day industrial system, has given birth to the evolution of a common management function where many functionaries had been working often at cross purposes. The effect was lower production and productivity. The effort towards this integrative approach has been aided by the successful combination of the related areas of materials control with fragmentary authority and this has then led to an integrated materials management system. Recent shift of emphasis on materials cost control has again made it incumbent on management to use Materials Management as an important tool to reach the basic management objective of economic control of product cost and better customer service. Therefore there is need to organise and plan, coordinate and control various activities concerned with materials for an integrated approach towards materials management for better materials cost control. Even in highly decentralised organisation there is an urgent need to integrate such functions as materials planning and programming, purchasing and materials quality control, inventory control, transportation and traffic as well as waste disposal and salvaging. For effective control, it only makes sense to have the whole data under a central department and this will probably require "monitorship" at a suitable level. One could visualise this role as Materials Manager who should look for smooth flow of materials thus trying to shorten the materials flow cycle. Therefore there is no doubt that materials management can contribute to productivity if this cycle can be shortened i.e. interval between conception of a product and ultimate delivery of the finished product. *Therefore there is a definite and urgent need for proper control of materials and inventories through systems in order to provide the basis for cost-reduction. Without proper control, it is impossible to ensure effective utilisation of materials.*

Problem of Materials Control

Control will require the participation and cooperation of several functions previously isolated.

(i) *Purchasing* must ensure timely availability of materials, determine cost and arrange for delivery and final disposition.

(ii) *Inspection and Quality Control* will inspect and verify the extent of defects and must determine the problems in order to resolve the quality problem.

(iii) *Receiving and Stores.* must adhere to specifications as to quality and quantity in order to guard against any possibility of faulty materials getting into the stores.

(iv) *Material control must* be in a position to identify losses, process and correct defectives. In materials intensive industries, materials account for about one third of the working capital and about 50% of the current assets on balance sheet as materials and inventories in one form or the other. Since it is the single largest item which is responsible for huge investment remaining idle, therefore there is definite need for proper control of materials and inventories through systems in order to provide the basis for cost reduction.

(v) *Materials Handling* must see that handling is kept to the minimum in order to keep down cost of Handling but without affecting operational efficiency.

(vi) *Product Development* must develop materials specifications within the total materials cost, keeping itself abreast of the latest technology and materials innovation.

Success of total materials management has to be evaluated with reference to the inventory turn over, materials availability, inventory accuracy and reduction of stock levels to an economic size. The success therefore can be achieved only if there is cooperation and coordination of highest order for which information must flow smoothly, quickly and accurately.

Chapter 7

VALUE ANALYSIS AND MATERIALS MANAGEMENT

Introduction

Value Engineering and value analysis mean the same thing and are synonymous terms. Value Engineering or value analysis had its birth during the Second World War. Value Engineering comprises a group of techniques aims at the systematic identification of unnecessary costs in a product or service and efficiently eliminating them without detriment to its quality and efficiency. It is a technique which is looking for the function; seeking alternatives; and developing it through practice and test till the cost-wise idea is ready for implementation.

Value analysis involves a creative approach for the systematic identification of unnecessary costs. If these costs are first identified and then systematically eliminated, the overall cost of the product or service can be considerably reduced, and the sales and resulting profit considerably increased. Value analysis is an effective tool for cost reduction and the results accomplished are far greater. It improves the effectiveness of work that has been conventionally performed as it examines into the very purpose, design, method of manufacture etc of the product with a view to pinpointing unnecessary costs, obvious and hidden.

Definition

There are almost as many specific definition of value analysis. Value analysis is the study of the relationship of design; function and cost of any product, material or service with the object of reducing its cost through modification of design or material specification, manufacture by more efficient process, change in source of supply, or possible elimination or incorporation into a related item. Value analysis is the organised, systematic study of the function of a material, part, component, or system to identify areas of unnecessary cost that can be eliminated without impairing the capacity of the item to satisfy its objective. Value analysis focus is on engineering, manufacturing and purchasing with attention to one objective—equivalent performance at a lower cost without affecting functional performance. Value analysis is to buy a function rather than to buy an item. Value analysis techniques are important because of competition; profit squeeze; value of a rupee saved, etc. Value analysis means better value through better purchasing techniques, better suppliers, design, re-evaluation and modification, better manufacturing methods, lower cost office operations, standardisation, substitution, better material handling, better traffic operations and better inventory control.

Applications of Value Analysis

The implementation of a value analysis programme is the selection of products to be analysed. Value analysis makes its impact during the maturity stage of the product. The two approaches for the choice of products for value analysis are through ABC analysis and contribution analysis. It involves the listing of the products in descending order of their annual consumption/production sales. Now select the first 10% of the items accounting for around 70% of the annual turnover of the company. Thus maximum efforts can be directed on these items in order to bring about cost reduction.

In the Contribution Analysis the products are ranked according to their contribution (Sales price-variable Expenses). The product with the least contribution per unit are selected for value analysis as these have a higher cost compared to their sales price. In India several public and private sector undertakings have applied value analysis techniques successfully for cost reduction and import substitution purposes. The use of aluminium in place of copper in the cable manufacture has helped the country to conserve valuable foreign exchange. Similarly aluminising in place of galvanising has helped reduce the imports of zinc.

Vim was packed and sold in market in tin packing, thereafter it was substituted with cardboard packings, saving a lot of money to the company. Value analysis is gold mine for developing country like India which should endeavour to exploit this technique to the fullest extent. This technique originally evolved when Armed forces were faced with shortage of supples and rising cost. It is indeed a valuable technique in the hand of Industrial Management.

Value analysis is neither a cost nor price. It involves some thing more than cost or price. it is relative value, can be defined as 'Lowest price" for a function at the desired time and place with the required essential quantities. It is an inquiry into the functional value or utility of a product for the particular endure. It is a matter of measuring a cost of performance of an item and to determine how a performance can be improved by improving the value by a process of substitution or modification. Value analysis does not necessarily means reducing a price of an *article, at time* higher price articles may be substituted to improve the performance of article, reducing the ultimate cost and thus improving the value. Essential feature of value analysis is the process of identifying unwanted cost and steps to illuminate these costs. Each article purchased has specific function to perform and therefore its utility for performing the required function can be related directly to the price paid for it. Every article has more than one function to perform. These functions can be : Primary functions, Secondary functions and Tertiary functions.

Value analysis is a tool for assessing the value of end products as well as value of incoming materials. It is an important tool of 'Material Management". It is a scientific technique designed to make possible the same or better performance and customer satisfaction at lower cost. Frequently the production is improved by the process. Value analysis may be applied to the design of a product or a component since design changes will often simplify production and make it possible to eliminate some of the processes used.

What is Value?

Value is a broad term often used to denote cost and price. The value of an item is its worth. The various aspects of value are: Use value, Esteem Value, Exchange Value and Cost Value. The emphasis is on use value and at times cost and use value are confused. The value concept possesses tremendous profit maming potential and represents and attempt to integrate the commercial skill, manufacturing skill. Design analysis and cost analysis constitutes the two fundamental tools of value analysis.

Value can be expressed as :

$$V = \frac{W}{C}$$

$$\text{Value} = \frac{\text{Worth of an item}}{\text{Cost of price of an item}}$$

The worth and cost have to be worked out subjectively from the point of view of the buyers or sellers or manufacturers. Worth is determined in terms of functional utility, esteem time, place factor and special advantages if any. There are three ways in which value can be increased by increasing worth, decreasing cost for the same worth and by doing the above two ways.

Value can be classified as:

(a) Use of functional value: The properties and qualities which accomplish a use, work or service.

(b) Esteem Value :The properties, features or attractiveness which cause us to want or to keep it.

(c) Cost Value: The sum of labour, material and various other costs required to produce it.

(d) Exchange Value: Its properties or qualities which enable us to exchange it for something else we want.

Thus value analysis is like a three legged stool with three legs as Performance, Delivery and Cost. All the three legs must be perfectly matched to keep the seat on an even position. The general causes of high costs are: Lack of information, lack of ideas, honest but wrong beliefs, temporary circumstances, habits and attitudes.

Value Analysis and Materials Management

The various analysis process on value develops many questionnaires and ultimately reaching the optimum solution. These analysis are based on its function values. If we analyse the total cost say (100%) it can be composed of following components percentage wise:

★ Bought out (Material and Component) Cost = 40%

★ Direct Labour Cost = 10%

- ★ Selling and administrative charge cost = 17%
- ★ Profit = 8%

On the other hand product cost are compared of 75% in design phase and 25% being materials, tooling, processing and factory overheads. Now from this it is very clear that design phase and Materials phase are controlled than 50% cost can be controlled.

Value Analysis Techniques

The most desirable alternatives for a given application depends on the use to which the product will be put to use. The best product is the one that will perform satisfactorily at the lowest cost. Value analysis procedure essentially follow the same pattern in all cases. First there is an analysis of the design of the item and its uses, and then the application of price analysis to the alternatives.

Value analysis or value engineering, as it is called, is one of the several specialised services recently offered as tools of management. *Value Engineering techniques differs from other cost reduction techniques, in the sense that it probes into the economic attributes of value.* The concept is that by continuous process of planned action, it is possible to improve the performance, increase the value in product and thus reduce cost.

Value engineering is defined as the relationship between what function is worth to a buyer and what it costs to him. There are three types of values having relationship with function (a) Use value;—the monetary measures of the properties or quality of an item which contributes to its salability. (b) Esteem value, the monetary measure of the properties or qualities of an item which contribute to its salability, but not to its performance. It does not include use value (c) Exchange Value—the monetary measure of the properties or qualities of an item which enable it to be exchanged for something else. The above concept can be put in a formula. Use Value + Esteem Value > Exchange Value.

Value analysis techniques can be applied to the following types of materials:

(i) Raw materials
(ii) Semi-finished product
(iii) Component parts
(iv) jigs and fixtures
(v) Production tools
(vi) Packing materials
(vii) Transportation cost

The objectives of value analysis is to increase the value by either increasing the worth for the same cost or decreasing the cost for the same worth or both. It is very important to bear this value concept in mind, in order to increase the productivity. Value analysis concept and techniques have revolutionalised the entire function of purchase department. An equivalent substitute used in place of imported substance may save a tremendous foreign exchange. Example—corn oil use in place of imported oil used in fermentation industries of India. Use of *Hydrol* (indigenous) in place of *Dextrose* which was being imported. The difference in costs of *two* is about Rs. 2500 per ton.

In Indian industry we are normally finding a problem of either to continue the imports of variety of small items or should become creative and look around for substitute. The substitution is an activity which involve high technical skill which a manufacturer himself cannot create. Since the responsibility of procurement is on him, so it is desirable that he should initiate the programme bye creating the technical department to bring about substitution may even be a sheer wastage. It should not be accepted even for a moment that every item of value analysis results in the successful imports substitution. In India value analysis is still a concept. It is high time that this gestation period should be over and enlightened management of various organisations should accept the concept of value analysis with confidence and should be put in practice.

Thus Value Engineering objectives is designed to coordinate the professional skill of design, production and purchasing personnel in an endeavour to minimize all the elements of costs that are within their control, while at the same time retaining the quality, reliability and salability of the product concerned.

Value Analysis places great concentration on the use value but many times cost and use value are confused. Value analysis is very important from the view point of cost accountant and termed as marginal costing. Marginal costing infact means only variable costing and to accountants marginal cost averaged over a large block of units. In practice analysis of marginal costing included direct costs which are related to significant changes in volume and type of output. It is indeed difficult to allow for all the increases in fixed costs which arise from changes in volume and type of output. Accounts do take into consideration the cost of costing, the time available fór making calculations, the degree of accuracy required and other special features of a business enterprise. There are following five reasons why unnecessary costs enter into a product or service:

(a) Lack of information
(b) Lack of utilisation of creative minds
(c) Temporary circumstances
(d) Honest wrong beliefs
(e) Habits and attitudes

The techniques of value analysis refers to those techniques which enable to determine the level of value in product or in expenditure. As a result of the value analysis techniques the value of preforming the functions or service comes to 25% or even more below the price currently spent. These techniques are brought into application through:

- ★ Organised approach
- ★ Employing creative thinking
- ★ Evaluating functions
- ★ Working on specific matters
- ★ Considering the rupee value of each tolerances
- ★ Getting information and facts
- ★ Converting idea into rupee value
- ★ Using accurate costs
- ★ Using good human relations
- ★ Using ones own judgement
- ★ Using industrial standards

★ Spending company's money as one's own money.

These techniques are, however, used in a framework which is called value analysis job plan which consists of following steps or phases:

(i) Information phase
(ii) Speculative phase
(iii) Analytical phase (Going back and looking at our ideas and converting to rupee value)
(iv) Programme planning
(v) Programme execution
(vi) Conclusion

Design Analysis

The design analysis procedure entails a methodical step by step study of all the phases of design of a given item in relation to the function it performs. Analysis of each component attempts to answer the following four questions :

(i) Can any part be eliminated without impairing the operation of the complete unit?
(ii) Can the design of the part be simplified to reduce its basic cost?
(iii) Can the design of the part be changed to permit the use of simplified and less costly production methods?
(iv) Can less expensive but equally satisfactory materials be used in the part?

The specific manner in which a value analyst approaches the problem of design analysis is highly creative method and different from one analyst to another. Most companies developed some checklist to systematize the analyst's activity. The following is the Value Analysis checklists suggested by **Material Association of Purchasing Manufacturer** to determine the function of the items:

(i) Can the item be eliminated?
(ii) If the item is not standard, can a standard item be used?
(iii) If it is a standard item, does it completely fit the application or is it a misfit?
(iv) Does the items have greater capacity than required?
(v) Can the weight be reduced?
(vi) Is there a similar item in inventory that should be substituted?
(vii) Are closed tolerances specified than are necessary?
(viii) Is unnecessary machine performed on the items?
(ix) Are unnecessarily fine finishes specified?
(x) Is commercial quality specified?
(xi) Can you make the items cheaper in your plant? If you are making it new can you buy it for loss?
(xii) Is the item properly classified for shipping purposes to obtain lowest transportation rates?
(xiii) Can cost of packaging be reduced?
(xiv) Are suppliers being asked for suggestions to reduce costs?

Cost Analysis

Cost analysis involves the investigation of a suppliers probable costs of producing a given product. It helps in negotiating an original price. In recent years cost analysis plays the two following major roles:

(i) Cost analysis is conducted for currently purchased items whose costs appear excessive. In such cases the informations developed from Cost Analysis is used as a basis for further price negotiations with the suppler :

(ii) Cost analysis also serves as a means of locating high cost posts which should be subjected to designs analysis.

Steps of Value Analysis

The technique of value analysis can be grouped as follows:

(i) Eliminates (ii) Retain or keep
(iii) Change (iv) Modification
(v) Incorporation (vi) Subdivision
(vii) Substitutions

(i) **Eliminate.** If after the examining of the utility of an item it is found that it is not contributing to the functioning of a job than the item can be eliminated.

(ii) **Retain or Keep.** Retain only those items whose marginal utility for primary, secondary and tertiary function contribute to the productive examples.

(iii) **Change.** An alteration in the specification can be achieved in the following profiles:

(1) Modification (2) Incorporation
(3) Sub-division (4) Substitution

(iv) **Modification.** At times it is advantageous to modify the specifications or design of an item or job if such modification can be achieved by cheaper and better alternatives than those must be introduced.

(v) **Incorporation.** We may be able to incorporate two or more than two items for the same job. In other words we may also be able to incorporate two or more than two processes in the manufacture of the items into one single process.

(vi) **Sub-division.** It is similar to the concept of make and buy. It is often possible to manage the requirements more economically by purchasing component than to assemble it.

(vii) **Substitutions.** Value concept has a greater reliance to the concept of substitutions from both material as well as social point of view. One of the examples which can be taken with precise metal like copper. Sheets at which copper is being consumed in the world is 8% of its total reserve and with the expanding requirements we may be able to consume the total reserve in another 10 years time. Aluminium conductor can replace or substitute the copper conductor. This way we will be rendering a social value to aluminium and at the same time conserving the value and life of the copper by preserving the reserve for longer time. Value analysis concept has revolutionized the entire function of Purchase Department. In Western India in one of the chemical industry depending upon fermentation technique needed a particular type of oil for its fermenter which was not available in India. Thus the import license were required and the oil was getting rare and rarer. Circumstance and hazardous were increasing day by day. The Organisation Production Deptt. collaborated with Purchase Deptt. and after a series of experiments select a particular type of corn oil which replaced the imported oil equally and efficiently. This way a company can save annually a considerable amount of foreign exchange.

In another example an organization which was consuming 100 ton of dextrose annually. The dextrose manufacturing company in the country were finding it difficult to meet the demand as it requires maize as a raw material and maize became a rare commodity due to the economic and political weather as we were depending upon PL 480 programme of USA. As the programme disturbed thus resulted problem for dextrose manufacturing company. This organization substituted dextrose by another chemical by the difference in the cost between the two is about Rs. 1500/ton so naturally there was a saving of Rs. 1.5 lacs annually.

In Indian industry we are normally finding a problem of either to continue import of variety of small items or should become creative and look around for substitute. The substitute in an activity which involves high skill which manufacturer himself cannot create. Since the responsibility of procurement is on him so its is desirable to initiate the programme. But creating a technical department to bring about substitute may be even a shear wastage. It should not be accepted even for a moment that every items of value analysis results in successful import substitutions.

Application of Value Analysis

There are various applications of value analysis. A few of them are :

(i) **Value analysis of end products.** The end products offered for sale should be value analysed.

(ii) **Value analysis before undertaking of a project.** In one of the project height between floor and ceiling was reduced to 11 feet instead of scheduled 14 feet height. This resulted in tremendous cost reduction without affecting the functional utility.

(iii) **Predesign value analysis.** In developing country like India the importance of predesign value analysis cannot be overlooked. It may bring about a substantial cost reduction and foreign exchange saving by the creative design. Blind copying of foreign design has often led to extra cost in procuring material cost, unwanted expenditure of foreign exchange, high inventory and wasteful methods of production.

(iv) **Value analysis before tendering.** Many firms are now introducing this concept and subjecting their tenders for big jobs or project to value analysis before submission so that they can offer better value to their competitors.

(v) **Prepurchased value analysis.** This is the last stage to use this concept. This is the final chance to save money and to obtain better value before we make over final commitments to prospective suppliers. Example. In ABC analysis, first point is to handle carefully item 'A' whose value is 90%. Thus value analysis in Industry is the latest technique available for producing at a lowest possible cost. It combines price analysis and product analysis.

(vi) **Price analysis.** It may be defined as buyers investigation of suppliers direct and indirect cost of manufacturing the product. This will help buyer to negotiate few prices with the suppliers near the actual (closed) cost of production.

(vii) **Production analysis.** It refers to buyer's investigation to determine the adequate quality of material. Its primary objective is to change the specification of product to correlate the product design with a most economical production sources of supply.

Stages in Value Analysis

The value engineering exercise proceeds systematically through following six stages. These are :

(1) Organisation (2) Evaluation
(3) Speculation (4) Investigation
(5) Recommendation (6) implementation

1. **The organisation stage.** It is composed of *product* selection and its analysis.
2. **Evaluation stage.** This is also called Information stage. It is desirable to design an **evaluation sheet** on which to record all the collected information. The information that is to be recorded on the evaluation sheets includes:
   - ★ Design
   - ★ Manufacture
   - ★ Purchasing
   - ★ Costing
   - ★ Derived information
3. **Speculation stage.** Speculation stage can be regarded as the heart of the matter. The essential technique of this is functional approach. This has the following steps :
   (i) The functional approach to cost reduction.
   (ii) Assessing the value of a function.
   (iii) Alternative actions following functional assessment.
   (iv) Further studies during the speculation stage:
      (a) What are the functions, whether essential or can be eliminated?

(b) What material is used or proposed or can another material be used?
(c) What factors control the amount of material used?
(d) How much of the basic material is wasted during manufacture?
(e) Is the component made from standard raw material, or is the component itself standard?
(f) Through what operations does the component proceed during manufacture?
(g) What labour operations are involved?
(h) What tolerance have been specified and if so, why?
(i) What surface finish is required to meet the function?
(j) What is the "brought out" content of the cost? This division is based on make or buy.

Thus the crux of speculation stage is only *creative thinking*.

4. **Investigation.** It has:
   (i) **Design Contribution.** This include change in design, the raw material used, the dimension and limits etc.
   (ii) **Production Contribution.** Covers process of production, use of standard components, reduction of labour costs etc.
   (iii) **Purchase Contribution.** To reduce the cost of material and parts which is supplied.
   (iv) **Applying the ABC of Value Engineering.** There are 10 points suggested by Miles as long ago as 1947. These heads are:
   A = *Actual* necessity or otherwise has 4 points.
   B = *Best* way or not has 3 points.
   C = *Competitive* cost or not has 3 points.
5. **The Recommendation.** The proposed alteration and comparison of costs before and after all to be submitted for final recommendation by management.
6. **Implementation.** This is the stage at which management revives and decides upon the value engineering suggestions submitted, and take advantage of any "trade offs".

Benefits of Value Engineering

Results are derived on two factors:

(a) Benefits to the company (b) Benefits to the customer

(a) Benefits to the company. It is again divided as tangible and intangible results.

Tangible Results. The results of value engineering will be of two sorts—tangible and intangible. The tangible results are the actual savings which can be expressed in monetary terms, and it is true to say that they seldom does a properly-conducted value-engineering exercise, achieve less than 50% saving in costs. The saving is usually much more than this. Cost reduction on an individual component can be of the order of 25, 50 or even 100%. Example : It is assumed that 5% saving on Rs. 100 selling, manufacturing cost of Rs. 75, and a profit margin of Rs. 8. There will be Rs. 3.75 cost reduction; which increases the profit to 8 + 3.75 = Rs. 11.75

Intangible Results. These are:

(i) Increased cooperation.
(ii) Enhanced states of the purchasing function.
(iii) Simulation of creative thought.
(iv) Increased Cost-Consciousness
(v) Mutual understanding
(vi) Development of latent ability

(b) Benefits to the customer. To live and to prosper, industry must provide the customer with what he wants, when he wants it, and at a price he is willing to pay. Value technique must, therefore consider the customer and his requirements. The crux of value analysis may be on the following factors:

(i) If we are in production, consider one of our company's products. What function does it perform for the customer? What values are important to performance, durability, appearance or any combination of these values?
(ii) What materials go into the product? What other materials might be substituted for them and what would they cost in comparison with the materials being used at present? If cheaper material could be used for any part of the product, would the values provided for the customer be lessened?
(iii) Could the parts be made or the product assembled in some simpler way than at present?
(iv) If you are not in production, consider some procedure your department or section is using. What is this procedure designed to accomplish? What does this cost? Is every step in the procedure necessary, or could one or more of the steps be eliminated and the same result accomplished?

Introducing Value Analysis

The first step for implementation of a value analysis programme is the selection of products to be analysed. Value analysis makes its mark during the maturity stage of the product. This means that one has to start thinking along these lines during the later part of the growth stage. What is important here is the switch from. Performance-Oriented thinking to Value Oriented thinking. The two approaches for the choice of products for value analysis are through ABC analysis and contribution analysis. In the ABC analysis, the products are classified according to their sales or consumption value and ranked in descending order. The product which offer the maximum sales or consumption value are selected. This would offer the best result in term of return when analysed. Critical and production holding items are to be subjected to value analysis in order to examine the rigidity of the specification.

Value analysis is concerned with the cost added due to inefficient or unnecessary specification or feathers. It makes its contribution in last stage of product cycle namely the maturity stage. At this stage Research and Development no longer make positive contribution in terms of improving the efficiency of the function of the product or adding new function to it. The prime task of manufacturer becomes one of tackling the value part of the job so well that product leadership will be maintained.

In order to answer the above questions three basic steps are necessary:

1. Identifying the function. Any useful product has some primary function which must be identified, a bulb to give light, refrigerator to preserve food etc. In addition it may have secondary functions such as with standing shock etc.

2. Evaluation of the function by comparison. Value being a relative term, the comparison approach must be used to eliminate functions. The basic question is "Does the function accomplish reliability at the best cost" and can be answered only by comparison.

3. Develop alternatives. Realistic situation must be faced, objection overcome and effective engineering manufacturing and other alternatives develop. In order to develop effective alternatives and identify unnecessary cost the following thirteen value analysis principle must be used:

- ★ Avoid generalities.
- ★ Get all available cost.
- ★ Use information only from the best source.
- ★ Brain storming sustains.
- ★ Blast, create and refine.
- ★ Identify and overcome road block.
- ★ Use industry specialists to extend specialize knowledge.
- ★ Key-tolerance, not to be too light.
- ★ Utilise and pay for vendor skills and techniques.
- ★ Utilise vender available functional products.
- ★ Utilise speciality process.
- ★ Utilise applicable standards.
- ★ Use the criterion "would I spend money this way."

Chapter 8

PROGRAMME EVALUATION AND REVIEW TECHNIQUES APPLIED TO MATERIALS MANAGEMENT

Introduction

Purchasing planning and research can be aided by use of PERT and CPM techniques. PERT stands for Programme Evaluation Review Techniques and CPM refers to Critical Path Method. Both are control techniques designed to make planning more effective. These are principally scheduling and cost control devices. These techniques can be used in other areas of purchasing research where complex relationships are involved. An increasing number of applications are being found in subcontracting, development work, construction contracts and project buying. Following are the primary advantages of these techniques:

(i) Providing a means for careful planning by specifying all the variables involved.

(ii) Providing a clearer understanding of the inter-relationships involved in projects.

(iii) Assuring a constant review to see that projects are progressing on schedule.

(iv) Identifying potential trouble spots early so that resources can be diverted to avoid cumulative delays.

(v) Identifying potential trouble spots early so that resources can be diverted to avoid cumulative delays.

(vi) Making it possible to predict the completion time of projects with reasonable accuracy.

PERT provides a means of keeping account of critical parts and materials whose delay would hinder production schedules. The PERT network makes it clear that production cannot start until all raw materials and components are in the plant. Many steps preliminary to production, however are taken by other departments simultaneously with purchasing's activities. When purchasing is supplied with a PERT network analysis, the most economical purchasing and traffic decisions can be made.

Application of PERT in Materials Management

One of the important problems concerning today's materials executive is planning for materials ensuring that the various stages of work are brought forward in a logical sequence with minimum cost and least delay. PERT represents a significant step towards an integrated management system comprising variables of time, resources, technical performance and other utilities.

PERT is extremely useful for precise planning and buying when force majure clauses are operating i.e. to plan in advance and allocate responsibilities to the different executives in case of fire, strike, earthquake, major accidents, floods etc so that each executive knows what precisely his responsibilities are and what he has to do in such situations without having to await instructions. In making the network plan valid, the manger himself must be involved in, and associated with the preparation of the network. A network is never really finished until the project is finished. It is dynamic living plan which needs to be revised as and when new difficulties are discovered. By anticipating the trouble spots likely to *appear, application of PERT results in improved utilisation of resources and hence aids better managerial decisions. Management decision normally limits its attention either to* paths that are already critical or to those about to become critical. In fact an entire PERT network is programmed into a computer. All transactions concerned with the network are then key punched and entered into the computer. The computer then will calculate and recalculate critical paths, focussing management's efforts on events that are likely to delay the entire programme. PERT is particularly useful for extremely complex products, while a simple Gantt Chart is usually adequate when there are no more than a dozen possible paths, while PERT is used almost entirely in defense-related industries or construction, where the end product is made in relatively small quantities and is extremely complicated.

Network Analysis

Network analysis is a synthesis of two techniques namely Programme Evaluation and Review Technique and Critical Path Method evolved independently during 1956-57. The tow methods have many features in common and are now combined and called Network Analysis. Following are some of the factors responsible for making the technique powerful:

(a) **A logical and disciplined basis for planning.** CPM and PERT are useful at several stages of project management starting from early planning stages, when various alternative programmes or procedure are being considered, to the scheduling phase, when time and resource schedules are laid out to final stage.

(b) **Simplicity.** They are straight-forward in concept and easily explainable to the layman with no background in network theory. Basic critical path data may be handled with reasonable speed for projects with 500 or 600 activities. Computer programs are readily variable for larger projects.

(c) **Improves coordination and communication.** The network graph displays in a simple and direct way the complex aspects of various subdivisions of project.

(d) **Pinpoints trouble spots and responsibility.** Network calculations pinpoint attention to the relatively small subset of activities in a project which are critical to its completion. Managerial action is thus focused on exceptional problems, contributing to more reliable planning and more effective control.

(e) **Better management of resources.** CPM enables the manager to reasonably estimate total costs of various completion dates. These various trade off possibilities along with other decision criteria, enable an executive to select an optimum or near optimum schedule.

(f) **Versatile in application.** CPM and PERT are applicable to many type of projects starting from new product introduction programme to missile procedures. Moreover, they may be applied at several levels within a given project form a single department working on a sub-system to multi-plant operations within a large corporation.

(g) **Scope for unseen changes.** As simulation tools, they enable the manager to project into the future effects of planned or unanticipated changes and to take appropriate action when such projections indicate the need for it. Thus for example the manager can quickly study the effects of crash programs and can anticipate in advance potential resource battle. Wisely used by a project manager who understands their strengths and CPM and PERT can be effective amplifiers of his managerial skills and help the executive in following manners :

  (i) It aids the manager in planning, scheduling, controlling the activities.

  (ii) In guiding and directing team efforts more effectively.

  (iii) It permits advance planning, indicates current progress, warns of potential future trouble spots when there may still be time to avoid them.

  (iv) It aids in handling uncertainties regarding time schedules, coordination of many activities and control of cost involved.

  (v) It shows its values most strikingly when a special project of new kind is undertaken.

Network Techniques

The need for management direction on a programme or job depends upon two factors—its repetitiveness and complexity. Simple jobs that occur infrequently do not require any involved direction. The techniques for direction of project-type jobs ar rather new. However, there has recently been an explosive growth in the family of these techniques and a number of network techniques have been developed which are named below:

(1) P.E.R.T. : Programme Evaluation and Review Technique.

(2) C.P.M. : Critical Path Method.

Nature of the Techniques

In any project there are usually three types of problems—

(a) *Technical* (b) *Executive Type* (c) *Human*

More complex the project, more difficult are the executive type problems. An example of vastness of this problems in complex projects is given by the polaris weapon system which involve 250 prime contractors and at least 9000 job-contractors. In such projects it is possible that delay in the delivery of a small component might hold up the progress of the entire project. These techniques help to coordinate efforts of different agencies to :

(i) *plan resources*
(ii) *anticipate the occurrence of bottlenecks*
(iii) *guide corrective action*
(iv) *forecast the likelihood of meeting target dates.*

The basic functions of management are to make decisions and enforce their implementation. The function still remains, not withstanding the new techniques. The techniques are merely tools in the hands of management—the tools that make the decision process more rational and less painful.

"CPM" and its Advantages

Critical Path Method is a technique employed to schedule and control project. CPM is applicable to both large and small projects. It is a widely recognized and most versatile management planning technique.

Some of the important advantages are given below:

(i) It helps in ascertaining time schedule.
(ii) With its help control by the Management becomes easy.
(iii) It makes better and detailed planning possible.
(iv) It encourages discipline.
(v) It provides a standard method for communicating project plans, schedules time and cost performance.
(vi) It identifies most critical elements and thus more attention can be paid on these activities.

Those techniques require a greater planning than required otherwise. Thus these methods increase the Planning cost, but this Cost is easily justified by concentrating attention on Critical Paths only and avoiding unnecessary expenses on the strict supervision over whole programme.

Steps in "CPM" Techniques

CPM employs the following steps for accomplishing a project planning.

(a) Break down the project into various activities systematically.
(b) Label all activities.
(c) Arrange all the activities in Logical sequence.
(d) Construct the arrow diagram.

(e) Number all the nodes and activities.
(f) Find the time for each activity.
(g) Mark the activity times on the arrow diagram.
(h) Calculate early and late, start and finishing times.
(i) Tabulate various times and mark EST and LFT on the arrow diagram.
(j) Calculate the total float for each activity.
(k) Identify the critical activities and mark the Critical Path on the arrow diagram.
(l) Calculate the total project duration.
(m) If it is intended to reduce the total Project duration, crash the critical activities of the network.
(n) Optimise the cost.
(o) Up-date the network.
(p) Smooth the network.

Difference between "PERT" and "CPM"

CPM is a technique used for the Planning and Controlling the most logical and economic sequence of operations for accomplishing a project. The project is analysed into different activities whose relationships as in PERT, are shown on the network diagram. The network is then utilized for optimising the use of resources, progress and control. PERT is a technique used for scheduling and controlling the projects, whose activities are subject to considerable degree of uncertainty in the performance time. The methods of start-finish critical path and project time of P.E.R.T. and C.P.M. are similar. CPM is an activity oriented technique, while PERT is the event oriented technique. Event means the beginning or exceeding of one or more activities. CPM has one-time estimate, while PERT has three times estimates. The fundamental network of PERT and CPM are though identical, yet there are certain differences in details as mentioned below :

S.No.	PERT	CPM
1.	A probabilistic model with uncertainty in activity duration. Expected time is calculated from to, t_m and t_p.	A deterministic model with well known activity (single times) based upon past experience. It assumes that, the expected time is actually the time taken.
2.	An event-oriented approach.	An activity-oriented system.
3.	PERT terminology uses words like network diagram, event, and slack.	CPM terminology employs words like arrow diagram, nodes and float.
4.	The use of dummy activities is required for representing the proper sequencing.	The use of dummy activities is not necessary. The arrow diagram thus becomes slightly simpler.

S.No.	PERT	CPM
5.	PERT basically does not demarcate between critical and non-critical activities.	CPM marks critical activities.
6.	PERT find applications in projects where resources (men, materials and specially money) are always made available as and when required.	CPM is employed to those projects where overall costs is of primary importance. There is better utilization of resources.
7.	Especially suitable in Defence Projects and R and D where activity times cannot be reliably predicted.	Suitable for problems in Industrial setting, plant maintenance, uction projects : expansion schemes etc.
8.	PERT has three-times estimates.	CPM has one-time estimate.

Thus PERT should be explicit intangible, capable of accepting changes and capable of being monitored.

Distinguishing Features of PERT

These techniques have several distinguishing characteristics:—

(i) They give management the ability to plan the best possible use of resources to achieve a given goal within overall time and cost limitations.

(ii) They enable executives to manage "one of a kind" programs, as opposed to respective production situations.

(iii) They help management to handle the uncertainties involved in programs where no standard time data of the Taylor-Gantt variety are available.

(iv) They utilize a so-called "time network analysis" as a basic method of approval to determine Man-power, interests and capital requirements.

Advantages of PERT

(a) It provides clear objectives.

(b) It provides an analytical approach to the achievement of an objective.

(c) It enumerates detailed plans and important programmes events.

(d) it establishes sequence of activities and their inter relationship.

(e) It focuses attention on important and critical activities and events.

(f) It provides a logical plan for formulating a realistic schedule of activities.

(g) It provides up-to-date status information of the project and enables quick review of the progress at all stages.

(h) It can point out improbabilities and may even predict before their occurrence, and they help remedy the situation.

(i) It can foretell the feasibility of a plan and can help in formulating new schedules if the one under consideration be found impracticable or wanting.

(j) It avoids slippage of plan and waste of time, energy and money.

(k) It is an aid for allocating the available resources for optimum results.

(l) It brings about time and cost consciousness at all levels of management.

Distinguishing Features of PERT

These techniques have several distinguishing characteristics:—

(1) They give management the ability to plan the best possible use of resources to achieve a given goal within overall time and cost limitations.

(2) They enable executives to manage "one of a kind" programs, as opposed to respective production situations.

(3) They help management handle the uncertainties involved in programs where no standard time data of the Taylor-Gantt variety are available.

(4) They utilize a so-called "time network analysis" as a basic method of approval to determine Man-power, interests and capital requirements.

Advantages of PERT

(a) It provides clear objectives.

(b) It provides an analytical approach to the achievement of an objective.

(c) It enumerates detailed plans and important programmes events.

(d) It establishes sequence of activities and their inter relationship.

(e) It focuses attention on important and critical activities and events.

(f) It provides a logical plan for formulating a realistic schedule of activities.

(g) It provided up-to-date status information of the project and enables quick review of the progress at all stages.

(h) It can point out improbabilities and may even predict before their occurrence, and they help remedy the situation.

(i) It can foretell the feasibility of a plan and can help in formulating new schedules if the one under consideration be found impracticable or wanting.

(j) It avoids slippage of plan and waste of time, energy and money.

(k) It is an aid for allocating the available resources for optimum results.

(l) It brings about time and cost consciousness at all levels of management.

Steps in the Technique of PERT Planning

1. Define clearly the end objectives.
2. Determine the major events that must be completed prior to reaching the end objectives.
3. Analyse and record the work to be done in between events.
4. The project is broken down into different activities systematically.

5. Arrange the events and activities in the order of sequence of their occurrence.
6. The network diagram is drawn. Events and activities are numbered and make sure no activity is left over.
7. Layout and finalize the network in a neat form. May be more than one attempt is needed.
8. Event numbers should be given with the starting event as 1, and progressing successively to the right in the order in which they occur.
9. Any dummy activity should be shown by dotted arrow times on the network.
10. Check your network it should not have loose ends. Network is always closed and all activities lead to the objective.
11. Each activity should have a single location.
12. Using three times estimates, the expected time for each activity is calculated.
13. Standard deviation and variance for each activity are computed.
14. Earliest starting times and latest finishing times are calculated.
15. Expected time earliest starting time and latest finishing times are marked on the network diagram.
16. Slack is calculated.
17. Critical path is identified and marked on the network diagram.
18. Subcritical Path are also identified.
19. Length of critical path or total project duration is found out.
20. Lastly, the probability that project will finish at due date is calculated.

Terminologies

Activity. A time consuming element occurring between two events and represented by an activity.

Event. A meaningful accomplishment or 'mile stone' usually represented by small, circle or box in network.

—Activity start and finish points are events.

—Events have no time values.

Critical path. In network the path with smallest amount of positive slack or largest amount of negative slack. The most rigorous time constraint for this path

$Te = Tl$.

Slack or Float. Difference between last event time and early event time *i.e.* $Tl\text{-}Te = Float$.

Negative slack. The amount of time which is not available to perform the series of activities in a particular slack path and still meet the required completion date.

Positive slack. The amount of additional time which is available to perform the series of activities in a particular slack path and still meet the required completion date.

Network. A flow plan containing the pertinent activities and events.

Dummy activity. An activity with no time value constraining the succeeding activity.

Estimation of Activity Duration

It is not always possible to estimate the duration of each activity accurately specially when a new project is undertaken. Since to start a network the determination of these durations is necessary, the following method is used—From the people who will be responsible for those activities or from the persons who have undertaken similar works in past, we obtain the following estimates for each activity—

(i) Pessimistic estimated time = b

(ii) Most likely estimate time = m

(iii) Optimistic estimate time = a

The early expected time for completion of activity is

$$Te = \frac{a+4m+b}{6}$$

If we draw a histogram for frequencies, various estimates of activities against duration it will lead to a bell shape curve which is normal distribution curve.

$$\text{Variance} = \left(\frac{b-a}{6}\right)^2$$

$$Vt = \sigma^2$$

$$\text{Deviation } \sigma = \frac{b-a}{6}$$

$$= \sqrt{V}$$

Te, *Vt* can be added up for various activities to find out total early expected time *TE* and total variance *VT* for a Project, while standard deviation σt for activities cannot be added up to give total deviation.

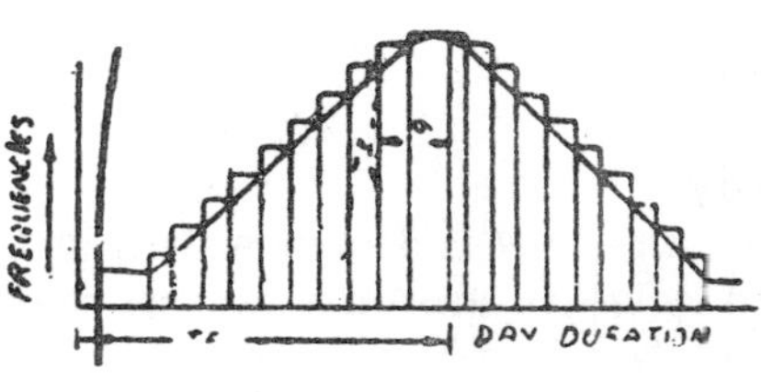

Fig. 8.1

TE = Early expected time for completion.

TL = Latest expected time for completion.

TS = Schedule time for completion.

$$Z = \frac{Ts - Te}{\sigma}$$

When $Ts = Te + 3\sigma$ probability of compleuon is 99.7%

$Ts = Te + 2\sigma$ " " " 95%

$Ts = Te + \sigma$ " " " 68%

$Ts = Te$ " " " 50%

Network Logic

To organise the activities into network, the following questions are asked concerning each activity :

(i) What activity must produce this one?

(ii) What activity can be concurrent with this one?

(iii) What activity must follow this one?

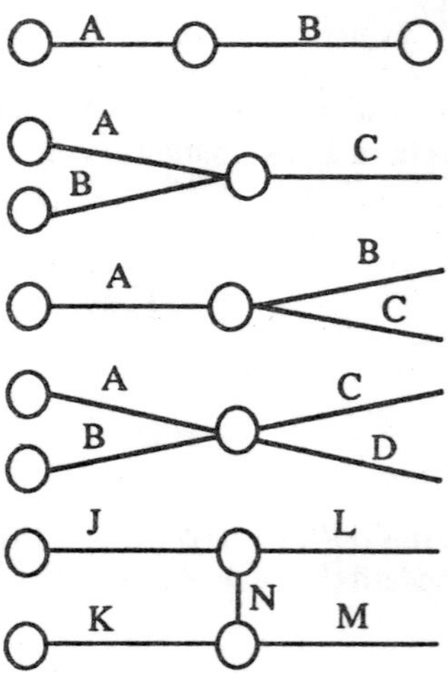

Activity *B* cannot start until activity *A* is completed.

Activity *C* cannot start until both activities A and *B* are completed.

Activity *A* must be completed before either *B* *or C* started.

Both *A* and *B* must be completed before *C* or D or both can start.

Both *J* and *K* must be completed before *M* can start, *L* can start only on completion of J and is independent of *K*.

Fig. 8.2

Dummy Activity

In network the activity *N* is dummy activity and always represented by broken arrow it always has zero time value and used only to describe logical connections.

A loop should never occur in a network as shown in Fig. 8.3

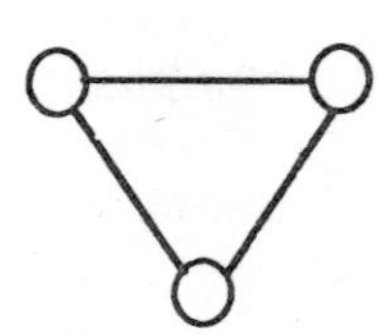

Fig. 8.3

Float or Slack

The term slack is used with an event *i.e.* in case of PERT and float is used with reference to an activity *i.e.* in case of CPM. But sill these terms are interchangeable.

Float or slack means spare time, a margin of extra time over and above its duration which a non-critical activity can consume without delaying the project.

Let us find Earliest Start Time—The time at which an activity can start and worked out by moving from first to last event in the network. The earliest finished time is the earliest possible time at which an activity ends.

$EFT = EST$ + Duration of the activity.

Latest Finished Time

It is worked out by moving backward from event 2 to event 1.

Similarly latest start time is the possible time by which an activity start

$LST = LFT$ – Duration of an activity

Free Float = (EST) Tail Event – (EST) Head event – Activity time

Total Float = ($LFT - EFT$)

($LST - EST$)

Illustration I

TABLE I

S.No.	Activity	to	tm	tp
		Days		
1	1—2	2	5	14
2	1—6	2	5	8
3	2—3	5	11	29
4	2—4	1	4	7
5	3—5	5	11	17
6	4—5	2	5	14
7	6—7	3	9	27
8	5—8	2	2	8
9	7—8	7	13	31

It is given that the scheduled date of completion of project is 38 days.

1. Find out the probability that project can be completed at scheduled time.
2. Find out the scheduled time for 94.5% probability of completion of the project.
3. Find out the probability of completion of path 1—6 ; 7—8.

Solution.

Te = Expected time for each activity

$$= \left(\frac{t_o + 4t_m + t_p}{6}\right) \qquad \dots (1)$$

$$\text{Standard Deviation} = St = \left(\frac{t_n - t_o}{6}\right) \quad \ldots (2)$$

$$\text{Variance} = V_t = \left(\frac{t_n - t_o}{6}\right)^2 = (St)^2 \quad \ldots (3)$$

$$Z = \left(\frac{D - T_e}{S_t}\right) \quad \ldots (4)$$

Z = Probability that the project will meet the schedule or due date.
Te = Total project duration
D = Scheduled date = 38 (days) given.

Using formula (1), (2) and (3) let us find out the value of *te, St* and *Vt* for various activities.

TABLE II

S. No.	Activity	te	St	Vt	Critical Path	Total Variance on critical path
1	1—2	6	2	4	—	4
2	1—6	5	1	1		
3	2—3	13	4	16	—	16
4	2—4	4	1	1		
5	3—5	11	2	4	—	4
6	4—5	6	2	4		
7	6—7	11	4	16		
8	5—8	3	1	1	—	1
9	7—8	15	4	16		25

Let us draw network diagram.

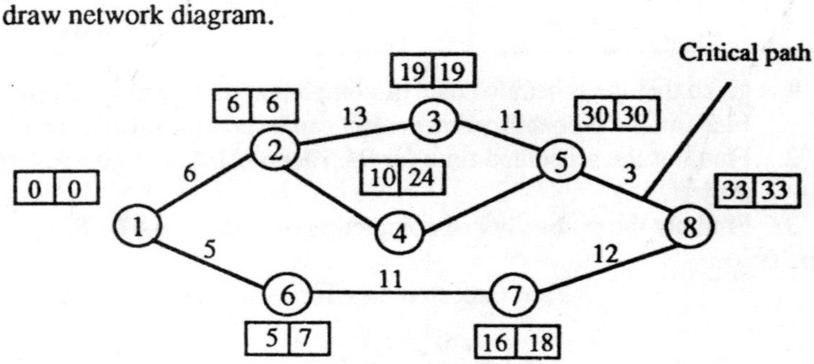

Fig. 8.4 On the Critical Path Total Stock is Zero.

Working out the *EST* and *LST* for the various activities as given in *Table I*.

TABLE III

S. No.	Activity	EST	LST	Total Slack LST – EST	Activity on on critical path
1	1 — 2	0	0	0	—
2	1 — 6	0	2	2	
3	2 — 3	6	6	0	—
4	2 — 4	6	20	14	
5	3 — 5	19	19	0	—
6	4 — 5	10	24	14	
7	6 — 7	5	7	2	—
8	5 — 8	30	30	0	
9	7 — 8	16	18	2	—

So critical path is 1-2-3-5-8

Project duration on critical path, we get

$T_E = 6 + 13 + 11 + 3 = 33$ days

Total variance on critical path = 4 + 16 + 4 + 1 = 25

Total project duration = 33 days

D = Scheduled date = 38 days

$$z = \frac{D - T_E}{S_t} \quad \ldots (4)$$

$$S_t = \sqrt{variance\ of\ critical\ path} = \sqrt{25} = 5$$

Substituting the value of *D*, *Te* and *St* in equation.

$$z = \frac{38 - 33}{5} = 1$$

After finding the value of Z, let us read table III we find that probability is 0.841. In other words there is a probability that project shall be completed in 38 days is 84.1%.

For the 94.5% probability of project being completed. Let us look at the value of Z for 0.945 value of probability.

So $Z = 1.6$

$$Z = \frac{D - T}{S_t} = 1.6 = \frac{D - 33}{5}$$

Thus $D = 41$ days.

Assuming critical path as 1 —6 —7 —8

$T_E = 31$ days

Variance of the path = 1 + 16 + 16 = 33

$$S_t = \sqrt{33} = 5.74$$

$$Z = \frac{D - T_E}{S_t} = \frac{38 - 31}{5.74} = 1.22$$

Now given the value of Z = 1.22 and read table I, the probability of meeting the due date is 0.888 or 88.81%.

Cost Concept of PERT

PERT tells us to achieve the committed objectives in best possible manner and also in the least possible cost and time. To effect this central, the management must know that :

(i) What is required to be done?
(ii) Schedule time required?
(iii) The estimated cost.

PERT provides a dynamic total for the execution of a programme and for developing a technique to control time and cost of achievement. The following functions are required to be carried out :

- To make a budget of expenditure for given time schedule.
- To assess the increase or decrease of cost in relation to decrease or increase in time.
- To arrive at optimum cost.
- To draw expenditure plan against time.
- To review the progress in terms of expenditure incurred and time spent.

The cost or expenses to be incurred in the performance of an activity is divided into two sub-heads:

1. **Direct Cost** . The cost incurred in compressing the activity completion time. Each of the activity in network can be performed in a shorter time than early expected time by providing additional resources. The resources can be evaluated in terms of money or cost. direct cost has the tendency to increase with decrease in time.
2. **Indirect Cost.** All overheads such as interest on capital, rent for various equipments, cost of supervision cost of storing materials etc. comes under indirect cost. It has the tendency to reduce with the reduction in time of an activity. Direct cost or indirect cost cannot be zero at any time.
3. **Total Cost.** It is the sum of direct and indirect costs and it can also be plotted against activity time. From graph shown in Fig. 8.5.

If an activity span is reduced, the direct cost increases. If we plot cost verses duration on a graph we will find a point where the further crushing of activity is not possible irrespective of the amount of resources applied. This cost is known as crash cost and denoted by *Cc*.

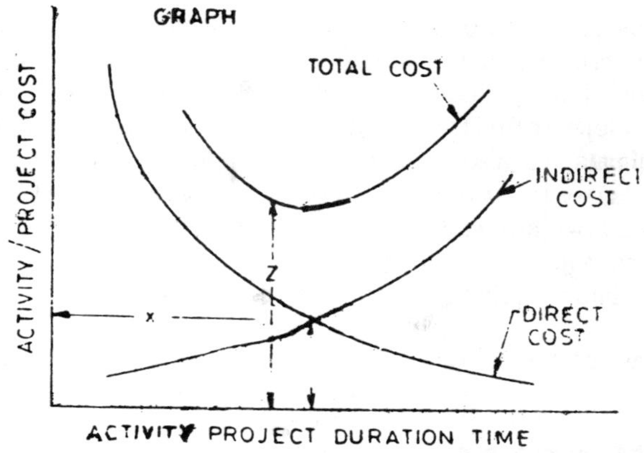

Fig. 8.5

Crash Duration

It is the minimum possible duration of an activity which cannot be reduced any more irrespective or resources applied.

Crash Cost

The minimum cost incurred for crash duration.

Cost Slope

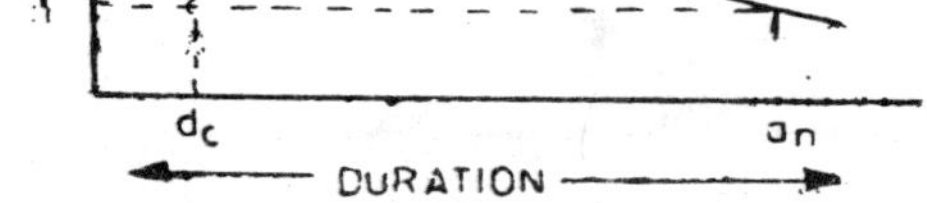

$$\text{Cost slope} = \frac{C_c - C_n}{dn - dc}$$

Where

Cc = Crash cost
Cn = Normal cost
dn = Normal duration
dc = Crash duration

Illustration II

TABLE IV

Activity	Normal time	Crash time	Normal cost	Crash cost	Cost slope
1—2	10	7	400	640	80
1—3	19	11	600	1160	70
2—3	10	8	500	600	50
2—4	19	15	700	1000	75
3—4	10	4	300	810	85
Total			2500	4210	

Analyse the feasibility of cost reduction for 22 days.

1. Find out critical path for the project which comes as (1 — 2), (2 — 3) and (3 — 4) the cost slope for these are Rs. 70, 50, 85 respectively.

From cost slope we find that activity (2-3) is having minimum cost slope of Rs. 50/- on critical path. It is also evident from the graph that in order to crash activity (2 – 3) by one day we have to crash either of the activities (1 - 3) or (2 - 4) along this activity. The cost of crashing the activities will definitely be more than activity (1 - 2) alone which is higher only to activity (2 - 3).

Hence minimum crashing cost for 1 day crashing the activity

(1— 2) = Rs. 80.00

Hence crash cost for 29 days = Normal cost + cost slope

= 2500 + 80

= 2580 ... (i)

Redraw the square network again for 29 days it is clear that activity (3 – 4) is most economical to crash.

Hence crashing cost for one more day by crashing activity (3 – 4)

by a day is = 8.5

Hence crash cost for 28 days = 2580 + 85

= 2665 ... (ii)

Again redraw new square network base on 28 days duration.

It is clear that for further crashing of critical path means crashing of more than one activity at a time. The possible ways of further crashing are—

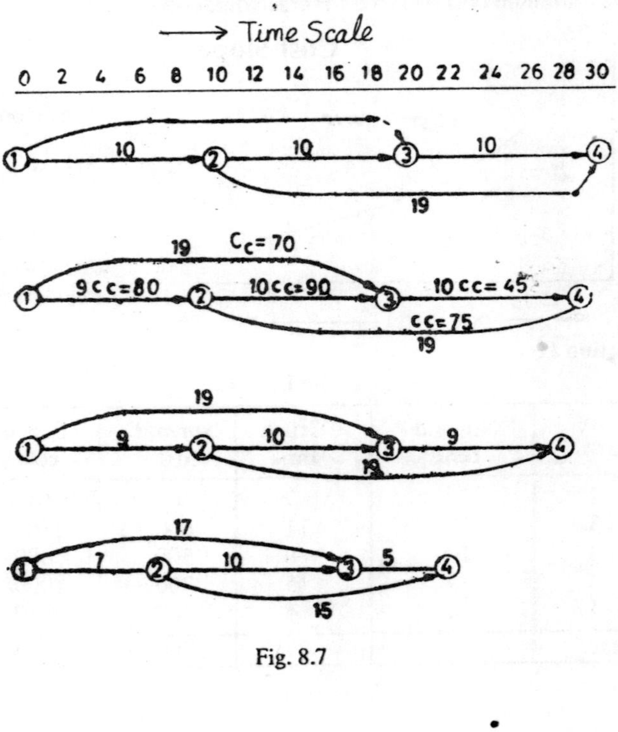

Fig. 8.7

Crashing activity	Total crash cost per day
(1 — 2) and (1 — 3) (1 — 3) and (2 — 3) and (2 — 4) (3 — 4) and (2 — 4)	80 + 70 = 150 ... (i) 70 + 50 + 75 = 195 ... (ii) 85 + 75 = 160 ... (iii)

Proposal (i) is most economical. Activity (1 — 2) can be crashed further only by 2 more days. Hence combination (i) can be crashed maximum for 2 days.

Crashing cost for 2 more days $= 2 \times 150 = 300$

Crash cost for 28 days $= 2665 + 300 = 2965$ ... (iii)

Further 4 days crashing can be done by adopting proposal (ii) which is 2nd most economical.

Hence crashing cost for 4 more days $= 4 \times 160 = 640$

Crash cost for 22 days $= 2965 + 640 = 3605$ ...(iv)

We also know that for 30 days normal schedule the normal cost is Rs. 2500.

Chapter 9

ELECTRONIC DATA PROCESSING AND MATERIALS MANAGEMENT

Materials Management by Computer

The electronic Data Processing has made possible speedy information flow under complex situations. The Electronic Data Processing should be so designed as to integrate activities from the receipt of order through planning and schedule to ultimate delivery. The need for Electronic Data Processing arises in order to optimise Materials Information System in four major areas of activities in which materials management has direct interest *i.e.* planning, data processing, problem solving and feed back information control. Electronic data processing has revolutionised materials management with in the last three decade. It is taking over control of the entire clerical phase of materials management. Computer can analyse, in no time, data that would take considerable time of a large force of ministrial staff. As a result, the materials manager can get more data for making decisions much faster than before.

Automation

Many of us do not understand the meaning of automation. The use of a computer is not automation. The employees have long made frequent use of the most common of all computers—the adding machine. This may be a form of mechanisation, but it is not automation. Mechanisation has gone on ever since man invented the simplest tool. The addition of power to tools increased man's mechanisation—but this still is not automation. Today the man is beginning to design tools that control themselves, and this is the essence of automation. Purchasing includes all aspects of procurement of materials from the time a possible need is known until the material is received and approved for use. There is difference in the functions of materials departments of various companies but common function that are designed to the purchasing department are:

(a) Determination of possible sources of supply
(b) Selection of the source
(c) Selection of the most economical method of delivery and routing
(d) Issuance of the purchase order
(e) Follow-up and expediting

While some of the functions of purchasing department which can be assigned to other departments are : (a) Receiving and inspection; (b) Invoice Checking and payment; (c) Materials and Inventory control; (d) Value analysis; (e) Salvage and Scrap disposal.

A review of these functions will reveal that automation of the production process has little effect on any of the functions. However, a much higher degree of mechanisation of purchasing is possible by ABC approach to inventory analysis and control. Inventory management involves the balancing of the cost of carrying inventory with the risk and cost of a stoppage because of being out-of-stock. Items of low rupee cost can be overstocked at no great expense. These items should not be followed closely by the purchasing agent. His attention should be devoted to type A items.

EDP And Purchasing

With the development of many kinds of electronic equipment ranging from the simple to extremely sophisticated, many business functions in the field of production, accounting and marketing have found the equipment useful in an increasing number of ways. But purchasing function which spends around 50% of company money has logged in the utilisation of computers and data processing equipment because of the following reasons:

(i) Survey of various industries revealed that purchase order writing could not be automated unless such purchases are repetitive. Only when purchasing was a support of a broader business system the higher degree of mechanisation was recommended.

(ii) Management thinking revolved around the concept that purchasing was entirely a non-routine, decision making function, often prevented serious consideration of adopting purchasing routines to computer. To a computer manager it appeared logical to place repetitious and routine business operations on the computer first.

(iii) The lack of knowledge on the part of purchasing managers of electronic equipment its capabilities and its application to purchasing activities has led to the fear of EDP and a reluctance to promote its use.

Object of EDP

The object of applying EDP to any operation is to distill pertinent and timely information for management from the mass of data available as a means of making better decisions. The objective of establishing an EDP system in materials management is togather, store, analyse and disseminate pertinent information to ensure an efficient purchasing operation. But to confine EDP objective to the writing of orders evaluation and preparation of reports would often fail to justify the EDP system economically. The greatest benefits of EDP come when all related elements of the business are integrated into a single system. The purchasing manager should take a broad view and consider the effects of EDP in purchasing on such related functions as accounting, inventory control, receiving, inspection, production control and production planning.

Materials management by computer normally starts with a magnetic tape that is, in effect, a list of items to be controlled and a programme that tells what to compute? What to do with this basic list and the variable data fed into it? The ability to think with the fantastic operating speed are what make a computer and electronic data processing different from punched-card mechanical processing. A well designed EDP system can handle all routine materials management functions such as

(a) **Provide up to date reports.** Current inventories of each item can be calculated and printed in detail. The computer can also be programmed to compile estimates of future inventories based on projected schedules of purchase and usage.

(b) **Complete materials transaction records.** A complete record of each transaction for each item can be compiled and printed automatically.

(c) **Compute economic order quantities and usages.** The computer can automatically analyse previous usage of an item and revise anticipated usages in accordance with some formula. It can recompose economic order quantity.

(d) **Can Handle routine Materials decisions.** The computer can review the lead time and planned usage of each item. When inventory drops to the reorder point, it can be programmed to print automatically a purchase requisition calling for a new buy and computer can be programmed to print a purchase order if there is no need to get competitive bids. Computer can also be made delivery conscious. The supplier's promised delivery date also can be fed into the computer and another expediting notice is generated if the material is not received before this time.

(e) **Update the Cost Data.** Computer can provide an accurate estimate of future cash needs to pay for deliveries against open purchase order. The computer can be programmed to provide information on all items where there is a price change.

(f) **Computer and Materials Management.** A computer can maintain information flow with basic data, coming from production planning, design and maintenance departments and environmental information coming from purchase and sales departments. It can give back the information of inventory records to the production planning department, can send purchase requisitions to the purchase department, remind purchase department for follow up and place direct purchase orders for standard repetitive items. It can check the actual consumption against the bill of materials and debit material cost incurred to user department. On the basis of record and basic data, the computer can formulate inventory levels. Inventory control is often the first application of EDP to materials management. In both large and small companies, EDP is typically used for scheduling and material control concurrent with its adoption for inventory control. The application of EDP to materials management varies from industry to industry. In general industries that use EDP in the materials management process are likely to have materials organisations headed by materials managers. The relationship between EDP and materials management will almost certainly become more pronounced when managements learn how to use their computers to manage materials in new ways. In order to understand the cost benefit analysis and how a computerized material system will work, let us study Management Information System and Computerisation and its application. A computer is all but essential to a system approach, since the concept is based on management's being able to react rapidly to changes in operating conditions. The systems concept is impractical without a computer. Non computerised information is too outdated to be more than a historical guide.

Management Information System

We perceive information as paper work, which means nuisance. This feeling is not correct. Information at present is one of the ingredient of industrial operations. In a simple organisation, the amount of information needed to provide efficient utilisation of men-materials and machinery is not very significant, but in a larger size production unit efficient production depends considerably on systematic flow of information regarding the sales forecasts, materials planning, production scheduling, costs and profitabilities at various production levels. Information is an action concept. When you want somebody to work, you must tell him what to do and how to do it. Modification for creative and intelligent work come only from job satisfaction and job satisfaction cannot be achieved without understanding the objectives of the job to be achieved which in turn can not be understood without information. Executives in industries normally complain of

(i) increasing amount of paper work.

(ii) Paucity of information available for decision-making.

The two are contradictory. On one hand, information is pouring in through papers, submerging the executives and on the other hand, there is not enough information for rational decision making. The information system is based on the analysis of each aspect of information with respect to different utility for decision making and the cost of getting the information.

The information system reflects the style of management. In many concerns, the management exists only at the top. All the decisions are taken by the top man himself. With this unitary style of management, there is a possibility of inefficiency in decision making or delay or no decision due to overwork rather than to share power and depend on the loyalty of others. Management normally has two options:

(i) Fire Brigade management and

(ii) Look ahead management

The Fire Brigade Management can ask for information when required. But look ahead management, believes in formulating carefully its needs for information ahead of time. The information is closely tied to the possible action to eliminate superfluous information. Thus there is a need to devise a system which provides symbolisation and information to substitute for seeing actual work.

The importance of professional managers has considerably increased during the last 30 years. Many factors are responsible for importance to information such as rapid change of technology increasing size of business, changing socio-political environment in which business have to operate. According to Peter Drucker managing of business goes a way beyond passive reaction and adoption. It implies the responsibility for attempting to shape the economic environment for planning and carrying through changes in the economic environment for constantly pushing back the limitations of economic circumstances and enterprise's freedom of action.

Need of Information

In order to provide this kind of creative leadership in a complex environment, the management needs information. Manager needs the information in order to perform following tasks:

(i) Setting of objectives
(ii) To establish the plan for achieving the objectives.
(iii) To execute the plans.
(iv) To evaluate the performance of the organisation.
(v) To have the feedback of the plans.

Thus management's number one task is to get the right information in the right form, at the right place and at the right time. The right information is that information which sis necessary for the effective functioning of the management. Thus the increased complexity of business has forced management to rely heavily on information systems. Following are the parallel developments which have increased the availability of the quantitative and qualitative information.

(a) Standard costing
(b) Marginal contribution and break-even analysis
(c) Flexible budgeting.
(d) Electronic data processing

Concept of Management Information System

We know that as a business grow in size and becomes complex it becomes impossible to pay attention to all the aspects of the business. At this stage we need the advice of functional specialists in the area of production planning, production control, accounting, work study, marketing, quantitative techniques etc. In addition to this the changes in the organisational structure had to be made to meet the various changes. The term management information can be defined as an efficient and purposeful system which have the capability to provide all levels of management, a timely, prompt, accurate and reliable information *M.I.S. is a nervous system of the organisation and any deficiency in this system is very likely to reflect of the functional and administrative efficiency of the organisation.* To understand the concept of management information system, let us understand each of the following terms:

1. Management 2. Information 3. System

1. Management. It is an essential part of any group activity. An organisation cannot survive without management. It is the management which makes people realise the objectives of the organisation and directs the efforts towards their achievement. Management is a multi-purpose organ of an organisation that manages the work and personnel at work. It is a creative and innovative force striving to secure the maximum result by the use of available resources. Management provides new ideas and vision to the work group and integrates its efforts in such a manner as to account for better results. The word Management refers to top, middle an lower level as well as different functional areas of management such as production, operations, marketing, finance, accounts, management services, personnel etc.

2. Information. It is sometimes which management expects to know at a given time. Information is not data, the data comprises of a host of information, which may be of little or no consequence to management. The information is needed to plan, organise, direct and control the business and suitably designed information pays for itself. The effectiveness of any information is dependent on the timing and content of the information presented and the management action. The need for management information is felt when the managers have to make decisions. The manager will have to rely on his judgement but he must have information on the basis of which he arrives at the decisions. The three important uses of information are :

(i) Process of management planning (decision making)
(ii) Execution
(iii) Control

Once the objectives of the business are decided than it is necessary to plan the course of action to be followed in order to achieve these. Such a plan need reliable information so as to obtain best results. The next step is to communicate the plan or decisions to lower levels for execution. This requires information from those higher up as to what action is to be taken all along the line to the lowest levels. The next is the control functions of management. After the plan has been made and executed one must have the information of the results and standards to evaluate whether objectives have been achieved or not. This calls for a regular flow of feedback information which will indicate in what way the results vary from planned targets. By examining these variances management can decide the corrective actions to be taken. Thus planning, executing and controlling the affairs of a business will require information. Information is required by all levels of management. At the top management level what is required is a very broad survey relating to areas where results have varied from plans. This is known as management by exceptions. Lower down the organisation structure the same principles will be followed by each executive and will be given more detailed reports directly bearing the responsibility.

Presentation of Information

Information can be presented by means of graphs, charts, (pie, charts. Bar charts, Histograms, Ideographs and Flow charts). The timing and frequency of reports depend on the nature of the report whether routine or special. In considering the timing and frequency of reports, the financial cost of preparation must be weighed and balanced against the anticipated benefits expected from the use of the reports. Reports normally present information regarding a period of time. Reporting is the physical aspects of manufacturing on its technological aspects and economic aspects. Reporting is a matter of planning and creation of record.

Following are the types of records which are usually created.

(a) Records of basic information

(b) Records showing what is available.

(c) Historical Records

(a) Records of basic information

(i) Blue prints.

(ii) Bills of materials.

(iii) Production routing.

(b) Records showing what is available.

(i) Raw materials.

(ii) Work in process.

(iii) Semi-processed stock.

(iv) Machinery and equipments.

(v) Finished stock.

(vi) Tools, jigs, fixture and gauges.

(c) Historical Records

(i) Records of production.

(ii) Records of waste and rejects.

(iii) Records of machine performance. (iv) Records of sales.

(v) Records of absenteeism.

The records exhibit information about actual production, inventory actual input as compared to pre-conceived standards. In a small organisation the reports are prepared on the shop floor and the management evaluates the daily report and takes prompt action. In a large plant the same course is followed by the production planning and control on an adequate scale relevant to the operational requirements.

Design of MIS

It is indeed a difficult task to design a suitable and efficient information system for the management. This demands a thorough knowledge of the organisational structure, working and system. It requires experience, skill and vision of the Information System. Designer who must understand, assimilate and foresee the information needs of the management. A few of the important steps involveed in the design of M.I.S. are :

1. Analysis Phase
   - Problem Recognition
   - Problem Identification
   - Problem definition
2. Synthesis
   - Problem of Flow Chart
   - Examination of the document flow
   - Working out quantities
   - Hardware and software consideractions
   - Establishing inputs and outputs
   - Fixing user responsibility
   - Running in Parallel.

Table An Information System and Corporate Hierarchy

Level	Organisation Identity	Activities	Information System	Outputs
Strategic Planning	Top Management	Set objectives	Special "one time reports	Goals and Policies
Manage ment Control	Departments heads	Allocate assigned resources	Many regular reports and Formats	Decisions "personal' leadership
Operational Control	Supervisors Foremen Clerks	Use resources to carry out tasks	Formal	Actions

Analysis Phase

(i) **Problem recognition**. The designer must recognise the potential areas which need to be served better and supplied with information which is better, prompt and accurate. This has to be accomplished by frequent and free discussion with the various levels of management. Enough time should be spent in the recognition of the problem, because it is preferable to have wrong solution for the right problem rather than the right solution for wrong problem.

(ii) **Problem identification.** This involves a further study into the areas which have been broadly recognised in the problem recognition phase and a closer scrutiny of the selected areas already identified a deficient areas.

(iii) **Problem definition**. This phase is further detailed study of the problem identification phase. For instance, it will point out the exact discrepancy.

Synthesis

(i) **Preparation of a document flow chart.** The purpose of the flow chart is to present the flow of different documents relating to the discrepancies of the deficient areas.

(ii) **A close examination of the document flow chart.** This is an exercise involving a careful examination of the several deficiencies thrown in by the document flow chart.

(iii) **Working out quantities.** This involves the computation of the record size and the data elements involved in the systems design. The total volume of data to be processed and maintained have to be determined. This will, in turn constitute the basis for identifying the type of information system that may be necessary and the kind of organisation and procedures which will be required to support an information system.

Impact of Management Information System

Following points give the impact of M.I.S on management:

(i) Information is power and a kind of *information or computer man* has grown in the organisation. Information man is consulted by the top management as well as heads of functional groups, in connection with the fulfillment of information needs of the organisation.

(ii) M.I.S. growth has resulted in centralisation. The availability of prompt, accurate and timely information about the various activities of the organisation to the management has enhanced their capacity to perform the control function.

(iii) M.I.S. with the growth of computers has changed the entire philosophy of the management. Certain problems which is used to be considered very complicated and almost impossible to solve are now a matter of fact. Production scheduling, Linear Programming, etc. are solved with computers.

Computer and Its Application

The information technology and high speed computers have a significant impact on the middle and top management of an organisation. The information technology should push upward in the organisation structure the boundary between planning and performance. The availability of high speed computers in conjunction with new mathematical techniques will enable large corporations to move to re-centralisation of the planning, organising and controlling functions. The information technology will draw a line separating top and middle management. The information technology will enrich rather than shrink the role of managers at middle level.

History of Computerisation

In 1944, the first automatic digital computer began its operation at Harvard University. By 1954, a few commercially available digital computers had appeared, the UNIIVAC I and the IBM 701 and 650.

Computer usage has led to savings of 10—25% in clerical costs in many cases, and savings of 10—20% in inventory costs. The greatest pay-off, however, will be

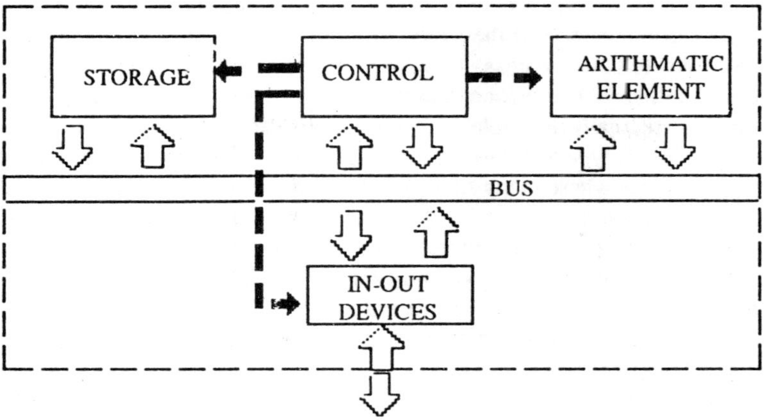

OUTSIDE WORLD

Fig. 9.1 Computer

in sophisticated total management information systems, employing advance management science techniques such as operations research and linear programming.

Output and Off-Line Operations

Computer output devices, must convert the electrical signals used within the computer to some other form of printed words, punched cards, graphical information, or magnetic type recordings. Ordinarily, the results must be presented as a permanent record in some tangible form. In some applications, the computer accepts voluminous input data and produces a very concise output. In other applications, a small amount of input produces a huge volume of output.

If a computer produces a voluminous report, assuming that it is a 700 page report, which might be equivalent of 20,0000 printed lines of 400,000 computer words. If a high-speed printer were used at 800 lines per minute, it would take 25 minutes to print out the report. This might seem like an excellent speed until you consider that the computer could transfer all that information to a tape unit in half a minute. If the computer were to control the high-speed printer while it is printing out this information, it would time up the computer for 25 minutes. However, if a suitable off-line equipment were available, the computer could transfer the complete report to a magnetic tape unit in about 30 seconds, then move on to other work. This off-line unit is connected to an off-line printer through a buffer unit. Although it would still require 25 minutes to print the report but the computer would not be involved now.

Equipment and Installations

Different computer generations can be reasonably distinguished by important differences in both hardware and software. As the industry continues to develop, it is unlikely that any clear distinction will be possible for future generations. The first generation computers used the stored program concept and programming was a difficult and tedious process. However, the mid-1950 is the development of improved software. The second generation began about 1959 with the delivery of the first commercially available, fully transistorized computers. During the second generation, batch-type operations became quite common, particularly at university computer centres where many small jobs were handled per day. The year 1965 is generally considered to be the dividing line between the second and third generation. Most computers that continued to be marketed after 1965 are considered at least by their manufacturers to be third generation machines. The characteristics of the third generation vary from one manufacturer to another. One major technical development is the use of integrated circuits. These represent a further development of solid state technology which permits more circuits to be packed in a smaller space and ultimately promises lower costs and higher reliability. By the beginning of the 1970's, the generation concept becomes confused. Another phenomenon of the third generation is the emergency of the mini-computers. They have a small word size and limited peripheral equipment. Mini-computers are designed so that they can function as a satellite processor connected remotely to a larger computing installation.

Economic Aspects

Computers equipment costs represent about one-half or one-third of annual operating costs. Other significant costs are associated with computer programming, planning procedural changes and training or retraining of personnel. The purchase price of the computer will normally be 30 to 50 times the monthly rental cost. The cost of maintenance service is typically 5 to 15 percent of the monthly rental charge. The decision to rent or buy depends to a greater extent on such factors as government policy, interest rates and availability of money, hours per day of expected usage-ratio of purchase price to rental price for the specific equipment selected.

The other cost consideration is the selection of optional or peripheral equipment. In large installations the cost of peripheral equipment frequently exceeds the cost of the basic computer. The preparation of the physical installation is frequently an important item of cost. Adequate provision must be provided not only for the equipment itself but for maintenance personnel and parts, for storage of tapes and other supples, for off-line equipment and for possible expansion of the configuration. Special electrical power is usually provided because most medium and large computer installations require 10 to 100 kw or more of electrical power.

The computer's program determines what the computer will do at any particular time. When that program is replaced by a different program, the same computer performs entirely different functions. Computer installations, therefore, are operated in a manner to make efficient and economical use of the equipment to insure that vital jobs are completed on schedule and to provide some flexibility for the immediate users.

Software

Software is an interesting and descriptive term and its general meaning is "everything other then hardware required to make a digital computer installation operational". More specifically it usually refers to the computer programs and programming aids which are an essential part of any computer programs supplied by the equipment manufacturer, thereby excluding those developed by the user. At any rate, it is a critical and expensive item which has given rise to a new industry which seems to be growing as rapidly as the computer hardware industry.

The programmer must state very explicitly the procedure to be followed by the computer. In a problem-oriented language, he should state only the problem. The compiler then chooses a procedure for solving the problem or accomplishing the result.

The compilers themselves are more complex than assemblers and require more time on a computer to perform their translating function. There are two major phases in the operation of a typical compiler program. The first is an analysis phase during which the source program is analyzed and broken down into self-contained information units. The second phase is the generator or synthesis phase which puts the overall program back together again. It generates the machine language instructions and is, therefore, more machine dependent than the first phase.

Hardware

Hardware computer resources include the processor itself main memory (core storage), auxiliary memory (magnetic discs, drums and tape) and output devices (line printer, graphic plotter, etc). Such a system notice that some of the auxiliary storage devices are able to transfer information back and forth to the main memory.

Computer Application

The digital computers had established itself as a useful mathematical tool capable of tackling problems that might otherwise require a lifetime of computational work.

Mathematical Applications

In one sense, mathematical applications are the easiest type to understand. Digital computers were developed originally to solve mathematical problems, and it would be surprising indeed if most computers were not well suited to handle mathematical problems.

Today computers are widely used for orbital calculations and computing trajectories to other planets. Statistical analysis usually involves a large mass of input data which must be sorted and organized in many different ways and the results summarized in many different forms. This was "natural" for the digital computer, and the processing of census data, for instance, was one of the first few applications. Today this type of analysis widely used in many other scientific and industrial problems. Many engineering design problems require the selection of optimum parameters. This selection of the best parameter is a design choice that must be made.

Actually, the area of operations research or operàtions analysis is very similar to the engineering design problem, except that instead of hardware design, it is more likely to be concerned with management decisions. Included among scientific applications is the general area of simulation. The concept of simulation by a computer is sometimes difficult to grasp, but it is a very important type of application.

Information Systems

The size and complexity of computer installations for business applications vary considerably. Since rather large files are usually involved, the magnetic tape has been widely used for this purpose, but there is a growing interest in magnetic disc type and other mass storage files which provide relatively large storage capacity with a much more rapid random access capability.

The general characteristics of information systems processing data are :

(i) Difficult to design the problem
(ii) Need random access to large storage capacity.
(iii) Organisation of computer storage is difficult.
(iv) Versatile inquiry stations desirable.
(v) Little reliance on punched card media.

In a control system, the computer's output is used to control, some process or activity which cannot wait very long for new instructions when the situation or the environment changes. Such systems are sometimes referred to as real time applications.

Computer For System Control

A computer is used to control the operation of a chemical plant, such control system might be made completely automatic, in which case the system is able to sense many variables on a more or less continuous basis. Typical variables might be the temperature, or flow rates at different points within the processing mechanism; and characteristics associated with the various products and waste. The computer is expected to control automatically many factors in the production process flow rates, temperatures, supply of raw materials, cycling procedures, etc. It attempts to optimize the overall process. More often the control system is semi-automatic and the computer works in partnership with one more operators.

Frontier Applications

Strictly speaking a computer does only what it has been told to do, but it can be directed to try many different ways of solving a problem. It can also be directed to improve its problem-solving performance, or to direct its systems of search in a more promising direction.

Linear Programming

This particular technique deserves mention as it has been applied profitably to a wide variety of industrial, military and engineering problems. This is the method known as linear programming. In this problem, a manufacturer has a certain number of warehouses stocking a particular items. He also has outstanding orders for this item from customers in different parts of the country. He wants to determine how many units should be sent from each warehouse to each customers in order to minimize the shipping costs. The linear programming has been discussed in depth in this book.

Data Bank

In almost every field of endeavour, we have come to rely on systematic records of some type. The principal characteristic of an information system is the large file or files of data must be kept up-to-date. This data bank is then used to prepare reports, notices, checks etc; to answer queries; or permit analysis of the stored data. In general, the data bank builds up gradually over a period time, and changes are made on a daily, weekly, or monthly basis.

The purpose of most information systems is to provide management with information to make decisions or plan operations. This information must be complete, accurate, and timely. Notice that all of these characteristics certain to the data before it gets into the system. The computer's contribution is to analyze and extract from the data base with negligible delay and relatively low cost. It can also make comparisons readily with past performance or other historical data.

If the MIS is to be really effective, management must do more than to give its support. It has been pointed out that many so-called management information systems serve the clerk not the manager. The reason for this phenomenon is often that the systems goals were established by the clerks because the managers were too busy with other matters or not willing to invest their own time or effort.

Classification of Computer Applications

Scientific Systems	Information Systems
★ General	Numerical
★ Statistical	Analysis of Census Data
★ Weather Prediction	Accounting
★ Reactor Design	
★ Orbital Analysis and Prediction	Project and Production Management
★ Linear Programing (optimisation	(PERT)
★ studies)	Sales and Advertising Analyis,
★ Engineering Design	Inventory and Quality Control
★ Simulation	Election Returns
★ War Gaming	Budgetary Control
★ Economic Games	Economic Analysis
★ Management Games	Reservation Control
★ Training Devices	Library and Scientific Data
	Reference
	Patent and Statute Search
	Language Translation
	Personnel Files
	Data Base Development and Use
	Medical Diagnosis

Control System	Frontier Applications
★ Air Traffic Control	Problem Solving
★ Air Defence Systems	Pattern Recognition
★ Communication Network	
★ Control	
★ Industrial Process Control	
★ Missile Guidance System	

System Design

System design is essentially the choosing between alternatives. Although the preliminary steps represent a considerable amount of hard work. The potential user should participate actively in this phase. It should be borne in mind that we are considering system design from an overall stand point; that is, we are including both hardware and software. In a computer system the two are interdependent in the initial design.

Data-Cost vs. Value

Many of the alternatives in computer system design pertain to the data that flow in the system. Decisions concerning data normally have the greatest impact on system cost and system effectiveness. There is a cost associated with collecting data, with processing it, storing it, retrieving it, reporting it, and even with using it. The cost will vary significantly with the type of data involved with the means of collecting and processing. The information capacity of a system or volume of data flowing in a system is an important element of cost. In trying to estimate the value of more information we have to consider the degree to which it relates to the problem at hand or to the goal of the system. One of the big potentials of digital computer systems is the ability to bring more information to bear on a particular problem without losing relevance.

Information Control

The idea in information control is very important in the planning of a computer system. Information is the raw material and the product of a computer system. It is essential to focus attention on the quality of this information as a raw material and as an intermediate or final product. This is necessary to establish user confidence in a system and to permit systematic improvement of overall system effectiveness.

Man vs. Machine

The factor governing system design is the area of man vs. machine. Should this particular function be performed by a man, by the computer, or should they do it together? This question arises often: sometimes, as a major decision; sometimes, as a minor decision.

Reliability is an important factor in system design. Strictly speaking there is always some uncertainty, some finite possibility that some data are in error or that some important item has been overlooked. Almost all computers being built today are solid state machine and the testing techniques have been developed to detect some types of failure before the failure actually occurs.

Flexibility And Growth Potential

In digital computer systems, there is an inherent potential for flexibility and growth. This should be rooted in the general purpose nature of a digital computer.

Personnel

A significant effect on system design is personnel acquisition and training. More than anything, else, the shortage of trained and experienced personnel acts as a restraining influence on elaborate plans for computer systems. Nobet Wiener said: "the computer is only as valuable as the man using. But he's got to have the ideas."

Chapter 10

PRODUCTION AND MATERIALS MANAGEMENT

Introduction

Production and Materials have a common goal of efficient and profitable operations. However their philosophies differ. A production executive quite naturally thinks in terms of having all he needs the best materials. This philosophy can easily lead to excessive inventories of unnecessarily high quality. The purchasing executive may find himself in an unpopular position when he must contend for a reasonable quantity of the appropriate quality. The relationship between the two departments can be harmonised through the exchange of information which each department develops in the normal course of its operations. Production must keep materials department informed, as far in advance as possible, about production plans and schedules. With this information, purchasing is able to plan its procurement programme intelligently so as to minimise such orders. The production department must be made to realise the "lead time" that exists between the issuance of a requisition and receipt of goods. In many companies the purchasing and production departments share joint responsibility for development of standards and specifications for materials and supplies to be purchased. The important thing is for the purchasing department to make sure that standards confirms to materials that are readily available in the market and avoid unnecessary deviations that add to the costs. The purchasing department has a valuable tool for the production department in its file of vendor's catalogs. These should be supplied on call to the production department. Purchasing also has the responsibility of informing the production department about the new materials, machines or methods that come to the buyers' attention through visiting salesmen or trade literature.

Production And Materials Control

Production control is the process of monitoring the performance of a group of workers or equipment and comparing the results of their efforts with a predetermined plan. The production controller's function is to see that the objectives of the plan are being met and that human and physical resources are being used as efficiently as possible. Production control is concerned with all the resources need to get a job done. The production control manager is concerned with having not only the materials on hand to do the job but also the labour and equipment. Production control is a part of materials management for the following reasons:

(i) For all the resources used in production, material is the only resource that is external to the organisation. Production control make sure that enough material is on hand so that workers and machines can be productively employed.

(ii) The skills required for materials management can readily be applied to production control problems involving labour and equipments.

(iii) The materials management is often considered part of operations management.

(iv) Production control problems involving materials, labour and equipment are inevitably interrelated. The production control problem is to bring all these resources together at the right time in proper quantities.

In order to understand the relationship of Production and Materials management department, it is important to understand the basic concepts of Production, Types of Production, Production Management and the role of Production Manger.

Production

Definition

The term production quite often means the same as manufacture. To carry out the process of manufacturing we need : Man to do the job; Equipment; Material.

However, if we have a lathe machine, a skilled operator, a metal bar for turning. Will we be equipped for production? Although we have now all the ingredients to start manufacturing but still we are not ready to manufacture. We do not know what is to make? When it is to be made? Do we have customer to buy the product? What will happen if the lathe machine breakdown? Are we making the right type and quality of the product? These questions show us that we need more than just the technical ability to manufacture. We also need: service activities and Control functions.

The service abilities are those which make sure that the manufacturing process can go on and control makes sure that it goes in the right direction. Economics defines production as utility creation. An activity which imparts from utility, time utility, space utility. Economists also define production as the act of making something with the object of satisfying human wants thus production is not only confined to goods and commodities but also include services. Consequently the economists definition of production is not restricted to the process of creation of physical items, but the transportation system, banking system, library and hospital etc. can also be considered as a production process. Present views of production are that it is a sequence of operations that transform materials from a given state to a desired state.

Objectives of Production. The main object of production is to ensure that it makes a product which can satisfy the needs of the customer by giving the right quality of the product at right place at the right time at right price. To achieve the above objective it is essential that production organisation is well managed.

Production Process

Production is a sequence of operations that transforms materials from a given to a direct form. The transformation may be done in one or in combination of the following ways:

- ★ Transformation by disintegration
- ★ Transformation by integration, and
- ★ Transformation by service.

Transformation by Disintegration It has one ingredient as input and producing several outputs. This transformation is accompanied by changes in the physical shape of the input, for example, making of steel bars from cast ingot, making components from standardised materials on machine taste.

Transformation by Integration. In this we have several components as input and one product as output for example producing of household appliances, automobile, T.V. set, Computers etc.

Transformation by Service. In this no change in object under consideration is perceptible, only certain operations are carried on the job, to change one of the parameters which define the object for example heat treatment of various jobs to increase tensile strength or other mechanical properties of the object, servicing and repairs of automobiles, loading and unloading of trucks etc. Many service operations are not considered as part of industry, but for the planning and control of these industrial operations. The objective of production management is the same as any other area of management that is to realise the overall objectives of the organisation.

Production Management

Production management is the process of designing, manning operating, servicing, and centralising the activities of a manufacturing organisation, responsible for the actual transformation of material inputs into marketable finished goods.

Production planning and control which is an integral and important part of the Production Management has to play a vital role. Production management is to decide the objectives of production. This will involve all the functions of planning, organising, directing and controlling the production activities from the short term and long term aspect. The area which help us in setting up our production facilities are :—

- ★ Method study,
- ★ Plant layout,
- ★ Work measurement,
- ★ Production planning and Control,
- ★ Stock Control,
- ★ Quality Control
- ★ Maintenance.

Production management is a sub-system of the business organisation. Production management is what a production-manager does.

Role of Production Manager

The production manager's role is that of a decision maker. After he has planned allocation of inputs, the creation of value through production process can begin. Once the production processes are started, it must be controlled. The control involves observing results and checking that they conform to the original plans. The checking is possible by feed-back mechanism. Thus production management is to plan, organise, direct and control the production activities of a business concern. Now we know that production is an art of making something with the object of satisfying human wants which include service in addition to goods and commodities. But the wants of the customers are not satisfied until the right quality of the products are in their hands with the result the marketing process may also be considered as part of the process of production. In certain organisations marketing of products is a minor task in comparison to the creation of product while in other organisations marketing process may be of greater importance and may dominate even the creating process. Clearly, the production and marketing are separate but still interdependent functions in a business.

Types of Production

There are three types of production which represent their basic approaches to production. The three types are :

(a) Job production.

(b) Batch production.

(c) Flow production.

Job Production

In job production the whole product is looked as one job which is to be completed before going on to next. The most common examples are building a ship or a large civil engineering construction job. Job production is not confined to large projects, it could be the making of a special piece of equipment or a tool.

Batch Production

If qualities of more than one are being made, it is sometimes convenient to split the production into a series of manufacturing stages or operations. Each operation is completed as one of the single items being made, before the next operation is started. In this way a group of identical products, or a batch are made, which move through the production process together.

If more than one types of product is being made, then batches of different products may be moving around the shop floor sometimes requiring operations from the same machine. This leads to problems of how long a machine should be processing a batch of one type of product before going on to the next process, a different one or which batch should be worked on first. This type of problem tends to make the planning and control of batch production of difficult task.

Flow Production

When there is a continuous demand for a product, it is sometimes worthwhile setting-up facilities to make the product and no other product. In these circumstances flow production may be best way of operating. Here the manufacturing is broken down into operations, but each unit moves, or flows, from one operation to the next individually, and not as one of a batch examples are motor manufacturing, fertiliser, pharmaceutical and urea manufacturing. Since only one product is being made there are no problems about priorities, but it is necessary to balance the work load at all stages of manufacture. Examples are motor car manufacturing.

Production Manager

The person who is given responsibility for the process of production is called Production Manager. Production manager should have both technical and managerial skills. Production manager needs to take two types of decisions:

1. Problem relating to production system like operation and technology.
2. Problems relating to planning and analysing.

Production manager must make decisions regarding lay out of equipments, techniques of material handling, location and size of the plant, motion and time study, process analysis and quality of the product. Once the production system has been designed and actuated the problems which production manager faces is the analysis and control of the production system. Routing, leading, scheduling, despatching expediting are the basic production planning and control activities. The production manager's role is that of a decision maker, after he has planned allocation of inputs, starts the creation of value through the production process. This is not the end but the beginning of production manager's activities. Once the production processes are started it must be controlled. The control involves observing results and checking that they confirm to the original plans. The checking is possible by feed-back mechanism. So the role of production manager in a production system is that of decision maker to plan and control the production processes.

Production Planning and Control

Production Planning and Control embrace all management decisions, policies, plans and actions which have something to do with optimisation of manufacturing objectives. Production planning must establish the basic relationship, among (a) Sales forecasts (b) Production capacity (c) Inventory levels (d) Working capital (e) Raw materials requirement (f) Production facilities (g) Product design and its manufacturing sequence (h) Manpower requirement etc. The objective of production planning is to strike the most economic balance between the above factors. The production planning and control systems are one of the basic activities that determine the effectiveness of a production enterprise. The production planning and control functions and its interaction with other functions is shown below.

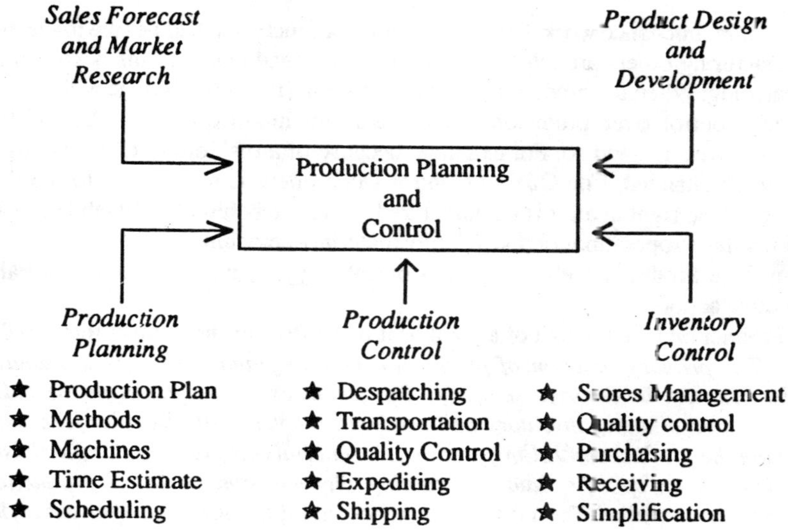

Managing Production

Production activity refers to the conversion of raw materials into finished product of desired quality and shape. In doing so, it must use the resources in such a way so as to produce the desired quantity of goods of desired quality at the right time and at the minimum cost. Production, Planning and Control Department helps in achieving this objective. Knowing the production requirements, this department plans for the resources, prepare route sheets determines loading and scheduling of machines. Once the production has started, it initiates control action to see that the work is being done according to plan. The type of layout and other supporting facilities like maintenance etc. dictate the type of production schedules one can make.

The production requirement of each product to be manufactured is first of all broken down into its sub-assemblies and component parts. However, all of the above components or sub-assemblies need not be manufactured within the plant. An important input to the planning functions is the make or buy decision with regard to these components and sub-assemblies. Based upon these decisions the Production Planning and Control department knows the requirements of each of the components or sub-assemblies that are to be manufactured within the plant.

Depending upon the sequence of operations and the layout, routine sheets are prepared which shows how the product will move within the plant. The time estimates for all of the operations are obtained from the work study department. This helps in loading and scheduling the machines. While scheduling, due attention must be given to the maintenance policy of the company is following. In case of preventive maintenance the machines should not be loaded when they are to be down for maintenance work. Once the detailed production schedules are made, the manufacturing orders are released to all the concerned people. This is known as despatching. When the production starts, continuous follow up is done with a view to keep control over production and make any modification in plans if the circumstances demand so. For example, because of a rush order the plans might have to be changed. The Quality Control Department is responsible to see that product of the right quality is manufactured. If we are behind the schedule it may be either due to operations or due to faulty material or machines or wrong planning. In any case Production Planning and Control suggests us to pin point and take corrective action.

Production is the output of a plant or it is the flow of the product through the plant. *The primary function of production planning and control is to manage production and inventories skillfully. This requires participation in the sales forecasts coordinating inventory and production levels with the sales forecasts, planning the product controlling production materials and supplies for purchases and delivery on specific data maintaining physical control of all production materials and supplies.* The most effective coordination is achieved when it is under one management namely production planning and control. The managing of production can be broken into three major functional areas:

1. Production Planning
2. Production Control
3. Material Control

The three major functional areas can be further subdivided. Production planning can be divided into long range planning and current planning. Production control can be divided into production scheduling, despatching and follow up. The material control is divided into planned control and physical control. The responsibilities assigned to each of these six functions can be further discussed in their logical sequence of occurrence.

Production Planning is a Joint Effort

In some companies the work of department called production planning and control is limited to the responsibilities shown in production control and material control with perhaps the additional responsibilities of sales order processing and production releases. The place of production planning and control as a department in the management of organisation depends upon the scope of its assigned responsibilities.

Production Planning and control is a joint effort. In production planning and control team every member has some responsibility for developing the programme and selling it out. Each member should know, understand and accept his responsibility and recognise the way in which it integrates with the responsibilities of others. The planning in many organisations is till left to chance. A successful organisation should think out where it wants to go, why it wants to go, how it can get there and when it should get there and then sets about doing so with minimum of dislocation. In this present era of increased competition and tight profits the practices of production1 Planning and Control are destined to give a desired progress. No nation can prosper if its industrial companies fail to make adequate profits. The industrial forecasting planning and control enable companies to operate safety and profitably. Production Planning and Control is the tool that coordinates all manufacturing activities. The management employs this technique to obtain the targets. The highest efficiency in production is obtained by manufacturing the required quantity of product of the required quality, at the required time, by the best and cheapest method.

Definition of Production Planning and Control

To understand Production, Planning and Control let us define each of these terms: Production; Planning, and Control.

- Production consists of a sequence of operations that transform materials from a given to a desired form. Transformation may be done by disintegration, integration or service.
- Planning begins with an analysis of the given data, on the basis of which a scheme of the utilisation of the firm's services can be outlined so that the desirable target may be most efficiently attained.
- Control invites and supervises operation with the aid of a control mechanism that feedback information about the progress of work.

Hence Production Planning and Control may be defined as the direction and coordination of the firm's material and physical facilities towards the attainment of prescribed production goods in the most efficient available way. Production planning involves a system to plan production, cost quality and time. In a simple language the production planning and control determines when, how and by whom the job is to be done. Production Planning and Control gets the job of sending a continuous stream of directions given to each of the steps and at all parts of the factory. Its directions are again minute and specific.

Production Planning and Control is not essentially a management function which comprise the planning, routing, scheduling, despatching, and follow up functions in the productive process, so organized that movements of the material, performance of machines and operations of labour, however subdivided and directed and coordinated as to quantity, quality, time, and place.

Production Planning and Control is the cerebellum of brain

An industrial plant could be compared with the human body, we could say that the building is similar to the skeleton because both provide a structural frame work. In the industrial body, the productive departments would be similar to the human muscles which do the work. Service departments such a industrial tool and engineering, maintenance, inspection and transport are similar to glands because they make constant adjustment to the physical body that are both corrective and preventive in their nature. Sales, product engineering, purchasing, personnel and accounting have functions that are similar to the five necessary organs because they react to external and internal events (sensory organs are touch, hearing, smell and taste).

The events which can and do stimulate our sensory departments are infinite in number, some of these events could arise or decline in the general economy and/or the company's sales, a new product idea or a desire to revise a product design, a rise in product cost or overhead, or an anticipated rise in material prices coupled with an opportunity to buy now at lower price.

The nervous system of the plant is its communication system. This is the complex of routes and channels through which ideas, information, and data are transmitted in speech, writing, signs or symbols by human or mechanical means from one person or point to another. *Production planning and Control frequently has been compared with the human brain, which is the controlling centre of the nervous system and more particularly with the cerebellum which is that part of the brain which coordinates the muscular activity and movements of the body. Therefore, we can say that production planning and control department is the controlling centre of the communications systems in a plant which coordinates the physical activities of manufacturing and guides their direction. Production Planning and Control functions are much the same as those of the cerebellum of brain.* It receives messages from the sensory departments, interprets and filter out non-essentials and relays these messages to the productive and service departments. In turn, it receives from the productive and service departments, messages of reaction to the original stimulates (feedback) it interprets and filters out the essentials in these responses. In this light, the primary function of production planning and control ar receiving, interpretations, decisive and communicative.

To perform these functions effectively the people in the production planning and control must have an objective point of view, an intimate knowledge of products and production processes, and most important an understanding of the persons in the plant who are responsible for responding to their enquiries. The broader their knowledge of products, processes and people, the keener their ability to listen, the more effective they will be in communicating the ideas information and facts to other people.

Objectives of Production

Planning and Control

It is well-known fact that the survival of any business organisation depends on how it can satisfy its customer. Thus, to satisfy the customer by quality and with regard to delivery date is one of the main objectives of any business organisation. This, however, becomes the primary objective of production control. It is clear from the above discussion that the objective of production control department is very closely linked to the objective of the business enterprise as a whole. Keeping in view the "customer satisfaction", the objectives for production planning and control should be, broadly, as follows:

(a) To deliver the product to the customer when he wants it.
(b) To promise delivery in the shortest time possible if we cannot deliver our product when the customer wants it.
(c) To keep our promises.
(d) To maintain flexibility in the manufacturing operations so that we can accept and deliver the occasional rush order for the odd product which gives for us a new customer or additional business from an old customer.
(e) To issue coordinated schedules and orders to the production departments with complete information to tell them what is expected to meet delivery requirements.
(f) To follow up production schedules to assure that delivery promises will be kept.
(g) To maintain adequate but not excessive inventories of production materi-also to support the continuous flow of production.
(h) To maintain inventory, production and employment levels that are relatively stable and consistent with the general level of sales.
(i) To plan plant capacities that will provide adequate facilities for future production and sales.

Planning and Control

The planning and control is an integral part of the system. Whatever be the type of the product to be manufactured the basic production control functions have to be done. The difference lies only in what to do, how to do, how often, where is to be done and who should do it. The difference, in the various kind of production control are classified as under:

Order Control. This is used for intermittent type of production. Each order is identified separately and all instructions and report form relating to the lot bear this number.

Flow Control. This is used for continuous production. Instructions and day-to-day directives are reduced to a minimum. Nearly all the functions requiring directives like what materials to use, how long it will take, what machines to use etc. are very carefully performed during the planning of the production time. Plant lay out itself involves a lot of production control functions. Production control instructs the manufacturing department as to the planned rate of production and receives their reports showing their actual rate accomplished.

Load Control. Similar process industries have their process like continuous industries but their control problem resemble those in intermittent production. The load on the key machines are properly allocated. No separate instruction is issued for every individual lot as all go through the same process.

Block Control. Where the products are somewhat varied, but all go through the same operations and where the variations have very little effect on processing time, plant loading and progress control can be simplified by using block control. A block is a collection of orders whose work load adds up to a fixed time duration say one half day. The manufacturing department gets orders only in block. Unless block no, 20 is out of the section in fuil, block 21 cannot go to that section, Garment making industry.

Control of Production Levels

Safety stocks give a short term protection against sales or demand uncertainty. The effectiveness of control, however, depends on the ability of the control system to restore these safety stocks in case of depletion. If total demand varies and stocks are being restored from production operations, the ability to restore depends in the ability of the production facilities to react to chance fluctuations in demand. The control of production rates and inventories requires a clear cut control system with well-specified rules of operation. Some times a company will devote great effort to "inventory control" setting economical reorder levels, fixing safety stocks or re-order points etc., without clearly taking the effect of production fluctuations into account. A sound production control system depends on :

(i) A forecast of demand, expressed in units of production capacity.
(ii) A production plan or preliminary budget which establishes the inventory and production budget.
(iii) A control procedure for deciding how fast to restore inventories to budget levels when errors in the demand forecast cause inventories to exceed or fall below budget.

The first requirement is to get a measure production that is useful and can be applied to production, inventories and demand equally well. On the other hand a company business can be thought of as selling time of the employees and time of use of its physical assets. The finished product demanded by a customer, or the finished or processed item in stock, is a block of processing time plus raw materials in more or less permanent form. Production-Control decisions are answers to questions about how much time to make available and how to use it in view of customer demand for time and time stored in inventory.

Objectives of Production Control

The objective of production control department is very closely linked to the objectives of business enterprise as a whole. Control of production levels means setting a production rate in view of both a fore cast of future demand and existing inventories i.e. reaching to past operating results as these influence the capability of achieving planned objectives.

Benefits of production Control

The advantages of production control includes the following:

(a) Helps to stabilise business by getting more and more customers through better service.

(b) Increased wages to employees as better service to customers results in huge profits.

(c) offers job securities to employees as plans are laid to maintain steady flow of production inspite of the seasonal fluctuations in the market demand.

(d) Increases the value of goods by way of product development which constantly aims at improving the quality of the product, at the same time tries to bring down the prices.

(e) Increases the productivity through more effective use of men, materials and machines.

(f) Ensure better utilisation of capital as a result of well balanced inventory control at all levels and

(g) Assures adequate return in the capital invested.

Production Planning

Planning means getting ready to make the product. Planning is an intellectual process in which creative thinking and imagination is essential. Planning includes setting objectives, policies, decisions and strategies. Planning is deciding in advance what to do? Where to do it? How to do it? When to do it and who is to do it? Planning bridges the gap from where we were to where we should go, planning makes things to occur which would not occur otherwise. Following are the important concepts about planning:

1. **Objectivity.** Realistic planning is essential conceptualisation of the objectives, the needs, the priorities, the approach and the activities involved. The objectivity requires a long far sight, correct visualisation and practical anticipation.
2. **Futuristic.** The trend in planning is based on the present and future than on the past. It is very similar to vehicle driving where one drives while looking ahead, anticipating judging and making decisions and rarely peeping into the rear view mirror.
3. **Planning Time.** At all levels of management one has to devote time for planning. The lack of planning or no planning creates increasing work loads piling up of unattended work which deprives him of his planning time and ultimately resulting in a vicious circle. The time spent on forward planning is more and more as one moves up the ladder of organisation. Let us assume the time spent on advance planning as 100%, then time spent by different level of management is given the following chart:

TOTAL PLANNING PERIOD 100%

Level of Management	Advance Planning							
	Weekly planning	Mon-thly	Six mon-thly	One Year	II Year	III	10 Year	Over 10 Years
1. Top Manage ment (General Manager)	2	5	15	20	25	18	10	5
2. Middle Management								
— Functional Managers	7	10	15	30	18	12	6	2
— Departmental Heads	12	15	20	35	10	6	2	—
3. Lower Management								
— Foreman	20	20	25	28	6	1	—	—
— Supervisors	35	40	15	8	2	—	—	—

Planning Horizon

Higher the level of management, more time is to be devoted for long range planning. The different levels of management is responsible for different nature of planning work as shown in the following table:

Level of Management	Planning Functions
1. Top Management	**Long Range Planning** (i) Strategic planning regarding — Growth — Research — Break through

	(ii) Policies planning regarding — Financial policies — Product policies — Inventory policies — Manpower policies — Marketing policies (iii) Decision and Forecasting.
2. Middle Management	**Short Term Planning** (i) Tactical planning (ii) Scheduling (iii) Resource planning (iv) Inventory planning
3. Lower Management	**Instantaneous Planning** — Loading — Progressing — Feedback

The planning has become a requisite for enterprise survival. The attribute of planning is to look into the future. Its tool is the forecasting method employed. The results are always accurate but if the tendencies can be clearly recognised, it is a good attempt. The Planning exercise is continuous. Closer approximation are possible as one travels in time. Complete accuracy is possible only when all the parameters are as nearly constant as this dynamic world will allow.

Since planning is an art, it has the capacity to enthuse people to undertake this work. To peep into the unknown area however tenuous, stimulates thinking of the present in the comparison of the future. Risk taking assumes a purpose. The definition of objectives has been one of the most important top management functions. Planning is, therefore, a top management activity par excellence.

One way to narrow the gap between estimates and ultimately actuals is to plan for along period on the basis of small interval (six months to one year) on a moving basis. Despite its obvious inaccuracies and the dynamism of situation planning occupies a permanent place in management activity. Plans are usually sub-divided as follows :

1. Perspective—for 10-20 years at a item divided into yearly based estimates.
2. Long Term master plans—for 2-5 years at a time divided into monthly broad estimates.
3. Short term master plans—for one year divided into monthly close estimates.
4. Monthly plans—divided into weekly or daily plans.

Whenever plans are prepared, assumptions underlying the figures adopted are always indicated in good plans.

Types of Production

Planning in production will have a different procedure depending on the type of production but it has certain basic features common to all types. These are :

(a) Availability of men, materials, machines and methods.

(b) Balancing of capacities.

(c) Balancing with market and profit planning.

(d) Optimisation of the Plan.

Balancing is one of the most important operations of planning. The strength of the chain is in its weakest link. Optimisation has to take into account the weak features and apply known techniques of analysis to improve them. These improvements in the short term, would be without incurring costs but may mean marginally additional capital costs in the long run.

An essential feature of planning as stated earlier is to recognise that dynamism is a part of life and changes must occur. Adjustments are, therefore, necessary. A good monitoring system will indicate trends of changes before hand. If they can be recognised, changes will be made in advance otherwise thy will overwhelm the planners. It is important that master plan be kept upto date to spot out any adjustments required to reflect changes in sales prospects, production demands, unforeseen changes in plant and equipment or available manpower. Getting ready for the first time is *original planning* and doing it over again is *repetitive planning*. Original planning deals with how products are to made, what materials to be used for various components, what machines and tools are required, etc. Original planning needs to be done over again for repeat orders only if a product's design or the manufacturing processes change. After a product is once made, the drawings, processing instructions, the necessary machines and toolings are all available. But still planning is to be done for each repeated order and this is concerned with deciding upon the material requirements and man and machine hours requirements for each order.

Prior Planning refers to whatever goes on in the planning phase prior to the first step initiating the activity. Planning for a product starts when a new idea is first presented. Everything is very tentative at first but different ways of doing things are considered and some methods are discarded while the product is only a rough sketch. Making these choices can be called *prior planning or pre-planning or early planning*. Thus, to think of how to make products, and how much they will cost are called early planning functions.

The planning is broadly classified as:

(1) Manufacturing planning.

(2) Factory planning.

(3) Production planning.

(4) Financial planning.

Manufacturing Planning

The production planning cannot **begin till following** two phases of planning are completed:

(1) Manufacturing Planning (2) Factory Planning

When a product cames out of a Pilot plant the manufacturing planning lays the ground for factory and production planning. Manufacturing planning involve following steps:

(1) To revise the specifications of the product to suit the equipments and technique.
(2) Develop a plan for new process and techniques.
(3) Determine the operation to be performed in manufacturing.
(4) Determine the equipments and trained personnel required for each operation.
(5) Determine the time required for each operation.
(6) Determine the materials required for each part.
(7) Determine the cost at various levels of activity.
(8) Finalise the planning based at the level of price and sales value.

Manufacturing planning calculates risks before subsequent plans starts. The manufacturing planning follows research, development and product engineering. It includes rationalising and adjusting the product designate manufacture equipment and methods that are known to be economical and effective. In manufacturing planning the essential manufacturing operations are listed in sequence in which they should be performed. The time required to perform various operations is established by estimates. Costs are estimated for the different methods of manufacturing. The relationship between the selling price and the sales volume will determine whether a given project is practical or not.

Factory Planning

After the manufacturing planning, the considerations will be given to factory facilities for production. In manufacturing planning, the arrangements of equipment the structure to house these equipments are designed. The general activities in factory planning are :

★ To determine the optimum size of factory.
★ The geographical study to find out the suitable location.
★ To prepare the layout.
★ To determine the type of structure required.
★ To determine the service facilities.
★ To determine the construction schedule.
★ To determine the equipment and installation schedule.

As the size of the organisation grow, next thing is to plan the factories for optimum size. After details of manufacturing planning are complete, the factory planning can begin. A schedule for equipment installation is very important. The Gantt charts can be used to schedule both construction and installation.

Production Planning

Production planning translates the sale forecast into master schedule. Production planning utilises the information developed in manufacturing planning and factory planning to perform the following functions:

- ★ To prepare production forecast.
- ★ To prepare master schedules.
- ★ To prepare procurement schedule.
- ★ To prepare area schedules.
- ★ To prepare personnel schedules.
- ★ To establish the finish goods.
- ★ To prepare alternative inventory plans for production.

The production planning is used for various operations, to continue the manufacture of goods that are already in production.

Financial planning

It deals with the preparation of financial budgets. A manufacturing organisation must have table of expenditure and receipts to get a reasonably accurate picture of each position. The working capital is the life blood of an organisation and working capital should be adequate to meet the day-to-day financial obligations such as pay rolls, pay for raw material, advertising bills and cost of sales promotion. Thus the need for the budget is evident. All financial requirements of a company must be planned in relation to the expected income and the plan is embodied in master budget. Financial budgets are essential in a business organisation for its operation. All budgets, plans or schedules are planned and used continuously for critical comparison of actual with planned performance.

After the engineering and processing of the product to be manufactured have been completed, the production planning and control department is in a position to authorise the works to formulate their programme. The programme of works has to be undertaken within the limits set by sources as estimated by the PPC department subject to the approval of the top management. In case PPC happens to be a part of the Works management, the Works Manager obtains necessary approval from the management.

The approval is with reference to :

(a) Priorities for customer satisfaction which management considers reasonable and feasible to attend. The normal rule is first come first served unless management considers it otherwise.

(b) Lead times for materials, bought out items and fabricating contracts.

(c) Technological limitations.

(d) Any special instructions which may be given by the management.

The Production Planning and Control Department is in a position to communicate full details of manufacturing instructions. this is done through routing and scheduling document.

Routing

In intermediate flow-production the routing instructions are prepared once before the plant is commissioned. They are normally called technological instructions. They indicate in detail the flow of processes type and capacities of equipment used, physical and chemical characteristics of inputs, norms for inputs or raw materials, intermediates, services, individual process times and cycles times of processes where necessary. The main function of routing is to utilise machine at their fullest capacity. *Routing* involves the determination of where each operation in a component part, assemblies or assembly is performed. The aim is to find out the route path for the movement of manufacturing lot through the factory. To find this path the emphasis is placed on determining operating data. Operating data includes planning of where any by whom work should be done. It gives the green signal. If not, the exercise is again gone over to see if improvement could be made. The schedule or programme of production must be ready by 15th of the month previous to which it relates. It should then be upto dated continuously and passed on to works well ahead of the period to which it relates. Depending upon the quality of product to be manufactured, production system used routing may be either be generalised or detailed.

In job order planning, routing is confined to each job but scheduling covers work in progress and new orders. Determination of routing is finally the best sequence of operations. Routing in job order planning is based on process engineering for the product. It must either have been worked out by the customer and checked by the manufacturers or the entire work would be done by the latter. In both cases, PPC should get a complete list of manufacturing drawing bills of materials, process technology and special instructions regarding specific points. They will also get a chart of inspection programme in respect of the product.

Its function is to list the operations required to produce a part or a product and the sequence in which there operations are to be performed. The routes must determine the specific machining which should perform specific operation. Router should not only see the machines but should select the machines which perform the job at the lowest cost. The final specification of routing is a production control function. The engineering aspect of the problem are another matter. The decision on what to manufacture, how to manufacture, what methods, tools and equipment used may be made by the production controls, engineering department, manufacturing engineering or methods group or by industrial engineering personnel. The identification section will give the product to which route sheet apply. If the route sheet refers to a particular order it may include such information as order number, number of pieces, delivery date. The heart of the route sheet is the list of required operations. The route sheet will provide space for the record of operating results spoilage, actual times etc. If it reaches the planning office before the completion of the job because the office provide information for purposes of control. it helps in compiling the cost data and may serve as a permanent record of the order.

Whenever a plant is engaged in job production new route sheets are required for majority of orders. In case of standardised production it is possible to keep a file of master route cards. Scheduling information include starting time, finishing time, etc. These time may be in week, days, shifts or in hours or whether they appear at all will depend on the degree of central control involved. The route sheet is a convenient vehicle for bringing these times to the attention of the dispatcher, foreman or production clerk.

Loading

Whenever a customer orders for any product his first question is when the product will be delivered to him. The manufacturing organisations which are manufacturing the stock can quote a date for stock on hand or work in process. The job order manufacture need to determine the total order time for each order. The first step in answering the question is to list the available equipment. The machines performing the similar operations are planned in one group. The number of machines in each group multiplied by the number of hours gives the number of machine hours available for loading. Although the availability of machine hours per day is worked out at the time of planning. If we have 20 machines in the group and they are operated on 7 hours shift per day without any already scheduled increase, the machine availability per day is only 140 machine hours or 20 machines shifts. Similarly planning for operators and supervisors must be completed before there can be any additional availability for production planning in terms of machine hours or additional availability for production planning in terms of machine hours or additional hours.

The Gantt charts can be used to show graphically the relation of availability to machine load. Machine loading can be simplified by using Kardex files equipped with plastic riders to designate how much of the available capacity of each machine groups has been allocated. Certain production executives often make hasty decisions to accept attractive orders without knowing available capacity of their manufacturing facilities. This way production men became frayed to accomplish the goals and even then fails to achieve them. The company earns a reputation for delayed delivery and there loses customer's confidence. The complex problems in equipment loading can be solved by Operations Research and Mathematical Programming. The complex factors such as delivery time orders, shift premiums, overtime premiums, night shift efficiency, overtime efficiency etc. can be arrayed in mathematical programming matrices to obtain optimal solutions.

Sometimes the loading problems are so complicated that electronic data processing equipment is required for their solution. The simple act of carrying of loading problem on a mathematical programming matrix provides a valuable aid into the problem. Dislocations caused by deviations in sales trends and cancellation of orders and requests for certain special orders calls for loading and scheduling to be recomputed. Machine load charts gives us an idea whether machine or equipment is fully utilised or not. A manufacturer who is involved in jobbing work may find from the machine load charts that his grinders are used only about half of the item while his planners, shapers, drills are overloaded. Now for a rush order involving only the use of grinders the manufacturer will not find it difficult to go about. So the need of machine loading is apparent even in simple situations but it is indispensable in case of complex situations. The machine load charts reveal equipments which are not fully utilised. This enables management to take corrective measures which may help to select orders that will result in balanced and profitable operations.

Scheduling

Scheduling is the prerequisite to production control phases namely despatching and follow up. Scheduling is the heart of production control because it integrates the work of other departments to produce a complete product at the promised date as shown:

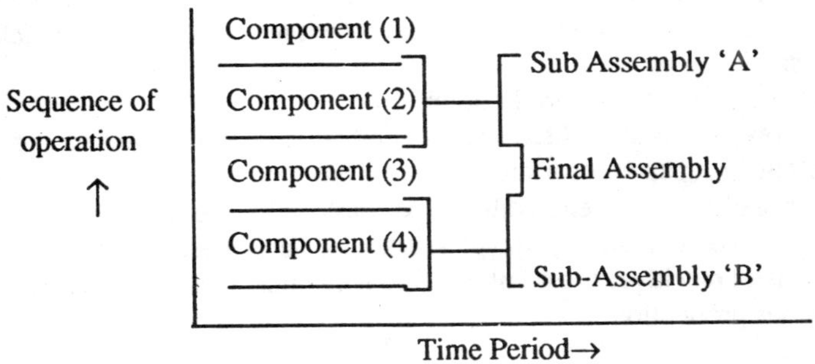

Function of Scheduling establishes the starting and finishing times for production action. The objectives of scheduling are:

- ★ Cost should be controlled.
- ★ Job should be taken up in proper sequence.
- ★ Final product must be delivered in time.

Scheduling problems exist whenever there is choice in which a number of tasks can be performed on one or more facilities by one or more men. The tasks, facilities may represent different things in different situations. Jobs to by processed in a manufacturing plant, patients waiting for a series of test in hospital, aircrafts waiting for landing clearance, a batch of orders waiting to be processed in a warehouse, bank customers at a row of teller's window and programmes to be run at a computer etc. are some of the examples of scheduling problems.

Scheduling is the last step in Production Planning. At this stage detailed plans are made which specify for each machine the time schedule at which different products will be processed on these machines. In fact a production schedule is the time table of the Production Department. Before a production schedule is made, the scheduler should know the quantity of each product to be manufactured, the delivery dates, type and number of machines and personnel available and an estimate of the processing times. A production schedule aims at choosing the best schedule so as to optimise the use of resources.

To compare different schedules, we must have some effectiveness criterion or the objective function. This criterion may be any one or combination of the following things: minimise the total schedule time, minimize in process inventory meeting, the delivery dates and reducing the total set up cost etc. Production scheduling problems are perhaps as old as the industries themselves. Before the era of scientific management, these problems were solved without getting a "formal solution" and so no one ever felt that there existed a problem at all. It was only in the early 20th century the "formal solution" to production scheduling problems were presented in this form of a graphic representation, more popularly known as Gantt Charts after the name of its originator Henry L. Gantt. In line production where all operations are of the same duration, and each piece of work moves smoothly on to the next machine on completion of an operation. By this means all machines are always occupied. Following are the principles of scheduling which apply to all cases:

(a) Operations should be of short duration.

(b) Different operations should have approximately the same duration.

(c) All machine groups, or departments, should have even load.

(d) As far as possible, work-centres should be employed in the same sequence.

It should be noted that these principles describe accurately the operating principles of a transfer machine, as assembly line, a paper machine and many other forms of continuous production.

Types of Schedules

Schedules are of two types: Master schedules and schedules employed to plan the manufacturing and assembly operations required for each product. Two important points with scheduling functioning to ensure production are:

1. It is simple 2. It is flexible

Scheduling problem in a process industry requires the calculations of plant capacities, availabilities of raw materials and forecasts of market demands which determine production lot economic quantities if a number of products are involved. Even where one product is involved and the demand is less than the production capacity, the phasing of production becomes very important. in case demand is more than the engineered plant capacity, various questions of cycle times may have to be investigated with a view to see whether additional production can be secured from the same resources.

Scheduling assumes a different character on an assembly line. In this one job immediately follows the other. The sequence of successive jobs is chosen to balance the total work load at each operation along the line. Parts and sub-assemblies required for final assembly should be coordinated so that they are available when needed. The scheduling problem for these items is to determine the proper start times.

Basic Scheduling Techniques

To coordinate and control various activities several basic scheduling techniques have been adopted. Many of these technique are Gantt chart or Bar chart; the Flow chart, the Line balance, the Milestone chart. The Flow chart is adopted in work study techniques for work simplification, method improvement and procedure analysis. The line balance is primarily a production technique and is not effective for construction projects. The Milestone chart is almost similar to Bar chart except that it displays the milestone rather than bars. These scheduling techniques are useful not only in the planning and scheduling of work to be accomplished but also following the progress of work in process.

The Gantt Chart

Henry L. Gantt developed a versatile charting technique. It is based on the principle of relating facts to time. It gives the relationship among different activities in a production process. It depicts on a plan of work in terms of time and servers as an effective communication device.

GANTT OR BAR CHART

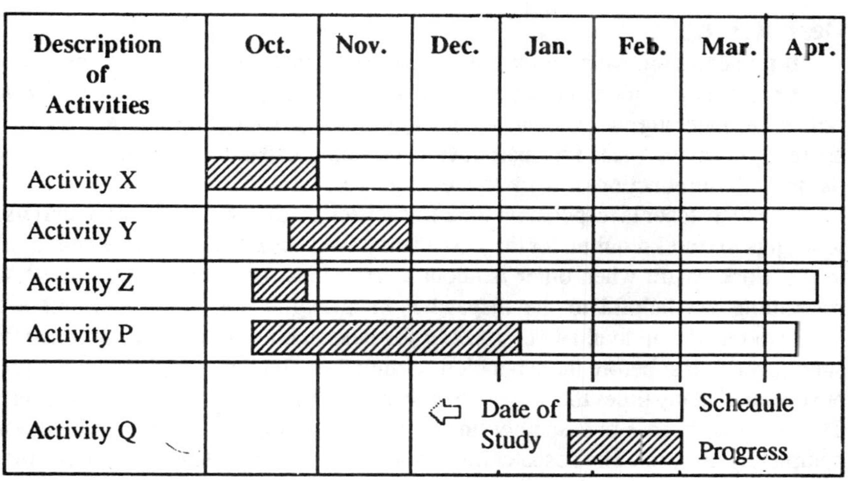

Fig. 10.1

The technique employs a horizontal axis of time measured in days or weeks or hours. The vertical axis may be used to list individual shop orders and departments through which they will be processed. In this form the chart shows both the planned and actual progress of job through several activities or departments as shown in fig. The visual array of information displayed by a Gantt Chart permits the user to absorb the information quickly. The principle of Gantt chart represent that an amount of work actually done in that time to amount scheduled.

Deficiencies of Gantt Chart

The conventional forms of Gantt Charts are now extensively modified to the visual control boards like production control schedule graphs. The deficiencies of Gantt Chart are :

1. Bar chart can indicate if some work is either behind or ahead of schedule.
2. Bar chart cannot show the inter-dependencies and the inter-relationships between the various activities.
3. It cannot predict the effect of delay in one area over another area.
4. Reporting with this chart require merely guessing or estimating.
5. It can isolate the critical areas of work.
6. Optimising the use of resources is difficult because it is not possible to identify the non-critical areas.

Due to these limitations and inadequacies of traditional planning techniques there is a need for effective planning and scheduling.

Despatching

It translates the paper work into actual production. Despatching coordinates and translates planning into actual production. Despatching includes of work orders. Despatching ensures that the right type of jigs, fixtures and other accessories are ready at correct place for a particular operation. Despatching is concerned with the smooth introduction of work to the stop floor.

The dispatcher is responsible for a final check on the availability of materials, tools, jigs, fixtures required for the job and may even ensure that these are delivered to the work centre when order is about to run. Most of the techniques used in scheduling are helpful to the dispatcher in arranging the work ahead of his department. The individual responsible for despatching an order to production should verify that before the scheduled starting date all parts, materials for the job are on hand. many times the despatching activity is controlled from a central point. This happens in case of assembly lines where the product is standardised but not completely uniform. The despatching problems involved are handled by transmitting messages to the stations simultaneously through teletype. The teletype is an electric type writer connected through a telephone circuit. in fact the despatching should be given due importance without which there would be little possibility of completing the production as per the established plan. The work orders as used by dispatcher contain the following information:

(A) Name of the product.

(i) Code No.

(ii) Quantity to be produced.

(B) Description of various operations.

(i) Machine to be used.

(ii) Special instructions in operating the machine.

(C) Departments involved.

Thus we see that some kind of despatching is necessary for all types of production, it is essentially needed for the scheduling and control of intermittent production.

Follow Up

After the despatching is completed, production of various operations has been authorised to begin at time as planned by the scheduling department, the follow up is to check on the progress of the order as it is being manufactured from the first operation until the order is converted into finished product. This comparison between the actual and standard progress is made to take corrective action. Follow up functioning checks and measure the effectiveness of previous production control function-routing, scheduling and despatching. Expediting is a special form of follow up. Expeditors are used to:

- ★ help to eliminate particular problems which are throwing production off scheduling.
- ★ speed the production of certain orders.

To summarize, the purpose of active functions of despatching and expediting are:

1. To release the production orders at the appropriate time and facilitate effective flow of information.
2. To record the flow of materials and tools and adjust whenever necessary.
3. To record progress of production operations and adjust whenever necessary.
4. To record amount of work in process and verify its effect on the schedule.
5. To record quantities produced and compared with required quantities.
6. To record amount of faulty work and scrap, issue orders for production of replacements.
7. To record machine idle time and check the reason for it.
8. To record stoppage and held up and classify them according to :
   (a) lack of drawings or instructions.
   (b) lack of materials.
   (c) work held up by previous operation.
   (d) machine break down.

(e) operator missing are not available.

(f) waiting for inspection to approve work on machine setting.

The system of follow up is governed by the organisation of the control system and the methods by which routings, scheduling and despatching are accomplished. The basic aim of follow up activities is that of preventing serious delays. An effective follow up system requires.

1. Recognition of delay.
2. Evaluation of reasons leading to delay.
3. Corrective action to remove delay.

The recognition of delays results from a comparison of planned with actual progress. The information of delay can be obtained immediately from the supervisors and operators concerned. In case of complex control system the department schedules may be marked in to stop to point out the position of various jobs which have been completed or which are well underway. The route sheet or detachable tickets may be sent back in the same manner when all operations have been completed. These tickets may be used for pay role purposes to provide instructions for the operator.

Chapter 11

COST REDUCTION AND MATERIALS MANAGEMENT

Introduction

The Materials Manager should have a program for the department to achieve these goals. In addition, he should require each of his key subordinates to develop programme to achieve similar goals. Authority to develop a program should be delegated to the lowest possible level in the organisation. In doing this materials manager ensures that the efforts of everyone in the organisation will be directed toward goals that are consistent with those of the whole department and of the company. The materials manger's plan is a composite of the plans of his subordinates and would also be submitted annually. If accepted by the top management it would become a standard against which the department's performance would be measured.

There are four basic steps in measuring the performance of any department: Define the limits of the job; Determine the objectives to be achieved within these limits; Develop a program to meet these objectives; comparing progress with the objectives.

The limits of the job are defined by the organisation structure and policies and procedures. The basic objectives of materials organisation are: Low Operating cost, Low prices of purchased materials; Minimum Investment in inventory; Superior supplier performance; Developing materials personnel; Good records. The performance measurements of individual parts of the plan might be made annually; quarterly; monthly; weekly, or even daily. In general, performance in achieving the qualitative goals would be measured less frequently than that in achieving the quantitative goals. The quantitative phases of performance measurement get more attention for several reasons. Among them are the following:

(i) **Quantitative data are more objective.** They are based on operating statistics where as the qualitative data reflect in large part the opinion of the observer. It would be hard for a materials manager to distort performance on cost reduction, where progress is measured in rupees.

(ii) **Quantitative Data Change.** The materials management goals and objectives can only be measured qualitatively are long range in nature. The progress on quantitative goals should be measured frequently so that remedies can be applied immediately should performance fall short of expectations.

(iii) **Quantitative Data Related to Company Performance.** Top management has an immediate interest in materials management goals such as cost reduction and inventory turnover which can be measured quantitatively.

Material Cycle

The material cycle commences from the time when its need is felt in the plant to the time when it is supplied either to stores or to the production service department. At the stage of materials planning, the requirements of all types of materials are estimated for a predetermined period. The industrial engineer, the production engineer, the R & D specialists; the designer and buyer all Joint hands in carrying out an effective value analysis. All repetitive items, their purchase, procurement, replenishment etc may be controlled through the application of ABC analysis. But non-repetitive items need a different treatment as the requirement for them is generally unpredictable. In this case the modern techniques of PERT and CPM analysis can be applied. In order to achieve better results, ABC analysis especially for 'A' and 'B' items, ignoring 'C' items. Application of value analysis in materials planning phases may be considered in two stages : Pre-design value Analysis and Pre-purchase value analysis. The materials management department is in a key position to effect substantial saving in materials cost. An efficient materials department should aim at obtaining: Right Quality; Right Quantity; Right price; Right source; Right delivery. These must also be constant market research and systematic effort for developing new sources of supply which would result in obtaining better quality at lower price, ensures earlier deliveries as also provide a second line of defence in case of a sudden dropping out of a regular source.

Buyer-seller collaboration and standardisation are the two other important aspects. Clear specification ensures right quality. Moreover, more than one manufacturer can supply standardised items, thus providing better availability, better price and better delivery. Since transportation cost constitute a large percentage of total material cost, the area also provides substantial saving if the principles of value analysis are applied here. Similarly for large volume transportation, the techniques of operations research could be applied and possibilities of cost reduction located.

Concept of Cost Reduction

Cost reduction is our prime concern but it should not be at the cost of product quality. Other values like use value, exchange value and esteem value of the product must be given equal importance. Every firm must try to continuously increase its productivity through cost reduction and quality improvement.

Direct costs. Direct cost of material is an important element in the total cost of product. It varies from 50-80% of the total unit cost. In the control of this material cost the method engineers, materials planners, industrial engineers, design engineers; who deal with direct material can play a significant role. They determine standard cost of the product, the Labour Cost; both "direct and indirect is an important element of cost. Performance standards may be set up through "Time and Motion" study. Actual performance should be compared with standard performance and in case of variation. Steps should be taken.

Indirect Costs. Overhead expenses such as indirect Labour, indirect Materials, Administrative and Selling expenses are controlled by budget. For the control of Indirect Materials, norms of consumption must be set up.

Works Cost and Works Overhead. This includes expenses on indirect labour, indirect material, power, rent, repair, depreciation etc. They are all indirect expenses right from the receipt of order to the despatch of finished goods.

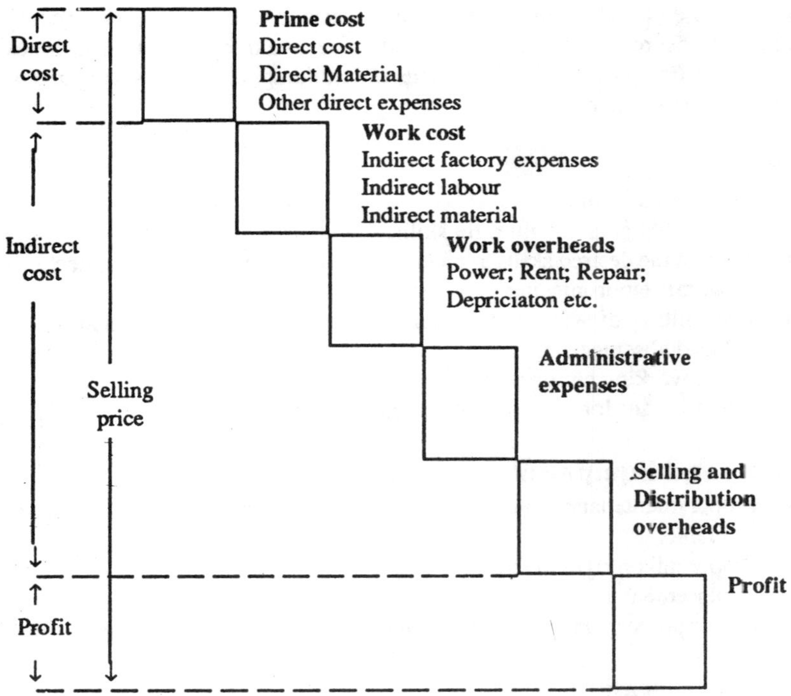

Fig. 11.1

Administrative Overheads. Direction, control and administration of an undertaking, rents and rates of office premises and furnishing if any, office lighting, salaries of office staff, stationary, postage and other expenses are covered under Administrative Overheads.

FACTORS CONTRIBUTING COST REDUCTION

Materials

- ★ Use of proper size and type of material
- ★ Vendor evaluation

- ★ ABC Analysis
- ★ Reduction in lead time as far as possible
- ★ Plan for minimum inventory levels to avoid stockouts and maximum inventory levels to control inventory carrying cost.
- ★ Proper storage to avoid change and ensure quick availability when required.
- ★ Minimum use of indirect material
- ★ Dispose of nonmoving inventory and waste to reduce the carrying cost.

Similarly cost reduction can be achieved in the area of Manpower; Machines and Equipment, Energy Conservation, Lands and Buildings and Time Management, which are given as under.

Manpower

- ★ Optimum utilisation
- ★ Select right person with right skills.
- ★ Train in the desired skills to meet the challenges of fast changing techno-economic environments.
- ★ Recognition of work and proper motivation for best performance and reduced absenteeism.
- ★ Better working environments.
- ★ Job redesign; Job enrichment and career planning.

Machines and Equipment

- ★ Proper maintenance so that (i) Downtime is minimum (ii) Full capacity is available.
- ★ Proper job on right machines.
- ★ Replacement at proper time.
- ★ Use of proper jigs and fixtures to reduce setting time and operating time.

Energy Conservation

Improving fuel consumption in boilers, furnaces and engines, effective plant maintenance, adoption of heat recovery system.

- ★ Good housekeeping in Industry gets priority.
- ★ To ensure compliance with energy conservation norms would be particularly worthwhile.

Lands and Buildings

- ★ Scientific layout to optimise area utilisation.
- ★ Better vertical space utilisation wherever possible.
- ★ Design of buildings to make use of natural light and ventilation.
- ★ Make use of gravity flow/feeding of materials and equipment wherever possible.

Time Management

- ★ A check list for the top management
- ★ Are company policies, objectives and mission well defined and made known to staff/employees?
- ★ Are responsibilities clearly defined and assigned?
- ★ Is there an established executive development programme?
- ★ Are vendors rated for services and quality?
- ★ Is a full organisational analysis made periodically to evaluate competence and redundancy?

Cost reduction embraces unit cost reduction by expenditure reduction in respect of a given volume of output and/or unit cost reduction by the increase in productivity. The another way of looking at cost reduction is to view it as the process whereby permanent savings are made without any reduction in the quality and/or usefulness of the products. There is a need to develop an attitude of mind which challenges all standards with a view to their improvement.

Areas of Cost Reduction

The success of any business depends primarily on the efficient use of those basic cost elements viz electric energy; per unit of production of goods; man-hour of labour; weight of raw material etc. The various constituents of total cost are shown in following diagram.

Fig. 11.2

Control of inventories of raw materials, semi finished and finished goods is essential in a well managed business. Speculation in inventory appreciation is hazardous and has no place in manufacturing. Integration of industrial processes under one management can reduce production costs through control of raw materials and selling costs through elimination of middle men.

Chapter 12

EVALUATION OF MATERIALS MANAGEMENT DEPARTMENT

Introduction

The evaluation consists of developing measurement criterions and then measuring performance against these criterions. The task of evaluation is difficult even in the simplest case because few functions can be accurately or completely measured in objective terms. We know that some functions can be objectively measured such as production in terms of unit of production, manhours of labour, unit of production, units of power consumed, rate of rejection and technical product tests. In evaluating departments that deal with people and ideas rather than things, the problem is more complicated because we do not yet know how to measure psychological factors accurately.

The materials management department is difficult to evaluate because, as in sales, much of its effective work for company is in the area of interpersonal relations. This is not to suggest that materials management department should not be evaluated, but rather that evaluation should be done with clear identification of the inherent problems that exist.

Evaluation Criterions

Following are some of the criterion's for an overall picture of purchasing performance:

(i) Cost Purchase Comparison
(ii) Cost per Order
(iii) Return on investment
(iv) Quality and Quantity criterions
(v) Price Criteria
(vi) Time and Place Criteria

Cost-Purchase Comparison A common measurement device relates to volume of production to the cost of operating the department. It is calculated by dividing the annual cost of operating the purchasing departments by the rupee value of annual purchases. The ratio of departmental cost to purchase volume has significance for evaluating a single department overtime, provided there is no change in the functional activities and department responsibility have remained fairly constant. Cost-Purchase comparison of similar concerns in the same industry are not likely to be revealing, since there are substantial variations in both factors of the ratio.

Cost per order. The evaluation of purchasing departments in terms of their cost-per-order is made by dividing total purchasing department costs by the number of orders placed. Beside establishing controls over the size of the order by the companies, the cost-per-order approach to evaluation is becoming less useful because companies are beginning to buy under open-end and annual contracts.

Return On Investment. The net savings per rupee spent on purchasing is referred as the "return on purchasing investment". Return on capital is a more significant measure of purchasing performance. Return on invested capital emphasizes purchasing's contribution to profits rather than its expense.

Quality and Quantity Criterion. Quality achievement may be measured in terms of the number of rejections of incoming shipments. Defects discovered during the production process should also be considered. In all such cases where the production or engineering departments, have designated a supplier, the purchasing department still share responsibility for poor quality because it should analyse suppliers thoroughly enough to warn the production and engineering department when they suggest poor sources.

Quantity performance can be measured in different ways. One criterion is the amount of 'downtime' resulting from shortage of materials. The number of emergency and rush orders processed in a purchasing department also is a measure of the efficiency with which the department is procuring the right quantity. Another quantity factor is the relationship between inventory and use. A related measure is the inventory losses occurring because of spoilage or obsolescence. A low level of spoilage and obsolescence is a reflection of purchasing efficiency.

Price Criterions. Purchasing performance can be measured by determining how close the department is coming to securing the right price. A comparison of the price index of company purchases with one of the standard price indexes can help in appraising price performance. a comparison of the market price at the time of use with the price that was actually paid for that item measures how well a purchasing department is anticipating price changes. Discounts obtained may also be considered in evaluating price performance.

Time and Place Criterions. Many of the criterions that measure quantity performance are also applicable in determining performance with respect to time and place. It is important to compare supplier's delivery dates with promised shipping dates and to estimate the amount of follow-up required to obtain performance with respect to time and place.

The other types of evaluation criterion include measure that indicate how well the materials management department is accomplishing its broad objective of securing the right quality; right quantity at the right "Price, Time" and "Place". The other such criterion, other than the money saved on quality; quantity; price; time and place considerations, is the total number of purchase orders issued, which is an indication of the work load of the department. One might subdivide the figure into the number of local purchases and non-local purchases, small orders and large orders, rush orders and regular orders and single item and multiple-item orders. The number of representatives or salesman of different buyers interviewed, the average time per interview, and the length of time that salesmen are required to wait before seeing the buyer are other factors that can be used in evaluating purchasing performance. The average item required to process an order from the recognition of need to the mailing of purchase order can be measured. The time involved in clearing invoices for payment and the number and amount of discount lost because of delays in clearing invoices are significant measure of purchasing performance in those companies where invoice checking is a purchasing department responsibility. In evaluating the purchasing department many companies also pass judgement on the relationships between the purchasing department and other departments, especially the relationships among the purchasing, production and engineering departments.

Evaluation Standards

Basically evaluation involves a comparison of what is being done with following standards:

(i) Past Performance
(ii) Budgeted Performance
(iii) Performance of materials management department in other companies.
(iv) Norms of ideal performance.

Past Performance. This approach is of particular value where size of the department and its assignments are stable from year to year. Comparisons are readily made by noting year-to-year changes.

Budgeted Performance. At the beginning of the budget period purchasing objectives ar established in view of the firm's total objectives. This approach is like management by objectives. The plans for a purchasing department for profit might include the following objectives:

(i) Reorganise flow of paper work to reduce clerical effort.
(ii) Value analysis with a target of reduction in material cost.

These purchasing objectives will contribute to the profit objectives of the company.

Norms. The use of non-budgetory purchasing performance has not been very common. This is primarily because there is such a wide variation in the specific duties assigned to individuals within purchasing departments and because of the way in which they perform their duties.

Evaluation Methods

Following are some of the methods or procedures in use:

(i) Internal Audits
(ii) Purchasing Department Savings
(iii) Variance from standard cost of Materials.
(iv) Outside Audit
(v) Variance from operating Budgets
(vi) Vendor Performance
(vii) Appraisal of Personnel
(viii) Inventory Performance.

Internal Auditing. The major purpose of the management audit is to determine whether the firm is functioning as an efficient whole. An effective audit requires that someone outside the departmental work areas view each department objectively to ascertain whether it is functioning in a manner that is best for the firm. In practice, outside consultants with varied training are often charged with the management audit task. In some purchasing departments, an individual within the department may even be charged with the responsibility of making periodic informal internal audits to ensure that the department's affairs are ready for a formal internal audit. The final aspect of an audit is to determine whether objective standards of purchasing performance exist and adequate provision is made for reporting of this performance to management. Even though a department is organised soundly and proper policies and procedure exist, there is no assurance that they are being followed unless the performance of the personnel is periodically reviewed and evaluated.

Purchasing Department Savings. Savings arising from purchasing operations are fairly commonly used as a means of evaluating performance. These savings are concerned with costs of materials, supplies and services being purchased.

Variance from Standard Cost of Materials. Some companies establish a standard cost of the more important materials and evaluate purchasing performance by comparing actual costs with the standard cost for the period under evaluation. The comparison is valid only if there is reasonable stability in the market price of the commodities being reviewed.

Vendor Performance. The purchasing department is directly and indirectly responsible for choosing vendors. If it does a good job of selecting vendors, this will show up in good vendor performance. Vendor evaluation should consider quality, quantity, price, time and place correctly. However these criterion should vary with commodities being purchased and their importance to the production process. Therefore it is not possible to develop vendor performance formulas.

Similarly we can carry out the "Appraisal of personnel"; Inventory Performance evaluations to assess the materials management department performance.

Profit Centre

The department that emerges may well become a separate profit centre. Earlier, materials management activities have been regarded as "services" that help other profit centres within the company do a better job and the department contribution has usually been too indirect and too difficult to measure. A profit centre is created by drawing an imaginary line around some part of the organisation and arbitrarily treating it as a separate business whose manger is responsible for profits. The purpose of profit centre is to focus managements attention on the most basic objective of the business: profits. Every profit centre has three basic criterions: (i) value is added, (ii) capital is employed productively and (iii) costs are incurred. The materials management organisation in any profit or non profit company can meet these criterions.

Purpose of Profit Center

Even more important, however is the impact that a materials management profit center may have on the ways in which materials are managed. Presently, the performance of the materials manager is directly related to the primary economic mission of the organisation to achieve maximum results with minimum resources. The efforts of the materials manager are automatically focused on economic performance. The materials manager behaves like other managers and ams at maximising his return on capital. Some of the areas where the materials manager successfully employ less capital to maximise return are : Inventory Reduction; Lower purchase Costs; and Improved methods. If the materials manager is able to make improvements in his operations, his return on capital will begin to increase gradually. Of the ground rules for measuring profitability are correctly constructed, then the relative improvement in materials management profitability is a fair measure of the materials manager's performance.

Advantages of the Profit Center

The materials management center is primarily a device by which materials management performance can be measured objectively. Some of the major ancillary benefits are :

(i) **Unified materials management is encouraged.** Purchasing, production control, traffic and other materials management activities have a natural tendency to operate independently of one another, even after they are brought together organizationally. The profit center approach tends to define materials management responsibility more sharply and to force materials functions to work together towards common objectives.

(ii) **Responsibility is defined clearly.** In real life situations, materials manager and other executives of the department are too quick to blame someone else when there is supply failure. The plain fact, is of course that using departments cannot be held responsible for supply failures unless they do their own materials management.

(iii) **Profit-Center problems.** The advantages of profit centre outweigh its disadvantages, the materials management profit center is not an unmixed blessings. The breaking up an organisation into a group of captive profit centres may create additional administrative costs. In the case of materials management profit center, there might be temptation to try to cut costs by purchasing merchandise of inferior quality while maintaining the same transfer price.

To summaries the logical starting point to appraise and control the performance of a completer operating department is an analysis of the objectives of the department. Once this has been done, the organisation structure and responsibility assigned to each work group should be examined in an effort to determine the impact each operating activity has on the attainment of each departmental objective.

Chapter 13

MAKE OR BUY DECISIONS

Introduction

This is an important policy decision of management and purchase department has a role to play in both cases. After preliminary investigation of cost a detailed study may be needed which can involve engineering, design, production planning, costing as well as purchasing. The final decision on a make-or-buy question is made by the joint efforts of several departments, the purchasing department will always have an important part in the determination. It needs no emphasize that no simple rule can be applied to all cases of make or buy. Some decisions are major, such as a paper manufacturing firm deciding whether to build or buy a pulp mill to supply its own raw materials or a pharmaceutical company to manufacture or buy the basic bulk drug from an outside. Each such case must be decided on its merits, but the important issues may be different in the two cases. In broad terms four relevant considerations are the elements in all purchasing decisions: Quality; Quantity; Cost; and Service aspects.. Make or Buy decisions are taken at the top level and the position of materials manager in the organisation hierarchy determine whether he is to play a key role or supporting role to deal with the problem of Make or Buy. Few organisations have formed committees to analyse and to recommend proposals. Make or Buy decisions arise due to a variety of reasons. Mostly such situations arise due to consistent failures on the part of the suppliers in the supply of items. The management then decides to make the item. Sometimes availability of items from outside suppliers in the supply of items. The management then decides to make the item. Sometimes availability of items form outside suppliers may not be adequate owing to staff competition from many end users.

Importance of Make, Buy or Lease

Every organisation has a choice of following three basic decisions in sourcing a new product:

(i) Purchase the product complete from a contract manufacturer.

(ii) Purchase some components and manufacture the balance.

(iii) Manufacture the product completely starting with the extraction of basic raw materials.

In practice no company can seriously consider the third alternative. Normally large companies rely on outside suppliers for at least some components and materials. Some companies choose the first alternative and obtain a new product completely from an outside supplier. The general rule, however is that an organisation will make something and buy others. This applies even to service organisations. For manufacturers, make or buy decisions must constantly be made and it is largely a matter of deciding at which stage of fabrication a component should be purchased.

Make or Buy Criterion

Companies will usually buy a finished component from an outside supplier when:

(i) They do not have facilities to make it and there are more profitable opportunities for investing company capital.
(ii) existing facilities can be used more economically to make other components.
(iii) Patent or other legal procedures do not allow the company to make component.
(iv) There is only seasonal demand of the components.

In addition following are some of the considerations which have a say in case for decisions "to buy".

(a) Drawing needs modifications.
(b) Quality to be manufactured.
(c) Fluctuation demand.
(d) Special manufacturing techniques involved.
(e) Frequent changes in the design involved.
(f) Jigs and tools, gauges etc are to loaned.

Companies prefer to do their own fabricating. They buy only raw materials or semi-finished parts.

(i) Components can be made more cheaply by the company than by outside suppliers.
(ii) The fabrication is vital to the company's product and requires extremely close quality control.
(iii) Component can be readily manufactured with the company's existing facilities.
(iv) Fabrication requires extensive investment in facilities that are not available at supplier plants.
(v) Product has a demand that is both relatively large and stable.

In addition following are some of the considerations which have a say in case of decisions "to make"

(a) Prices obtained are the best.
(b) Quantity to fabricate is optimum.
(c) Some other items can be produced along with the product and thus reducing production costs in the whole.
(d) The material to be fabricated is readily available.

Other Important Factors

Some companies, by tradition prefer to make almost every component of their products. Other prefer to buy as much as possible from outside suppliers. In general, an aggressive company in an industry that is expanding very rapidly will prefer to buy many of its components from outside suppliers. In some companies making an item is effectively prevented by its own labour relations policies. If it is extremely generous with wages and fringe benefits for its employees, there will be some industries where it simply is not competitive even if its methods are better than those of potential competitors. When a company decides to make an item that it has been buying, it always eliminates the suppliers sales expenses and usually eliminates some freight cost. If its production costs are identical to those of the suppliers the company also gains the suppliers profit and usually at least part of the fixed overhead expenses incurred by the supplier.

Illusory Savings

Companies often continue to buy the item even though they may be capable of making it. In most cases it is not to their advantages to make the item for a number of reasons, including:

(a) **Start Up Cost.** The company's direct costs may be substantially higher than the direct costs of the supplier. The supplier presumably is one of the most efficient producer of the item and has achieved his existing costs only after management have acquired considerable experience. Assuming that buyer can produce as efficiently as the supplier, his saving will be reduced by **start-up cost.** No company can immediately produce a new item at peak efficiency, costs on initial production runs are always above standard.

(b) **Flexibility.** Company which has invested in equipment to make the item has less flexibility with make items. But if the company has not invested in equipment, it can exploit changes in market conditions on buy items and take advantages of lower prices offered by suppliers eager for new business.

(c) **Savings in Overhead.** Savings in overhead are often illusory. When business expands to capacity operations, fixed overheads increases and must be absorbed by each component that is produced. Similarly if business slumps, fixed overhead is under absorbed and unit cost rises. It has been observed that fixed overheads rarely rises immediately after a company starts using idle facilities to make a part it has previously purchased but eventually it creeps up.

(d) There may be better profit opportunities in other areas. Each make part requires some investment in facilities, inventories, and top management time. Even though this investment is profitable the company may be able to earn even higher by using its resources to expand the business it knows best.

(e) Some companies decide to buy items that they have been making. In some cases they even dispose of plant and equipment used to make the item. Such decisions are almost economic if the suppliers price is lower than that of company's direct cash cost of making the part. Similarly when a company facilities are temporarily taxed beyond capacity, it may decide to buy part of its needs from a outsider supplier.

Factors Governing Make or Buy decisions

Following are the four factors in the context of make-or-buy to show how it might bear on the decision.

Quality Consideration

It has been observed that quality available in an item being purchased differs in no important respect from the quality the company could impart to the same item if it make it. However often there will be sufficient quality differences between the two alternatives to warrant weighing the quality factor in making the decision. If the supplier consistently fail to meet the quality requirements, then the firm may decide to make it. Firstly, it is essential to find out whether such exacting quality requirements are necessary at all. Another important aspect is whether the buyer will be able to make the item to such quality standards when established vendors are unable to do so. A vendor enjoys the benefit of specialisation and probably the item in question is his main product line. Buyers also have the option of changing the supplier and hence there is lot of flexibility.

Quantity Requirements

When the quantum is small, such as specialised jigs and fixtures, it may be worth while to make them especially if the existing facilities and the little amount of sub-contracting is adequate for such manufactures. It is not paying proposition for the supplier to accept such small jobs. Sometimes demand for items may not be certain and it may be advantageous to make it using a flexible production schedule. When the requirements are very large, buying would be desirable.

Cost Aspect

Advantages and disadvantages will have to be quantified and a cost analysis has to be done. The problem of estimation accurately the cost of making an item stems from the nature of overhead costs manufacturing plants. If the make or buy decisions were concerned with an item that was clearly separate and apart from all other items made in the plant, the allocation of overhead would be a simple matter.

Fixed costs do not vary with output and are often referred to as overhead or unavoidable costs. They include such items as management salaries, taxes, depreciation, and insurance. Variable costs fluctuate with output and are often referred to as direct costs. Examples include the direct labour and raw materials required to produce additional units of output. In evaluating the estimated cost of making an item, it should be recognized that the accuracy of estimate depends on the skill and case with which the cost estimates are compiled. The smaller the item in terms of either value or quantity, the more difficult it is to arrive at an accurate cost figure. A plant with excess capacity can increase production by merely adding incremental costs that are variable in nature, where as a plant being fully utilised can increase production only by increasing its capacity, thereby adding incremental costs of both fixed and variable nature.

Similarly cost of transportation; economics of scale and cost of capital must be given a thorough analysis in arriving at a make or buy decision. An adequate return on investment should be considered as a cost of making an item because money invested in raw materials and equipment is tied up and therefore a real cost, since other opportunities must be forgone. Management should ask itself; If as a result of a buy decision, we can free money? what return can we expect from it? On the other hand, if a make decision required an increase in investment, what will be the implicit cost of this money? It must also be remembered that a firm that produces for itself may have only itself as a customer, and therefore its production runs must be large enough to take advantage of economics of scale.

Chapter 14

MATERIALS HANDLING FUNCTIONS

Introduction

It has been observed that no value is added to the end product through material handling. Materials handling can be defined as the function dealing with the preparation, placing and positioning of materials to facilitate their movement or storage. Materials handling includes every consideration of the product except the actual processing operation. Many organisations have used industrial engineering techniques such as "flow process charts" to design effective integrated internal material handling systems. When layout and handling are designed in an integrated manner valuable insights can be developed on the selection of handling equipments, number of equipments and maximum utilisation of floor space. In the two basic layout, viz Product layout and process layout, it has been found that material handling is kept at a minimum in the case of product layout. Layout and Material handling should be considered as an integrated system since there is lot of interdependence between the two which necessitates the planning of layout and material handling as an unitary problem. A good plant layout and material handling system improves the economics of production by reducing wastage in materials and improving utilisation of man and material. It also results in reduced accidents; good house keeping and increased, employee morale. Material handling is an important area of study with a view to effect cost reduction by suitable material handling. Material handling has now become a specialised function. In the pre scientific management period the material handling was only *manhandling* and handling was done in most uneconomical way by human labour only. It is important that material handling should have no congestion of materials, in process inventory and bottlenecks and this could be achieved by the study of layout and material handing systems.

PLANT LAYOUT

Introduction

Production results from the working of men, materials and machinery. One or more pieces of materials are taken and their form, nature or chemical characteristics are changed by using machinery including tools and equipments to give a product. The product has a greater value than the sum total of all the inputs that goes into the making of it as it serves a need and is functional. The value is created by incurring the cost in the process of production and using of varieties of production facilities. While physical arrangement of production and other facilities have a bearing on the cost due to maintenance, quality control etc. They have also a direct effect on the cost due to the handling of material and movement of men and other facilities. *It is estimated that in the cost of production about 30% is the cost of material handling at various stages in various steps.* Let us study the effect of systematic and good plant layout and material handling system.

Definition

The layout of a factory, workshop or working area means the position of the departments or shops in the factory and of the machines, work places and storage points in the working areas, including offices and staff facilities relative to one another. A bad layout can add a good deal of time to the total work. Contents of a process which causes unnecessary movement of material and consumes time and energy of the worker without any value addition in completion of a job.

Many establishments have never thought of any change in the layout ever since they were established. Machine, pieces of plant and even whole departments have been added from time to time wherever space could be found. The result has been that material takes often long time and round about journey in the course of process.

The importance of layout to the production of process varies from industry to industry. Equally important variable is the extent to which it is possible to alter the layout once it has been established. These two factors must be borne in mind while studying the flow of material or movement of workers about the plant.

Objectives of Layout

If a finished layout is to present an effective arrangement of related work areas in which goods can be economically produced, it must be planned with objectives of plant layout well placed in mind. The major objectives are :

(i) Facilitate the manufacturing process.
(ii) Minimise the material handling.
(iii) Maintain flexibility of arrangement of operations.
(iv) Maintain high turn over of works in process.
(v) Hold down investment in equipment.
(vi) Promote effective utilisation of labour.
(vii) Provide employee convenience and comfort in doing the work.

Minimizing Material Handling

The material should travel from the one machine to the other as little as possible, specially the heavy components should flow in line only because excess flow of material require manpower as well as equipment for lifting and carrying the material. Following are factors minimising material handling.

(i) **Flexible Layout.** The layout should be flexible for the following causes:
(a) Design Change.
(b) Increased production.

(c) Adding a new product.

(d) Maintaining high turn over i.e. the storage time of the material inside the line should be minimum.

(ii) **Economical use of Area.** Each square feet area costs money. Unaccepted waste or idle floor is burden on rest of the plant spacing between machines after necessary spacing required for movement of men and material.

(iii) **Effective use of labour.** Labour may be wasted through poor layout. Following factors should be considered for effective use of labour utilisation:

(a) Reduce manual handling.

(b) Minimize walking.

(c) Balance machine cycles so that man and machine are not idle.

(d) Laying the machine in such a way that supervision is simplified.

(iv) **Employees comfort.** The layout should be such that the worker is not effected by heat, moisture or dirt. Direction of light should also be considered for laying the machines. Equipment causing more noise should be isolated as far as it is possible. Equipment which vibrates should be cushioned or specially mounted to prevent transmission of vibrations to floor or surrounding areas.

Plant layout problems

Ordinarily when one thinks of plant layout, then comes the problem of planning a complete layout for a new product, that is planning a new plant, starting from scratch. This is usually not the case as more frequently problem involves the re-layout of existing plant or alteration of some sort of arrangement. Following are the main problems of plant layout.

(i) **Design change.** Frequently change in design of a part calls for change in process of operations to be performed. This change may require only alternations of existing layout, or it may cause extensive re-layout programme depending upon nature of change.

(ii) **Enlargement of a Department.** If for one reason or the other it becomes necessary to increase the production of certain part of product, a change in the layout may be called for. This involves the addition of a few machines which call for entirely new layout so that, product need not to travel long.

(iii) **Reduction of a Department.** Problem is a reverse of the stated above. If products demand are reduced drastically and permanently then few machines have to be removed and rest of the machines have to be rearranged.

(iv) **Adding a new Product.** If a new product is to be added to a line then it is similar to the product already being done, the problem is similar to enlarging a department. However if, the new product differs considerably from those in production, a different problem presents itself. The present equipment may be used by adding a few machines or completely new department may be desired.

(v) **Moving a Department.** Moving a department may or may not present a new problem. If present layout is satisfactory it is only necessary to shift to another alternative position. If, the present layout is not satisfactory, an opportunity presents itself for correction of past mistakes.

(vi) **Planning a new Plant.** This presents a largest problem in plant layout. Building can even be designed to suit the layout.

The additional area has already been provided by removing the receiving department from its present position.

Types of Layout

There are three types of layout:

Layout by fixed position or by fixed material location. Here the material or major component remains stationary. The complete job is done herewith material, men and machinery brought to the location, *e.g.* ship building.

Layout by Process or Layout by function. In this case, all operations of the same process or type of process are grouped together, like all welding in one area, all drilling in one area.

Layout by product or line production. This layout places one operation adjacent to the previous operations. The equipments regardless of process are arranged as per the sequence of operations.

In ideal conditions the raw material comes in at one end of the factory, travels through it in a straight line and comes out at the other as a finished product ready for dispatch. Ideal conditions are not often possible in real life. There is no harm in the work travelling around the factory, provided that it follows a fixed path, that the distances between successive operations are kept as short as possible and that the work moves steadily forward.

In factories where many products are made, or where the products are made up of many different parts, a good layout is much more difficult, especially where batch quantities are small and there is a choice of processes. This situation is generally found at its worst in the engineering industry. A decision may have to be taken between having a *process* layout and a *product* layout.

A process layout is one in which all machines or processes of the same type are grouped together. A product layout is one in which all machines or processes concerned in the manufacture of the same product or range of product are grouped together. The following are the advantages and disadvantages of both layouts.

Process layout: Advantages and Disadvantages

(i) The sequence of manufacturing is flexible and a minimum investment in machines is involved. More floor space is usually occupied than in a product layout.

(ii) Machines can be kept busy most of the time, low and medium-volume production costs can be kept down.

(iii) There are no definite physical channels along which work must flow. The results of this are more handling of materials, larger banks of work in process and a more complicated system of production control than with a product layout.

(iv) Workers and supervisors become skilled in the operation of a single type of machine but require longer training to be able to deal with varied jobs. Thus specialisation can be achieved.

(v) Machine breakdowns do not hold up a succession of operations; work can be transferred to other similar machines.

Product layout: Advantages and Disadvantages

(i) The flow of work over direct physical routes cuts out delays: there is less material handling, and the definite sequence of operations over adjacent machines simplifies production control and cuts out forms and records.

(ii) The total time of production is kept low, less floor space is occupied and the capital tied up in work in process can be kept down. The capital investment in machines may however, be raised by duplication of the same machine on several lines.

(iii) Manufacturing costs are low at high volume production but rise steeply as it drops. If one or more lines are running light there is considerable machine idleness.

(iv) It is easier to train workers inexperienced in industry upto a certain level of skill.

(v) A single machine break down may shut down a whole production line.

Classification of Layout

Layout by fixed position—This type of layout is suitable where—

(a) Operations require hand tools or simple portable machines.

(b) Making only one or few pieces.

(c) Cost of moving the major pieces is high.

(d) Skill of workmanship lies in the ability of workers or where we wish to fix responsibility for product quality to one workman.

Layout by process—this layout is used where—

(a) Expensive machinery is involved.

(b) Variety of products are made.

(c) Operations are unbalanced or in other words wide variation in time required in different operations are encountered.

(d) The demand for the product is small or intermittent.

Layout by product or line production—this type of layout is used when—

(a) There is a large quantity of pieces of products to make.
(b) Design of the product is more or less standardised.
(c) Demand for the product is fairly steady.

The graph shows the cost comparison between product and Process type Layouts.

Factors affecting layout

Whatever be the type of layout being contemplated, the following factors influence the selection in every case.

(i) Material; (ii) Machine
(iii) Man; (iv) Movement
(v) Waiting; (vi) Service
(vii) Building; (viii) Flexibility.

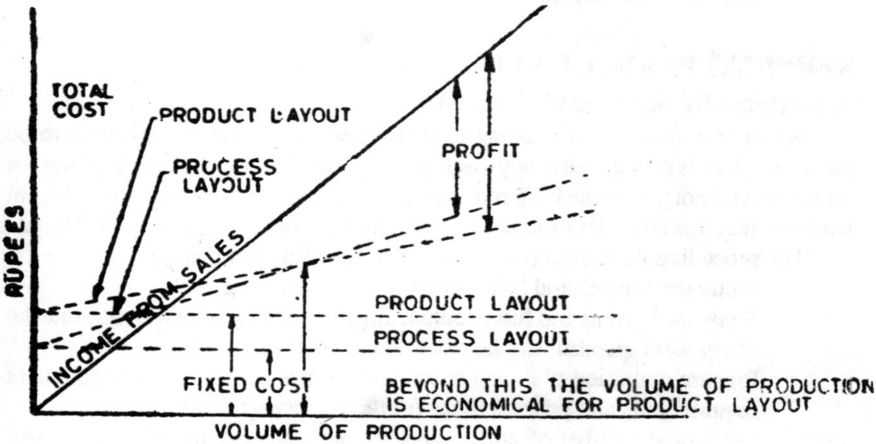

Fig. 14.1

(i) **Material.** This include the design, variety, quantity, necessary operation and their consequence. These are affected by : (a) Design and specification, (b) Physical and chemical characteristic, (c) Quantity and variety of products and material and (d) Component parts or material and how they go together.

(ii) **Machine.** This include process or method, machinery tools and equipment, machine utilisation and requirement of machinery and power.

(iii) **Man.** This include safety and working conditions, manpower requirement, man utilisation etc.

(iv) **Movement.** This includes the flow pattern reduction of unnecessary handling, space for movement and analysis of handling methods and equipment.

(v) **Waiting.** This include location of storage or delay points, space for waiting, method of storing, safeguard equipment for storing and delay.

(vi) **Service.** This include services for personnel such as fire protection, lighting, heating and ventilation etc., services for material such as quality control, production control and services for machinery such as maintenance and utilities like gas, steam, water supply etc.

(vii) **Building.** This includes features like Railway siding, yard areas for parking and storing, shape of building, numbers of floors,facilities of elevation stairs etc.

(viii) **Flexibility.** This includes consideration due to changes in material, machinery and process, supporting activities and installation limitations etc. It means easy changing to new arrangement and is facilitated by mobile or mounting or movable machinery, self-contained equipment, readily acceptable service lines, standardised equipments.

STEPS TO PLAN A LAYOUT

A Systematic Approach To layout

Whether a new layout is being contemplated or an existing layout is to be changed, there is a systematic approach in doing so. Dis-coordinated thinking for movement do not pay in the long run. A systematic approach, ensures to the layout engineer that due consideration has been given to all factors affecting the layout.

The procedure for layout project will entail the following steps:

: Study the 'make' and 'buy' items in the material list.

: Study the current and future output target for each product. Determine the component quantities to be stocked and manufactured.

: Prepare operation planning sheet. Obtain production routine equipment requirements and process times from other departments.

: Determine number of equipments of each category required and direct man power requirement.

: Determine space requirement at each work spot and make tentative work place layout.

: Study the stock policy and find out the storage requirements for raw materials, work in process, 'Buy' items and finished goods.

: Obtain packaging informations to determine the quality of packaging materials and the final shape of material for shipment, obtain also the shipping schedule.

: Prepare operation process chart, flow process chart and an overall and detailed diagram of the flow.

: Make tentative layout by trial and error.

: Choose handling procedure. Determine the size of the unit load number of units to be moved and the distance. Also calculate the indirect man power required.

- : Provide adequate gangways for movement.
- : Discuss with line management and incorporate their suggestions.
- : Prepare detailed layout drawings with as much visual aid as possible. Locate all services facilities like gas, compressed air, water etc.
- : Explain to line management.
- : Prepare a detailed cost analysis sheet for all equipment additions movements installations etc.
- : Draw up a work schedule for your course of action for the installation.

Any layout problem requires that these steps are properly taken care of. At some stage or the other, whether scientifically or by guess work and approximation all the data entailed in the steps have to be collected before a change or a new layout is brought into effect. The various steps are discussed in detailed below.

Techniques of Plant Layout

One of the mathematical techniques used for making a layout is known as Travel Chart method. This method can quantitatively compare various layouts by finding the total weighted distance of each layout. The method consists of making three matrices known as *Volume matrix, Distance matrix and Volume-Distance matrix. Volume matrix gives the total flow of material from one department to another*. This is an input data to the problem and remains unchanged throughout the solution procedure. It is independent of the layout. Distance matrix gives the distance to be travelled in moving the product form one department to another. It is dependent on layout. Volume Distance matrix is calculated from the above two matrices and is used for finding the total weighted distance. The method of Travel Charting may be explained with the help of an example.

Example

Suppose we have four product groups I,II, III and IV requiring the services of some or all the five departments A,B, C, D and E. The problem is to determine the location of these five departments. The five departments are required in different sequences for each product group as given on next page.

Group	Sequence	% Volume of the Product
I	A B C D. E	30
II	A C B E D	35
III	A C D B C	20
IV	A E D C	15

The volume matrix for this problem is given below :

Volume Matrix

From \ To	A	B	C	D	E
A	—	30	55	—	15
B	—	—	50	—	35
C	—	35	—	50	—
D	—	20	15	—	30
E	—	—	—	50	—

Now a tentative layout may be made and inter-department distances calculated. Suppose we obtain the following distance matrix, which shows the distances in feet between various departments. Distances between tow departments, where there is no flow of material between them are not needed hence they are not shown in the Distance matrix.

Distance matrix

From \ To	A	B	C	D	E
A	—	20	15	—	40
B	—	—	10	—	25
C	—	10	—	30	—
D	—	25	30	—	15
E	—	—	—	15	—

Distance Volume matrix is determined by multiplying the corresponding all the above two matrices.

Distance-Volume Matrix

To From	A	B	C	D	E	Total
A	—	600	825	—	600	2025
B	—	—	500	—	875	1375
C	— .	350	—	1500	—	1850
D	—	500	450	—	450	1400
E	—	—	—	750	—	750
					Grand Total	7400

Total weighted distance in this case is 7400. A number of layouts are developed and the weighted-distance for each one of them is calculated. The layout with minimum weighted distance is then selected. The layouts are also compared on the basis of qualitative factors like safety and aesthetic aspects etc. if there is no significant difference between them on the basis of weighted distance.

Definition of Material Handling

Material handling has been rightly defined as an Art and Science involving the moving, packing and storing of substance in any form. Material handling is the preparation placing and positioning of materials to facilitate their movement or storage. The total cost of material handling formed is indicated in the following diagram.

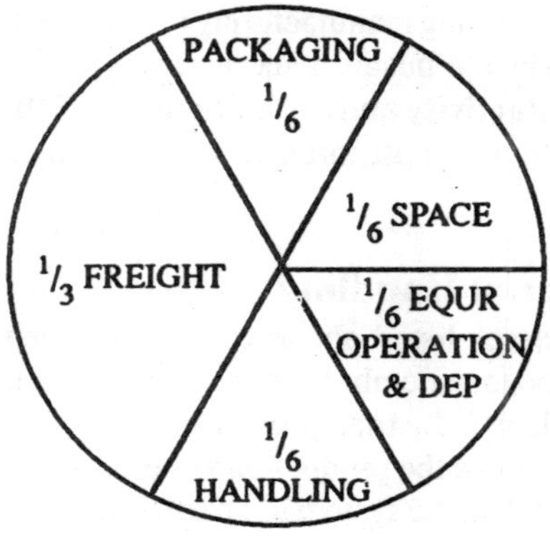

Fig. 14.2

Material handling is the moving of material from the raw material storage through production to ultimate consumer with the least expenditure of time and effort, so as to produce maximum productive efficiency at the lowest material handling cost.

Objective of Material Handling

(i) Reduction in wastage of machine time.
(ii) Reduction in manufacturing cycle time.
(iii) Avoiding disruption in production schedule.
(iv) Bring safety to workers and provide for safer working conditions.
(v) Bring customer satisfaction.
(vi) Enhances productivity and avoid high costs.

(i) **Reduction in wastage of machine time.** Proper material handling system would ensure regular supply and distribution of raw material and finished product. This will not create the problem of idling of machine and eliminate problem of wastage of machine time.

(ii) **Reduction in manufacturing cycle time.** Keeping the loading and unloading time of machine at minimum enable the completion of manufacturing cycle at reasonably short time.

(iii) **Avoid disruption in production schedule.** In mass production system, all parts or materials must come in the assembly line in correct quantity and at precisely the right time to avoid risk of shut down.

(iv) **Safety and safe working conditions.** Correctly designed material handling system enables utilisation of proper material handling device and training workers in safe material handling practice It is tangible saving in reduced insurance rates, payment of compensation and boost to worker's moral.

(v) **Customer satisfaction.** Regular market supplies, by avoiding disruption in production schedule, shortening manufacturing cycle time, timely deliveries lead to customer satisfaction a key to business success.

(vi) **Enhances productivity and avoids high cost.** Efficient material handling system results in reduction in cost through various steps which results in higher productivity.

Principles of Material Handling

The various objectives listed above can be achieved by following certain principles. It will be good to remember that these are the general principles only and in practice the individual industrial problems affect the evolution of material handling system. Factors like the production system, types of building and cost of various devices largely effect the system in a particular industry. General principles are:

(i) Materials should be moved over the shortest distance possible. Short movements require less time and cost less money than long movements.

(ii) Do not retrace your path. The aim of material handling system should be to move in forward direction or clockwise direction.

(iii) Terminal time should be kept as short as possible. It is time taken for picking up the finished product.

(iv) Loads should be carried both ways on material handling trips whenever possible.

(v) Partial loads and manual handling should be avoided.

(vi) Utilise gravity as moving force as far as possible.

(vii) Utilise containers and unit loads. The unit load means the product to be moved should be grouped into units of a large and constant size.

(viii) Materials should be already marked to help save time in sorting and avoiding mixing up.

Factors affecting Materials Handling System

The following four factors affect material handling system.

1. Production system.
2. Product to be handled.
3. Type of building within which material is to be handled.
4. Cost of material handling device.

1. Production system. There are two basic types of production systems. One is intermittent or job-lot production; the other is continuous-production. Intermittent systems are used where a variety of jobs are being done at the same time on a variety of machines and in a variety of places. Since a great deal of flexibility is necessary it is likely that variable path equipment will be used more than fixed-path equipment. In terms of materials-handling devices lift trucks, pallets, hand trucks and trolleys would be more useful in intermittent production system in continuous production systems. These materials-handling devices would not be so commonly used in continuous-production systems, because fixed-path equipment would be more reliable and more economical in many cases. In mass production or continuous-process systems, one would find extensive use of conveyors, cranes, hoists, pipelines and in modern plants, automatic of transfer machines and tape-controlled indexing machines.

2. Type of Products to be Handled. The type of products being handled greatly affects materials handling decisions. Powders, liquids and gases are well suited to transport by pipelines. Automatic transfer machines should be used in automatic processes where a sufficiently high volume of production is available to offset the high cost of the equipment. Cranes and hoists are best suited to very heavy lifting jobs, where the material to be used cannot be easily lifted from below. Conveyors should be used where high volumes of products move from one fixed point to another. Trucks should be used where flexible destinations are required and where the volume of material to be moved may be low. The characteristics of the products, including weight, size, shape, perishability and whether it is a solid, liquid or gas have significant bearing on the selection of the type of device which should be chosen to move them.

3. Types of building. The number of floors has a direct effect on the devices which should be used. Single-storey building, the most common type being built today lend themselves to the use of lift trucks and conveyors. They also eliminate the need for elevators, which often prove to be a bottleneck in materials-handling. Multi-storyed building, however, find themselves to the use of gravity flow with pipelines and shutters which is the most economical method of materials handling.

4. Cost of Material Handling. The last major factor is the cost of various devices which are available for use. Cost comparisons among various alternatives are often difficult to make. The initial costs of alternative devices should be considered. The usual life of equipment will also affect the decision. Resale or scrap value is the other factor. Perhaps most important are operating costs which include fuel maintenance, repair, insurance and labour costs. These costs must be determined for the alternatives before estimates of the value of one device versus another can be determined. The graphical representation given in Fig shows the relation between cost per unit of load moved and distance moved.

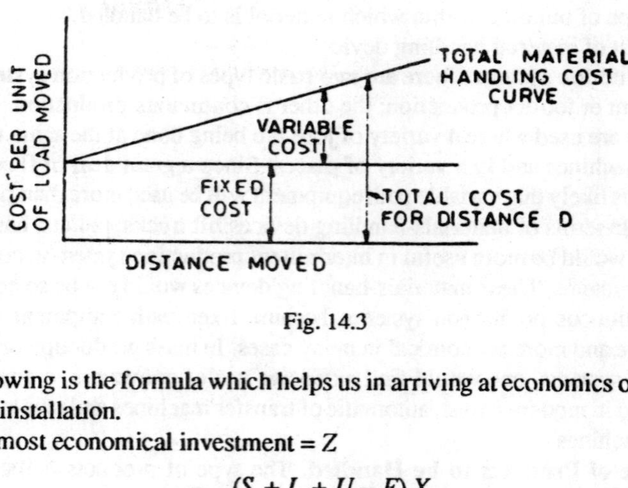

Fig. 14.3

Following is the formula which helps us in arriving at economics of a material handling installation.

The most economical investment = Z

$$Z = \frac{(S + L + U - E)\,X}{A + B + C + D}$$

Where A = Interest on investment

B = Percentage allowance for insurance

C = Percentage allowance for maintenance of material handling equipment

D = Percentage allowance for depreciation of equipment

E = Annual power cost to operate the equipment

S = Annual saving in direct labour cost

L = Annual saving in fixed and variable overheads
U = Annual saving or increase in earnings
X = Percentage of year the equipment is used
I = Initial cost of equipment.

The cost of maintaining the equipment (excluding labour) to operation is:

$$Y = I\,(A + B + C - D)$$

The yearly profit V made from operating the equipment is:

$$(S + L + U - E)\,X - Y$$

Materials Handling Problems

Following are the various important factors which need to be studied to analyse the handling problems.

Establish the Scope of the study

(i) What is the degree of thoroughness expected of the study?
(ii) Should the study includes related functions such as manufacturing, financing, personal relation etc? If not what are should be included?

Pinpoint what Physical boundaries of the study

(i) What areas in the plant layout should be covered by the study?

Determine Production Forecasts

(i) What volume of material is expected to be handled by the equipment?
(ii) What is the expected range of expansion?

Determine the most-handled items

(i) Which material require the most of the handling work?
(ii) What is the total handling cost of these items in relation to the others?

Compute the cost of the present handling method

(i) What are the functional elements of the system?
(ii) How many man-hours are spent for each element?
(iii) What are the other costs directly related to the handling operations?

Analysis of Material Handling

Materials handling problems vary from situation to situation. The gravity of the problem varies according to whether production is continuous or intermittent. This in effect means only that a detailed analysis of various aspects of materials movement is necessary.

1. What to Move. Data is collected on what materials are to be moved. The bill of materials coupled with the production schedule would give this information. Additionally all information regarding weight, size, shape, quantity etc., of the materials to be transported is to be collected. The following form could be used.

ITEM SPECIFICATION LIST

ITEM				UNIT				HOW MOVED			
Description	Size	Wt.	Qty.	Qty.	Size per unit	Wt.	No.	From units Reqd	To	Dist.	Eqpt.

2. Where to Move. Once the data is available as to what to move, the details of where to move are to be collected. It is necessary that information is collected in the form of distance ¥ weight since this is the most pertinent information. The information could be collected in the form given below:

To / From	DEPARTMENTS A	B	C	D
A				
B				
C				
D				

3. How to Move. The data required to be collected is (i) the equipment used for movement, (ii) whether material is moved individually or in units like tray, pallets, bundles etc. and (iii) the time taken for the movement. Details of equipments used are to be collected, *viz.* (i) capacity, (ii) speed, (iii) flexibility and (iv) maneuverability. Hence the factors affecting material handling can be summarised as follows:

What to move	:	Materials-form, characteristics, quantity.
In what	:	Containers
Where	:	Routing
How often	:	Frequency and duration
How far	:	Distance

How fast	:	Speed
On what	:	Paved gangway, curves
By whom	:	Type of labour
By what	:	Equipment.

Materials Handling Surveys

These surveys are of mainly three types:

(a) Plant-wide survey

(b) Department survey

(c) Area survey.

(a) Plant Wide Survey. It is there to provide a material handling system in the plant. It can be carried out in following steps:

(i) Prepare a plant activity drawings

(ii) Prepare a plant-layout drawings

(iii) Draw the flow of samples of major materials, assemblies and products.

Department Survey. After selecting the appropriate department of plant-activity we should prepare a material-handling chart showing methods of transportation, quantities, distances moved, times and frequency of movements.

Area Survey. In the areas survey we are able to analyse each material handling situation in the department. In this we use the predetermined times and activity samplings.

The survey of material handling reveal—the kind, the type, the volume, the weight and other characteristics during processing, storing and shipping. In carrying out the survey following information should be available:

- ★ How often handling occurs.
- ★ Number of times each type of material is handled.
- ★ The type of the material to be handled.
- ★ The form in which the material is received, moved and despatched.
- ★ The dimension of the material handled.
- ★ The nature of route the material follows.
- ★ The probability of plant accident that can be contributed to handling.
- ★ Cost of material handling at each place.

Material Handling Equipments

The material handling equipment will provide three types of services:

- ★ Material loading and unloading
- ★ Inter-departmental movements.
- ★ Intra-departmental movements

The choice of the equipment requires a thorough knowledge of all available equipments. The various types of material handling equipments can be grouped into four major heads as shown in the following diagram.

- Floor operated group
  - Movable
    - Manual (Hand and platform trucks)
    - Power (Rider and pedestrain)
  - Fixed
    - Non-powered conveyors
    - Power conveyors
- Vertical handling group
  - Vertical
  - — Portable Elevator
  - — Inclined Conveyors
  - Hoists
- Overhead handling group
  - — Cranes
  - — Overhead Conveyors
  - Monorail System
- Allied Equipment
  - Skides
    - Platform
    - Box
  - — Palletes
  - Bridge Plates

Evaluation of Material Handling Problems

Normally in a plant there are lot of problems with which an employee is bombarded but, with passage of time he develops a habit to tolerate the inconveniences at that place and accept the problem as inevitable. However, a survey of plant would bring out several facts which need a systematic study. Certain points will show us the need of a study of the Material Handling Problem.

In Receipts and Stores

(i) Does the area where materials are received give a look of bad house keeping? Are materials being dumped all over the space?

(ii) Are materials piled up in the receiving yard to be moved?
(iii) Are the members of group, handling materials are uniformly loaded? How many men are engaged?
(iv) Are the materials moved twice in the receiving yard before they are finally sent into the plant?
(v) Has the storage area been divided into sections for storing different materials?
(vi) Are the records of materials stored maintained properly so as to locate them properly?
(vii) Are floor loading capacity and ceiling height used properly displayed?
(viii) Are the items of more frequent use kept near the gate?
(ix) Is the floor properly levelled so that the movement can be made without the danger of accident or obstruction?
(x) Does the distance of the store from the production department ensure shortest distance moved?
(xi) Are the packages ready in time to avoid deberrage of wagons?
(xii) Are there any damages to the materials during handling?

In Production Areas

(i) Do skilled workers handle material or heavy object?
(ii) Are there proper demarcation lines for material movements areas?
(iii) Is the production area clustered with parts and materials for use rejects?
(iv) Are in process material kept on floor?
(v) Has the storage area been divided into sections for storing different materials?

If the answers to the above question are observed to be in affirmative then general diagnosis is that there is need for studying in detail the material handling problems.

Develop better Methods

After the charts have been prepared, following questions must be answered before selecting a handling system.

Materials

(i) What material is handled and why?
(ii) Can it be handled in any other convenient form?

Location

(i) What is existing location of the material?
(ii) Is there a better alternative exists?

Timing

(i) Why must this material be moved now?

(ii) Will other operations be effected if this does not reach in time?

Handling

(i) Can the operators be relieved oi handling!

(ii) Does material travel effect the pace of operation?

The evaluation of material handling system can be measured in terms of the ratio of the time spent in the handling to the total time spent in production. Equipment utilisation ratio is an important indictor for judging the material handling system. The ratio can be computed and compared with similar firms or in the same form over a period of time.

$$\text{Materials Handling Labour ratio} = \frac{\text{Personnel assigned to Materials hadling}}{\text{Total operating work force}}$$

In order to ascertain whether the handling system delivers materials to work centres with maximum efficiency, it is desirable to compute

Direct Labour Handling Loss ratio

$$= \frac{\text{Materials handling time lost by divert labour}}{\text{Total divert labour time}}$$

It should however be emphasized that the efficiency of materials handling mainly depends on the following factors : (a) Efficiency of handling methods employed for handling a unit weight through a unit distance (b) Efficiency of the layout which determines the distance through which the materials have to be hauled. (c) Utilisation of the handling facilities (d) Efficiency of the speed of handling.

Therefore to conclude effective materials handling system depends on the design of layout and equipments to suit specific requirements.

Chapter 15

QUALITY DETERMINATION AND CONTROL

Introduction

In purchasing, quality is a function of use. All components used in production process demands a certain level of quality. Therefore, inappropriate quality may mean that a component either is too good or too poor for a given application.

Quality is an expression of the measured properties, conditions or characteristics of a product or process usually stated in terms of grades, classes or — specifications and determined by—the application that is involved. It is important to determine what quality is the right quality for a given purpose. Similarly it is a matter of defining the quality in such a way that it is clearly understood by both buyer and seller. It is important to measure the quality of goods delivered to see that it conforms to specified quality.

Quality Control

Quality is never an accident. It is always the result of an intelligent effort. In any organisation the quality function involves all departments and all groups of personnel. Quality control is a deliberate and planned activity to integrate the quality development, quality maintenance and quality-improvement efforts of all the various groups in an organisation. Quality means the very survival in a competitive world. The quality is not the only means for enlarging the share of export and also the sale of goods in the internal market where there is a growing inter firm competition but also a means for providing the right quality of the goods to the customer with satisfaction. Term 'Quality' conveys the meaning that there is something good or desirable in the product. Quality conveys the impression what consumer expect from the product. Quality is the fitness for the purpose at the lowest cost and quality of any product is regarded as the degree to which it fulfils the requirement of customer. Quality can be determined by the characteristics of design, size, material, chemical composition, mechanical functioning, workmanship, finish and so on. Quality signifies the several attributes of product such as durability, colour, intrinsic properties etc. Quality means the characteristics of materials, parts, assemblies, processes and processing conditions and product including its packaging.

The word quality has a variety of meanings these include: the degree to which a specific product satisfies the wants of specific consumer or it is called consumer's preference. The degree to which a specific product conforms to a design or specification (quality of conformance).

Importance of Q.C.in Industry

Quality Control is based in the concept of variability, whether large or small which is inevitable in any manufacturing process. The variability can be classified as one which is inherent to the process, and the one causes for which can be assigned. This knowledge enables us to detect the causes of external variation almost instantly during the course of manufacture, and eliminate them before much damage is done to the process. The approach of quality control is, therefore, to prevent the defects by simply inspecting them after the manufacture. The various benefits of Quality Control are given as under:

(a) Better understanding of processes and product.
(b) Helps in building information system for improving quality and reducing cost and coordinating the activities of various departments.
(c) Increased production under same set-up.
(d) Reduction of cost per unit.
(e) Reduction of scrap.
(f) Saving in excess use of materials.
(g) Reduction in inspection.
(h) Evaluation of scientific tolerances.
(i) Maintaining operating efficiency.
(j) Less customers complaint.
(k) Increasing quality consciousness.
(l) Building quality into the product rather than inspecting it.
(m) It helps in planned collection and effective use of data in studying "Cause-Effect" relationships which lead to corrective action on the process.
(n) Reduction in overhead expenses.
(o) Increase in yield and efficiencies.
(p) Increase in goodwill.
(q) Reduction in idle time loss of machine and equipment as well as operational staff.

Quality control, aims at achieving quality standard with existing facilities by determining, maintaining and improving. Thus systematic and continuous application of Q.C. would lead to better quality, increased production, reduced cost through reduction in scrap and rework, saving in consumption of material, reduced inspection and above all greater consumer satisfaction.

Problems of Quality Control

Quality Control is a systematic and scientific system involving the application of all known industrial and statistical techniques to control the quality of the manufactured product. The meaning of Quality Control will be different from one individual to another and also differs from time to time. The various problems of quality control can be grouped into the following three classes.

(a) Engineering. the development of a product is basically engineering; the development of quality evaluation through improved inspection procedures, the knowledge of causes of defects and their rectification is engineering.

(b) Statistical. The concept of the behaviour of a process, has brought in the idea of 'prevention' and 'control' is statistical. Based on this we can build an information system to satisfy the concept of prevention and control and improving upon product quality.

(c) Managerial. The efficient use of the engineering and statistical concept is managerial. The introduction of quality consciousness in the organisation is also the management. The effective coordination of the quality control function with those of others is managerial.

Principles of Quality Control

The principles of quality control are : Principles of co-ordination, Principles of prevention, Principles of building quality in the product.

The concepts of quality prevades all along the length of an organisation and thus it is absolutely necessary to conceive of the quality control function as coordinating the quality activities in the various departments. Even coordination principles is very important in the production cycle of a product. Here the coordination is based on SQC concepts. In any production cycle, there are three major functions—design, manufacture, and inspection. These three functions were treated as almost independent until recently the knowledge of capability of processes, came to light. The second principle is the principle of prevention. It is important to consider in any actual manufacture to eliminate the causes of defects as manufacturing is going on. The routine inspection procedures should sort out the items produced as good. This approach must be replaced by a new technique of corrective action as and when manufacturing is continuing. Following are certain important ideas regarding principles of building quality.

(a) The idea of building quality into the product rather simply inspecting them.
(b) Feed-back information which assists in coordinating the activities of the various departments.
(c) The use of data in studying cause-effect relationships which lead to taking action on the process.
(d) Importance of planned collection and effective use of data.

Development of Standards

The systematic control of quality and development of standards had their inception with the industrial revolution and the mass-production techniques that accompanied it. The need for consistent quality of process materials led to the setting up of standards that described the chemical and physical characteristics, such as size, colour, hardness, weight, finish and purity, that buyer would accept. Standardisation has continued to play an important role in advancing technical progress. It has substituted common measurement methods for "rule of thumb" criteria, enabling parts made to be interchangeable.

Standard

A standard is the description of an acceptable level of quality; design and composition of a particular item, which evolves as a result of study and experience by industrial firms. Standards are widely publicized and are readily available to any buyer who wants to use them or to any supplier who needs them to develop a quotation. Most buyers find that they can adopt industry or government standards to their use.

Brand or trade Name

A brand name is the mark or designation that a manufacturer uses to distinguish his product and to identify its origin. In putting a brand name on his product, it is the manufacturer's intention to ensure proper credit to his product for any good will developed in satisfied customers. To build and retain goodwill, it is important for the manufacturer to provide consistent quality. In ordering by brand, the purchaser is depending on the integrity and reputation of the supplier. Purchase by brand is necessary if a product to be used as fabricated part and it had been advertised that its inclusion in a finished good makes that good more stable.

Specifications

Specifications are detailed description or listing of the characteristics of an item. Compiling specifications often requires considerable time and may prove costly in comparison with other methods of communicating to the supplier. Buying by specifications is one of the most common methods used in business purchases.

Advantages of Specifications: The main advantages of specification buying are :

(i) Drawing up the specifications requires careful thought and a review of the buyer's needs.

(ii) Specifications ensures the identical nature of items purchased from two or more sources.

(iii) Specification buying is a necessary step toward industry, wide standardisation programme which hold the promise of substantial savings.

(iv) Purchasing to specifications gives the buyer's inspection department an exact standard against which to measure the incoming materials and results in accurate inspection and uniform quality of materials.

Disadvantages

(i) It is not desirable to prepare specifications for small-lot purchases.

(ii) Specifications buying adds to the purchaser's responsibility.

(iii) In specification buying the cost of inspection is greater than in purchasing items by brand.

(iv) There is also the danger of assuming that after specifications are established, the characteristics of the item have been permanently set.

Cost-Value Concepts In Quality Control

If the marketing department has indicated the consumer's requirement with respect to some product which should include at least in some degree an indication of the price which he would be willing to pay to obtain such a product. Fig (15.1) gives the idea that higher the technical excellence higher shall be cost. As we increase the technical excellence of our product, necessarily the cost of product increases at an increasing rate. The low degree of technical excellence may be attained at a correspondingly low cost of production. It may also carry with it just not a low but even a negative value. That is, a product may be so poor that one would have to pay consumers to take it away.

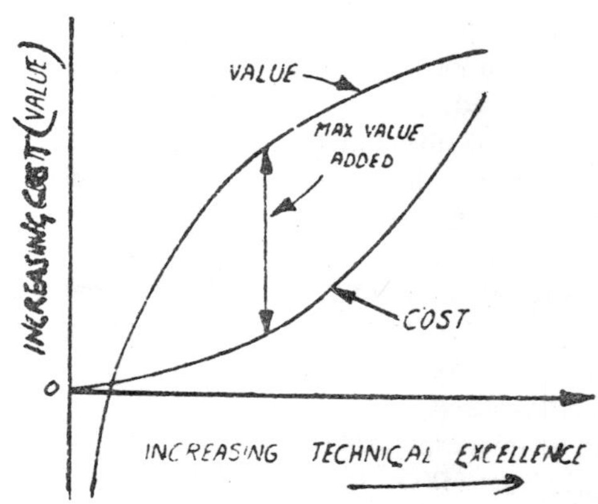

Fig. 15.1

As one moves to the right, that is, as technical excellence is increased, costs increase at an increasing rate while value increases at a decreasing rate. Even though one design may be superior to another in terms of its technical excellence, it may not have increased value in the market-place in terms of the service it renders. There exists some desired degree of technical excellence as shown at the point at which marginal value equals marginal cost, that is, the maximum value added occurs when the slopes of the two curves are equal.

Processes must be designed to produce output according to the desired specifications and these production processes must be monitored to assure conformance. As is shown in figure one may obtain a greater degree of conformance by operating more costly processes, but these more costly process result in decreasing losses due to lack of conformity at a decreasing rate. It is quite possible to buy processes which are too good, given the most economical specification. A processes obtainable at lesser cost may result in a higher rate of defective output, that is, low conformance. Thus the problem of assuring quality consists of two inter-related design phases. First, the design of a product whose reliability is economic in terms of its end use, and second, the design of a set of procedures which will at economic levels assure the attainment of the defined reliability. Establishing proper balance between these two is difficult.

Inspection

Inspection is concerned solely with the acceptance or rejection of output based on a comparison of the attributes of a unit of output with specifications. Inspection in some degree is an integral part of any production process. The purpose of this inspection may be different even at different locations with the same process. Inspection is economical only when the expected cost of a defective is greater than the cost of inspection necessary to detect the presence of defect. It is necessary to inspect in order to gain assurance that the process s producing at a level at which rectifying inspection is not required.

Inspection is concerned with estimating the degree to which output conforms with established specification. The process by which degreed of conformance is determined may range from the simplest possible comparison of a unit to output with a specification by measurement with a standard instrument all the way to life testing under actual operating conditions of a sample of output followed by rigorous statistical analysis of the result of the experiment. The degree of conformance can be measured by measurement of:

Tolerance, and **Allowance.**

Tolerance refers to any permissible variations in size. For example, a dimension which is specified as 2.0000 inches may be given with many different tolerances. A tolerance of +0.0001 inches would specify that all output within the limits 1.999 inches 2.0001 inches would be acceptable for use.

Allowance refers to difference in size between parts which fit together. For example, a shaft to be fitted in a hub might be specified with a maximum diameter of 4.001 inches and the hub with a minimum diameter of 4.002 inches. So in this case the minimum allowance would be the difference between these two dimensions that is, 0.001 inches. So by now we know that the basic quality function is to decided whether a product or material conforms to its specification. This function is generally known as 'acceptance'. The inspection functions constitutes the following.

(a) Interpretation of the specification.
(b) Measurement of the product characteristics.
(c) Comparison of the above two.
(d) Judgement as to conformance.
(e) Disposition of the materials/product.
(f) Recording of the data obtained.

The individual who conducts the above activities is known as inspector and the department which guides this inspector is known as inspection department.

Methods of Inspection

Inspection on acceptance basis can be carried out either by:

1. 100% inspection or
2. Sampling inspection

Sampling inspection is preferred to 100% inspection because of:

(a) Cost
(b) Time
(c) 100% inspection fails to provide 100% assurance against the acceptance of bad quality due to inspection fatigue. To ensure the correctness of acceptance to the best possible extent, one should ensure the following:

(i) Sampling should be done on random basis representing the total lot.
(ii) Proper sampling sizes.

When is Inspection justified

Fundamentally, the decision hinges as practical economics of each specific situation.

Two basic Costs are involved.

(a) Cost of Inspection.
(b) Cost resulting from defective parts entering the production or wrong parts reaching the customer. The object is to minimise the sum of these two costs is the major criterion in arriving at the basic inspection decision.

SINGLE SAMPLING

Lot-by-Lot Acceptance-Sampling

In any sampling plan following three values must be specified.

(a) The number of units in the incoming lot of material.
(b) The number of units to be inspected in the sample.
(c) The maximum number of defective items allowable in the sample.

The procedure of inspection

1. Determine from the purchase order the applicable sampling plan and lot size.

2. Using this information to determine the sample size and the acceptance number to be used.

3. Draw the sample randomly from the lot, several technique can be used in doing this, although the more formal approach is one based on the use of table of random numbers.

4. Inspect each of the sample items in accordance with the inspection specifications, noted in the purchase order.

5. If C unit or fewer defectives are found in the sample the lot is accepted. If more than C units fail to meet specification the entire lot is rejected.

The Operating Characteristic Curve (OC Curve)

The performance ability of a statistical sampling plan is described by its operating characteristic curve. This helps the manager to know what to except from a particular sampling plans. Figure shows *OC* curve for sampling plan with N=1000 and n=135; C=3. The figure was constructed by making this computation individually for a 1% defective lot, 2% defective lot, and 7% defective lot. The OC curve is obtained by connecting the plotted probability points. *OC* curve inform us whether to accept or to reject lots of 1000 items. If the in-coming lot contains 1 per cent defectives items there is 95% probability that sample will contain 3 or more defectives, thus telling him to accept the entire lot. There is also a 5% probability that the sample will contain more than 3 defects thus telling him to reject the lot.

The *OC* curve in reality tells the user how well the sampling plan discriminate between good and bad lots. The steeper the slope of the curve the more discriminating is the plan discriminate between good and bad lots. The steeper the slope of the curve the more discriminating is the plan. *Either by increasing the sample size or by reducing the acceptance number*. In practice several points on the *OC* curve have been chosen as bench marks n the design and indexing of sampling plans. The first of these is the *P* value which corresponds with approximately a 95% probability of acceptance, this is commonly called the acceptable quality level (AQL). The second point is the P value which corresponds to 10% probability of acceptance this is commonly called the lot tolerance percent defective (L.T.P.D.)

Average Out-going Quality (AOQ)

If we assume that all 100% inspected, and that all defectives found are replaced with good products the AOQ for each value of *P* can be given by

AOQ = Number of defective items accepted by the Plan average lot size after 100% inspection.

$$= \frac{P\,(Pa)\,(N-n)}{N}$$

Probability that the incoming lot will be accepted by the sample

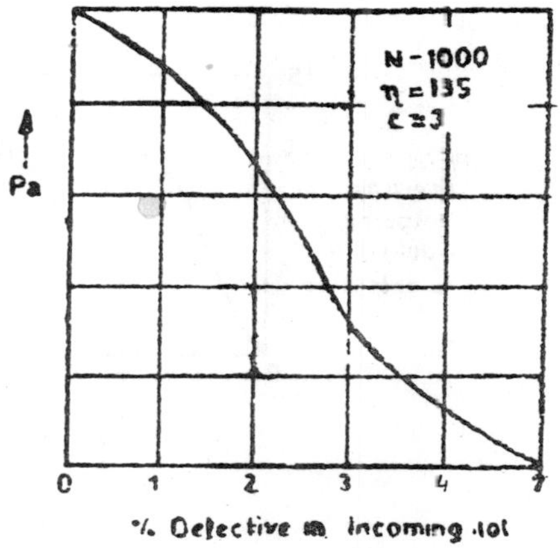

Fig. 15.2

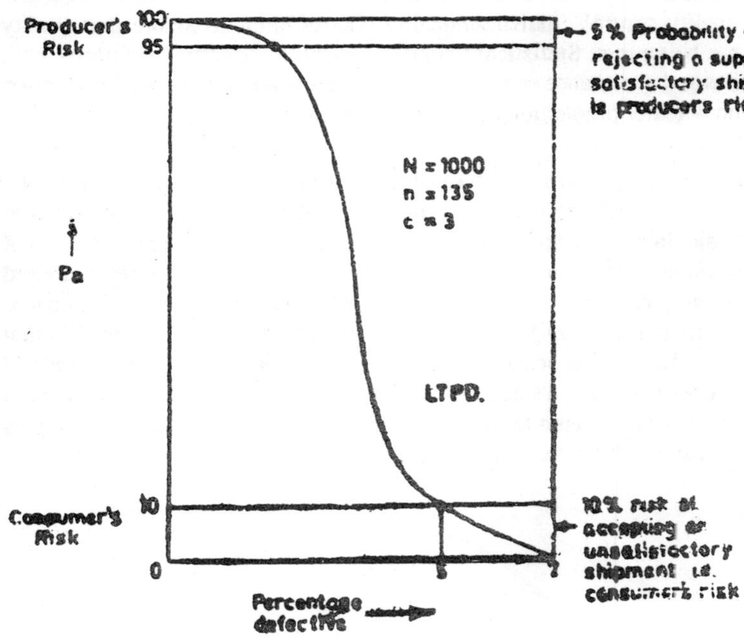

Fig. 15.3

AOQ reaches its bad level when incoming lots contain 2% defectives. This is called the average out-going quality limit (AOQL).

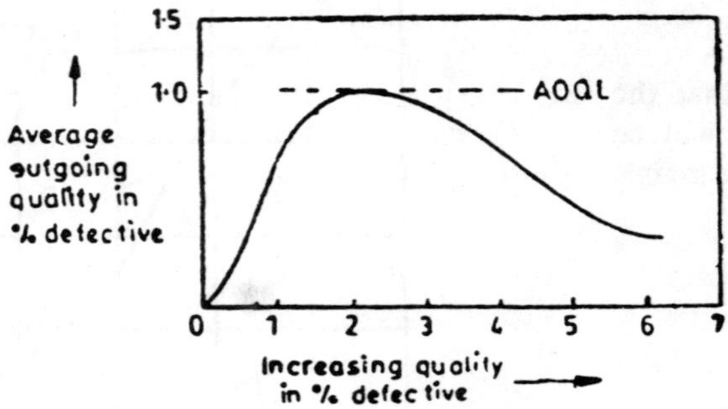

Fig. 15.4

Sampling and Statistical Quality Control

Sampling is the best known branch of statistics in management. It chief application, one that has been used successfully in business for several decades, is statistical quality control. Statistical quality control helps to assure that quality standards are being met. Statistical Quality Control is concerned primarily with control charts and acceptance sampling. Control charts are used during production to determine whether production quality of being maintained.

Control Charts

In many cases, the most useful control charts deal with the mean and the range. Suppose, again, that we are manufacturing 1.2" slabş and from past production figures, we calculate the mean length of slabs and call it *X* or the estimated mean of the universe. Suppose that samples of five slabs are taken at regular intervals and that for each sample, the mean length X and the range are computed. Since no two slabs are exactly the same length, there will be variations in the different X's that are obtained. If these variations are due to chance (random variations), the sample means will be distributed in a statistical pattern. Now let us remember that this is a distribution of sample means and not of individual items. The means of the samples will tend to cluster around the means of the universe.

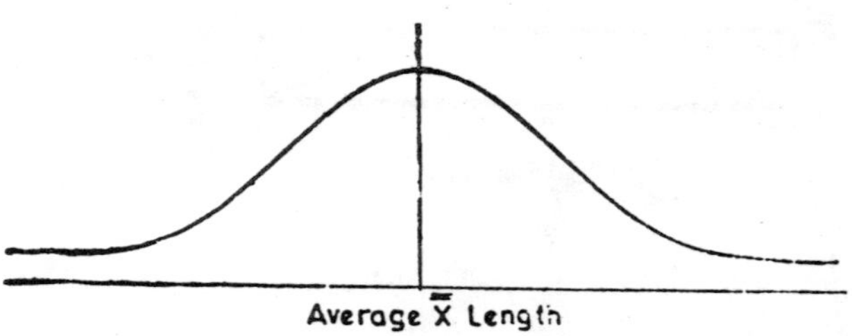

Fig. 15.5

Now we need an upper control limit (U.C.L.) and a lower control limit (L.C.L.) to tell us when the average length of slab has changed. To illustrate this, assume that X is 1.2001 inches. Let us take a sample of five slabs from the production line and the average length of these five slabs happens to be 1.1998. If the point falls above the UCL or below the LCL we assume that this much variation in sample means from their mean is not due to chance; an investigation is made to find an assignable cause.

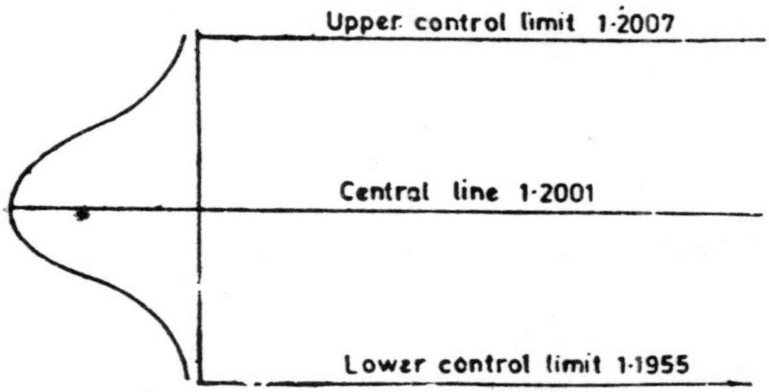

Fig 15.5

The *X* Chart alone is not enough because it says nothing about the dispersion of the process. Changes in dispersion can signal that quality standards are not being met. So along with the *X* chart, we must have a range chart. An example of an *R* chart, is shown in figure. The central line is shown as *R* or the estimated average range of the universe. This can be computed from past experience. As in the *X* chart, there is a UCL and LCL for the *R* chart. The *R* chart gives the limits of the range that can be expected if the dispersion of the universe does not change. Both the *X and R* charts make use of the exception principle. The charts are simple enough to be plotted, only when control limits are exceeded is the service of the supervisor or engineer is required.

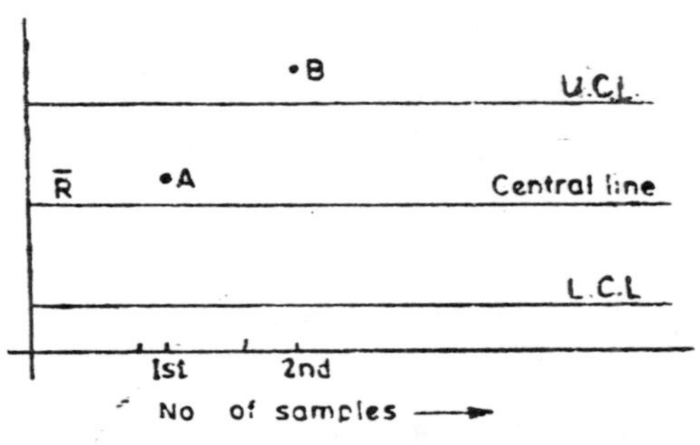

Fig.15.6 (a) Samples number 3 and 5 are out of control.

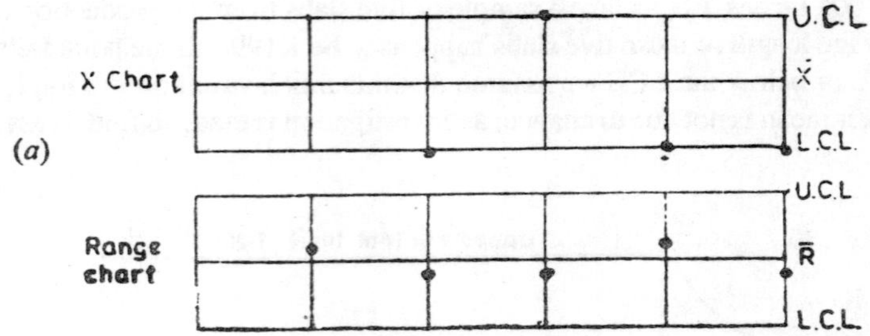

Fig. 15.6 (b) None of the points is out of control but there is cause for concern

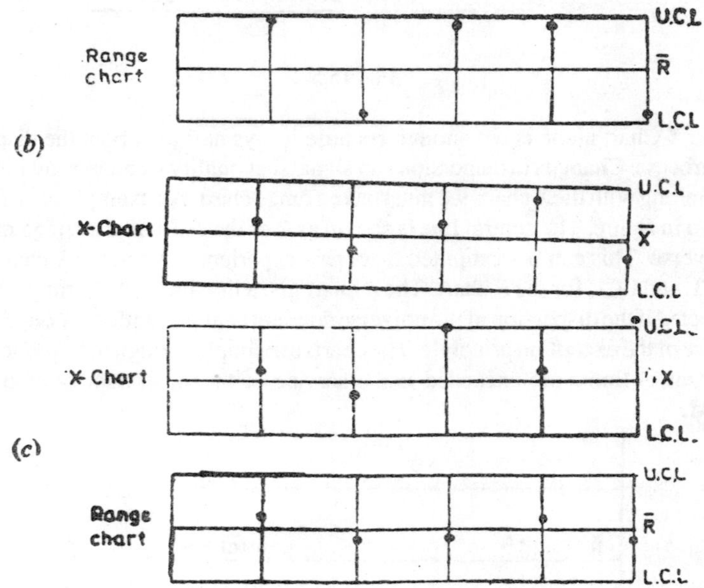

Fig. 15.6 (c) All Points are out of control

Fig. 15.6 (c) All points in the X charts are out of control. This could mean that the quality cannot be achieved or that improper production methods are being used.

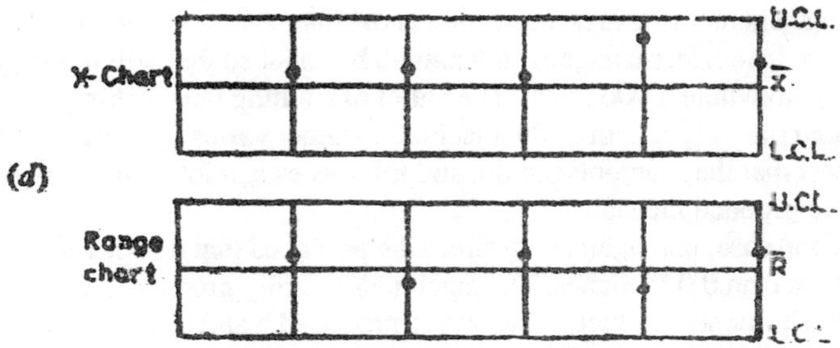

Fig. 15.6 (d)

Fig. All points out of control, but since they all are above the presumed mean of the universe, the actual mean of the universe has evidently shifted upward.

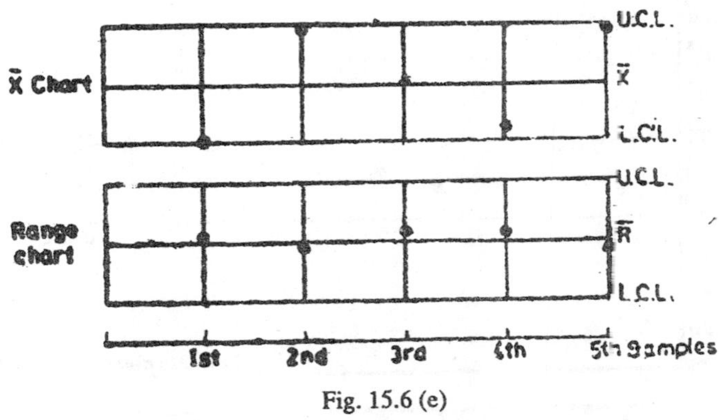

Fig. 15.6 (e)

We can see that there is a great variation within the samples. This indicates the strong possibility that similar items are used in each sample.

Economics and Quality Control

Control limits are determined by the machine's capabilities rather than by management. For example, is a machine can produce products with great precision, control limits would be narrow. If, however, the machine is not capable of precise production, control limits would be wider. The relationship between tolerance limits and control is an important one. These relationship can be classified into three general cases.

1. Tight tolerance limits and loose control limits.
2. Loose tolerance limits and tight control limits.
3. All other cases.

If the management desires more precision than the machine is capable of producing. For instance, management wants slab produced that will not vary from 1.2 inches by more than 0.0001 inch. Then after examining the machine's capabilities, it is found that 60 per cent of the machine's output varies by more than this. If this is the best that the machine can do, and tolerances cannot be revised, we will not be able to produce the slab.

The second case, management desires slab produced that do not vary from 1.2 inches by more than 0.025 inches. The machine generally produces slabs that vary by about 0.0020 inches. In fact, it has never produced a slab that varied from 1.2 inches by more than .01 inch. In this case, if control limits were determined by routine methods, we would try to keep production 'too perfect'.

The third samples mean exceed the upper control limit. There is no need for a tight control on output since we are well within the tolerance limits.

This case is illustrated in Figure.

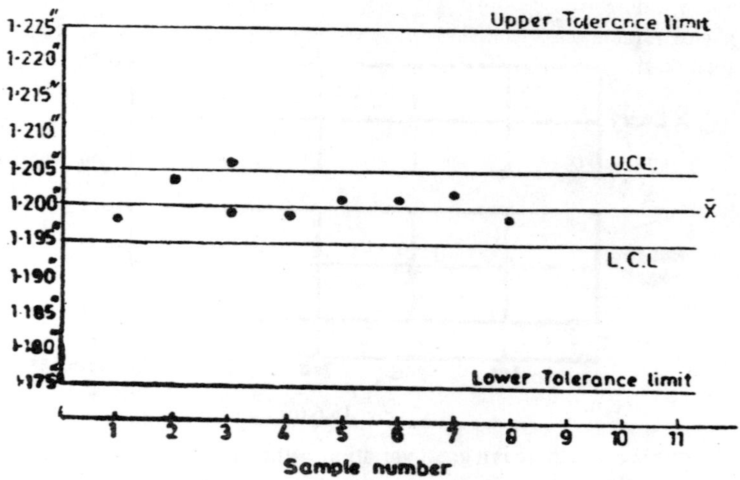

Fig. 15.7

CONTROL CHARTS

The techniques of Quality Control

A process may be such so that it is capable of producing output which is economically acceptable or acceptable after some rectification.

The Control charts, describe a pattern. The pattern of points of the control charts will lead to a proper interpretation of the working of the process. For nay process, it is possible and will be useful to prepare a list of causes which might give rise to particular pattern of points.

The control chart consists of a series of points taken at different intervals of time plotted in the sequence of time. These points could be gathered into a frequency distribution as shown in Fig.

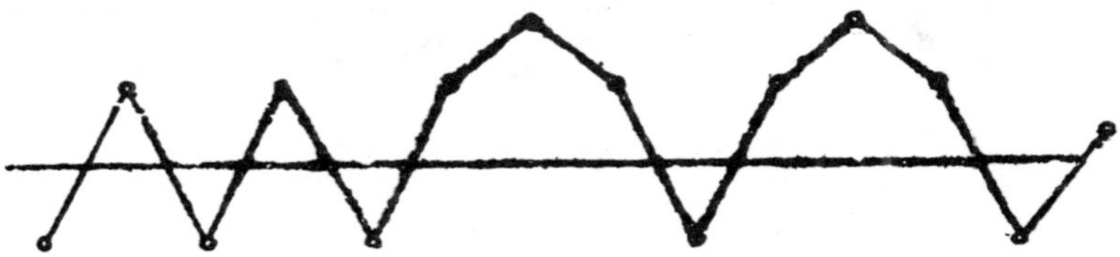

Fig. 15.8 (a)

In order to understand the behaviour of any process, it is essential to understand the pattern it describes on the chart. Ability to interpret the charts depend on the ability to distinguish between the natural and unnatural patterns of the processes as described on the chart.

It has been seen that when the process is in a state of control, the pattern of variation can be represented by a frequency distribution called the Normal Curve. If the same causes are at work, the same pattern of variation will repeat itself day-in and day-out and this situation constitutes a state of control as shown in Fig.

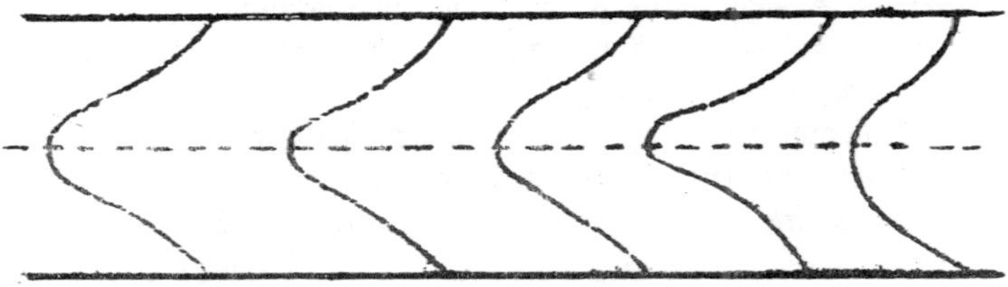

Fig. 15.8 (b)

The various type of distribution show that most of the points will be at the centre of the distribution. If the distribution is symmetrical it is natural to expect equal number of points on either side of the central line.

A central chart having a natural pattern of variation will have all the three characteristics mentioned above as shown in Fig. 15.8 (a), (b) and (c).

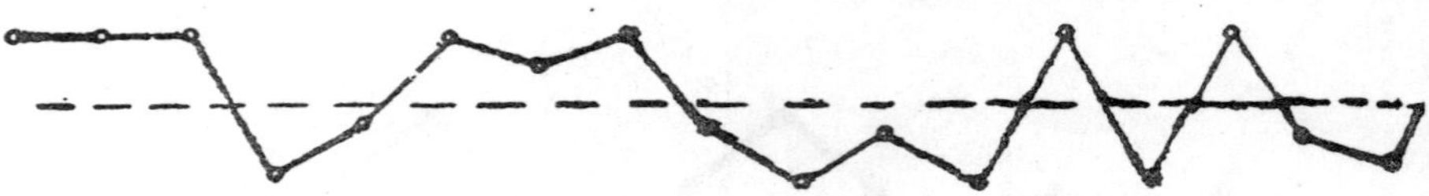

Fig. 15.8 (c)

A very important and difficult task in quality control is to determine how and at what stage in the production cycle to apply process control. Applying quality control where it yields little benefit is a waste of time, efforts and money. Quality control often involves the collection of datas, which may be absolutely vital for analysis and data collection should be geared to the amount of variation that occur. The more stable an operation, the less observations are required to provide adequate information about its parameters.

Statistical Control

Following is the procedure followed to keep the operation in the control limit. A number of samples of the product coming out of the process are taken over a period of time. Each sample consisting of a number of units taken at random. For each sample the average value X of all the measurement and the range *r* are calculated. The grand average X and the average range *R* are then found, and from there we calculate the control limit.

(a) Wide tolerances compared with process capability.
(b) Tolerances comparable to process capability.
(c) Tolerances are comparatively tight resulting in excessive scrap.

(*a*)

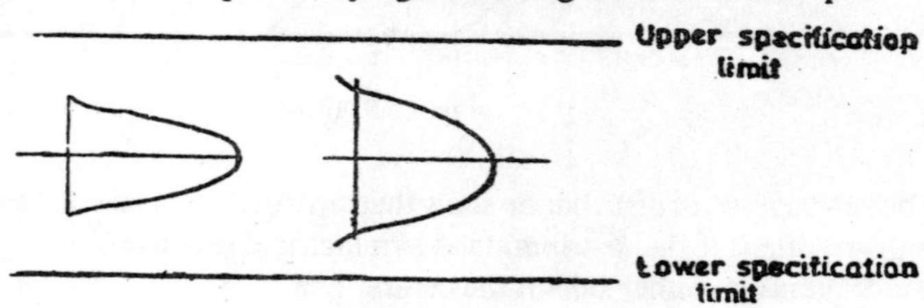

Fig. 15.9 (a)

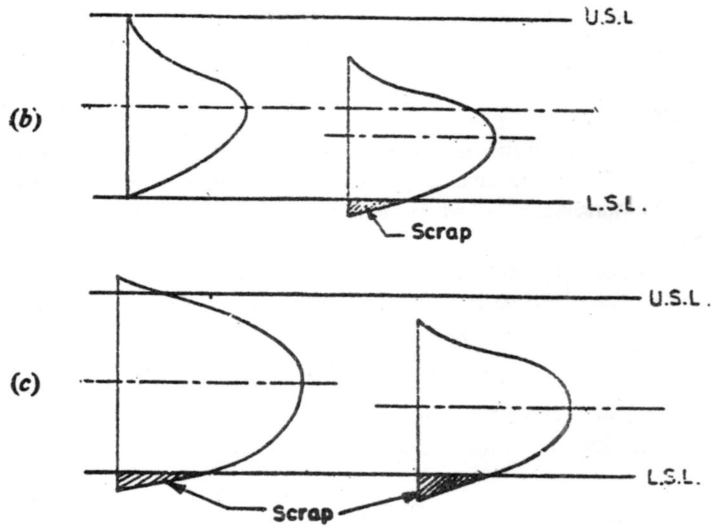

Fig. 15.9 (b)

The P-Chart

The fraction defective Chart is used to control the general quality level of the product and to find whether quality level of the product is due to chance alone. The basic difference between X and R chart is that former is based on control by attributes. The *P* chart, on the other hand, keeps a record of the percentage of defective. It can replace X and *R* chart if say, go-no-go-gauges are used without actual measurement of attributed being recorded.

$$UCL\ P = P' + 3sP'$$
$$LCL\ P = P' - 3sP'$$

where *P'* is the ratio of total number of defective to the total number inspected. **σ*P'*** is the standard deviation of the desirable distribution of fraction defective and from statistic theory.

$$\sigma P' = \sqrt{\frac{P'(1-P')}{N}}$$

N = Number of units inspected.

To start *P'* chart is estimated by *P'* which is the ratio of total number of defectives actually found in all samples to the total number inspected in all samples. Let us substitute *P'* by limits of *P* chart.

$$UCL\ P = \bar{p} + 3\sqrt{\frac{P'(1-P')}{N}}$$

$$LCL\ P = \bar{p} - 3\sqrt{\frac{P'(1-P')}{N}}$$

The C Chart

The *C* Chart is used for the control of the number of defects observed per unit.

The difference between *P* chart and *C* chart is that former takes into account the number of items found defective while the later records the number of defects in a given sample size.

In *C* Chart the control limits are based in Poisson distribution, which has often been found fit to describe distributions of defects.

$$UCL\ C = C' + 3\sqrt{C''}$$
$$LCL\ C = C' - 3\sqrt{C'}$$

C' is the desirable level of number of defects per unit and
$\sqrt{C'}$ is the standard deviation of the Poisson distribution.

Selecting amount $\overline{X}$, *R*, *p or C* Charts

Choosing a particular type of chart is to choose a balance between cost of collecting and analysing the type of data required to plot the chart against the usefulness.

The $\overline{X}$ and *R* chart, in which upper control limits are worked out.

$\overline{X}$ Chart

$$UCL\ \overline{X} = \overline{X} + A_2R$$
$$LCL\ \overline{X} = \overline{X} - A_2R$$

R Chart

$$UCL\ R = D_4R$$
$$CLR = D_3R$$

Terms A_2, D_1 and D_3 depend on the Number of items per sample.

As long as the X and R values for each sample are within the control limits the process is considered to be in statistical control. Soon after drawing the charts, it is necessary to determine whether the process is in statistical control. If it is not, there must be a cause that throws process out of control. Reasons for the process being out of control may be faulty tools, change in properties of materials in the present consignment, breakdown of the lubrication system, faults in speed mechanism etc. Reaching the cause may be difficult if it is subject to the combined effect of several external causes. If the process is found to be statistical control, a comparison between the required specifications and the process capability may be carried out to determine whether two are compatible. There are three possible alternatives.

(i) Re-evaluate the specification to find tolerances really necessary for effective performance or could they be relaxed.

(ii) If the relaxation of the specification is not acceptable, choose accurate process.

(iii) If the previous alternative are out of questions a 100 percent inspection must be undertaken to sort out the defective products.

Example

S. No.	Date		(A) Number of pieces	(B) Number of defectives joined	Fraction defective p = B/A
1.	Ist	January	400	30	0.075
2.	2nd	January	400	25	0.0625
3.	3rd	January	400	30	0.075
4.	4th	January	400	35	0.0875
5.	5th	January	400	40	0.10
6.	6th	January	400	45	0.112
7.	7th	January	400	35	0.0875
8.	8th	January	400	35	0.112
9.	9th	January	400	35	0.0875
10.	10th	January	400	40	0.10
Total	10 Days		4000	360	

Upper control limit (U.C.L.) $= \bar{p} + 3\sqrt{\frac{\bar{p}\,(1-P')}{n}}$

Lower control limit (L.C.L.) $= \bar{p} - 3\sqrt{\frac{\bar{p}\,(1-\bar{p})}{n}}$

$$\bar{p} = \frac{\text{Total number of defectives}}{\text{Total number inspected}}$$

$$\bar{p} = \frac{360}{4000} = 0.09$$

n = Number of pieces inspected on each day = 400

$$\text{U.C.L.} = \bar{p} + 3\sqrt{\frac{\bar{p}\,(1-\bar{p})}{n}}$$

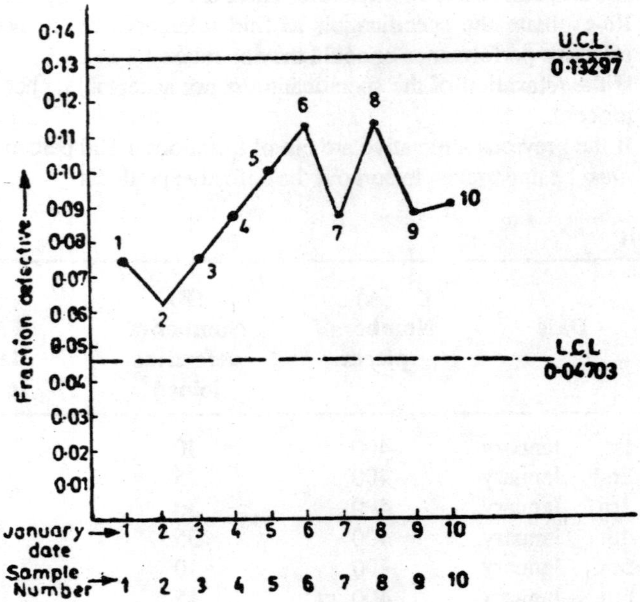

Fig. 15.9 (c)

Let us first and find out the value of

$$= \sqrt{\frac{\overline{p}\,(1-\overline{p})}{n}}$$

$$= \sqrt{\frac{0.09\,(1-0.9)}{400}}$$

$$= \sqrt{\frac{0.09 \times 0.91}{400}}$$

$$= \frac{1}{20} \times \sqrt{0.0819}$$

$$= 3\sqrt{\frac{\overline{p}\,(1-\overline{p})}{n}} = \frac{3}{20} \times \sqrt{0.0819}$$

$$= 0.2865 \times \frac{3}{20}$$

Thus U.C.L. $= 0.09 + 0.04297$

$$= 0.13297$$

$$\text{L.C.L.} = 0.09 - 0.04297$$

$$= 0.04703$$

Let us draw U.C.L. and L.C. L on the graph paper as per Fig. 15.9 (c)

Quality Control and Value

The challenge to the success of quality control in all its implications is to make "quality" synonymous with "value". It requires an approach that carefully bridges the gap between customer satisfaction and business economics. Many industrial mangers have started realising that quality control can be valuable asset. Quality control, should be capable of causing positive management action and should be dedicated to the theory of prevention, and should be dedicated to the theory of prevention, and should be dedicated to the theory of prevention, and should be designed not only for profit but also for customer satisfaction. The essential ingredient that must permeate the entire quality control activity is excellence in management. If quality control is to be capable of constructive involvement in management problems, it must earn respect for its own ability to manage.

We know that industrial worker is not intimately aware of how his skill interacts with others, he can never be sure that he is fulfilling his responsibility. To be knowledgeable is a necessary and important starting point. The second element is the "strength of your own convictions." It means much more: being action-oriented, always taking a clear, timely, and decisive position and giving employees positive support and displaying a willingness to commit oneself to action. The third element of excellence in management is a demand for performance. In quality control, enforcement must be a way of life, both within the quality control organization itself and in those other areas where it is responsible for ensuring control. Knowledge, strength, and a demand for performance therefore are the keys to the initial establishment of excellence in management.

Planning for Quality

Quality planning is the management portion of the total quality control effort, responsible for formulating the policies, procedures, techniques and detailed plans necessary to achieve all quality control objectives. There are three ways by which total quality costs can be reduced to a minimum by the quality control organization; these are best envisaged as the three basic objectives of quality planning.

(i) to make maximum use of available quality control effort.

(ii) to exert maximum influence on the planning of others in an all-out effort to make the control of quality.

(iii) to review the results of the total efforts periodically and present them to management in such a way that improvements can be forthcoming.

The evidence of the work of quality planning can be found in inspection plans, in documentation systems, in quality status reports an din procedures for the control of quality. The attitude of other planning groups with respect to the importance of quality control is also very important. A planned inspection is essentially a trade-off between protecting from errors and risking failure to find errors. Once the parameters to be inspected have been defined, the step in planning is to determine where to perform the inspections. From a manufacturing viewpoint, inspections should be performed at the earliest possible point in the progress. The last step in planning is to determine how much inspection to perform. Certain critical parameters such as material condition for aircraft structural parts will always require 100 percent inspection and verification. Planning should be specifically aimed at using today's knowledge to prevent, or at least to reduce, the production of scrap and rework. An equally important ingredient for each inspection plan is the documentation of results.

This device-known as a quality logbook. A log-book is the accumulation into one large package of specific pertinent data combined with information on the status of supplementary data physically field elsewhere. The use of log-books, has simplified the overall quality planning effort and has improved inspector's ability to control total equipment status on a current basis. Without log-books as they have been developed, the task would be far more cumbersome and costly, and timeliness would be almost impossible. Quality planning must develop a close working relationship with broadest possible spectrum of company activity. The magnitude and importance of the total quality control effort make cooperation between quality planning and other company planning groups mandatory. Quality planning must be dedicated to the reduction of paper-work yet at the same time be trained to take each directive seriously. Quality planning, therefore, provides the principal liaison with the customer and has the first opportunity as well as the obligation to develop good customer relations.

The principal objective of quality planning is to create and to develop business and management systems designed to make the quality control function a respected, useful and effective area of management. This objective is accomplished through inspection plans, training, data systems, manual of operations, introducing new techniques, problem-prevention, liaison with associates and customers, and sound administration of the purely business aspects of quality control.

Zero Defects

Zero defects performance have attracted much credit and considerable controversy to the quality control profession in recent years. Zero defects is a motivation program having its concept of working which is beneficial to groups but particularly to the individual. Originating in the aerospace industry during 1961-62, it grew out of the many perplexing problems facing the aerospace industry in those days. ZD holds that people are conditioned throughout their lives to accept the fact that they are not perfect and will, therefore, make mistakes. By the time they begin working in industry this belief has become firmly rooted and finds its normal expression in the statement: "People are human and thus make mistakes. Nothing can ever be perfect so long as people take part in it." People make individual to establish a personal goal of superior performance and to strive conscientiously for personal excellence in everything he does. The crux of the challenge is to achieve perfect results by preventing and eliminating defects.

Errors are measures of the importance a man places on things; he takes better care of certain things than he does of there. In short, man has developed a dual attitude. In some things he is willing to accept errors; in other he is not. Mistakes have two causes : lack of knowledge and lack of attention. Knowledge can be measured, and shortcomings corrected, through established methods. Lack of attention is an attitude problem; it must be corrected by the man himself—who must take a conscious effort to do things right the first time. The most significant feature of zero defects, is the opportunity if affords every employee—from factory floor and office upto top management—to participate in the program and to develop self-improvement.

The materials manager and his buyers are catalysts in zero defects programmes. They are administered by the quality control department and applied to both purchased and manufactured items. The materials department is responsible for getting the message through the company's suppliers, and it works with quality control in arranging seminars and other programs designed to make suppler personnel conscious of the need for zero defects. The end result may not literally be less defects but at least a higher quality level than prevailed before the zero defects programme was begun.

Quality Certification

When buyer and seller agree on quality levels, it is sometimes possible to eliminate a great deal of extra inspection with quality certification. A supplier whose quality control procedure meet the buyer's standards then supplier can simply ship the material, which gets little or no incoming inspection by the buyer.

With quality certification, much duplicate inspection is avoided, since for most shipments the buyer's receiving inspection can be quite superficial. Companies with quality certification programs are careful, however to limit their use to suppliers of proved reliability. Most other organisations settle either for a quality certification programme or conventional receiving inspection.

Chapter 16

MATERIALS COMMUNICATIONS SYSTEM

Business Reports

An effective materials communication system can assist materials department by directing its attention to exceptions that occur in the execution of its responsibilities and by providing an objective base for improved performance. While the increasing complexity of business tends to make purchasing personnel "fire fighters", an efficient communication system enables them to be orderly by supplying them with: organised information; Ready reference nformation; Relief from clerical details, management by exception; Guide lines for improved performance. We all know that one of the significant problem facing business today is the communication. The need arises in the complexities of large and highly specialised business firms. Communication provide the unifying force to coordinate the inter-departmental efforts. With the introduction of Electronic Data Processing equipment more facts and figures are available to all departments, greater emphasis has been focussed on the means of presenting material in a manner that will be most productive to the departments and the firm. Business reports are a basic means of communication within a firm. Reports are vertical communication system; move from a lower level to a higher level of management and constitute a one way flow of information, however an effective communication system demands two way communication. The top management has become more cognisant of the need of two way communication in the enterprise and is using such devices as written policy statements, news letters, and staff meetings to communicate downward. All of these can be of value in overcoming the problem of communication, both upward and downward, in a company. Let us study upward communication system through reports from materials department. The various materials reports can be classified as : Interdepartmental reports; which are designed to inform the head of the department about departmental matters; directed to higher levels of management.

Object of Reports

The purpose of various management reports is: to provide information; assisting in evaluation, and aiding self analysis.

To Provide Information: A report is an instrument of managerial control which provides the information on which an executive can base a decision or judge an activity. In complex business organisation the senior executives receive a condensed version of the significant factors affecting the decision and based on this information take sound decisions. Since oral discussions may not be complete and planned therefore written reports are essential for this purpose, and good reports are a mark of the well-run materials department. in performing an information function, management reports interpret the actions, motives and plans of the purchasing department. An important outcome of this information flow is the development of cooperation through mutual understanding of the operations of the departments.

Assisting In Evaluation: The other important reason for submitting reports to management is that they enable management to evaluate the performance of the department. By the submission of reports a materials manager can inform and educate the management concern the activities of his department. A report that shows the contribution of materials department to company profits will do much to gain management recognition of the purchasing function.

Aiding Self Analysis: The preparation of various reports by the department requires collection of data, analysis and interpretation of data which helps the materials manager to uncover methods and procedures that need improvement. As a result the overall efficiency of the materials department can be enhanced.

Need of Periodic Reports: The need for reports varies from firm to firm but following are some of the key factors indicatives of periodic reports : Analysis of general business conditions and their probable effects on the company; Performance evaluation of materials department including an evaluation of training and improvement of techniques for personnel, Vendor reports, including analysis of their supply performance, delivery performance, price reductions and so forth. Interdepartment relations directed toward profit improvement including value analysis quality improvement and quality circles programmes.

The significant of periodic reports is to reveal the trend of performance of the department over a substantial period of time. The periodic reports help the management to evaluate the present performance of the department. The first step in the preparation of periodic reports is the gathering of the data to be used in the report. The data for the periodic reports will be available from the daily departmental records. A good periodic report will cover: Price performance; Administrative performance; Inventory performance and Procurement performance. In each of these four phases of materials management the data from departmental records is compiled.

Price Performance Covers: Average unit price of the product purchased; Cash discounts earned and cash discounts lost; Saving realised from quantity discounts taken; Saving realised as a result of cost analysis, Value analysis, system analysis, cost of transportation per rupee spent.

Administrative Performance: Departmental operating cost; Ratio of total department cost to value of purchases; number of purchase orders issued; Average cost per purchase order; Average man-hours per order; Number of requisitions processed; Number of unprocessed requisitions on hand; Number of personnel in department; Amount of telephone bills.

Inventory Performance. Rupee value of inventory; Ratio of inventory to sales; Rupee value of purchases received during period ; Ratio of purchases to sales.

Procurement Performance. Number of production shutdowns due to shortage of materials and supplies; Number of out of stock occurrences; Number of emergency purchases made; Number of rejections; quantity and value of scrap and surplus goods sold; Reports on strikes at vendors' plants; Reports on material substitution and import substitution.

The above refers to some of the reports but some companies will have certain peculiarities that lead them to want certain information, and the periodic report should be designed to conform to such management requirement.

Format of Reports

The main objective of format should be to secure the initial attention of the recipient and thereafter to hold executive's interest until he has completed reading the report. A good report should have the following elements.

(i) Titles
(ii) Summaries
(iii) Text
(iv) Recommendations
(v) Appendix
(vi) Illustrations

Titles. For an effective communication of reports it is a usual practice to begin clear and descriptive title that may immediately tell the reader whether or not he is interested in the report. A long title is likely to discourage a prospective reader. The readers normally want to know who prepared the report; hence the name of the reporter should appear in connection with the title.

Summaries. The first part of the report should be a summary. This is an important, but often neglected, part of the report. The summary should contain all the important point of the report in highly condensed form.

Text. Following the summary should come the mainbody or text of the report. This is the part of the report in which the writer's ability, originality and conscientiousness will show up.

Recommendations. The writer's recommendation should appear at the end of the body of the report if they have not been made a part of the summary. A report should not be used as a device for shifting responsibility.

Appendix. Following the body of the report should come the exhibits and appendixes needed to support the statements in the report.

Illustrative Techniques. Illustrative techniques help the reader to grasp the significant changes and trends without executives having analysed the detailed figures. It has been observed that very often the essential points of the report can be summarized in one or two diagrams. The various illustrative techniques are: Picture diagram; Pie diagrams; Bar charts; Line diagrams; Graphs; Maps; Flow charts; PERT diagrams etc.

Some of these techniques have been discussed in other chapters and a few of them are mentioned below:

Picture diagrams: The pictures are generally used to portray changes in quantity by altering their relative sizes or numbers.

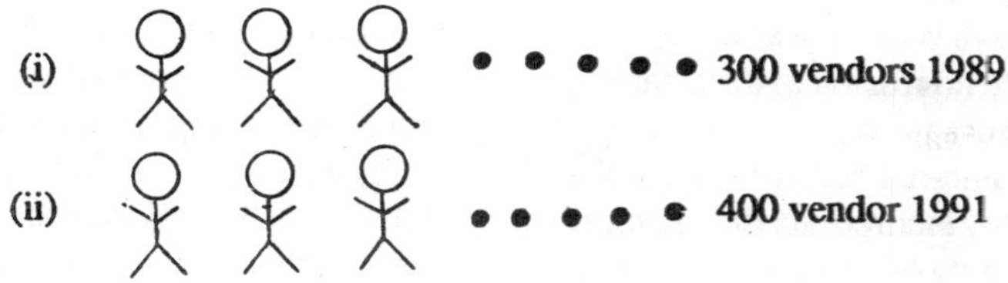

Figure above illustrates the use of a change in number of vendors during two alternative years.

Pie Diagram: Pie diagram are used to express a whole and the sum to its parts. The Pie diagram bellow explain the variance expenditure/cost associated with Production, Maintenance; Administration, Materials, Selling and R & D etc. showing distribution of various Expenditure costs to the total cost/expenditure.

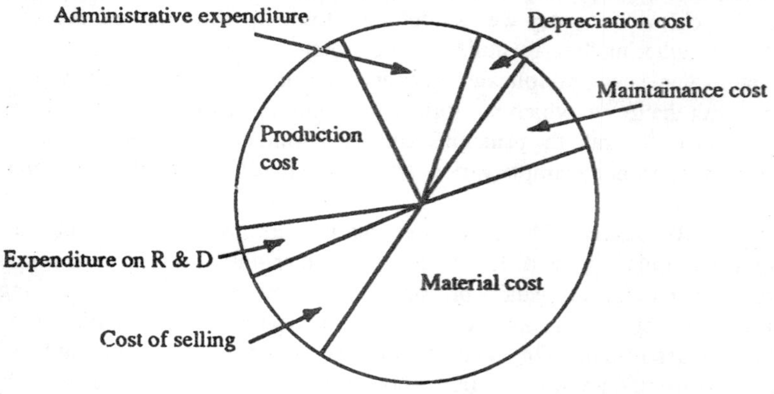

Bar Charts. It is an effective way to compare quantities. The length of bar represents the quantity and variation in length provide instant comparisons.

Line Diagram. It represents data that vary over a substantial period of time. The "Quantity" and "Time" parameters are represented on vertical and horizontal axes respectively. Line diagrams are useful when an attempt is made to project the future on the basis of the past.

Maps. Maps are used when the data to be presented follow some geographic division. When data appear on a map, the visual effect is instant and clear.

Flow Diagram. A flow diagram can be used to indicate a sequence of operations or series of work procedures.

The illustrative techniques can add clarity and vividness to any report.

Materials Management Forms

Forms are designed to help the materials management department to function efficiently. It expedites the communication within the department with other associated with the department. Forms are the tools of the materials management department and particularly the purchasing department. The problems of the materials executive is to have as many forms as will be used effectively and not so many as to create confusion and red tape. The number of forms required depends in the size of the organisation the materials management system employed and the accounting and internal control methods in effect. Regardless of forms use, it is important that they incorporate the principles of good design such as: Forms should facilitate the entering of data required; forms should impress the executives who use them; forms should try to reduce the possibility of errors in entry of data; Forms should be economical to reproduce; Forms should help to centralise the data on which decisions are to be made. Forms should also be designed with adequate and properly placed instructions for filling it out. A good form will create a favourable mental attitude on the part of the executives who must use it. After forms are filled out. It is submitted to executives as the basis for business action. The actual use of a sample form is a useful step in designing a form that will serve its intended purpose. To achieve economy we can combine forms to eliminate unnecessary duplication in gathering data, by utilising standard-size dimensions of paper stock, by eliminating unnecessary duplicate copies and by using paper stock of a durability consistent with the use to which the form will be put. Following are some of the forms selected to illustrate the principles and are definitely not meant to illustrate the ideal form but rather a simple variety and type that will frequently be encountered.

Purchase Requisition. The requisition usually bears the prominent heading or title "Purchase requisition" to differentiate it from other similar forms or the actual purchase order. The form is usually prepared in duplicate, the original copy going to the purchasing department, and the carbon copy being retained for the files of the requisitioning department. On many companies, two basic types of purchase requisition are used. One of these, frequently called a "Travelling requisition" is used for inventory items that are ordered repetitively and was mentioned previously as constituting the simplest step toward automation. The second which is used for all other requirements, might he called a "Descriptive requisition". As stated earlier, the travelling requisition includes a complete description of the item to he ordered, a listing of the preselected vendors, a space to record the purchase order number, date ordered and the vendor selected. The quantity to be ordered may be specified by the stores department or may be determined by the purchasing department in accordance with Economic order Quantity procedures. The buyer selects the vendor to be used and prices to be paid. After the purchase order has been prepared, the travelling requisition is returned to the person originating it.

Request for Quotation: This form is used when a potential supplier is asked to furnish prices and terms on a contemplated purchase. To make sure that it will not be mistaken for an order; it bears very clearly across its face an imprint to that effect. The form ordinarily specifies a date by which the bid must be received in order to be considered. Many organisation permit a prospective supplier to quote on the basis of alterations or substitutions in the original specification, provided that such changes are clearly denoted and accompanied by complete specifications.

Purchase Order. A purchase order is the commitment by a buyer to pay for goods ordered and the seller's authority to charge the buyer for them. It becomes a legal contract if it is submitted in acceptance of formal quotation or offer. It becomes such a contract in other cases when it is accepted by the seller.

Follow Up Forms. It is an important responsibility of the purchasing department to obtain the material at the time required. This makes it essential to establish a follow up procedure that can be used effectively by staff members.

Receiving Forms. This form is dated to show when the shipment was received. It contains information for the name of the vendor and mode of transport or carrier; who made the delivery. The form contains information for noting the amount paid, the carrier if shipment was not prepaid.

Rejection Forms. Many Companies require that all material received be forwarded to the receiving inspection department. This department makes a detailed inspection of the materials against the specifications on the order. If the material does not meet the specifications it is rejected or must be modified. The report suggest the return and replacement of the material or it may state that the material is usable but with certain discrepancies.

Public Relations and Materials Management

The importance of public relation in a large organisation like DGS & D can not be over emphasized. In recognition of the need to establish public relations on a proper tooling for handling complaints for supplier on centralized basis, the public relation department are being set up.

In addition to internal relationships, the purchasing department maintains important relationship outside the firm. Much of a firm's reputation for integrity and fair play comes from the manner in which its purchasing department deals with vendors. Vendors are capable of rendering valuable financial assistance, technical aid, and service to their customers. Whether a buying company receives this help or not depends in large measure on how capably it exercises its purchasing function. The company that fails to capitalise on these attainable vendor benefits is losing money because of poor purchasing practices. If a vendor is to render the most effective help to customers, he must understand the materials requirements of his customers. He must understand the purpose for which his materials is used. He must understand the buyer's manufacturing processes in order to offer suggestions that may lead to improved materials specification or to more economical substitutions.

As it applies to the buyers, public relations may be described as the sum total of all the efforts of the purchasing executive and his subordinates in working and communicating with the various publics with whom the purchasing department comes into contact. In general it may be said that unless a buyer has empathy he is unlikely to have good public relations. Unless one can put himself in another's position and look at a situation from another's point of view his public relations can not be good because it will not be sincere. Public relations is good morals and good manners. Good morals are the relations of a company and its executives toward its employers, its customers, its competitors, its owners and the general public. Good manners mean the intelligent presentation of these morals in the written or spoken word, as well as in everyday actions.

Public relations is the continuing process by which management endeavors to obtain the good will and understanding of its customers, its employees, and the public at large, inwardly through self analysis and outwardly through all means of expression.

Internal Public Relations: A successful material management, operation depends heavily on the soundness of its internal relations. Rapport with other functional areas with in the company determines to a large extent whether purchasing external relations will be satisfactory. Understanding the inter relationships between departments is essential to success. The interdepartmental problems that inevitably arise can be overcome much more early if a co-operative attitude exists. Problems of specifications, quality levels, delivery times, and vendor qualifications can be much more easily dealt with if materials department exhibit an awareness of the fact that there may be more than our solution to a problem. A friendly atmosphere can be promoted by certain techniques available to all employes. These may range from formal reports to company success stories, to bulletin, to company boards announcements. Every organisation has its informal communication network, and employing it is an effective way of achieving good public relations. The informal communications system can be used to gain useful information for the purchasing department from with in the company.

External Public Relations. Sound external relations are built on a foundation of internal acceptance of purchasing organisation. A purchasing executive can not convey to external public an image of effectiveness, co-operativeness, and responsibility if its internal position is weak. Thus good external relations are dependent on good internal relations. This good external relations are dependent on good internal relations and the results of co-operation are expanded through good relations between the purchasing department and its vendors. Some of the important public relations tool that has come into service in recent years is vendor analyses, which when combined with an informative report to the vendor are extremely helpful in advising him how he rates in the areas of service and delivery. Another important means available to the purchase executive is visiting vendor's plants. If visit is done with proper preparation and by mutual agreement, good public relations will result.

Chapter 17

INVENTORY MANAGEMENT

Introduction

The pressure for operating capital has made business an increasingly aware of inventory as a form of earning investment. Why are we always out of stock? A complaint from a large numbers of businessmen faced with the dilemmas and frustrations of attempting simultaneously to maintain stable operations, provide customers with adequate service, and keep investment in stocks and equipment at reasonable levels. In order to get at the answer to this question as a basis for taking action, it is necessary to step back and ask some rather different kinds of questions: Why do we have inventories? What affects the inventory balances we maintain? How do these effects take place? From these questions a picture of the inventory problems can be built up which shows the influence on inventories and cost of various alternative decisions which the management may ultimately want to consider.. The basic problem of inventory policy is to strike a balance between operating savings and costs of capital requirements associated with larger stocks. Striking this balance is easier to say than to do.

What Is Inventory

Inventory constitute one of the most important elements of any system dealing with the supply, manufacture and distribution of goods and services. The concept of inventory control is very old but it came in light when Harris F.W. published his work on classical order size model. This work was extended by Raymond F.E. (1931) and Wilson R.M. (1934). But only after the second world war with the development of operational research and computer technology that the theoretical concepts got a practical application. The basic purpose of inventory holding stocks in a material flow system is to decouple successive stages of system. Following are important purpose of inventory:

(i) Existence of time lags between manufacturing, and transport operations.
(ii) The need to schedule various stages of the system independently.
(iii) The need to meet the fluctuation in demand and production rates.
(iv) The need to maintain control over the quality of the finished product.
(v) The need to exercise influence over changes of material prices particularly basic raw materials.

All the above factors involve costs. The inventory control mainly concerned with making optimum decision with respect to the variables which are subject to control. Inventory control is a multi-item, and multi-stage in nature. *Inventory is an idle resource which is useable and have value. The idle resource may be men, money, materials, plant acquisition*. The manpower, capital and plant acquisition problems are essentially inventory control problems.

The scientific inventory management helps the purchase department to determine when to buy and how much to buy. The problem before the management is to balance the following opposing costs.

S. No.	Cost to have Inventory	Cost not to have Inventory
1.	Return on Investment	Stock out costs
2.	Storage cost	(Demand × Profitability × Future)
3.	Handling cost (Labour and Industry)	Loss of customers.
4.	Handling Equipment	Down time cost.
5.	Obsolescence	Idle Labour and idle Production.
6.	Spoilage and Shelf life	Capacity and other cost.

The scientific control can also be defined as a system of internal check to control. We know that inventory tie up a sizable part of working capital and also cost a good deal to carry them. Money resources are scarce and efforts should be directed to conserve it by all means. Inventory is money but is it not at all like money in the bank but it is the money in which the we pay interest instead of earning interest. Arriving at a level between too much and too little stock is a real challenge to the management. The uncontrolled inventories are dangerous and at times it is called as grave year of business.

The inventory control exist in some form in every plant. the system in a particular company may be formal or informal, cheap or expensive. In one case control may depend upon the efforts of a large control staff while in another the responsibility may rest with the plant manager and the foreman. Even systems used in similar plants, differ in outward appearance at least. Production planning coordinates the production department with other department of the business. Production control promotes effective shop operation through its control of activities within the production department itself.

Inventory control determines the levels of composition of inventories of parts, materials and products which will protect most effectively the production, sales, and financial requirements of the business. A system of production planning and control is not and end in itself. It can only be justified because it:

(1) Provides the means for effective coordination of the Production department with other departments of the business; and

(2) Promotes effective shop operation through its control of activities within the production department itself.

In any given company a good system of planning will strike the best balance possible between the required amount of control and the overhead cost entailed in achieving it. If tight control cost no more than loose control management would of course try to attain the maximum control possible in a particular situation. This is not the case. The tighter the control a system produces, the more overheads is required to create it.

Every businessman must have faced the problem of either being out of stock or a large amount of money tied up in the form of inventories. Inventory is an evil which cannot be eliminated. On the other hand large level of inventories hamper the growth of the company. Inventory control is to determine the optimum level o inventory which is essential to carry out the various operations of the organisation efficiently and effectively.

Inventory control is essential for effective plant operations. The inventory carrying charges from 12% to 22% of inventory value with the average near 18%. A company with restricted working capital is always in a dangerous position and there is no easier way to dissipate working capital than to build up excessive inventory.

Definition of inventory

(1) Inventory is wider sense is defined as any idle resource of an enterprise. It is commonly used to indicate materials—raw, in process, finished, packaging, spares and others—stocked in order to meet an expected demand or distribution in the future. Even though inventory of materials is an idle resource in the sense it is not meant for immediate use, it is almost a necessity to maintain some inventories for the smooth functioning of an organisation.

(2). Inventory is made of all those items ready for sale or of items which keep the process running.

Why inventories are essential

In some circles inventories are thought of as a sign of wealth, even excess inventories in relation to the magnitude of production and distribution function are considered advantageous. On the other hand, the wise businessmen place more emphasis on having working capital in the form of cash and securities. In recent years a greater emphasis has been placed on having the means of purchasing materials than having the materials themselves. Excessive inventories have been the death of many a business and very high inventory levels have tipped the scale in our economy.

The finished product after packaging are first stored and sent to the market as the need arises or orders are received. Also the raw materials needed for the finished product cannot be directly fed to the production department from the market. These have to be stored first after procurement. These things put together give an idea of storing these items. This process of storing is called inventory.

Necessity and Advantages of Inventory Control

There are various reasons why organisations should maintain inventories of goods. The fundamental reason for doing so is that it is either physically impossible or e economically unsound to have goods arrive in a given system precisely when demands for them arises. Without inventories customers would have to wait until their orders were filled from a source or were manufactured. In general, however, customers will not or cannot be allowed to wait for long periods of time. For this reason alone the carrying of inventories is necessary for almost all organisation that supply physical goods to customers.

There are, nevertheless, other reasons for holding inventories. For example, the price of some raw materials used by manufacturers may exhibit considerable seasonal fluctuations. When the price is low, it is profitable for him to procure a sufficient quantity of it to last through the high price seasons and to keep it in inventory to be used as need in production. Another reason for maintaining inventories, a reason particularly important to retail establishments, is that sales and profits can be increased it one has an inventory of goods to display to customer. Furthermore to even out the work loads on the shops in the event of fluctuation loads and a protective buffer against transportation delays and production rate changes.

Advantages

(i) Introduction of a proper inventory control system helps in keeping the investment in the inventories as low as feasible.

(ii) Ensures availability of material by providing adequate protection against uncertainties of supplies and consumption of materials.

(iii) Allcws full advantage of economies of bulk purchases and transportation.

(iv) Reduces changes of going out of stock.

(v) Leads to reduction in inventory levels.

(vi) Releases more of capital for other operations.

(vii) Increases profitability of an organisation.

(viii) Adequate customer service.

(ix) Advantage of price discounts by bulk purchasing.

(x) Providing flexibility to allow changes in production lines due to changes in demands or any other reason; and

(xi) Even out the work loads on the shops in the face fluctuation demands.

Evils of Excess Inventory

- ✯ Essential though they are, inventories also mean lock up capital of an inventories which could be invested in more profitable operations.
- ✯ Excess inventory adds to the cost of carrying the inventory more store

space, equipment and personnel, insurances, taxes, pilferage etc.

★ Excess inventory invites risk of deterioration and obsolescence.
★ Changes in the prices of inventory materials sometime go unfavorable.
★ Maintenance of cost money.

Control Aspects of Inventory

A company which finds that different portions of its inventory present different problems will have three general methods of control to choose from. These are:

★ Elimination of certain inventories
★ Semi automatic routines.
★ Periodic review.

Elimination of Inventories

At first glance, elimination inventory may seem a strange form possible. It is more feasible to eliminate the inventories entirely if little advance information is available on exact specifications and quantities. Steel plate is one item required in the manufacture of every unit, if the firm did carry inventory this would be one material it would have to stock, however where one customer specifies I" plate, another calls for 1.5". In the view of these facts the company does not order steel plates until the actual specifications for each order are at hand. This solution is possible because the manufacturing interval is very long and vendors can provide the required plate in a reasonable period.

Semi-automatic routines

The semi-automatic types of control are usually variations of the maximum minimum system. They are most applicable for standard items with fairly stable prices and steady usage. For materials which do not possess these characteristics, maximum-minimum control offers few advantages. This system is usually established by considering the minimum balance desirable, the re-order point, the standard order quantity, and the maximum allowable the minimum balance is the point below which the minimum represents is determined by the rate at which an item is used, its size and cost its size and cost its similar factors, importance in the process, whether substitutes are available and by Ideally, a new shipment should arrive just as stock reaches this minimum. Slight variation in usage or delivery intervals will prevent such exact operation in practice. The order point is located somewhere above the minimum. Its exact location will depend upon the delivery or manufacturing intervals required after an order is placed and upon the usage rate of a particular item. When the available balances reaches the order point, a clerk will note this fact and place an order. The standard order quantity is that amount of material which will be requisitioned each time available balances drop to the order point. This quantity is determined by considering such things as vendors' discounts, economic lot sizes, storage and handling costs, order processing costs, the danger of obsolescence and desired rates of turnover. The maximum minimum type of systems offer semi-automatic should be emphasized because it is the key to successful operation of the system. The precise amounts established as minimum order points and adhering to them, give the system an appearance of exactness and automaticity which it does not always possess.

Periodic Review

The third type of inventory control might be called 'periodic review' for want of a better term. All the factors considered under the maximum-minimum system are applicable here. But definite points are established in advance. The interval will be shortest where:-

★ Price of usage fluctuates widely.
★ cost in high.
★ shortages are apt to be critical.
★ there is considerable risk of obsolescence.
★ Materials are bulky.
★ delivery or manufacturing cycles are long.

These three methods of control are not mutually exclusive. One company may use any or all the them to control different categories of inventory. Some commodities, such as special motors,may not be ordered until their use and specifications can be established exactly.

The inventory control system is a composite of many routine operations.

Types of Inventory

1. Transaction inventory
2. Speculative inventory
3. Precautionary inventory

(1) **Transaction inventory.** It is formed basically of those items which are basically needed for transaction for example transaction of finished saleable products or transaction of raw materials.

(a) *Delinking Production with purchasing Department* is one of the function of this for example receipt of raw material is stored in the form of inventory and whenever production department needs raw material it put indent to inventory organisation rather than to purchase department.

(b) *Delinking production with sales organisation.* Similarly it delinks sales and production departments.

(2) Speculative Inventory. It is basically kept as a measure of speculation of increase in the price of raw material or increase the sale price of finished goods. It is generally resorted to before the budget proposals.

(3) Precautionary Inventory. The machines are to be kept running. There may be breakdown of machines at any time due to damage of any part due to wear and tear. At that time it cannot be purchased immediately. Therefore,such items which are essential to keep the process running are to be stored like machine parts, tools, etc. It is also called maintenance repair and operation inventory.

Classification of Inventory

There are another way of classifying various types of industrial inventories such as:

(1) Production Inventories. Raw materials parts, and components which go into the manufacturing process of the company products.

(2) M.R.O. Inventories. Maintenance, Repair and Operating supplies which are consumed in the production process but which do not form a part of the product (often known as consumables).

(3) In-process Inventories. Semi-finished products at various stages in the production operation.

(4). Finished goods Inventories. Completed products ready for shipment.

Inventory Control Systems

Control over inventories means good long range and intermediate planning of production operations good production scheduling and good methods of control. A comprehensive inventory-control system, including production planning, scheduling and control must be closely coordinated with other planning and control activities such as cash planning, capital budgeting, and sales forecasting, since it impinges on a wide range of production, sales, and the financial policy and operating decisions. The essentials of an inventory-control system can be grouped into three broad classes:

(i) **Long-range planning:** In order to budget capital for facilities and inventory investment, to arrive at a balanced capital budget in view of long-range business forecasts and possible errors in these forecasts.

(ii) **Intermediate policy making and planning as a basis for short-term scheduling:** Decisions should be made on what money is currently worth, what current service requirment are. Therefore short term scheduling consistent with inventory policy lays the ground rules.

(iii) **Short-term scheduling:** In short-term scheduling of work assignments to keep facilities and men employed and stock balanced in view of demand for output as it actually materializes. This must be done within a consistent framework of policies governing the levels of production and employment to be maintained.

The inventories serve as cushions in each of there stages of planning to absorb the shocks of demand forecast errors to permit more effective use of facilities and staff in the face of demand fluctuations and to isolate one part of the system from the next to permit each to work more effectively. Fig () analyses the three planning functions and the flow of information. The figure illustrates, the long range plan making use or demand forecasts and preliminary policy decisions. On capital allocation and value and on the amount of risk to be assumed to show the implications of policy choices. The purpose of production planing is to resolve the general planning questions within the limitations of operating resources, with the objective of maximising profits or return on investment rather than to define precisely how much of what item to be made on what machine.

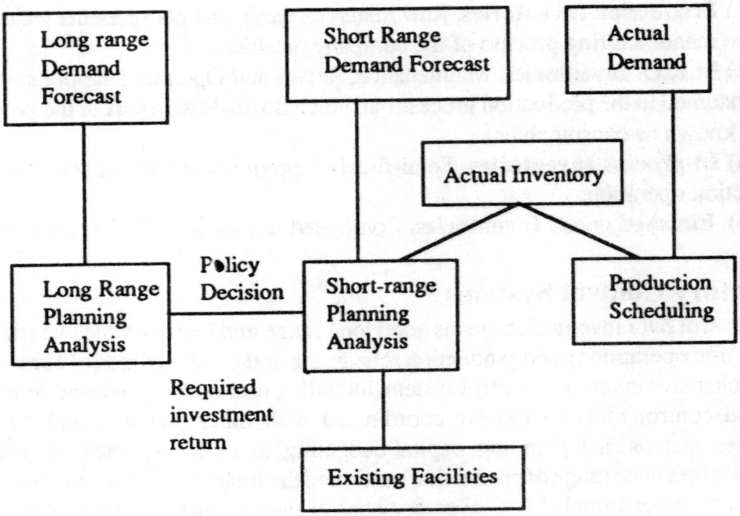

Fig. 17.1 Inventory planning.

Role of Forecasting

Fig (17.1) shown in detail are essential in inventory management. The forecasts may be hidden, crude, intuitive, but they are there. The important forecasting period is that just ahead, the time needed to make any current production or purchasing decision effective. In case of seasonal items of forecast at least through the next cycle is needed if stock are to be build in anticipation. Forecast errors cost money; the bigger the errors, the bigger must inventories to be guarded against them. But forecast errors or limits of error, is not enough . Sometimes specifying a maximum sales forecast, the maximum which the production and distribution organisation will be required to service, is a satisfactory way of accounting for forecast error.

The ABC Analysis

Introduction

The basic reason underlying ABC analysis is to exercise selective control on inventories thereby economising the efforts and cost involved in inventory management without materially reducing the extent of control exercised. Materials managers rarely, worry about stock outs of some stationary items. This is not in case with many other items, particularly production parts and materials. In many cases a stockout of even a minor production part can be costly. Safety stocks almost always are better value for low cost items then they are for expansive ones. Modern inventory control system take this into account by classifying items by value of usage The high value items have lower safety stocks because the cost of production is so high. The low-value items carry much higher safety stocks. The basis of the "ABC" approach to inventory control which provides maximum overall protection against the stockouts for a given investment in safety stock, assumes 10 percent of items and 70 percent of value of inventories for the most costly items. The 10 percent that are most costly are A items; the next 20 percent are B items; and the balance are C items. In every case the A items will amount for a heavy percentage of total expenditures and C group will account for a surprisingly small percentage. The relationship of percentage of items and percentage of value of each category is given as under:

Category	Percentage of items	Percent of value
A	10	70
B	20	20
C	70	10

Although here are one seventh as many A items as C items, seven items as much is spent A items as on C items. Thus the average expenditure of an A item is 49 times greater than the average expenditure for a C item. Investment is safety stock for A item must be 49 times gráter than for a C item in order to afford the same protection against stockouts. The ABC system permits selective inventory control. Safety stocks are kept low for high-value items, which should be subject to extremely close control by materials personnel; stock-outs are prevented by maintaining much higher safety stocks. With ABC control, it is possible to risk fewer stockout and reduce investment in inventories. This is proved by comparing ABC control with overall control inventories are divided into three classes: The expensive A items account for 10 percent of the total and roughly 70 percent of the value; the B items for 20 percent of the total and about 20 percent of the value; and the C items for 70 percent of the total and about 10 percent of the value. In other words on costly items, tight control is substituted for the protection of inventory. This is economic since it permits reductions is inventory investment with the low cost items, it is cheaper to carry inventory than to pay salaries of the personnel needed for close control. It would take seven times as much effort to maintain tight control.Over the 700 C items as it would for the 100 A items, and it would be possible to reduce investment for C items by only one seventh as much as the reduction in the investment for A items.

With the B items, a middle of the road policy would probably be followed. There would be some control, but the company would also rely to a greater extent on inventories to protect against stockouts than it would with the A items.

Objective of ABC Analysis

The object of carrying out ABC analysis is to develop policy guidelines for selective control ABC analysis enables the materials manager to exercise selective control when he is confronted with a large number of items. The tighter and accurate procedures are essential for 'A' value items. The degree of control should be regourous for 'A' items and should be minimum for 'C' items. ABC analysis is helpful to rationale the number of orders and thus reduce the overall inventory cost. It is also common to further subdivide 'A' items as A_1 and A_2 or A^+ and A^- and similarly categories for 'B' and 'C' items for exercising finer control. For 'A' items there should be weekly control statements; Rigorous value analysis; Accurate forecasts in materials planning; Central purchasing and storage; Multiple sources and should be handled by senior officer while for 'C items there should be a follow up and expediting is exceptional cases; Decentralized purchasing; Minimum value Analysis; Rough estimates for planning and can be fully delegated.

Methodology of Handing ABC analysis

Following mechanics can be used for classifying 'A'; 'B'; and 'C' categories:

(i) Calculate the Rupee value for each item is inventory and the annual consumption.
(ii) Arrange all the items is descending order; value wise.
(iii) Prepare a list of items according to annual rupee value.
(iv) Compute a total running total item-by-item.
(v) Computer print for each item the cumulative percentage for the item could and cumulative annual issue value. A graph can be drawn based on the above data and we can visually see the ABC categories as ABC analysis is based on the principles: Analysis based on annual consumption value; Dose not depend on the importance of the item and limits for ABC categorisation are not uniform but will depend upon the size of the undertakings.

Concept of ABC Analysis

Any average medium-size organisation consumes a few thousand tons of stages. An organisation choosing high degree of control of each item would, therefore, neither be practical, considering the work involved, nor worthwhile since not all items are of equal importance. Hence it is desirable to classify or group the items depending upon their importance and subject each class or group the items depending upon their importance and subject each class or group of items to control, commensurate with importance. This is the principle of selective control as applied to inventories and the technique of grouping is termed as A.B.C. analysis or classification which it said to be "Always Better Control". The basis of analyzing the annual consumption cost goes after the principal "Vital Few"—"Trivial Many" and criterion used here is the money spent and not the quantity consumed. The Following Fig 17.2 brings out clearly the concept of the ABC Analysis.

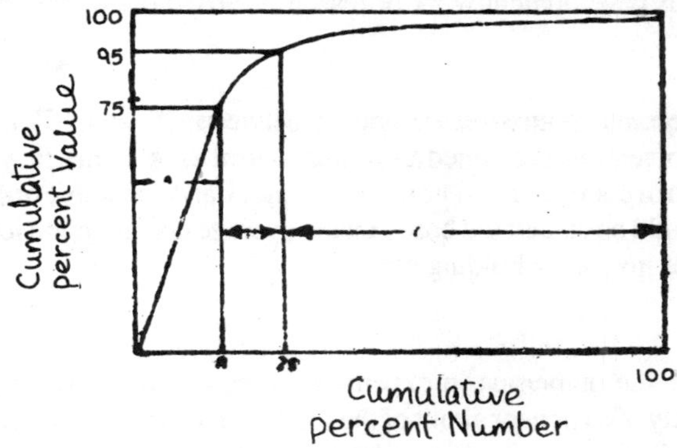

Fig. 17.2

'A' Items

From the graph and analysis it may be found that about 8% of items cost more than 75% of the cost on inventory. This is classified as *'A'* items. These are the most important items form the control point of view.These should be ordered and scheduled for receipt on a monthly, weekly or even daily basis in order to keep the investment on them as low as possible. Their movement through the shop should have high priority and the movement time kept at a minimum. Safety stock or reserve stock on such items should be kept to an absolute minimum. A close watch on he ordering, follow up stocking and issue of these items are a must for economy on Inventory.

Control policy for A Items

The measure to taken on *'A'* items can be briefly put down as follows:

1. Annual or half yearly contracts for supplies with as frequent staggered deliveries as is economical.

2. Develop and revise more often ordering quantities, reorder points and safety stocks for items not covered by long terms contracts as indicated in items I.

3. Frequently reviewing of stock position and consumption patterns and maintenance of records of issues and stock to enable to get the up-to-date position of stocks at any time.

4. Precise quality specifications or material standard.

5. As far as possible, two or more suppliers should be sought for each item so that the dependency on one supplier is not here. Due to any contingencies the other supplier could be approached.

6. The control of *'A'* items should be directly under the charge of Purchasing Manger himself.

7. As these items are to be stocked to a minimum level, the purchase department should pay maximum attention to expedite the delivery of the items.

8. Waste control measures to reduce the scrap, rejection, rework and sub-standards.

9. Continuous development work or research carried out whenever possible.

'B' Items

These are secondary importance and in between *'A'* and *'C'* items. Even though, they do not require as detailed and close control as *'A'* items, they need more attention and control than *C* items. The minimum stock and economic order quantity of these items should be calculated based on the average consumption lead time for prominent, cost of inventory holding etc.

'C' Items

'C' items are the numerous in expensive items i.e about 70% of the items contributing to only 50% or near about of the total cost on material. However, these items may be critical items which may hold up production in case of their non-availability. These items are to be purchased in large quantities in order to secure purchase discounts and minimise time and effort required by order clerks, store keepers and accountants, the company should carry say six months to one year stock of these items taking into consideration storage facilities available and storage costs.

Advantages of ABC Analysis

1. Preference for keeping inventory can be placed properly after ABC analysis.

2. Stores personnel are placed better with this analysis i.e. their time can be utilized better.

3. Storing, handing and delivery of material to production department become better.

4. We known I'*C'* items take more time in review as they are more in number. Review can be decided accordingly.

VED-Analysis

The analysis specially pertains to the classification of maintenance spare denoting the essentiality of stocking spares.

V—Stands for vital-items when go out of stock or when not readily available, completely bring the production to a halt.

E—Stands for Essential-items without which temporary losses of production or dislocation of production work occurs.

D—Stands or Desirable-all other items which are necessary but do not cause any immediate effect on production.

SDE-Analysis

For developing countries and especially where certain items are in scarce supply, this analysis is very useful.

S—Stands for Scarce items, especially imported items and also those which are very much in short supply.

D—Stands for Difficult items which are available in the market but not easily available. For example, items which have to come far off cities.

E—Items which are easily available; mostly local items.

HML-Analysis

The cost per item (per piece) is considered for this analysis. High cost items *(H)* Medium cost items *(M)* and low cost items*(L)* help in bringing controls over consumption at the departmental level.

FSN-Analysis

Here the quantity and rate of consumption is analysed to be classified as Fast-Moving *(F)*, Slow Moving *(s)* and Non-Moving *(N)* items.

Chapter 18

FACTORS INFLUENCING INVENTORY

Introduction

Materials account for over 50% of the production costs. In addition, frequently as much as one third of company's total investment is in the form of work-in-process, finished goods and stores inventory. Out of the three inventory forms, the stores inventory usually represents the largest share and this is the area in which the purchasing department, either directly or indirectly, can contribute significantly to company profit by efficient management of quantity and timing of purchases. There is one right quantity to buy for any given transaction but since there are many different kinds of transaction, the determination of correct quantity is a complicated matter. Similarly there is only one right time to purchase the right quantity. The issue is important because, if too small a quantity is purchased the unit cost will usually be higher, shortages are likely to increase, expediting work will necessarily be greater, and the relationships between vender and purchaser will suffer. On the other hand if too large a quantity is purchased, the excess inventory will raise costs, obsolescence will become a more serious problem and the need for additional storage facility will create investment problems.

Inventory Control

It may be defined as planning, ordering and scheduling of materials used in the manufacturing process. These are four major reasons for maintenance of sound inventory control procedures:

(i)	Unit Cost	:	quantity purchases permit lower unit costs.
(ii)	Operating Costs	:	quantity purchases permit efficient use of manpower; machines and facilities.
(iii)	Customer Service	:	quantity purchases assure optimum customer service and provide for efficient scheduling of internal options.
(iv)	Efficient use of Invested Capital	:	The balancing of unit cost; operating costs; customer service with cost of capital.

Right Quantity

Buying the right quantity is one of the most important as well as the most complicated tasks of purchasing. A company's ability determine the right quantity and is influenced heavily by basic managerial planning, organisation, co-ordination; and control. An effective inventory control system must be integrated with other company wide planning and control activities such as cash flow planning; capital budgeting; sales forecasting and production planning, scheduling; and control.

Types of Inventory Control Systems

There are two basic systems controlling inventories: (i) Cyclical ordering system and (ii) Fixed order quantity system.

Cyclical Ordering System

It is a time based system which involves scheduled periodic reviews if the stock level of all inventory items. When the stock level of a given item is not sufficient to sustain the production operation until the next scheduled review, an order it placed replenishing the supply. The frequency of reviews varies from the company to company. Stock levels can be monitored by physical inspection; by a visual review of perpetual inventory cards, or by automatic computer surveillance. In operations where a small quantity of material is involved, the simplest method is a periodic physical count of stock. In practice, the cyclical ordering system is well suited for materials whose purchases must be planned months in advance because of established and infrequent production schedules maintained by suppliers. The cyclical ordering system tends to peak the purchasing work loads around the review dates. This disadvantage can be avoided to some extent by regulating frequency of reviews. In this system the unexpected changes in secular trends are so gradual that they rarely have any effect on short term materials forecasting and planning. Errors in cyclical forecasting are far more likely to affect materials management. An unexpected shift in the business cycle works like a two edged sword on materials management: it affects both the lead time and the lead time usage.

Fixed Order Quantity System

It is based on the order quantity factor rather than on the time factor. The design of this system recognizes that each item possesses its own unique optimum order quantity. The major advantage claimed for the system are that (i) each material can be procured in most economical quantity (ii) Purchasing of items/materials is when required (iii) Positive control can easily be exerted to maintain total inventory investment at the desired level simply by manipulating the planned maximum and minimum values. The system functions correctly only if each of the materials exhibit reasonable usage and lead time. In fact irrespective of the system inventory policy for different groups of items 'A'; 'B'; and C there are two basic problems: what quantity of an item should be ordered each time; and when should an order be placed. In order to find a solution to these problems we should try to analyses the four cost factors: Cost of Material; cost associated with keeping the materials in stock (Inventory Carrying Costs); Cost associated with placements of purchase order (ordering costs); Carrying Inventory: The cost of material is the most important and for items with frequent unexpected price variation. While cost of materials and inventory carry costs are totally dictated by the price of the items. The inventory carrying cost arise out of the following factors.

: Interest charges (4 to 5%)
: Insurance Cost (1 to 3%); Protection against theft and fire etc.
: Properties Taxes (1 to 3%)
: Obsolescence and deterioration cost (4 to 10%)
: Stationery and consumables used in stores
: Depreciation and repairs cost.

These cost come nearly 20 to 25%. These costs are arbitrary and vary from industry to industry and from item to item even in the same industry.

Ordering Cost or Acquisition Cost of Items

Placement of a purchase order for a material is associated with certain obvious cost due to advertising, consumption of stationary and postage, telephone charges, telegrams etc. In fact all the annual expenditure of the purchasing deptt. of a company can be considered to be on the purchase orders it places during the year. The cost associated with ordering would, therefore consist of

(a) Salaries of the staff n administration and purchase deptt.
(b) Rent for the space used by the purchasing deptt.
(c) The postage, telegram and telephone bills.
(d) The stationary and other consumable required by the purchasing deppt.
(e) Entertainment charges on vendors.
(f) Travelling expenses.
(g) Lawyers and court fees due to any legal matters arising out of purchase.

These all usually come to 20-25% as ordering cost. Obviously more the number of orders placed in a period, the more would be the stationary and postage consumed, more staff and officers will be required for handling the work, the more will be the space required for accommodating them and so on. Thus the total expenditure on purchasing or ordering would depend on the numbers of orders placed. It is assumed that the expenditure on ordering of material is directly proportional to the number of orders placed. The ordering cost is expressed as the cost/order and is calculated by dividing the total ordering cost during a year (or a period). These are about 20-25%. Following are the components or elements of Inventory carrying cost and Procurement cost which are the most important costs in inventory management.

Components of Inventory Carrying Cost

The components of inventory carrying cost are:

(a) The salaries and wages of storing, receiving and issue of the material personnel.
(b) The loss by way of interests in the capital invested in the stocks of materials.

(c) The rent of the stores premises.
(d) Taxes on inventories.
(e) The depreciation and repairs cost for the stores facilities and handling equipments.
(f) Loss of materials through pilferage and deterioration, obsolescence.
(g) Stores insurance cost.
(h) Stationery and other consumables used by the stores.

The cost generally varies from 10 to 20%.

Procurement cost

This includes:

(a) The salaries and wages of the purchase staff purchasing the materials.
(b) The expenditure on travelling etc.
(c) The expenditure on the use of Post and Telegraph services such as postage, telegrams and telephones.
(d) The expenditure on stationery and other consumables.
(e) Entertainment expenditure on receiving of suppliers.
(f) Rent for the premises used by the purchase department.

Certainly it can be sad that more the number of orders are placed the more shall be the above expenditures.

The ordering cost is generally dependent on the purchasing procedures of the individual organisation. The procurement or ordering cost generally have no relation with the value of an order.

Carrying Inventory

Cost of carrying is not the same as carrying inventory. Carrying inventory results where there is stock left on hand after the demand for the item has terminated. This cost is called the overstock cost. The inventory problem can be static or dynamic. Static inventory problem is with retailer who wishes to sell greeting cards. His sale season is very limited and few cards left over at the end of season will have a very little or no salvage value. Thus if he has too much stock he will have a cost due to the loss he will suffer for each greeting card he overstocks. The dynamic inventory problem could be for household items such as towels etc. There is always a demand for towels so any towel left over after one time period can be sold in the subsequent periods thus there is no overstock cost to a greater extent. The similar examples, holds true for high fashion items, woman clothes. If only one order can be placed we have the static inventory problem if several orders can be placed during a season then we have dynamic problem. There will be no overstock cost involved until last order period of the season.

Procurement and Consumption Cycle

A simplified procurement and consumption cycle for an item having a steady consumption all through the year and which is available immediately on placing an order is shown below:

At time *A* the stock is zero and hence an order would be placed and the delivery being immediate, the stocks would be brought upto a level say *Q*. These would be steady issued upto time B and another order would be placed at *B* to bring up the stock to *Q* and so on. The inventory at the beginning of the period *A-B* would be *Q* and at the end of the period zero or the average inventory would be *Q*/2 and orders would have to be placed of *A*, *B* and *C* etc.

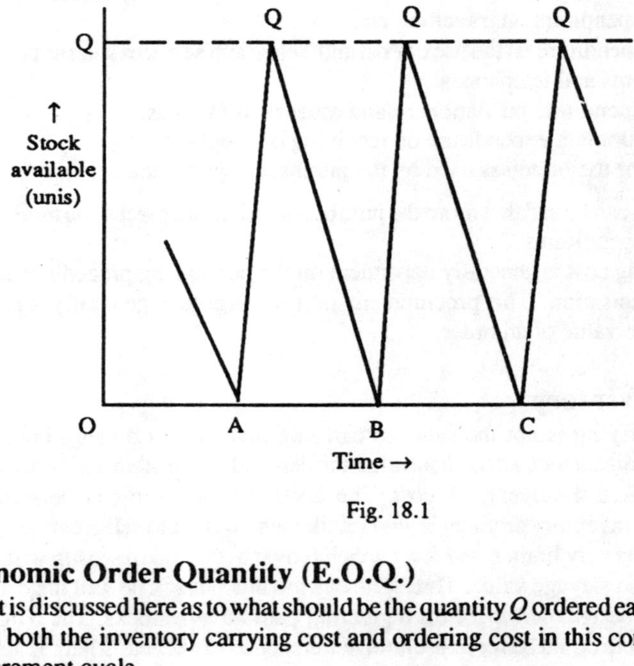

Fig. 18.1

Economic Order Quantity (E.O.Q.)

It is discussed here as to what should be the quantity *Q* ordered each time to keep down both the inventory carrying cost and ordering cost in this consumption and procurement cycle.

Consider the procurement of the entire annual requirement of an item under the procurement and consumption cycle. For keeping the inventories and inventory carrying costs low it would be better to procure the item in as small consignment as possible. But this would mean larger number of orders and so more ordering cost. This has been graphically shown below. The requirements are thus conflicting and there is a particular quantity at which the sum of both the ordering and inventory carrying costs is minimum and this very quantity is called EOQ (Economic Ordering Quantity).

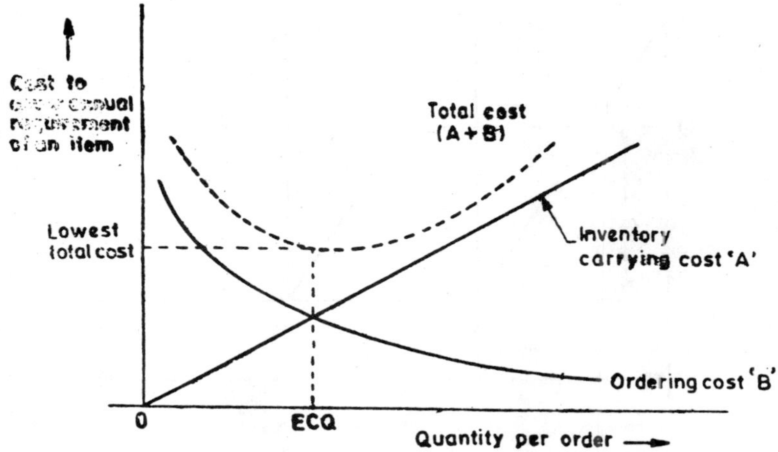

Fig. 18.2

Let us now derive the formula:

Let A = Ordering cost/order

Q = Quantity/order

λ = Total quantity ordered in the period under consideration.

IC = Inventory carrying cost per unit.

TIC = Total procurement and inventory cost or total inventory cost or No. of orders in the period under consideration would be = λ/Q.

TIC = Ordering cost + inventory carrying cost

= Cost per order × No. of orders + (average inventory × inventory carrying cost per unit)

$$TIC = A \times \frac{\lambda}{Q} + \frac{1}{2} Q.I.C. \qquad \text{... (1)}$$

Differentiating (1) with respect to Q, for the total cost to be minimum and then equating to zero.

$$\frac{d(TIC)}{dQ} = -\frac{\lambda A}{Q^2} + \frac{1}{2} IC = 0$$

or
$$\frac{\lambda A}{Q^2} = \frac{1}{2} IC$$

or
$$Q^2 = \frac{2\lambda A}{IC}$$

$$Q = \sqrt{\frac{2\lambda A}{IC}} = EOQ$$

$$EOQ = Q^* \times \sqrt{\frac{2 \times \text{Annual consumption} \times \text{ordering cost}}{\text{Inventory carrying cost as a fraction}}}$$

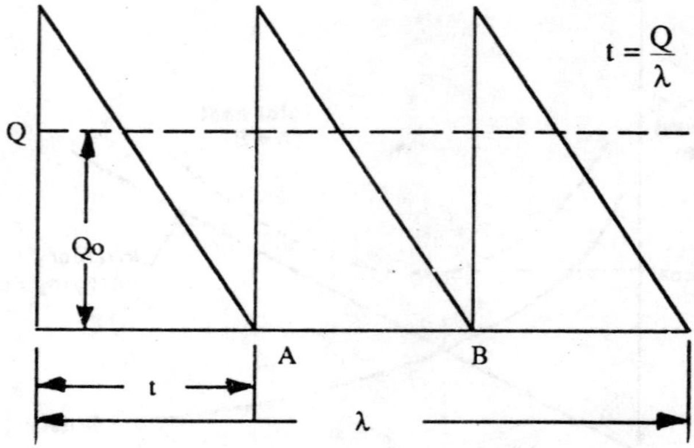

Fig. 18.4.

It can be proved that at *EOQ* the ordering cost and inventory carrying cost are equal.

$$Q = \sqrt{\frac{2A\lambda}{IC}}$$

or

$$Q^2 = \frac{2A\lambda}{IC}$$

or

$$\boxed{\frac{QIC}{2} = \frac{\lambda A}{Q}} \text{ at } EOQ \qquad \text{... (2)}$$

Equation 2 indicates that at *EOQ*, inventory carrying cost and ordering cost are equals.

It may be noted here that shape of the total cost curve is fairly flat near $Q = EOQ$ in other words if little more or little less is ordered than *EOQ*, the total cost only increase slightly. In practice 25% less or more than *EOQ* makes very little difference in the total costs. Also the formula is quite general and '*A*' need not necessarily be annual consumption. '*A*' could very well be for 6 months consumption cost. When simultaneous consumption is there and the rate of which is *X* then the formula for *E.O.Q.* becomes,

$$Q = \sqrt{2A\lambda / IC\,(1-\lambda)}$$

Problem 1

Given

Annual consumption (λ) = 36,000 units

Inventory carrying cost (*I*) = 20% per annum

Ordering cost (A) = Rs. 25
Cost/unit (C) = Re. 1
Find Q at EOQ and total cost of Inventory.

Solution

$$Q = \sqrt{\frac{2A\lambda}{IC}}$$

Here

$$\lambda = 36{,}000$$
$$A = 25$$
$$C = 1$$
$$I = 0.2$$

Putting the values of $\lambda, A, I, C,$
We get,

$$Q = \sqrt{\frac{2 \times 36{,}000 \times 25}{0{\cdot}2 \times 1}}$$

$$= \sqrt{36{,}000 \times 25} = 600 \times 5 = 3000$$

This means that for the order quantity 3000 units company will incur the minimum total cost on ordering and carrying inventory. This is explained below:

Qty. per Order (Q)	No. of Orders	Inventory levels (Rs.) (Q/2)	Ordering cost (Rupees) (A)	Inventory Carrying cost (Rs.) (B)	Total cost (A × B)
3000	12	1500	12 × 25 = 300	1500 × 0.2 = 300	600
2400	15	1200	15 × 25 = 375	1200 × 0.2 = 240	615
3600	10	1800	10 × 25 = 250	1800 × 0.2 = 360	610

When 12 orders are placed and inventory is maintained at an average of Rupees 1500, the total cost is the minimum is

$$(300 + 300) = \text{Rs. } 600$$

Problem 2

In the above example, it is forecast that the next year consumption will increase to 144,000 units *i.e.* 4 times. On this basis calculate EOQ and TIC.

Solution

Given

$$\lambda = 144{,}000$$
$$A = 25$$
$$Q = 6000$$
$$I = 0.2$$
$$C = 1$$

$$EOQ \text{ (for new consumption)} = \frac{2A\lambda}{IC}$$

$$= \sqrt{\frac{2 \times 25 \times 144{,}000}{0{\cdot}2 \times 1}}$$

$$= 5 \times 1200 = 6000 \text{ units.}$$

Note. Sometimes deviations from economic order quantity have to be made for variety of reasons. In such cases some believe that deviations towards a quantity less than the economic order quantity is more desirable than deviations towards a quantity greater than EOQ. This however is not correct. In our example if the deviation is great than the EOQ by 20% total cost of ordering and carrying inventory increases by Rs. 10. If the deviation is less than EOQ by 20%, the increase in total cost is Rs. 15. Thus we have noted that deviation towards a greater quantity than EOQ increases total cost of ordering and carrying inventory by lesser amount than what the same % deviation of 20% towards the lower side would increase the total cost of ordering and carrying inventory.

$$TIC = \frac{A\lambda}{Q} + \frac{1}{2} QIC$$

$$= \frac{144{,}000 \times 25}{6000} + \frac{1}{2} 6000 \times 0{\cdot}2 \times 1$$

$$= 24 \times 25 + 600$$
$$= 600 + 600$$
$$= 1200$$

Problem 3

A sewing m/c manufacture buys from a nearby foundry the body casting in which the m/c is assembled. The foundry provides usually good service and always makes delivery on 8th day of the receipt of the order. The normal consumption of casting is at an average rate of 100/day. The consumption varies from 80—120 casting/day. The management decides to set an order point and safety stock so that under the present operating conditions they do not run out of stock.

Solution

Average number of casting needed $= 8 \times 100 = 800$
Maximum number of casting needed $= 8 \times 120 = 960$
Buffer stock or safety stock $= 960—800 = 160$

The management has concluded here that they should not run out of stock by establishing this order point at the level of 8=960 units. The safety level stock is 160 unit.

Lead Time—6—10 days

Average no. of casting used during the lead time	$= 8 \times 100$	$= 800$
Minimum ,, ,, ,,	$= 6 \times 80$	$= 480$
Maximum ,, ,, ,,	$= 10 \times 120$	$= 1200$
Safety Stock	$= 1200 - 800$	$= 400$
Order pt—minimum use	$= 1200 - 480$	$= 720$
Order pt—maximum use	$= 1200 - 1200$	$= 0$

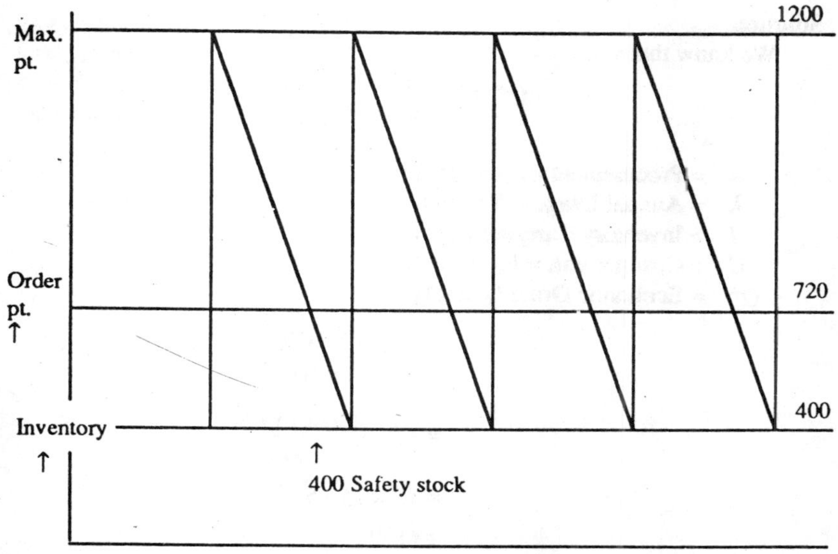

Fig. 18.5.

Problem 4

An oil engine manufacturer purchases lubricators at Rs. 42/piece from a vendor. The requirement of these lubricators is 1800 per year. What should be the order quantity per order (A = Rs. 16 and I = 0.2)

Annual requirement is = Rs. 1800 × 42 = 75600

$$A = \text{Rs. } 16$$

$$I = 0.2$$

$$EOQ = \sqrt{\frac{2A\lambda}{IC}}$$

$$Q^* = \sqrt{\frac{2 \times 1800 \times 16}{0{\cdot}2 \times 42}}$$

$$= 82.8 \text{ or } 83 \text{ lubricators}$$

Problem 5

Calculate the value of Economic Order Quantity. Given the following:

Annual usages	= 50 units
Procurement Cost	= Rs. 15 per order
Cost per price	= Rs. 100 per item.
Inventory Carrying Cost	= 10%

Solution

We know that

$$Q^* = \sqrt{\frac{2A\lambda}{IC}}$$

A = Procurement Cost = Rs. 15/order
λ = Annual Usage = 50 units
I = Inventory Carrying Cost of 0.1
C = Cost per unit = Rs. 100
Q^* = Economic Order Quantity

$$= \sqrt{\frac{2 \times 15 \times 50}{0{\cdot}1 \times 100}}$$

$$= \sqrt{\frac{2 \times 10 \times 15 \times 50}{100}}$$

$$= \sqrt{2 \times 15 \times 5}$$

$$= \sqrt{150}$$

$$Q^* = 12.21$$

Taking the whole number. The most Economic Order quantity where the inventory carrying cost and inventory procurement cost are minimum are 12 Nos. per order.

Problem 6

The annual consumption of an item is 12000 per year. The procurement cost is Rs. 15 per order and inventory carrying cost per unit per year is Re. 1.

Find out the most economic order quantity and the total cost of inventory also.

Solution

We known that

$$Q^* = \sqrt{\frac{2A\lambda}{IC}} \quad \text{... (A)}$$

A = ordering cost per order.
Q^* = Economic order quantity.
λ = Annual consumption.
I = % of inventory carrying cost.
C = cost of item.

If we substitute the value in (A) we find the economic order quantity is

$$Q^* = 600.$$

So everything order is placed the number of units to be ordered are 600. Since the total requirement is 12000 per year, 20 orders at an interval of 18 days are to be placed assuming 360 days in one year. The total cost of the inventory consists of two parts:

(1) Total procurement cost.
(2) Total inventory carrying cost.

Total ordering cost = Rs. 20 × 15
= 300.

Similarly total inventory carrying cost
= 300

Total inventory cost is Rs. 600

Any other policy will increase the total cost. If each item cost Rs. 10 then total usage value per year is Rs. 120,000 inventory carrying cost I is 0.10 and Q^* can be calculated with the formula given before.

In calculating the economic order quantity only the cost of ordering and stock holding have been taken into account. In certain cases the ordering quantity might have to be adjusted taking into consideration:

(a) Bulk.
(b) Available space.
(c) Package size.
(d) Shipment size.

The economic order quantity is suited in a static equilibrium or when there is no uncertainties.

To deal with economic order Quantity in the real situation following terms should be discussed.

(1) Lead time
(2) Re-order point or level
(3) Safety stock.

Lead Time

The procurement and consumption cycle has got two elements in it—(1) Lead Time (2) Safety Stock.

In the earlier simplified cycle the supplies of material were assumed to be immediate on order but in practice this is not so. *From the time the requisition for an item is raised, it may take several weeks or months before the supplies are received, inspected and taken into stock. This time is called as lead time* and involves the time for the completion of all or some of the following activities.

(a) Raising of a purchase requisition.
(b) Inquiries, quotations, scrutiny, and approval, (Import license procedure for imported item).
(c) Placement of an order on supplier/suppliers.
(d) Suppliers time to make the goods ready (may have to be manufactured or supplied ex-stock).
(e) Transportation or clearing.
(f) Receipt of goods at the company.
(g) Receiving inspection.
(h) Taking into stock.

Obviously, in order to receive supplies before the stock reaches zero level, it is necessary to order the materials much in advance i.e. when the stock available is sufficient to last during the lead time. This is shown graphically in Fig. No. given on next page.

Suppose an item has a lead time of 15 days and the monthly consumption of the item is 500 units, then a recorder must be placed when the stock available is sufficient to last 15 days is 300 units.

In graph above Q = Order Quantity.

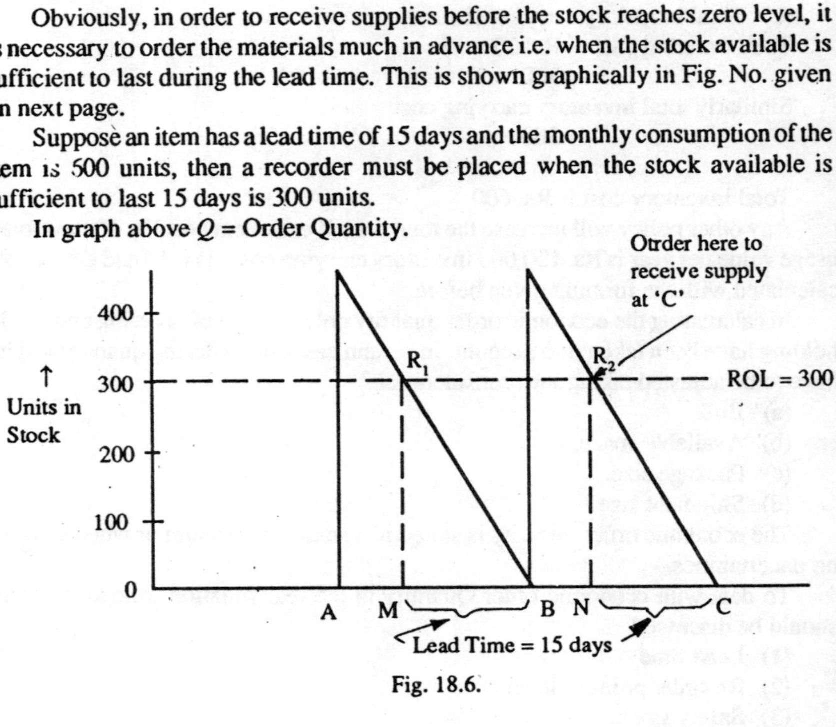

Fig. 18.6.

NC = MB = 15 days is lead time Re-order level
(ROL) = stock sufficient to last during the lead time is 300 units.

Safety Stock (Buffer or reserve)

It is well known that neither the consumption rate of a material is constant throughout the year nor is the lead time. Hence in the earlier example though recorder is placed at a stock level of 300 units, the consumption rate may rise subsequently and the stocks may well be exhausted in 7 days instead of 15 days or it may be that the supplier fails to supply after 15 days as expected. In either case a stock out would be experienced resulting into hampering of production to guard mainly against these uncertainties in consumption rate and lead time, an extra stock is maintained all along the this is called as buffer stock or safety stock or reserve. This stock also comes in use when:

(1) Any excess in process rejections.

(2) Rejection at the time of receipt or goods due to damages or substandard quantity.

Since safety stock is a part of inventory, it should be maintained just sufficient to guard against the uncertainties and not too excessive (especially for *A* items).

Before deciding how much the safety stock should be analysis of the following aspect is essential :—

(1) •Is the variation in consumption more predominant in the lead time.

(2) If the variation in consumption is more predominant way it is so and can it be forecasted in advance.

(3) If the variation in lead time is more predominant is it restricted to a particular period (say monsoon) or spread all over the year?

In most cases it is found that the variations in consumptions can be predicted fairly in advance accurately by good production and maintenance planning and does not present much of a problem. But in the present Indian conditions, it is the lead time variation that is more erratic and unpredictable.

Uncertainty

The safety stock is needed because of uncertainty. The uncertainty can consist of:

(a) Uncertainty of demand i.e., how much the actual demand differs from what you expected.

(b) Uncertainty of delivery, i.e., how long the lead time is going to be.

(c) Uncertain quantity, i.e. how many scrap or imperfect items the ordered quantity is going to contain. Uncertain quantity is usually small and will be neglected in the discussion.

Determining Safety Stock

One simple method of determining safety stock in such cases is to approximately estimate the maximum lead time and the normal lead time for an item in consultation with the purchasing personnel and from the past records. The safety stock should then be sufficient to last the periodic difference between maximum and normal lead time period.

Suppose for an item monthly consumption is 100 units, the normal lead time is 15 days and maximum lead time is estimated as one month. The safety stock would be,

(Maximum lead time in a month—Normal lead time in a month)—(monthly consumption)

$= (1 - \frac{1}{2})\, 100$

= 50 or say 50 to be on safe side.

Or for an imported item with a normal lead time of 1 year and maximum estimated lead time 15 months, the safety stock would be

(15—12) = 3 months or say 4 months for additional safety.

It should be well understand that safety stock is meant only to provide for above normal lead time and above normal consumption rate. The normal lead time and consumption rate is already taken care of in setting Re-Order Level (ROL). If normal lead time consumption is 300 and safety stock is 100, the reorder level is set at 400 units (i.e. safety stock = lead time = ROL).

Optimum Safety Stock

If the safety stock maintained is inadequately low, the inventory carrying cost would be low on the safety stock but stock-outs will be very frequently experienced and the stock out cost would be very high. As against this, if safety stock maintained is rather large stock-outs would be rather rare but the inventory cost would be high. An optimum stock is better. Stock outs may give rise to following cost:

(1) Customer loss or customer dissatisfaction.

(2) Loss of production.

(3) Idling of machines or man.

(4) Emergency purchases at high prices.

(5) Extra transportation changes for speedier modes of transportation.

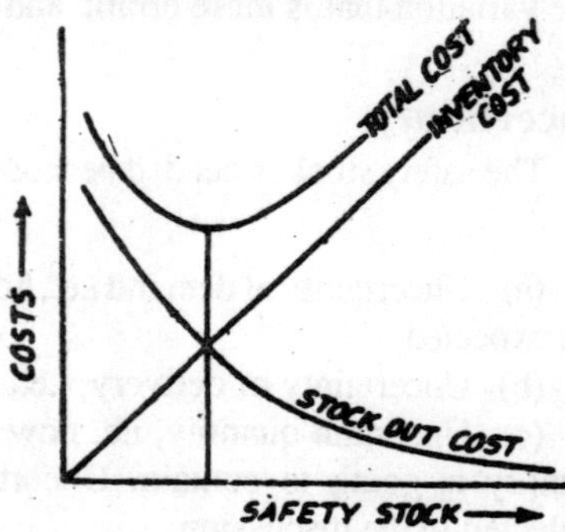

In fact the cost of holding high levels of stock must be weighed against the cost of having stock out. The problem is of calculating the two costs. The cost of running out of stock is often difficult to assess. If the management decides it could not run out of stock on more than 2% of the orders. In other words, management policy is that 98% of orders must be met from stock, *i.e.*, the defined service level is 98%. We must know what service level is defined before one can workout what safety stock should be hold.

Forecast

The expected demand is a forecast of demand. In this difference between the actual demand and the expected (forecast) demand is known as the forecast error. To compensate for this forecast errors we hold safety stock and so the level of safety stocks is, to a large extent, based on the extent of the forecast errors.

Service level

We hold safety stock to make sure that we can satisfy the demand but because of the uncertainty we won't be able to satisfy all the demand all the time. So we must decide what proportion of the demand we want to satisfy, *i.e.*, how often we will allow stock-outs to occur. In other words we must decide on the service level we desire.

Forecast Errors

Since the safety stock depends on forecast efforts and the desired service level, we would like to find the forecast error. For this we study the past data on forecast efforts and try to see what pattern they fall into. In statistical terms, we want to find out the distribution of the forecast efforts. Once we have found how the forecast efforts are distributed, we can go on to draw conclusions about the probability of getting errors of any size.

Suppose we have a record of the last 30 forecasts of the demand made for an item. We can group the errors and draw up a table given below.

Forecast Error	Frequency	% age frequency	Cumulative
— 100 to — 50	12	40	40
— 50 to — 0	6	20	60
0 to 50	5	16	76
50 to 100	2	7	83
100 to 150	1	3	86
150 to 200	0	0	86
200 to 250	1	3	89
250 to 300	0	0	89
300 to 350	1	3	92
350 to 400	0	0	92
Over to 400	2	7	99
	30	100	(Approximate)

From the table we can see that 18 times the actual demand was less than the forecast. It means that more than half the time the actual demand was less than the forecast demand. We are not much worried about the occasion when demand turns out to be less than what had been the forecast, since the safety stock is not affected.

The table also shows that 89% of the errors were less than 250. Hence if we had safety stock of 250 units we would have been able to satisfy the demand 89% of the time *i.e.* the service level would be 89%.

If the distribution of forecast errors is one of several well known statistical distributions or can be approximated, then we can calculated the safety stock for any required service level quite easily from statistical tables.

Techniques of inventory control (Ordering System)

Having discussed all the basic elements of a procurement and consumption cycle we can now depend on various ordering systems.

1. **The fixed internal System/cyclical review System/Replenishment System.** The basic type of state control is known as the fixed internal system. In this system the stock level is reviewed on a regular cycle say once a month. The interval between review is known as the review period. From the cycle shown in the figure below can be explained how the system is determined.

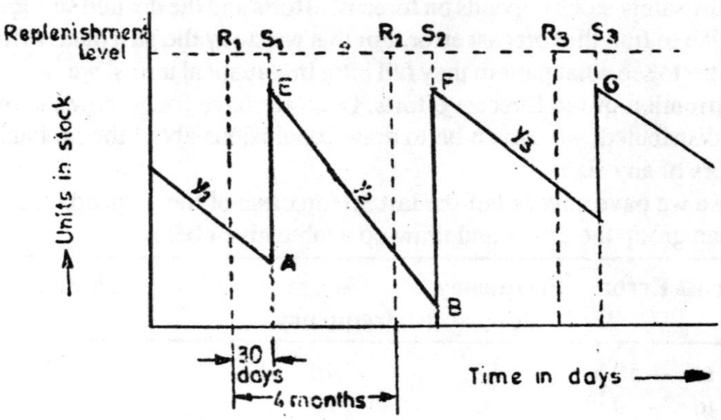

Fig. 18.7.

Suppose 4 months is fixed as the review period for an item and lead time for the item is 30 days. Then the order would be placed every 2 months *i.e.*, at ordinates R_1, R_2, R_3 etc. and the respective supplies would b received at ordinates S_1, S_2, S_3 etc. (30 days after R_1, R_2, R_3 etc.). At R_1 the stock available to be Y_1 then this stock together with the quantity ordered at R_1 (supplies received at S_1) should be sufficient to last till the next supplies are received at S_2 *i.e.* to last for a period of 5 months (1 Review + 1 lead time). In addition some buffer/safety stock would also be necessary to take care of any increased consumption or increase in lead time.

To find out how much to order, we calculated a figure called stock required. The stock which we have in hand and an order immediately after a review date must be good enough to last until the order which we lace at the next review date is available. This order would not arrive till one lead time after the next review date. So stock required = (Lead time + review period) × usage + safety stock on each review date the stock in hand plus that an order is compared with "Stock Required" and an order is placed to bring to stock upto the "Stock Required" level.

In a fixed internal system the combined cost of stock holding and placing orders will always be higher than a fixed order quantity system because the stocks have to last only over the lead time but also over the review period.

2. **Fluctuation In Stock Level.** The following diagram, in a simplified form should the stock level of an item fluctuates.

The amount used over a period is the usage in that period. As the stock is used up over the period, the stock level falls until it reaches a level at which an order is placed. If × is the re-order level. When the stock falls to re-order level, an order is placed for a certain amount. This is known as the order quantity and is shown as *OQ* in the diagram.

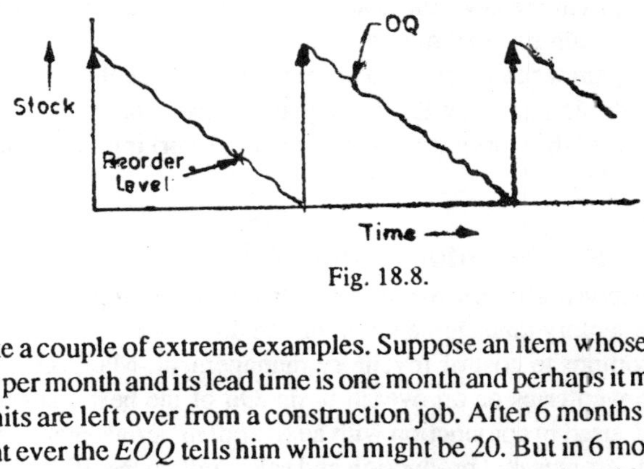

Fig. 18.8.

To take a couple of extreme examples. Suppose an item whose consumption is 10 number per month and its lead time is one month and perhaps it might be possible that 150 units are left over from a construction job. After 6 months the store keeper orders what ever the *EOQ* tells him which might be 20. But in 6 months he has used only 60, so he is reordering at 90. With usage of 10 per month and 1 month lead time store keeper will still have 80 on hand when the ones he ordered arrives. That is 8 months supply.

The other extreme : if the store keeper waited until he got down to 10 before reordering he would run out of stock just about the time the newly ordered ones arrive. No protection against variation in lead or in usage. If these were never any variation in usage or lead time he would reorder when stock was depleted to 11 units. Which is a best set up; minimum inventory and never a stock out. But there are bound to be fluctuation in lead time and in usage so there is a need to set the Reorder point high enough to provide protection against those fluctuations.

If the reorder point were 15, for instance, still 5 are on hand in the normal course of events (10 per month usage 1 month lead time). The inventory would vary between 25 and 5 averaging 15 of which 10 is "working stock". The 5 is called safety stock? A normal 2 weeks' supply in the example which might be adequate if there were very little variation in lead time or usage, but might not be nearly enough wide variations.

Reorder Point should be whatever one determines one should have as a safety stock for each item, plus the number of that item which normally be used during the lead time. ($RP = SS$ + Usage during lead time) obviously, the more uniform these factors are the fewer pieces needed as Safety stock protection and wider the fluctuation the more is needed for comparable protection. In the example given above suppose once every 5 years, the monthly usage would exceed 15 units. By setting the Reorder Point at 15 protection have been provided equivalent to one stock out in 5 years.

It an order quantity does not arrive immediately after is has been ordered. The time which elapses between the stock reaching the reorder level and the arrival or order quantity is known as the lead time. Stocks go on falling during the lead time until the order quantity arrives and is in the stores. In an ideal situation, the stock should reach zero just as the new stocks arrived. Then when an order quantity come in the stock level would rise to a maximum.

From the diagram we can set that the maximum stock level is equal to the order quantity and the minimum stock level is equal to zero. The stock we have been talking about, is called the working stock. The average working stock is equal to half the order quantity.

Responsibility For Inventory Control

The basic responsibility of Inventory control lies with top management. The effects of poor inventory management will not be directly visible on the operating statement as a composite cost of inventory management. Management can only hope to control inventories on an overall basis. On of the best ways to do this is through standards used in conjunction with an overall materials plan. For example, suppose the plan assumes that production and sales will be Rs. 10 lakhs per month for the first three months of the year and then will increase steadily to a peak of Rs. 15 lakhs in June. Obviously some inventory built up is necessary to accommodate the sales increase. However, it is not necessary to increase inventories in proportion to increase in output. Plants can operate with higher stock turnover ratios as production increases to near-capacity levels. What happens in fact is that materials move through the plant more rapidly when production increases. Thus the need for inprocess inventory may not increase as rapidly as out put. Raw-material inventories may not change at all. The extra demand causes stocks to drop more rapidly to their re-order points. Outstanding purchase commitments would grow, but, if everything goes accordingly to plan, actual stocks of purchased increase. It has been seen that routinization of the daily operation often camouflages the importance of sound management in this area.

Nevertheless in most companies these indirect costs, dispersed and hidden throughout the operating statement can have a significant influence on profit. Top management should, for this reason, carefully formulate and periodically review the basic political, mans and forecast which constitute the frame work with in which the daily inventory control operation functions.

The Inventory control functions are usually assigned to materials management department or production control department. A production inventory is the reservoir which operationally connects these two departments. The materials management department, feeds the inventory reservoir and production control utilises the inventory by utilising production facilities.

To summarise the need is to have high degree of co-ordination between materials and production control department relative to inventory control policy and operations. This is essential for optimum utilisation of results and efforts of materials and production groups.

Chapter 19

COST REDUCTION TECHNIQUES

Cost Reduction and Materials Management

On a manufacturing industry material takes a major share (50 to 70%) of the total cost. Therefore comapany must aim at a material cost reduction. It has been observed that material cost gets enhanced by defective design of the product; wrong selection of raw material ; poor manufacturing methods and this can be controllled by shop supervision. The responsibility for controlling direct material cost can be divided amongst; designer; purchaser; and supervisior. However, the greatest scope for cost reduction throughout industry lies at the stage of product design. The cost of manufacturing, warehousing and distributing will depend greatly on the decisions taken at this stage. The effect of design upon product cost makes it imperative that systematic consideration should be given at this stage at all aspects contributing to its cost. Some of the factors are: standardisation and variety reduction; compactness of the finished product leading to economy of packing; use of materials considering their cost; influence of design upon manufacturing cost interms of tolerances, tools, jigs and fixtures and processing time.

Standardistaion

Value analysis programmes are usually designed to reduce the cost of an item. Standardisation programmes may eleminate the item entirely. Standardisation is essential to a modern mass production economy. Almost every major industry has standards to classify its products. A standard is definied as that which has been established as a model to which an object or an action may be compared. The purpose of a standard is to provide a criterion for judjement. Companies are concerned with standards both for the products they design and for the materials designed by their suppliers. Standardisation is therefore required not only for ensuring procurement of the right quality of incoming material, but also for cost reduction.

Aims of Standardisation

The aims of standardisation should be to have uniform standards for similar items, and the standards evolved should take cognizance of the indigenous availability of materials to the maximum extent possible. Standardisation enables the materials manager to achieve overall economy and ensures inter-changeablitiy of parts. Since more than one manufacturer can supply standard items, it will imply better availability, better price and better delivery. Standardisation also implies routinising purchase efforts, less stock and hence less obsolete items. Standardisation also means less inspection efforts. To understand the concept of standardisation, let us understand the term standard. Standard is defined as a model or general afreement of a rule established by autority consensus or custom created and used by various levels of interest. A firm may similarly prepare, by consulting different departments, a standard for guiding the activities. Similarly, at the industry level, the related industry may also prepare industrial standards. At the national level, by consulting manufacturers, scientist, users and government departments, national standards are evolved. Such national standards are discussed to form international standards.

Standardisation and Materials Management

We all know, the fewere the items that need to be controlled the simpler and more efficient the materials management process. It is in the interest of materials management department to promote standardisation and simplification of specifications. The engineering groups are primarily responsible for standards and specifications but materials personnel can make a substantial contribution streamlinign the methods and standardisation of productivity and thus reduce cost.

Simplification

The process of standardisation logically leads to simplification or variety reduction. This implies unnecessary varieties and standardising to the most economical sizes, grades, shapes, colour, types of parts and so on. The items can be analysed by their frequency of usuage or movement analysis over the last few years. On the basis of analysis, a firm could set standards to these items. The setting up of standard depends on the effect the diamension variation has on the performance of the product. Simplifying work methods requires caseful study of each operation in order to find shorter or more advantageous ways to reach the same goal.

Benefits of Standardisation

Quite a large number of Public Sector organisations have started using standardisation as it leads to variety reduction. Standardisation has been successfully used in forms, purchase orders and contracts. Standardised sampling and testing has also resulted in reduced inspection costs in a large number of organisations. Some of the important benefits are:

(i) Standardiation reduce inventory cost.
(ii) It helps in better communication.
(iii) It helps in inventory analysis.
(iv) It makes quality control more firm.
(v) It helps in the promotion of export and creating confidence in the international market.

Linear Programming

Sometimes costs can be reduced without making any changes whatever in design, price or number of items carried in inventory. Operations research techniques can help the companies to have a competitive edge. Linear Progamming and Simulation techniques of operation research are very helpful to materials management. In materials management, linear programming can be applied to make or buy; Inventory management; Scheduling and physical distribution problems. The most important application of operations research has been the transportation and physical distribution.

Linear Programming is an extremely useful technique used for the purpose of maximising some objective such as profit or minimising, some objective such as costs in order to achieve the objectives of the organisation. Linear programming is now used increasingly to solve management problems. Linear programming is used in situations where numerous activities are competing for limited resources. The person responsible for developing linear programming was George B. Dantzig, who in 1947 developed the simplex method of Linear Programming. Since World War-II; the linear programming models have been used increasingly to solve management problems. Teh term linear reveals that the technique is mathematical and involves linear functions and the term programming refers to certain mathematical procedures to get the best solution to a problem involving limited resources. Linear Programming is a technique of numbers and the application of the numbers to arrive at a better decision. It is a tool in the hands of managers to take better decision among the number of alternatives.

Definition

Linear Programming is a technique of selecting the best possible (optimal) strategy among a number of alternatives:

(i) Linear Programming is an important tool used by the management, involved in choosing most appropriate (best possible) alternative among a number of alternative actions.

(ii) Linear Programming helps the management discover whether the maximum profit or the least production programmes open to it.

(iii) It is applied to problems which involve interaction between alternatives.

Uses and Applications of Linear Programming

(i) Linear Programming helps in determining the optimum combinations of several variables with given constraints.

(ii) It provides additional information for proper planning and control over various operations in the organisation.

(iii) It also helps the managers to have better understanding about the phenomenon and various activities of the organisation for the organisation construction of suitable mathematical model visualizing the relationship between variables if any and making improvement over them.

(iv) It also contributes the development of executives through the technique of model building and corresponding interpretations.

(v) It provides a clear specification of the management problems by defining:

(a) the objectives to be persued by the organisation.

(b) the various restrictions imposed by the system.

(c) the various alternatives and relationship between various variables.

(d) the contribution made by each alternative to the objectives of the organisation.

(vi) Linear Programming has found useful avenues in the fields of agricultural, industrial, military, space and research etc.

(vii) Specific areas where it can be fruitfully applied are:

(a) Production scheduling and inventory control satisfying the demand and minimising the cost of production and inventory cost.

(b) Blending operations and problems—where basic components are combined to produce a product that has definite set of specifications and one may be interested in calculating best possible combination of these components which maximises the profit or minimises the cost.

(viii) Other important applications of linear programming techniques can be in the area of:

* Purchasing and materials management.
* Routing and scheduling.
* Assignment problems.
* Marketing.
* Space exploration.

The problem of linear programming can be formulated with the help of the following terms.

The Transportation Problem

Many firms buy materials from several suppliers that is shipped to several plants. In considering how business is to be divided, they must take in to account not only the price charged by each supplier but also the cost of shipping the material to each plant. Transportation model helps to solve the problem to decide on the qualities to be purchased from each vendor and where they are to be shipped so that plant's requirement will be met at overall minimum cost.

Transportation Method: With this method problems of Plant location; Machine assignment material transportation and Products Mix can be solved.

Example

Plant	**Warehouses** 1	2	3	4	**Output (Weekly production in plants A & B)**
A	3	4	9	2	23
B	6	5	8	8	27
					0
Demand (Customer demand at each warehouses	12	13	15	10	50

3. 4. 9, 2 and 6, 5, 8,8 are the costs in Rupees per tonne of distributing product from plant *A* and *B* to respective warehouses 1,2,3,4.

Solution

The first step in the transportation method is to load the basic matrix without bothering whether the solution formed is optinal or not. There are various mehtods to do it but we shall be considering only tow common mathods:

(1) Northwest Corner Rule

(2) Vogel's Approximate Mehtod.

Northwest Corner Rule

In this method the initial assignment starts by loading the cell located in the upper left hand corner of the matrix and filling the non-requirements to the right and downward until all the requirements of the problem have been satisfied.

Ist Solution

Plant	Warehouse 1	2	3	4	Output
A	3 (12)	4 (11)	9 0	2	23
B	6	5 (2)	8 (15)	8 (10)	27
Demand	12	13	15	10	50 / 50

The transportantion cost involved in the first solution can be evaluated as

$= 3 \times 12 + 11 \times 4\ 2 \times 5 + 15 \times 8 + 10 \times 8$

$= 36 + 44 + 10 + 120 + 80 = 290$ (rupees)

In order to ascertain whether the solution *I* is optimal or not the empty cells in the solution must be evaluated. Following is the procedure to evaluate the empty cell:

1. Shifiting 1 unit from loaded cell into the empty cell.
2. Comparing the cost of orginal schedule with the cost of new schedule involving the empty cell.
3. The loaded cell which is selected must have following two characteristic:

(i) Loaded cell must be situated in the same row or columen of the empty cell.

(ii) The route used for evaluation would not require more than one emply cell during same evaluation.

The effect of shifiting 1 unit from plant *B* to warehouse 1 would be

$+6-3+4+5=$ Rs. 12

The plus sign indicates that the total costs cannot be reduced by adding one unit to B_1 combination.

Evaluation of empty cell B-1

Plant	1	2	3	4	Output
A	3 (11) −	4 (12) +	9	2	23
B	6 (1) +	5 (1) −	8	8	27
Demand	12	13	15	10	50

Further Evaluation
Evaluation of Cell A-4

Plant	1	2	3	4	Output
A	3	4 (10)	9	2 (1)	23
B	6	5 (3)	8 (15)	8 (9)	27
Demand	12	13	15	10	50

Evaluation of cell A_4 follow the route

$-4+2-8+5=$ Rs. -5.

(Assigning positive signs to the cost of those cells which gained one unit and negative signs to those cells which loses one unit.)

Evaluation of A_3 Cell

Plant	1	2	3	4	Output
A	3 (12)	4 (10)	9 (1)	2	23
B	6	5 (3)	8 (14)	8 (10)	27
Demand	12	13	15	10	50 / 50

Moving one unit to A_3, we remove one unit from A_2. In order to restore one unit to warhouse 2, we shift one unit from B_3 to B_2.

The cost associated with these moves are :

$-4 + 9 - 8 + 5 = + 2$

Thus adding one unit to cell A3 would not reduce the total costs. Thus evaluation of empty cells give the following inference:

(i) If the evaluation is positive, then the cost of new solution would be greater than the cost of present schedule.

(ii) If the evaluation is negative than the cost of new solution would be less than the cost of present schedule of the evaluation result into zero value than the cost will not change by using these empty cells.

The second feasible solution and optimum solution afte analysing empty cells is given below. Now the evaluation for all empty cells involve costs greater than zero. So any change in the solution would result into increase of total costs.

Plant	1	2	3	4	Output
A	3 (12)	4 (1)	9	2 (10)	
B	6	5 (12)	8 (15)	8	
Demand	12	13	15	10	50 / 50

If the evaluation revealed negative costs then another feasible solution could have been constructed. The evaluation process is complete when all evalutions are positive. Thus an optimal schedule has been obtained.

(2) Vogel's Approximate Method

This method was developed first by W.R. Vogel. This method gives a good approximation and provides an optimum solution to most of the simple problems. Following are the various steps used for Vogel's approximate method:

1. Construct the basic matrix
2. Find out the difference in each column and row between the minimum and the next higher to minimum.
3. Select a row or column containing the largest difference.
4. Select maximum unit in that square or column which carries the lowest cost.
5. The steps (2), (3) and (4) are repeated till all units are distributed satisfying the capacity and requirement constraint.

Vogel's Method

Let us find with the help of Vogel's Method.

Ist Step **ware-houses**

Plant	1	2	3	4	Output (Weekly production of the products A & B difference)	
A	3	4	9	2 (10)	23 23 – 10 = 13	4 – 3 = 1
B	6	5	8	8	27	6 – 5 = 1
Demand	12	13	15	10	50 / 50	

Difference 6 – 3 = 3   5 – 4 = 1   9 – 8 = 1   8 – 2 = 6

↑

IInd step

Plant	1	2	3	Output	Difference
A	3 (2)	4	9	13 13 – 12 = 1	4 – 3 = 1
B	6	5	8	27	6 – 5 = 1
Demand	12	13	15	40 \ 40	

Difference 6 – 3 = 3   5 – 4 = 1   9 – 8 = 1

↑

IIIrd Step

Plant	2	3	Output	Difference
A	4 1	9	1 1 – 1 = 0	9 – 4 = 5
B	5	8	27	8 – 5 = 3
Demand	13	15	28 \ 28	
Difference	13 – 1 = 12 5 – 4 = 1	9 – 8 = 1		

Difference 13 – 1 = 12

5 – 4 = 1   9 – 8 = 1

IVth Step

Plant	2	3	Output	Difference
B	5 / (12)	8 / (15)	27	8 – 5 = 3
Demand	12	15	27 / 27	

Let us combine step I, II, III and IV to get the initial solution.

Plant	Warehouse				Output
	1	2	3	4	
A	3 / (12)	4 / (1)	9	2 / (10)	23
B	6	5 / (12)	8 / (15)	8	27
Demand	12	13	15	10	50 / 50

Let us evaluate the empty cells, B_1, B_3 and B_4. Evaluating square B_1.

Plant	Warehouse				Output
	1	2	3	4	
A	3 / (12) –	4 / (1) +	9	2 / (10)	23
B	6 / +	5 / (12) –	8 / 15	8	27
Demand	12	13	15	10	50 / 50

If we transfer 1 unit from square B_2 to B_1.
The change in the cost of transportation will be
$+6-3+4-5=+2$
Thus transferring one unit to cell B_1 is not economical.

Evaluating empty sq. A-3

Plant	Warehouse				Output
	1	2	3	4	
A	cost 3, (12)	cost 4, (1) –	cost 9, +	cost 2, (10)	23
B	cost 6	cost 5, (12) +	cost 8, (15) –	cost 8	27
Demand	12	13	15	10	

Transferring one unit from square A_2 to square A3. the new cost of transportation will be

$9-4-8+5=+2$

Thus the new set of assignment is not economical.

Evaluating empty sq. B-4

Plant	Warehouse				Output
	1	2	3	4	
A	cost 3, (12)	cost 4, (1) +	cost 9	cost 2, (10)	23
B	cost 6	cost 5, (12) –	cost 8, (15)	cost 8, +	27
Demand	12	13	15	10	

We are not considering the occupied cell B_3.

Transferring one unit from square A4 to sqaure B4, the new cost of transportation will be

$8-5+4-2=+5.$

Thus transferring one unit from square A4 to square B4 is not economical. The evaluation for all empty cells involve cost greater than zero. So any change in the solution would result into increase of total costs. We can also conclude that Vogel's approximate method gives a good approximation and provides an optimum solution to most of the simple problems.

Simulation

One of the most important functions of management is to make decisions. While some of these decisions may be taken on a day to day basis and be only significant in the short term, other decisions may be of critical importance to the long term future of the company. The simulation with decision model provides two important advantages to the decision maker:

(i) It offers an inexpensive method for analysing the behaviour of the system under different conditions.

(ii) It attempts to predict what would happen in real life.

Simulation duplicates the esential features of a system without actually obtaining reality. This duplication may take one of the following model forms.

(i) **Physical models:** Examples of theses model forms include the ways in which a praticular design or operation might work. The purpose of building such models is two fold: firstly to have a better understanding of the design relationships and secondly, to identify any area of weakness in the model so that the design may be corrrected before the actual real-life product is built.

(ii) **Analogue Models:** Analogue models represent the essential characteristics of the problem under analysis by physical representation. Physical analogue models have also beeb used in economics.

(iii) **Symbolic Models.** Symbolic models make use of mathematical and statistical notation to represent problems. The symbolic models can be further expanded into:

  (a) *Analytical Models:* with there models the solution can be derived directly from the model, as is the case when simulation is carried out by hand.

  (b) *Numerical models.* The solution is given in the form of numerical output as is the case when simulation is carried out by computer.

As with any model, simulation focuses on the important characteristics of the system and hence by implication largely ignores those parts of the system which is assumed to be unimportant. One of the main areas of difficulty, therefore is constructing a simulation model to know what to leave out. Simulation can be applied even by smaller materials management organisation. Simulation is a device that permits the materials manager to predict what will happen to a system when demand changes. At any given time the materials management is concerned with efficient use of available resources subject to fluctuating and often unpredictable demands. Simulation is the device that permits a company to measure what will happen when a particular group of resources is subject to input that varies at random. Materials manager simulates operation of the system by subjectign it to random variations of input using the Monte Carlo technique.

Organising Cost Reduction

There is no way to accomplish cost reduction or no one method that is going to lead to the ultimate in a cost reduction programme. The success of the cost reduction programme is assured provided there is organisation of people behind the cost reduction derive. Effective organisation for cost control is based on the psychology of the individual. Reducing cost and improving the profit picture are invariably the results of many small measures properly applied. Organisation for cost reduction may be defined as a systematic arrangement of a dynamic element essential in operation of any successful business. Broadly speaking, there are seven basic areas in a company which are subject to cost reduction analysis viz. Finance and Control, Sales and Marketing; Manufacturing products and service; purchasing and personnel. The areas mentioned concern every facet of the business organisation. When considering cost reduction there is no business area which can be eliminated. Therefore, cost reduction programme should involve every member of the business organisation and should reach at all levels in the organisation hierarchy. In otherwords company should take the approach to cost reduction through consideration of all its people or cost reduction has to go to every employee in the organisation.

For the success of an organisation of cost reduction following point must be considered:

(a) An/executive has to be responsible.

(b) The top management must have interest, cooperation, consideration and firm belief that cost reduction is worthwhile and necessary for the success of an organisation.

(c) The cost reduction awareness must be inculcated in the employee and must encompass all employees—each person that is part of the organisation.

(d) Cost reduction is a continuosu operation. It cannot be started and stopped at will but must be worked on constantly. There must be constant effort to improve, and to think of new methods.

Chapter 20

PURCHASE MANAGEMENT

Introduction

The scarcity of raw materials has practically put the people in purchasing department in a very tight position. The Purchasing department can be in a better position if the designers take a little pain to consult the purchasing personnel about the technological capabilities of the vendors. It has been observed that drawings are sent to purchase department for components with high degree of close tolerance. But we should ensure that high degree of tolerance is really needed because close tolerances not only make procurement difficult but also contribute to high price. The main outset of company's cash goes in materials purchase thus purchasing people should take greater responsibilities and should analyse the existing procurement policy and should tune with the overall organisational objectives and policies. The various activities associated with Purcahse are shown in Fig. 20.1. Materials supplies and equipment are the lifeblood of any industrial concern whether Govenrment or Commercial. These are used for converting raw material into forms that have higher utility and value to the consumer. Thus a value is added by the manufacturer which result into profit. Teh efficiency of any business activity depends upon having materials, supplies and equipment available in proper quantity with proper utility at the proper place and time and the proper price.

In India approximately 60 paise of every rupee of manufacturing is spent on

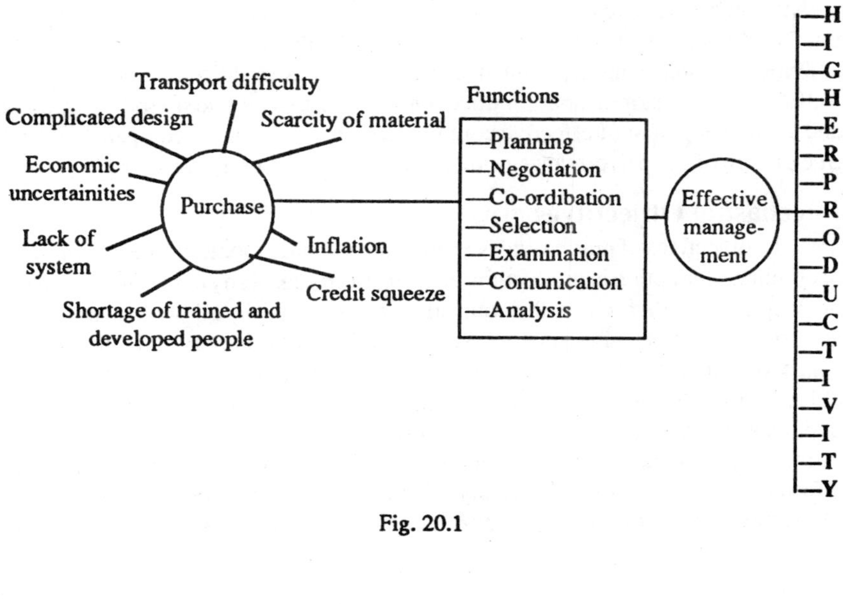

Fig. 20.1

material and about 90% of net working capital of industry is tied up in inventory. The improvement in purchase management by the help of standardisation, value analysis, material substitution, transport saving, cost reduction by packing modificatin and scrap reclamation all can contribute to the profitability of an organisation. Purchasing in its narrow sense refers merely to the act of buying an item at a price. A broader meaning of purchasing makes it a managerial activity that goes beyon the simple act of buying and includes the planning and policy activities, research and development, service selection etc.

Importance of Purchasing.

Purchasing Management, best reflects the role of purchasing in corporate operation and organisation. There is a trend toward introducing materials management in industry today, but to say that it has superseded purchasing would be to anticipate the future more than we feel is warranted. Purchasing is still a clearly identifiable function in most business organisations. The term "management" suggests that purchasing decisions involve the weighing of alternatives possibilities, and many of these alternatives involve the influence of other functions on the purchasing decisions. No organisation can operate without materials, supples and equipment. The efficiency of any business activity is contigent upon having materials, supplies and equipment available in proper quantity with proper quality at proper place and time, and at the proper price. Purchasing is a managerial activity that goes beyond the simple act of buying and includes the planning and policy activities covering a wide range of related and complementory activities such as research and development; proper selection of materials and sources from which those materials may be bought. The follow up to ensure proper delivery for inspection of incoming shipments to ensure both quantity and quality compliance with the order; the development of proper procedures; methods and forms to enable purchasing department to carry out established policies; the coordination of the activities of purchasing department with other internal dividiosn of the concern as traffic, receiving, storekeeping and accounting so as to facilitate smooth operations; and the development of effective communication system in the company so that a true picture of the performance of the purchasing function is presented.

Purchasing Objectiives

The objectives of purchasing is to conduct purchase function so as to minimise or eliminate disruption in production resulting from lack of any materials equipment or supplies. Further more this objective must be achieved with a minimum investment in reserve inventories. Another objective of purhasing is the maintenance of adequate standards of quality for items purchased. The purchasing objective is lowest ultimate cost rather than the lowest initial cost. Another objective of purcahsing is the avoidence of duplication, waste and obsolenscene with respect to the various items purchased. The mission of purchasing organisation is the effective commitment of the company's funds. Its objective is the economic success of the business organisation. Sound procurement is itself the proper management of the materials rupee investment. In other words the objective of purchasing is not so much to procure the raw materials at the lowest price but to reduce the cost of the final product. To ensure these objectives a large number of parameters such as right price, right quality, right contractual terms, right time, right source, right material, right place, right mode of transportation, right quantity and right attitude have to be considered jointly. The objectives of purcahsing is to procure goods that are best suited than those that rank highest in quality. Avoid duplication, waste and obsolensce with respect to various items purchased. Maintain competitive position of the company, develop good relations with suppliers and develop internal relationship that lead to understanding and harmony among the various organisational units within the company.

According to A.G. Pearson the prime objective of Purchasing Organisation is "Effective commitment of the company's funds" and having goods of the Right Quality, form Right Source, at Right Price and at Right Quantity and Time.

(i) **Right Quality.** Cost and Quality are critical dimensions. The inter-action between two is very complex. A right quality is not necessarily a best quality. To a large degree manufacturers determine the quality of goods by the desired quality of product to make. The considerations are basic materials, workmanship, grades, sizes, designs, colours, patterns,durability. For the purpose of purchase quality of raw materials etc., need to be established.

The quality must be described precisely so that vendor should understand what is exactly needed. The exact specifications of items have to be given, preferably in terms of market grades, brand or trade names, commercial standard, on blue prints, chemical or physical characteristics, material and method of manufacture. Use of national standards shall be made to the extent possible. Alternately, materials standards shall be fixed by the committee set up for the purpose in the organisations. Simplification (variety reduction) is a great boon for purchase department and is repaid in terms of reduced inventory investment, greater quality discount, better competitive prices, reduced clerical and handling costs, besides less recording, controlling, receiving and inspecting. It is prudent to obtain samples along with question or a sample of such material be available to supplier before quoting the price. This will help in building buyer supplier relations besides, scrutiny and decisions of choosing the supplier.

(ii) **Right Quantity.** Quantity to be purchased varies with the production strategy and planning. For running operations, P.P.C. determines the volume of production in advance, and in such cases it is desirable to enter into annual or bi-annual contracts specifying periodical supplier at regular intervals. This leaves the burden of ensuring the uninterrupted supply with the suppler and lot of energy of purchase department is saved. In case of varied strategy of manufacture, the techniques of E.O.Q. is followed to save the producer from the danger of stock outs as well as carrying cost of surplus inventory. Other strategical considerations in determining quantities, are combination of items to reduce transportation costs, anticipation of market conditions both of the raw materials/spares as well as the minimum quantitity of finished goods.

(iii) **Right Source.** The source of supplier is determined normally by calling quotations and the lowest bidder is selected provided he has quoted as per the requirement of producer in terms of quality, quantitiy and period of delivery. But such ideal situations do not appear in all cases and selection of supplier involves a strategic considerations of various factors. It is always prudent to select a manufacturer in case of patents standard products even if it means a little extra transportation. Secondly, the past records, financeial capacity, technical ability, and other resources play important role in the selection of supplier. Testing facilities of supplier eases, inspection of goods and all other problems arising out of inadequate supply at the producer's end.

The purchase department has to maintain a vocabulary of suppliers of different goods and develop it further from the knowledge/data collection through journals, bulletins, and newspapers, trade directory, and exchange of information through buying associations.

(iv) **Right Price.** The right price is the worth in terms of quality, time and adequacy of supply of an item obtained. It is no doubt easy and safe to go for standard products at a higher price but then one has to keep in mind the utility of item in the ultimate worth of product.

There is a tremendous growth in the number of varieties specially spares, fixtures and such other goods after the Industrial Revolution and innovations have put forth cheaper brands in the market. This has developed a situation where the new industries have to use their skill in selection of new brands who are attempting continuously towards recognition and standard brands who have proved their utility and due to increased demand are constantly pushing up their prices.

(v) **Right Time.** The ideal time of purchase period would be the minimum time for which the goods remain unconsumed. This could be achieved if the stockist or manufactureer of raw materials supplies the day-to-day requirements in regular instalments. This would save the storage. But the geographical and market conditions do not permit and it is where the ordering system comes into existance. The timing policies will depend upon fluctuating prices as well as problems arising out of monopolistic trade and sellers' maturity.

For large industries, located in interiors, "hand to mouth" buying is not practicable and as such long lead times have to be given to allow cheaper mode of transportation and economical bulks. It is the practice to remain in touch with the production department to know the expeditions/delays in schedule. The modern purchasing needs follow up actions right from the beginning of demand to ultimate supply stage including despatch and chasing of transporters through special messangers. These costs have to be weighed in terms of actual delays in production and purchase department cannot just afford to rest with telegraphic reminder or trunk calls.

Types of Purchasing

Purchasing is primarily a buying activity and therefore types of purchasing vary with the purpose of buying. There are four types of buyers:

1. Industrial buyers,
2. Buyers for wholesalers,
3. Buyers of merchandise for retail stores,
4. Ultimate consumers buying from the retail stores.

As such purchasing fundamentally is aimed at resale and consumption or conversion. Above four types will fall in one or both of these categories *viz.* Industrial buyers, and consumers (buying from retail stores) will purchase for consumption or conversion whereas Buyers for wholesalers and merchandise for retail stores aim at distribution or resale. As for the purpose it is evident that buyers of type (2) and (3) above are opportunist and mainly concerned with the market conditions. Ultimate consumers, a large percentage have to go by a necessity and the quantity purchased is small. The main activity of purchasing in terms of technique or scientific management rests with industrial buyers.

'Induastrial Purchasing' is defined by Dr. Watte as *"the procurement by purchase of the proper materials, machinery, equipment and supplies or stores used in the manufacture of a product adopted to the marketing in the proper quantity and qality at the proper time and a the lowest price consistant with quality desired."*

In most organisations normally the consumption of materials anges between 60% to 70% of the cost of products (Sales Value). These percentage vary from industry to industry, *e.g.* in the mining industry the consumption of materials would be proportionately lesser than another production unit but all the same the supply function remains vital and important. Besides Industrial Undertakings Central and State governments and other local bodies have to make large purchases. The important aspecthere is public accountability in the sense that those who spend public money must be responsible to the public representatives. This leads to added precaution ensuring that all purchases are made without any favour and form the most compective biddders. The very nature of purchase activity places the officials concerned in contact with the suppliers and thus call for judgement and decisions which are very important not only from purchasing angle but also from the fact that those concerned have to display the highest sense of recognition.

Purchasing Principles

Folowing are some of the important principles:

(a) The acceptance of order is to be specific and not implicit. Preferably this should be acknoledged by either side before it is binding.

(b) Ambiguity and mis-interpretation should be avoided specially in respect of quality, delivery, service, discount or any other such changes.

(c) The Indian Sale of Goods Act lays down that unless a specific provision is made regarding the time of payment or any other stipulation as to time of payment or any other stiputaltion as to time being essence of contract, the same is not implied. It has to be stipulated.

(d) The supplier takes warranty of goods as per specifications laid down in tender and not whether these are fit for intended use. If it is so required the detailed information has to be stipulated well in advance or through negotiations.

(e) The other features are buyer's right to reject unwanted goods, liquidation for damages, passing of ownership etc., are covered in legal aspects.

In case of major contracts, involving large sum of money or, extending over long periods of time it is advisable to avail of professional and legal opinion. Familiarity with law provisions will enable personnel engaged in purchasing to decide in which situation it will be desirable to take legal opinion. Summarising with *ethics* of purchasing, the following code be kept in mind by purchase manager:

(i) To be aware of company's interest.

(ii) To be recepient to advice from his colleagues and be guided by such counsel without imparing the dignity and responsibility of his office.

(iii) To buy without prejudice-seeking to oobtain maximum value for each rupee.

(iv) Eager to seek knowledge of materials and process at the same time establish practical methods for conduct of his office.

(v) Accord prompt and couteous reception.

(vi) To respect his obligations.

Role of Purchasing Manager

Unlike production, manager, purchase of capital equipment is decided by a committee constituted by top management normally called as purchse committee. The committee usually consists of members representing production, Design and Engineering, Finance and Purchase. The recommendations of this committee are then finally approved by the General Manager or Chief Executive of the company before the capital equipment is purchased. The next important role of a purchase manager is to apply the qualitative information regarding the image, the technical capabilities, the financial soundness and the reliability of the supplier. He should also find out whether the supplier is capable of providing technical know-how mainly in regard to the installation, commissing and after sales service. A purchase manager has to get complete details regarding offers of potential suppliers, tabulate them and supply them to the finance department so that they can make a thorough analysis. He shold also in collarberation with te finance department, come up with a suitable payment terms with the supplier. On the whole, the role of purchase manager in the procurement of capital equipment is that of a liasion man.

A New Approach to a Better Purchasing Management.

We all know that the responisbility of minimising cost revolves on purchasing management. It has been observed that for a steel plant the cost of converting raw materials into saleable products is only 8% while purchased materials, supplies and services account for 37%. It is therefore evident that much lies in the economy of purchase. In case of purchase, various factors that come into operation included purchase procedure, freight, quality of goods, vendor selection etc. In order to study the effects of each one of these factors a common measure is needed. In many organisations particularly Government, one is accustomed with the method of purchasing from the lowest tenderer. It remains to be seen how fallacious is the criterion of purchasing from the lowest-tenderer. The lowest tenderer need not necessarily be supplier of the right type of material and that too at the right time and in right quantity. This may at times lead the purchase manager to face situations which results in stock outs and defective products.

Visible and Invisible Costs. There are visible and invisible costs associated with purchasing. Visible costs include net price, freight, delivery date, etc. where as invisible costs are related to quality and delivery date which are hidden in the vendor's past and future expected performance. In order to study the influence of invisible costs, one can start with the terms of payment. At times the vendors offer discount on large quantity purchases and facilities for deferred payments. In such situations, large scale purchase leads to locking up of capital in inventory. One has to balance between discount for bulk purchase with that of cost of borrowing money for the purchase. In case of freight cost, one faces alternatives of carrying the inventory by different modes of transportation. In this case also one has to predecide as to whether the materials shall be shipped by premium or lowest cost transportation. The cost of transportation may also vary form time to time. In case the purchaser has to balance between the advantages of different modes of transportation with that of cost of borrowing money. The next factor which is of importance is quality of raw materials. Bad quality raw materials leads ultimately to the cost of prefering claims. Here again the cost of litigation for claims have to be balanced against the cost of borrowing money. The early shipment cost as well as late delivery cost also causes trouble for the purchaser. A new technique called Vendor Cost Imporvement Contribution is also used by enlightend purchaser. This involves helping the supplier in reducing the cost of raw materials through alternatives by suggesting for Make or Buy, standardisation, inventory, transportation, respecification etc. In effective purchase management a technique known as **"Hidden Cost Ratio"** has also become quite popular. This is a measure which enables the purchaser to compare the cost of purchasing from various suppliers. The hidden Cost Ratio shows the cost of freight, Claims, early shipment minus cost of improvement contribution over the rupee value of total purchase. If the hidden cost ratio of a supplier is Rs. 0.05 it means that the cost of doing business with this supplier is Rs. 1.05 for Rs. 1.0 quoted price. Such an analysis helps the purchaser to select a supplier. The hidden cost ratio can be calculated when the data pertaining to the behaviour of the suppliers over a long period of time is available. Therefore, for successful purchasing management the various techniques of determining the influence of factor like Vendor Selection; Transportation, Improvement Contribution, Quality etc are determined through the common measure of cost. The success for implementation of scientific purchase method will largely depend on the performace of the vendors which can be ascertained inter alia on maintenance of computerised historical performance data of vendors.

Chapter 21

PURCHASING PROCEDURES

Introduction

Purchasing procedures refers to the way in which a purchase transaction is carried through from its inception to its conclusion. Purchasing policies outline the broad objectives to be accomplished and guidelines within which the procedures must accomplish the desired results. Procedures outline in detail the functions to be performed by the people involved in the purchasing operation. Forms and records used to implement procedures and policies. Since there are wide variations among industries, firms, products and personnel with the result there are different set of procedures that apply to all cases. Some of the common steps to complete purchasing transaction are Recognition of need; Description of requirement; Selection of possible sources of supply; Determination of price and availability and placing of order; Follow up and expediting of order; checking the invoice; Processing discrepancies and rejections; closing completed orders; maintenance of records and files. Let us examine these basic steps one by one to understand purchasing procedures.

Recognition of the Need. Any purchase transaction starts with the recognition of the need for an item by someone in the company. The need may often be satisfied by a transfer of materials from another department or store room, however the store room must also replenish its supplies of the item. For many items a well run purchasing department, will anticipate the needs of the using department, anticipating advance needs is one of the consideration that determines the size of the order for an item. In such cases purchase officer buys a quantity sufficient to reduce the likelihood of such orders in case of sudden increases in the rate of consumption of item. A purchase officer has to develop alternate source of supply and potential alternative materials.

Description of the need. Once the need has been recognized it must be so accurately described that all parties will know exactly what is wanted. An improperly or poorly described need can be costly. Securing an adequate and complete description of needs calls for the exercise of tact or skill on the part of purchasing officer. He must have enough knowledge of the item being purchased to be able to recognise inadequate descriptions.

Selection of the Source. The next is the selection of the source for requisitioned items. For branded or patented items there may be but a single source but in most cases there will be number of alternative suppliers. For regular purchase consideration like goodwill, price, company's policies etc. are considered for selection of source.

For items that has not been purchased with regularity, there are several things a purchase officer may look for viz:

(a) Prepare list of supplier, by reference from salesman, user department, vendors catalogue etc.

(b) Narrow the list by discussing with the salesmen, interview, investigations.

(c) Negotiate the price with one or more based on company's policies.

The process consists of selecting the desired number of suppliers, in accordance with established guidelines from whom quotations will be requested. For non routine purchases, the procedure involves a careful survey of potential sources of supply.

Ascertaining the Price. Purchase department must ascertain price information on the item being purchased. Price will be one of the important factor on which the final choice is based. For many items it s possible to keep current price information, in the form of manufacturers catalogue, price lists and discount schedules. Such source of information must be kept uptodate. A second method of securing price information is to negotiate with the seller until agreement is reached or price and terms. This method is specially suited to goods made to the specification of the buyers. The third method is competitive bid. This method is widely used by governmental purchasing departments because of statutory requirements but also applied by industrial Purchasing department.

Placing of order. All orders should be in writing and should be on the buyers purchase order to avoid the possibility of level difficulties. When order is placed by telephone it is the practice to confirm the order by sending the supplier a regular order.

Follow up of the order. It should not be supposed that once an order has been placed, the purchasing department has no further responsibilities. Every purchasing department has the responsibilities for following up orders that it places *e.g.* seller may not receive order even though it has been mailed. Thus it is necessary to institute a follow up procedure for all orders placed with supplier. Responsibility for follow up is generally assigned to the buyer who placed the order. Follow up consist essentially of holding a supplier to his promise of delivery. Follow up procedures should be employed whenever the costs or risks resulting from delayed deliveries or non-deliveries are greater than the cost of follow up procedures.

Checking invoices. Invoices checking is a part of purchase function since receipt of invoice constitutes the usual notification that the suppliers has made shipment. Further it is the responsibility of buyer to see that his orders are accurately filled and billed though it is an accounting procedure yet in order to avoid delay it should be done by purchase department.

Maintenance of Records and Files. purchase orders are legal contracts and as such should be preserved for as long as they have legal significance. Requisitions and similar documents should be preserved by the purchasing department, since they constitute the authority on which purchasing department had taken its actions to a given item.

Maintenance of Vendor relations. Good relations are based on mutual trust and confidence, these grow out of the dealings between buyers and sellers over a period of time. The purchasing department effectiveness is measured by the amount of goodwill with suppliers.

Automatic Purchasing Procedures

The large volume of orders processed through the purchasing department, many of which are repeated several times during a year has led purchasing executives to seek ways of minimising the paper work. The automation of paper work has made great strides in the field of purchasing, maintenance of inventory stock record cords. Several machines and techniques have been developed to simplify and speed up the entering of inventory receipts and disbursements and to secure reports and disbursements and to secure reports on inventory levels. The use of such equipment saves considerable time and ministerial efforts and brings to the attention of the purchasing authorities current information inventories of materials. The other development in the area of automatic purchasing procedures is **travelling requisition.** This is a form that contains identifying information with respect to an item that is repeatedly purchased and includes the names and addresses of approved suppliers as well as prices paid on previous purchases. Executives have a common opinion that in the field of purchasing are in agreement for major purchasing innovations are being developed in automatic purchasing procedures.

Specialised Purchasing Procedures

Most specialised purchasing procedures relate to maintenance, repair and operating supplies. Specialised purchasing procedures deal almost exclusively with reducing the cost of handling small purchase orders. The small-order problem is not one that can be solved by eliminating all small orders. Better planning and scheduling can reduce such small orders by combining several into a single-purchase transaction. Whatever procedures are adopted by a firm to meet its small-order problems, such procedures must be designed to meet the specific-needs of the firm. No standard answer can be applied to all firms and all situation. It has been observed that many small orders occur because of carelessness, errors and ignorance on the part of purchasing personnel or related departments. Improvements in internal efficiency and management of purchasing function would automatically improve this problem at the same time that other purchasing practices are being corrected. The proper approach to solving the problems created by small orders involves at least three steps.

(i) Analyse and categories the small orders that have been processed in the department for a specific time to determine whether the orders had to be small orders.

(ii) Determine if any procedure could be adopted that would reduce the costs of handling such orders.
(iii) Exercise ingenuity in proposing and testing alternative procedures for handling small orders.

The majority of purchase orders involve small sums of money, since a substantial part of the operating cost of a purchasing department which involves the paper work required to place orders. Some of the procedures to be described completely eliminate the carrying of inventory by purchasing firm and thus eliminate this cost for the purchaser.

Blanket Orders

The blanket order is the most popular alternative to the single item, fixed-price order. A blanket order may be an agreement to provide a designated quantity of specified items for a period of time at an agreed price. A second type of blanket order is an agreement to furnish all of the buyers needs for particular items for designated period of time. Under this type of blanket order the quantity is not fixed until the time period has elapsed. The blanket order is best for items with low unit value, but high annual usage, whose rate of usage can not be accurately planned. The blanket order may be written to cover categories of goods that are broadly described, for example fasteners. Price is handled in number of ways in a blanket order. Firm prices may be negotiated for each item covered. The blanket order may specify market price and include a method of determining such price. The advantages of Blanket Order Procedure are:

(i) It releases the buyer from routine work.
(ii) It requires fewer purchase order which reduce the clerical work in purchasing, accounting and receiving.
(iii) It often achieves lower prices through quantity discounts.

Stockless Purchasing

Under this system the buying company has no financial responsibility for inventory of the good being purchased. The inventory is owned by the supplier. The goods may be located either at the supplier's or buyer's location. Under stockless purchasing system it is probable that prices will be slightly higher, since the suppliers assumes most of the warehousing and inventory costs. However the cost at the point of use may will be lower, because the seller may be able to perform these functions more economically than the buyer since he is a specialist in the products and handles his own inventory in any care. Stockless buying is advantages to both the parties and therefore likely to continue to spread and become a standard rather than specialised purchasing procedures:

(i) Buyer gains significantly as he no longer is required to tie up captain inventory.

(ii) Purchasing routine is significantly reduced.

(iii) Vendor's salesman do not have to solicit orders, they can devote more time to aiding buyers through service.

(iv) Lead time is considerably reduced and may even be eliminated under consignment buying.

(v) Buyer is lively to get a lower price because the seller is willing to make price concessions when he knows that he will have all customer's business for contract period.

(vi) The supplier can also eliminated more rapidly from his inventories spare parts that may became obsolete.

Re-ordering

Systems Contracting

A system contract is a total corporate technique designed to assist the buyer and seller to improve re-ordering of repetitive-use materials or service with absolute minimum of administrative expense and with the maintenance of adequate business controls. There is some confusion as to whether a systems contract is different from blanket order buying, automatic purchasing arrangements, and similar ideas. The essential difference is that in practice the system contact has been long-term in its operations, where as the other arrangements are if shorter duration, with changes in suppliers being relatively frequent. Following are some of the points which differentiate between systems contract and other methods of purchasing:

Choice of Vendor

Under the systems concept not only will the agreement be of longer duration but much more formal method of selecting the vendor will be employed to eliminate personal considerations. The chosen vendor should be a specialist in the materials covered by the contract so as to be able to offer maximum quantity to a large buyer of such items and discounts to the buyer.

Materials Covered by System Contract

In this system the prior rate of usage of particular products must be determined as well as the frequency of reordering over some pest period. The records show not only transactions with that supplier but also previous purchases from competitive sources. One could argue that transactions have no bearing on the choice of system contractor which has already been made.

Standardization

Under the system contract the buyer receives only the brands produced or sold by the contractor. This means that standardisation programme must be adopted.

Requisitions

In the system contract, the vendor guarantee delivery and, to remain a contractor, there is no need to requisition more than the buyer's immediate needs: There is no need for multiple copies of a requisition as is the care with most purchasing procedures.

Order Filling by Vendor

In system contracts the vendor assigns a number to requisition when it is received. The vendor prices the requisition, since it comes to him unpriced. He selects the method of shipment, since on-time delivery is a crucial element in the systems contracts arrangement.

Advantages of Systems Contracting

The following are some of the advantages of systems contracting:

(i) Systems contract substantially reduces store records, requests for quotations, bids, purchase orders; follow up and expediting procedures shipping notices, invoices and so on.

(ii) There is reduction in store room requirements, it nets a saving in personnel and space cost.

(iii) Opportunity for errors in ordering is reduced.

(iv) Obsolescence due to changes in requirement, is reduced. In addition without risk of materials in inventory, changes that would have obsoleted such materials are made more rapidly.

(v) A systems contract has significant advantages to the vendor as well as the buyer.

(vi) There is savings in paper work for the vendor under a systems contract.

(vii) In systems contract the supplier can concentrate attention on new ideas and materials not covered under the contract.

Small Order Procedures

All organisations have a significant volume of purchase transactions that are non recurring nature and involve insignificant sum of money for an individual transaction. It is difficult to anticipate the need for small, non recurring purchases because the situations that generate such needs are usually unrelated to one another. Frequently the item involved can be rough only from a single supplier, thus precluding the possibility if combining orders to increase total value.

Petty Cash Systems

It is system that virtually eliminates paper work. Petty cash is a monthly set aside to meet minor expenses of a business. Where this technique is employed, the general petty-cash fund or a special find for small purchases must be under the control of the purchasing department to preserve the advantages of centralized purchasing.

Telephone Orders

The use of telephone ordering of small value, non recurring purchases is thoroughly logical. Frequently when buyer receives a requisition from a using department, he must in any event, telephone a supplier to determine the availability and price of the item.

Chapter 22

SELECTION OF SOURCES OF SUPPLY

Introduction

The essence of purchasing process is the rational selection of sources of supply. In selecting sources of supply the purchase officer makes decisions that influence not only his firms economic success but livelihood of the supplier and the efficiency of the entire economy.

After the list of possible suppliers has been compiled, the next step is to evaluate each suppliers has been compiled the next step is to evaluate each supplier so that the list may be narrowed down to the predetermined number with whom the buyer chooses to place his business. This process of evaluation is conducted by comparing the suppliers in terms of their ability to provide the desired quality, quantity, price and service. In purchasing context, quality refers to the suitability of an item for its intended purpose. In purchasing therefore the best quality is not necessarily the highest quality; in fact sometime the best quality may not necessarily be the highest quality. The quality must always be judged in the light of the use to which the product will be put. In purchasing, as in all economic activity, price is a measure of value. The important thing to keep in mind is that price is meaningless considered by itself. A price is a good price only if it is the lowest price offered for a desired quality, in the right quantity and accompanied by sufficient useful services.

Selection of Prospective Suppliers

As selection is the essence of the purchasing process, it is imperative that final authority rest with the purchasing department. In some companies improper selection causing inferior goods and services has resulted in authority being shared with the using department.

Procedure

The procedure of source selection involves the preparation of an extensive test of prospective suppliers and the successive elimination from the list on various grounds until the number has been reduced to one or few to be favoured with the business. The produce is therefore one of searching for all likely suppliers and then sorting for one or ones with whom to do business. Some of the important factors responsible for selection of the prospective suppliers are: Experience; Catalogs; Trade directories; Trade Journals; Associates; Trade shows and conventions;

Requests for quotations.

When a new item is under consideration, a buyer should therefore, first of all inquire whether any of his present or past suppliers are likely prospects. Most purchasing departments maintain vendor files which contain the the names and addresses of all vendors with whom the company has dealt throughout its history as well as a notation of classes of goods that have been purchased from each vendor. Frequently the files are set up to include additional data on such things as the reliability of the supplier in meeting commitment dates, willingness to handle emergency and rush orders, and defect or reject ratios on shipment received in the past.

Catalogs

For standard production items such catalogs frequently are one of the most effective and efficient sources of potential suppliers. All buyers make some use of their catalogs and a substantial percentage of buyers use them extensively. A master card is then prepared for each catalogue, listing the catalog by the vendor's name and a second card on which the catalog is indexed according to vendor's major product lines. Many organisation appoint a librarian who maintains the catalog file as one of her official duties.

Trade Directories

A trade directory is a publication that list and classifies suppliers according to the products they make. Frequently it also gives a minimum amount of information on such matters as the financial status of the companies, their method or distribution and location of their offices. Some trade directories are specialised by industries as, for example a directory of all companies manufacturing paper and paper products. The better known directories, however, cover all industries.

Trade Journals

Trade journals or business magazines ar other very fruitful sources of supplier names. There are thousands of such publications, and no purchasing department can subscribe to more than a small fraction of total number. In general they are not useful as directories to be consulted as the need arises. Rather, they are general sources of information on new products, developments, and methods which are described in the editorial and advertising pages.

Trade shows and Conventions

Another source of information about suppliers that is available to all buyers is the trade show or convention. At the trade show the members of an industry display their wares in an attempt to attract buyers, build up their wares in an attempt to attract buyers, build up their interest, and, if possible, make sales.

Requests for Quotations

Finally information on prospective suppliers can be secured through a request for quotation form. such requests contain a blueprint or written specifications including quality requirements and estimated usage. The procedures is usually used annually on all significant parts and services that are being purchased. Bids are solicited from at least three potential suppliers, there by providing an opportunity for equitable comparisons among competitors.

Vender Rating

The objective assessment of vendors demands a systematic analysis of their past performance. But reassessment at regular intervals is a time consuming process and thus did not receive adequate attention. The systematic assessment of suppliers ability to meet the quality, delivery schedules, product price and service giving an appropriate weightage to each factor can help us in designing Vendor Rating system. The overall Vendor rating could be prepared to evaluate the vendors. Following are the there methods normally used for rating vendors.

(i) The categorical method
(ii) The weighted point method
(iii) The cost-ratio method

(i) The categorical method: This is a functional method giving emphasis on the cost of value analysis. In this method the functional utility is given more importance in vendor selection. We can device a system with three levels based on the value viz High value; Middle value; Low value. In each of these value system a list of factors is made for the purpose of evaluation, for example delivery; price and quality are given high value. The geographical location suppliers reputation are given middle level value. The categorical method relies heavily on judgement of the individual carrying out the rating.

(ii) The weighted Point Method: In this method the number of factors such as the objectives of the organisation, its products and economic conditions of the organisation are included. The relative worth of there factors are compared to each other will give a composite performance index. The relative worth of there factors as compared to each other will give a composite performance index. The relative worths of these factors vary from products to product, organisation to organisation. The following are the maximum but average points for the best performance.

Factor	Average Points
(a) Quality	35
(b) Price	30
(c) Delivery	20
(d) Service	15

The points are allocated based on the nature of product for example for toys quality is less important but the attraction and price are of main consideration while for aircraft components quality aspect is more important as compared to the price.

(iii) Cost Ratio Method: In this method a list of suppliers services is established in relation to the price. In this method the object is to evaluate the suppliers on the basis of proceeding considerations which may not be practical considerations. The small differences in the point score among various suppliers may not be of a great significance to justify their reactive merits, for example suppliers, X.Y.Z. have scored 60, 62 and 63 points respectively. In such cases price the orders with one of the suppliers as long as his performance is satisfactory. It has been observed that it is extremely desirable to develop good public relations with vendors. While choosing a particular vendors for a particular commodity one may have to look to one's previous record. The three factors involved in vendor rating and their weightage are given as under:

Quality rating	45%
Price rating	35%
Service Rating	20%

Quality rating is determined by the number of rejections in a particular supply i.e. working our percentage performance and multiplying by its weightage. Similarly price rating is determined by comparing the suppliers price with the estimated minimum price and multiply by its weightage. Service rating is determined by the ratio of number of timely delivery against total deliveries and again it has to be reduced to its weightage. The overall rating of vendors are made by working out total of all three ratings in case of each vendor. Normally the ratings of vendors remains between 80 to 90 points while 100 points are rating. The best suppliers do more than meet quality standards and ship according to schedule. They offer shorter lead times than their competitors; their prices are lower; and they offer more new products, ideas and miscellaneous services. The various materials managers have attempted to weigh all these factors and develop numerical ratings for each of their suppliers. A suppliers price performance can be calculated by comparing his price with that of the lowest bidder on the order. A similar comparison can be made for lead time. In each case, the suppliers rating is calculated by averaging performance on a series of orders. The formulas are:

$$\text{Percentage of Price Performance} = \frac{\text{Lowest Price bid}}{\text{Actual Price}}$$

Percentage of lead-time performance =

$$\frac{\text{Shortest Lead Time (any vendor on comparable item)}}{\text{Actual Time}}$$

Some companies consider only quality and delivery in developing delivery rating, others take price and lead time into consideration. The relative importance of various factors depends on the materials managers judgement. In view of the above facts the weight to rate Quality, Delivery, Price and Lead time by another company is as under:

Quality	=	40%
Delivery	=	20%
Price	=	35%
Lead Time	=	50%

Similarly knowledge of vendors financial condition can after all save the time and effort of further investigation. It is not unusual for small business to aspire unwisely to large orders, financing such orders after exceeding the capacity of the firm's working capital and borrowing ability. Buying locally is sometimes an important factor in vendor selection. Most buyers prefer to patronise local sources whenever possible. Local buying normally assures better service, quick delivery, and greater ease for resolving misunderstandings.

Vendors Relations

A company standing in the business community is to a considerable degree determined by the manner in which it deals with its suppliers . A company with a good reputation in suppliers relations is more likely to attract customers than one with a bad name. Suppliers relations is more likely to attract customers than one with a bad name. Suppliers can make a direct contribution to a company's success, their product development and research efforts can be of tremendous assistance to their customers. One of the major problems of materials management is sudden shifts in the demand for materials requiring either rapid cancellation of existing commitments or extra output to prevent shortage. Co-operative suppliers can do much to help the materials manager with such problems.

Reciprocity and Trade Relation

Reciprocity and trade relations continue to play an important part in vendors selection. In fact, increased competition, increased product diversification, plus the decentralization of management, and the complicity of management decision making are causing an increased use of reciprocity and trade relations. Trade relations executives view reciprocity as an economic process of trading. In contrast they view trade relations as a management function, which deal with complex logistic and industrial intelligence factors in purchasing decisions, beyond the factor of quality, service and price. Some buyers disapprove of reciprocity because it usually constraints the purchasing departments opportunity to increase profits by reducing materials costs. It can be reasoned logically that if all factors are equal it is good business to buy from companies that are also customers because to do so strengthens the relationship and mutual understanding between two companies. To buy from customers when Quality, service and Price are equal is the stated reciprocity policy of the majority of the companies. The concept of reciprocity has been a part of the business scene since trade began and it is still a potent force in industrial marketing. However in recent times the old concept of reciprocity has given way to the development of a new concept called trade relations. The major factors which contributed to this change of concept include managerial decentralization, diversification of products and processes.

LETTERS OF INTENT AND IMPORT OF EQUIPMENT

The letter of intent is a device that can reduce thee risk of cancellation charges and misunderstanding between buyer and supplier. It is particularly useful when a buyer finds it advantageous to define purchase terms and conditions before he can formally commit himself to buy anything.

Import of Machinery

Importing is an essential economic function which cannot be completely eliminated. The international trade is undoubtedly governed by political motives and as such a country can not totally rely on another country for its requirements of specific items. Government of India from time to time review the import policies considering various aspects such as trade balance, raw materials positions etc. Recently import policy has been liberalised as shortage of raw materials have led to under utilization of capacity.

Procedure

If a company is importing for the first time, the first and foremost step for it would be to check whether the item is allowed to be imported. In case the import clearance is obtained or the item is not banned for imports, a company has to go through the following stages to accomplish the purchase:

(i) **Localizing the Foreign Source of Supply:** This has to be done by contacting the Ministry of Trade, Foreign consultants and Embassies having a commercial attache who is well versed with the list of suppliers in his country.

(ii) **Procurement of the Items:** At this stage the importer will be involved with foreign source of supply, manufacturing unit of company, engineering department and governmental institutions like DGTD; MMTC & STC.

(iii) **Documentation:** Special documents, not used for indigenous purchases, the commonly used documents are:

(a) BIll of leading
(b) Invoices
(c) Certificate of origin
(d) Weight certificates
(e) Insurance policy
(f) Marking of packages

Nature of Document

Bill of Lading: The bill of lading is the most important document which accompanies bill of exchange drawn under letter of credit. The bill of lading is a document signed by the master of a ship or by the ship-owners or their agents, acknowledging the receipt of certain specified goods for carriage or to his order or assignee, or merely to order. Bill of lading are prepared by the ship on terms supplied by the shipping company. Bill of lading are usually made out in sets of four, three copies signed and one left unsigned. goods are released at destination only against surrender of the bill, and when one copy has been surrendered the other copies become void. the bill of lading possesses some characteristic of a negotiable instrument. It can be transferred by endorsement to another person. Good shipped under a bill of lading are often deliverable to a person or just to order, in which case the title to the goods can be transferred by endorsement and delivery of the bill of lading. It a foreign trade contract provides for payment of freight by the consignee, the bill of lading mast be marked. "Freight paid" or a freight receipt must be attached.

Nature of Insurance Policy

Marine Insurance Policy is a contract between the insurer and insured, whereby the former in consideration of the payment of a premium by the letter agrees to identify the letter against loss incurred by him in respect of goods exposed to the "perils of the sea".

Packing List

A packing list serves to indicate the exact nature, quantity and quality of the contacts of each package in a shipment. Banks may require such a list when they have financial interest in the merchandise. Clearance of goods through customs is also facilitated by packing list.

Clean Bills of Lading

A bill of lading which indicates that the goods are in apparent good conditions without any qualification is known as a "clean" bill of Lading.

Foul Bill of Lading

A "foul" bill of lading is not an acceptable document, unless specifically provided for in the foreign trade contract.

Invoices and Certificates

Among the documents the accompanying bill of exchanging drawn under letters of credit in foreign transaction are the commercial invoice; the consular invoice, the certificate of origin and packing list.

The commercial Invoice

The invoice describes the merchandise, indicate the price; and other details of the transaction. The financial terms of sale; such as whether under letter of credit, sight drafts etc. are given. The number of packages and identifying marks and numbers on them are clearly is not a document of title, nor is it negotiable.

Payments

The importer is involved with Banks; Ministry of Finance; and Reserve Bank of India The documents involved are: Letter of credit; Terms of Payment; Rate of exchange; Payments under various credits and agreements. The letter of credit is an arrangement whereby the obligation to pay an exporter is undertaken by Bank. The liability for payment is really that of the Bank issuing the letter of credit and the Bank that honours the drafts drawn by the exporter, gets reimbursed by the Issuing Bank. The essential functions of letter of credit are: Name of the Bank, Issuing letter of credit; Instrument mentioning the name and full address of the beneficiary is clearly stated; The name of the importer for whose amount of credit is opened; The letter of credit has an expiration date i.e. a date upto which the instrument is valid; the type of credits opened whether revocable or irrevocable etc.

Problems in Import

Language

Language is often the biggest barrier to successful foreign purchasing. Industrial purchasing is highly technical process. It is essential that buyer and seller be genuinely fluent in the same language.

Legal and financial

Purchase law is different in each country. Consequently, buyer and seller must exercise much greater care in negotiating contracts because each is working from a different legal framework. Trade terms must be carefully defined.

Quality Standards

The industrial buyer likes to get precisely the quality that he needs. Poor quality products will perform unsatisfactorily; premium quality products will be wasteful if the extra quality is not needed.

Government Procurement

The basic principles of materials management are as applicable to government procurement as they use to private industry. In every case, materials management should be oriented towards the objectives of the organisation it serves. The fundamental objective of the materials manager in government is not significantly different from that of his counterpart in industry. The materials manager in the private firm strives to maximise his company's profits over the long term. The public purchasing executive attempts to get maximum value for the taxpayer's rupee.

Difference In Approach Between Government and Private Industry

Difference between government and private industry procurement is not basic principles but in legal environment. The private purchasing official has tremendous flexibility; the public official is regulated by a myriad of laws. The tight regulation makes public procurement inflexible and not always efficient, but it is politically essential for the two basic reasons viz: To protect the tax payer against corruption; To promote non economic objectives.

To protect the taxpayer against corruption

The public purchasing executives are atleast as honest as their counterparts in private industry, but they remain circumscribed by literally hundreds regulations designed to prevent malpractice. In some cases, these regulations protect the professional public purchaser from political pressures, in other they simply make it difficult for him to do a competent role.

To Promote non economic objectives

Legislative bodies have always assumed that public purchasing should take social as well as economic factors into account. The state purchasing executive may be forced to buy locally even when better values can be obtained from a supplier in another city or state.

The DGS & D

The Directorate General of Supplies and Disposals constitute the central purchasing organisation of India. It is responsible for the procurement and purchase of supplies required by the identifying departments of the Government of India, including the Defense Organisation; Railways; Post and Telegraph Department. The DGS & D services are also utilized by State Governments; Public Sector Enterprise and Quasi-Public bodies. The DGS & D, being a government department is accountable to the Parliament for its action. DGS & D also scrutinizes proposals for the purchase of stores from abroad with a view to ensure encouragement of Indian Industries and to prevent as far as possible purchase of stores from outside India when goods of suitable quality are indigenously obtainable. DGS & D also inspect stores purchased direct by Government Departments and other bodies when purchasing departments want to make use of the services of DGS & D. Although the majority of DGS & D purchase are made within the country, DGS & D also imports from East European countries.

In order to ensure expeditious supplies of critical items to major indentors, periodic meetings are held to consider issues lake coverage of indents, supply positions of contracts and bittlenecks which may hold up supplies. The disposal way of DGS & D is charged with the responsibility of the disposal of stores declared surplus by various government departments. DAG & D promotes standardisation not only by purchasing the stores according to some standard specification, but also by directly assisting, encouraging and insisting upon the suppliers to maintain the standards in manufacture and quality control techniques. No supplier is registered with DGS & D unless it is verified that he has got the necessary technical know how and he is manufacturing the stores to relevant standard specification so that these can be objectively tested at an independent laboratory. The firms registered with DGS & D enjoy the following advantages;

(i) Demands which are not advertised are normally met from registered firms.
(ii) In case of advertised demands copies of the notices are sent to registered firms.
(iii) Operational priority demands are normally reserved supply by registered firms.
(iv) Registered firms are not required to deposit any security deposit.
(v) The state Government and Public Undertaking may at their discretion waive the requirement of security deposit from firms registered with DGS & D.

Advertised Bidding

Government procurement executives operate in a fishbowl; every act is a matter of public record. State Governments are required to advertise for bids whenever possible. Exceptions to this basic rule are possible only when the purchase is too small to be worth the time and expese of advertised bidding or when the nature of the product makes advertising impractical.

Mechanics of Bidding

Advertised bidding requires highly detailed specifications. Once the specifications are available, the advertised bidding process becomes available, the advertised bidding process becomes highly mechanical, while going through the following steps:

(i) The government agency that is to do the buying gets a budget authorisation and specifications from the indentor who is to use the material.
(ii) Invitation to bid are prepared which set-forth, a specific place; date and hour for opening of bids.
(iii) At the specified hour, bids are opened. Under normal circumstances no bidder can withdraw a bid once it has been submitted.
(iv) The bidder is required to perform precisely in accordance with the term of the contract.

There are basic advantages of advertised bidding there are following weaknesses even for certain types of public purchase. These include:

(i) The contracts is automatically awarded to lowest bidder who possesses the minimum qualification to do the job. This may not be the best firm in the business.
(ii) The public purchasing executive using advertised bids tries to get bids from a maximum number of firms. In some cases it may be necessary to evaluate several hundred bids.
(iii) Advertised bidding is costly and time consuming compared to private method of buying
(iv) Highly detailed specification are needed.

Despite these serious limitations the advertised bidding is highly effective public purchasing technique when

(i) Specifications are detailed
(ii) there are many qualified bidders
(iii) the purchase is important enough to be worth advertisement.

Thus, there is good reason why most government procurement agencies will advertise except on purchases where it is clearly not workable.

Chapter 23

CAPITAL EQUIPMENT PURCHASING

Capital Equipment

Capital equipment refers to those items of machinery and equipment whose long life and high value require that they be carried in balance sheet and depreciated over a period of time. Capital equipment are boilers, pumps, electric generators, machine tools, mechanical conveyors, rail road engines and cars, steel rolling mills and generators.

Characteristics of Capital Equipment Purchasing

The purchase of capital equipment differs from the purchase of raw materials, supplies and other items in that each purchase is the result of careful negotiations, requiring the consideration of many more vendors than is usual for other purchases. The other difference between capital equipment and other purchases concerning the lead time, is the interval between the placing of an order and the delivery date. As a general rule, the lead time requirement for capital equipment is much greatet than for other materials and supplies. Similarly the specifications for standard capital equipment frequently are not so flexible as the specifications for raw materials and supplies. If a buyer insist on rigid specifications, he would reduce competition and probably pay a higher price as a consequence.

We know that materials manager is both a user and buyer of equipment and relies almost entirely on the Judgement of users of the equipment for engineering evaluation. The financial evaluation of equipment is primarily a responsibility of the organisation's controller. However, materials management should also play a major role in the economic evaluation of proposed equipment purchases. **The materials manager should also serve as catalyst to acquint others in the organisation that might help reduce costs.** The materials department normally buys capital equipment to specifications developed by company's manufacturing engineering department. The engineering department plays a more active role in buying equipment than they do in the purchase of parts and materials. The materials department has a special interest in capital goods purchases, however, because of the opportunities they offer for cost reduction.

The buying decisions for capital equipment are usually based on an analysis prepared by the finance department which in turn, is based on data submitted by manufacturing engineering and purchasing. The unit value of capital equipment is high because equipment contains a higher proportion of labour to raw material than almost any other kind of purchase. The high unit value is most significant for financing. The top management must usually budget and authorise such expenditure before they can be made.

Procedure for purchasing capital Equipment

The first step in the purchase of capital equipment is the evaluation of need.

Evaluation of Need

The recognition of the need originates with the using department and the evaluation of this need requires the study of alternative methods, a cost analysis of alternative methods, a search for equipment that will do the job, and a second cost study to determine the savings made possible by the use of the proposed equipment.

Specification

Once the need has been established and the type of equipment determined, the next step is to draw up specifications. The manufacturer's representatives are also consulted in designing the specifications.

Negotiations

The materials management department, which has so far arranged the contacts with Vendors, determine which vendors to solicit for quotations. The specifications are provided to selected vendors and they are invited either to quote or to send a representative to survey the job before quoting.

Ordering

After deciding the supplier, it is necessary for the purchasing department to work out with that vendor all details of the purchase order. An experienced buyer knows that, although he may be reimbursed money for any damages incurred he can save himself much trouble, cost and work by taking precautions before placing the order.

Follow-Up

Because the purchase of capital equipment usually covers an extended period of time, follow up of the order is an important responsibility of the purchasing department. The follow up of an order should be performed by the executive who placed the order.

Factors Favouring the Purchase of Capital Equipment

The various considerations favouring the purchase of New Equipment are:

Long Life Expectancy

One of the important reasons for buying new equipment rather than used is that the life expectancy of new equipment is longer.

Uniform Life Expectancy

The nature of a particular project may justify the purchase of new equipment. It would be unwise to install an item of used equipment with an uncertain life which could cause a breakdown operations.

Technological Innovations

The new equipment is usually of more modern design. The manufacturers are constantly striving to improve their products, not only because of competition for the product, but also in an effort to improve their own manufacturing efficiency.

Reduced Maintenance

The new equipment quite naturally requires less maintenance than used equipment. This is strong argument for the purchase of new equipment. Related to lower maintenance cost for new equipment is the fact that lessor stock of spare parts is needed for new equipment. Similarly it is much easier to evaluate competitive bids for new equipment than to compare bids on used equipment or bids that involve some of each. Similarly for new equipment, specification play a very important part in the purchase of major equipment. Once careful specifications have been worked out, it is a relatively simple matter to relate them to new equipment being considered.

Factors Favouring Purchase of Used Capital Equipment Cost

Low Cost is perhaps the major consideration favouring the purchase of used equipment.

Delivery. Sometimes a compelling reason for the purchase of used equipment is its immediate availability. When production is required on short notice, and the only possible way to achieve it is by the purchase of used equipment. Similarly when the equipment long life is not required it is satisfactory to buy used equipment. Another factor for the choice of used equipment is that the buyer can inspect the equipment before purchase.

Economic Analysis

Approaches to Capital Equipment

The company considering the purchase of new equipment makes a careful cost analysis to compare the operation of the proposed equipment with his present equipment. Because of the large size of capital equipment expenditures, most companies use detailed economic analysis procedures to calculate the expected return from the purchase against the expected cost.

Payback Period

Payback period is calculated by relating the cost of the equipment to the profit it earns and then estimating the number of years it takes for the equipment to pay for itself. The basic objective is to purchase the equipment with fastest payback period. Payback period is simply the time it takes to cover the cost of the equipment and is expressed in the formula $P = \frac{C}{R}$ where P = The payback period; C = cost and R = the cash return from the investment, or the present value of the future return. This simple approach assumes the return each year to be constant, does not allow for depreciation or taxes, and ignores returns after the original investment is recovered.

Discounted cash Flow

According to this approach the management assumes that a minimum return must be made on their capital, and an investment is not made if this standard is not met. For example, a lot of companies assume that they must earn a 20 percent return after tax on new investment in plant and equipment. They then discount the value of future cash flows to the present at this rate. The discounting factor assumes that the return is spaced out evenly during the year. The discounted cash flow refers to the rate of discount which when applied to the future cash flows will equate their sum to the supply price of the assets. It is given in the formula.

$$C = \frac{Rs}{1+r} = \frac{R_1}{1+r} + \frac{R_2}{(1+r)^2} + \ldots + \frac{R_n}{(1+r)^n} + \frac{S}{(1+r)^n}$$

where r = discounted rate of return

R_1; R_2; = cash flow after taxes in years 1, 2, ... 4.

n = life of association

s = salvage value

After the discounted rate of return on the investment has been calculated it is compared with the cost of the capital to be invested. If the return is greater than the cost, the purchase is economically sound, because the discounted return is greater than the return that could be obtained from the invested capital in alternative use.

Present Value

Any investment calculations involve two things: the expected pay off; or savings, which extends over many years, and the cost of the capital invested. Because capital equipment will usually produce savings over a long period of time, it is necessary to determine the worth of the future savings today. The present value of anticipated savings can be obtained by several means, the simplest of which is:

$$V = \frac{R_1}{1+i} + \frac{R_2}{(1+i)^2} + \ldots + \frac{R_n}{(1+i)^n} + \frac{S}{(1+i)^n}$$

where V = Present Value

i = the interest rate on capital

R_1; R_2; R_3; .... R_n

= cash flow after taxes in years 1, 2, 3, ..., n

n = life of asset

s = salvage value in year n.

If the present value of the investment, V, exceeds the cost of the equipment, the purchase is economically sound. The determination of the present value of estimated future savings is an integral part of any capital equipment economic analysis.

Return on Assets

The approach relates the cash savings anticipated to result from the purchase to the amount of money invested.

$$\text{Return of Assets} = \frac{\text{Present Value of Savings}}{\text{Rupee investment}} \times 100$$

This approach is subject to all conceptual difficulties already mentioned viz. Estimated if of equipment; estimated future returns, etc.

Therefore variety of economic analysis techniques is great, and they often involve quite detailed and complicated procedures. It a new machine has a greater out put or a faster rate of operation, one might assume this to be a greater value. But this is nob necessarily true if there is no need for the faster or greater output.

Leasing

At times the capital equipment or items of major equipment may be leased instead of being purchased. The principal difference between the two types of transactions is that title to the equipment remains with the original owner.

Factors Favouring Leasing

One of the important reasons for leasing equipment is the temporary nature of certain needs. The example of items normally taken on leasing are; Metal scaffolding; Wheel barrows. Pneumatic tools and many other such equipments whose life is longer than the project. Similarly leasing for temporary use is the rental of power equipment, such as transformer, for emergency service until other equipment can be delivered or repaired. Companies with very high opportunity costs of capital often prefer to lease many of their assets. For example, a company that earns 20 percent on its own capital might prefer to lease a fleet of cars for its salesmen rather than buy them. The leasing company might be willing to settle for 10 percent return capital. Leasing has grown enormously in popularity in recent years. The tentative percentage of leasing by different industry as showed by a survey is; Transportation Equipment (23%); Materials-Handling Equipment (18%) Machine tools (17%) and other machines and equipment (11%).

Advantages

Companies that lease do so both to avoid the responsibility of ownership and to make capital available for other purpose. On the other hand if a company owns equipment it must capitalise its costs. Depreciation charges deductible as operating expense must be spread over the life of the equipment. Normally lessor pays not only an adequate amount to cover probable maintenance, depreciation; taxes; and other expenses but also a healthy profit for the lessor. Decisions to make or buy; or lease affect both manufacturing and materials activities and should not be made without the approval of both the manufacturing and the materials manager.

Sometime the nature of the equipment may make outright purchase impracticable. Similarly the fact that certain equipment has a high rate of depreciation is another reason for leasing. Companies operating fleets of trucks and passengerscars often resort to lease for this reason. It has been found that, because of high depreciation of such automatic equipment, it is often more economical to rent the fleet and leave the problem of replacement to the lessor. It should be remembered that, by leasing equipment, the buyer is spared the large cash outlay required for out right purchase.

There are some unfavourable aspect of leasing that should be taken into account before decision to leasing equipment is made. Over an extended period of time it probably will cost a company more to lease than to buy equipment. This is so because the lessor expects to make a profit proportionate to his risk, and the risk supplier is greater from leasing than form selling. A lessee should also recognise that he will have to grant the lessor access to leased equipment for repair and maintenance. Such free access can prove embarrassing to a company that has methods and processes which it desires to keep private.

Mechanics of Leasing

Equipment available under lease may be available directly from the manufacturer, an outside sales agency, and firms specialising in financing and leasing equipment. Leasing arrangements are evidenced by a contract. The contract describes the equipment so that it can be positively identified, defines the duration of the lease, sets the rental rate and terms of payment, and defines the responsibility for maintenance of the equipment. Frequently the lease agreement includes an option of outright purchase with the provision that rental payments may be applied against the purchase price.

Chapter 24

DETERMINATION OF PRICE (RIGHT PRICE)

Introduction

Price is value expressed in terms of money. In a buying decision there is always a tendency to think in terms of process as being either high or low in an absolute sense, where as a buyer should concentrate his attention on the value of the product for his purpose and then ask himself whether the price is an accurate measure of that value to him. The relation of price to value is a primary responsibility of the purchasing agent.

Right Price.

Determining a fair and reasonable price and negotiating to get it requires a very high degree of skill and judgement. It is true because most prices are determined from estimates and judgements and not precise facts. Because a supplier cannot precisely forecasts his sales and production volumes, he is unable to calculate his costs precisely. Hence he is unable to calculate the precise price he needs to maximise profit and is thus forced to rely on his business judgement. Judgement of costs, profits and prices are always subject to analysis and negotiation. The market also plays a dominant role in pricing. When business is booming, manufacturers can generally increase their prices. Sales go up and during such times there is little effort, the most skillful buyer can do to gain price concessions. On the other hand when the market turns downward, circumstances change radically. The supplier, for survival reasons must review his costs and be willing to make price concession. A professional buyer has a comprehensive knowledge of cost, production booms and recessions. He has also the knowledge of negotiating principles, make or buy analysis, techniques of group ordering, and selection of the appropriate type of contract. Competition is the mainspring of good pricing for one overriding reason. All suppliers do not have the same costs of production. The sales from all products must recover all costs, plus a little more if a profit is to be made. However, individual product do not always sell at a profit. The sum of all out-of-pocket costs is the lowest price at which a firm can reasonably accept business. Break even analysis may enable a buyer to further his pricing objectives in three ways:

(i) To sharpen his perception of purchasing role in his own company's profit and loss performance

(ii) To gain clues on the timing of future price changes and

(iii) To obtain assistance in determine the reasonableness of a vendor's price quotations.

Pricing Tools—Break Even Analysis

Break even analysis is a planning tool and used by top management. Break even analysis helps management make intelligent decisions about proposed changes in the firm's product mix, about the pricing of individual products and about the purchase of new production equipment.

A business is said to break even when its income equals its expenditure. The break even point means the level of output or sales at which no profit or loss is made. It represents the position at which marginal profit or contribution is just sufficient to cover fixed overheads when production exceeds the break-even, business makes a profit and when production is below the volume of production at break even point, the business makes a loss. *The following problems are solved with the help of break even analysis.*

★ Total profit of business is ascertained at various levels of activity and different patterns of production and sales.

★ Reporting the top management the affect on net profits of introducing a new line or discontinuing the existing line.

★ Where severe competition is being met and it is desired to reduce the selling price, the affect of any reduction on profits can be easily ascertained.

★ Where the reduction in selling price is intended to increase sales, the increase necessary to allow to earn the previous profit can be calculated. The controllability and postponability of expenditure can be worked out from the break even point.

★ It helps in planning and managerial control and can be helpful in detecting the effect of gradual changes that may have crept into the operation of budget planning and evaluating new proposals and alternative courses of action.

Thus the utility of Break-even analysis to the management lies in the fact that it represents a cross-sectional view of the profit structure. It highlight the areas of economic strength and weaknesses in the firm.

Assumption Underlying Break Even Analysis

Following are the assumptions which are taken into consideration before drawing the Break Even Analysis.

a. All costs are perfectly variable over the entire range of volume of production.
b. All costs are absolutely fixed over the entire range of volume of production.
c. All revenue is perfectly variable with the physical volume of production.
d. The volume of sales and volume of production are equal.
e. For multi-products firms the product mix should be stable.

Following are a few terms which are commonly used in Break Even Analysis. These are:

(i) Margin of safety.
(ii) Angle of incidence.
(iii) Contribution.

(i) Margin of Safety. Margin of safety is output at full capacity—the output at break even point (it is the difference between output at full capacity—output at break even point) which may be expressed as percentage of output at full capacity. If the margin of safety is small, a small drop in production capacity will reduce the profits considerably.

(ii) Angle of Incidence. It is the angle at which income line or sales line cuts the total cost line. If the angle is large it is an indication that profits are being made at a high rate. On the other hand if the angle is small it indicates that profits are being made and are achieved under less favourable conditions.

(iii) Contribution. Contribution is the difference between sales and marginal cost. It is also called as marginal profits or gross margins. The marginal profit provides the contribution towards fixed cost and profit. If the contribution is less than the fixed cost the loss is incurred. If the selling price is reduced, contribution will also be reduced assuming variable cost remains unchanged.

Break Even Analysis—An Aid to Management

Break even chart is an aid to management in decision making. It is a graphical representation of sale and cost informations. It shows the manager the profitability of an undertaking at various levels of activity.

The break even chart is needed where the business is new or a new product is introduced. In fact the concept of break even assist the management to appreciate

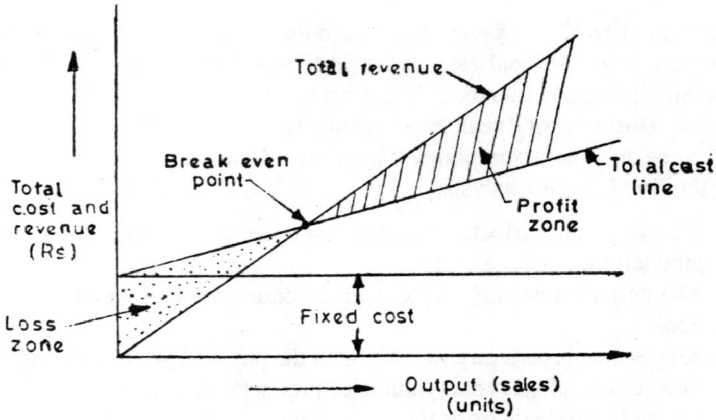

Fig. 24.1

the significance of quantity in relation to price. The objective of the chart is to indicate what happens to total costs and total revenues as output and sales change from one level to another. The genuine structure of the break even chart shows on horizontal axis the measure of output such as physical volume of production, percentage of full capacity output or sales volume. The sales lines relates total revenue on the vertical axis to total output on horizontal axis and is always drawn as straight line. There are usually two components variable costs (assumed to vary with output) and constant costs (assumed in independent of output) the vertical distance between total sales and cost is total profit at output greater than break even point and at the output less than this represents losses. The break even chart is shown in Fig. 24.1.

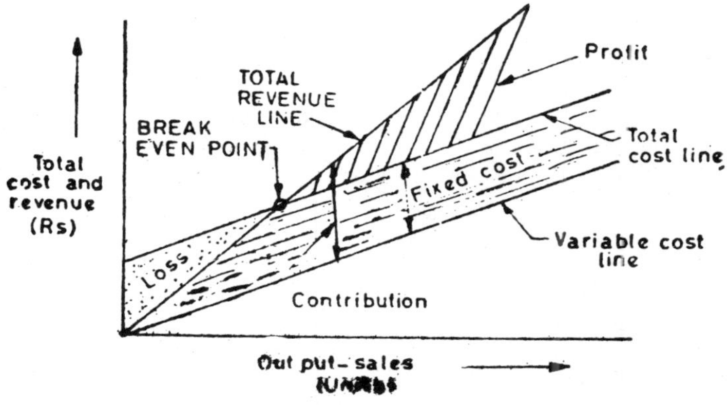

Fig. 24.2

Contribution to Overhead and Profit

Fig. 24.2 readily gives us at glance the contribution to overhead and profits. The short term decision making is more concerned with contribution to both overhead and profits than it is to the profit figure alone.

Construction of Break Even Chart

The plotting of Break even chart is normally in the following two ways:

1. Analytical Approach. In this approach we take one single income statement for the firm. The manager confines himself with the concept that if output is increased it will increase the expense also and he estimates the amount of increased spending. This process may have to abandon the linearity assumptions upon which the break even chart are constructed as shown in Fig. 24.3.

2. Statistical Approach. It is also called as historical approach because in this approach series of income statements periods which reflect varying levels of output and costs are taken. In this approach the output and cost relations are plotted on a scatter diagram and if the cost output relation is linear we can draw back the total cost line back to the vertical axis.

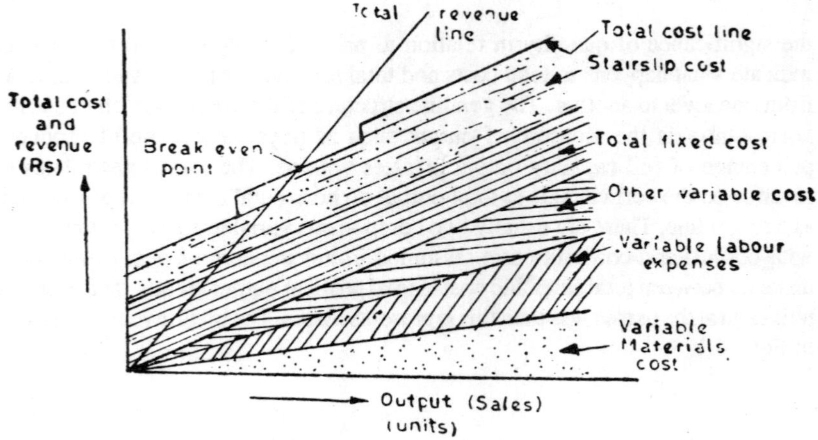

Fig. 24.3

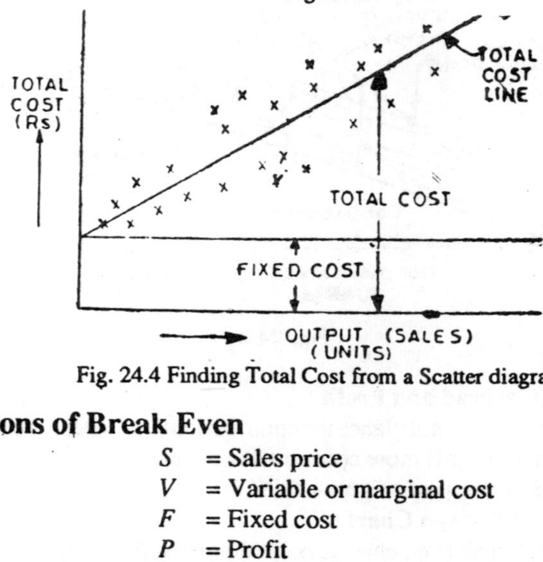

Fig. 24.4 Finding Total Cost from a Scatter diagram.

Calculations of Break Even

Let S = Sales price

V = Variable or marginal cost

F = Fixed cost

P = Profit

Let $S - V = P + F$ ... (i)

At break even $P = 0$

Equation (i) reduces to

$S - V = F$ ... (ii)

Let us multiply both sides of Equation (ii) by S

$S(S - V) = F \times S$

$$S = \frac{F \times S}{S - V} = \frac{F \times S}{\frac{S - V}{S}} = \frac{\text{Fixed Cost}}{\text{Contribution per unit}}$$

$$\text{Sales at B.E.P. (Rupee-Value)} = \frac{F \times S}{S - V}$$

$$\text{Sales at B.E.P. unit} = \frac{\text{Fixed Cost}}{\text{Contribution per unit}}$$

$$= \frac{\text{Fixed Cost}}{\text{Marginal Profit per unit}}$$

Example:

A company "A" sold 2,50,000 gallons paints with variable cost of Rs. 4.20 per gallon. Each gallon contribute 30% of its revenue to fixed costs and profits.

This year the company is contemplating a price reduction of 5 per cent.

(i) How many more gallons will the company have to sell at years 5 per cent price reduction in order to earn the same profit this the as lost?

Solution

Total Revenue = Fixed cost + Profit + Variable cost.

divide both sides by numbers of units.

Sales Price = Fixed cost/units + Variable cost/unit + Profit unit ... (i)

Let us assume that sales price be - Rs. x

It is also given that 305 of contribution goes to the fixed cost and profits per gallon of paint.

(Fixed Cost + Profit) = 0·3x ... (ii)

Putting the value in equation

$$x = 0{\cdot}3x + 4{\cdot}20 \quad \text{... (i)}$$

$$(x - 0{\cdot}3)x = 4{\cdot}20$$

$$0.7x = 4.2$$

$$x = \frac{4.2}{0.7} = \frac{42}{7} = 6$$

x = Selling price = Rs. 6

So putting the value in equation ... (ii)

(Fixed cost + Profit)/Gallon = 0.3 × 6 = 1.8

It is given in the problem to cut down the price by 5 per cent.

So the selling (New) price per unit

$$= \frac{6 \times 5}{100} = 30 \text{ Paise}$$

New Selling price = 5.70 Paise

We know that

$$Q = \frac{F + P}{S - V} \quad \text{.. (ii)}$$

With change in the selling price

$$Q_n = \frac{(F + P)}{S_n - V}$$

$$Q_n = \frac{1.8}{5.70 \times 4.20} \times Q = Q \times \frac{1.8}{1.1} = 1.2$$

$$= 2{,}50{,}000 \times 1.2$$

$$= 3{,}00{,}000$$

$$Q_n - Q = 3{,}00{,}000 - 2{,}50{,}000 = 50{,}000$$

In order to reduce the price from Rs. 6 to Rs. 5.70, we are to produce 50,000 additional units.

Principles of Break Even Analysis

The break even analysis involves following principles.

1. To find the safety margin with proposed volume.
2. To find the quality needed to have desired profit.
3. To find the effect of change in price.
4. To find the effect of change in costs.
5. To find whether to accept an order or not.
6. To find whether to add or drop a product line.
7. To find whether to make or buy.

1. Finding safety margin

The safety margin refers to the extent to which the company can afford to decline in sales before it starts incurring losses. The safety margin can be represented by the percentage ratio of sales over break even volume to volume of sales.

$$\text{Safety Margin} = \frac{\text{Sales} - \text{B.E.P.})}{\text{Sales}} \times 100$$

2. Quality needed to have desired profit

This is one of the most common application of break even analysis.

The formula used to find the desired quantity is:

$$\text{Target Quantity} = \frac{\text{Fixed cost} + \text{Target profit}}{\text{Contribution per unit}}$$

3. Effect of change in price.

This problem with which the management is most often faced whether to reduce prices or not. To take this decision the management will have to consider the following points.

Reduction in price leads to reduction in contribution margin and thereby increasing the sales volume. But at times reduction in price may not always lead to proportional increase in the volume of sales which depends on the elasticity of demand of the product. The information about the elasticity of demand may not be easily available. The change in the break even point due to change of price is drawn below.

A different price levels, total revenue lines can be drawn as shown in Fig. From the chart one can then estimate the volume that will be sold and produced at each price and thus profit at each price value.

$$\underset{\text{(B.E.P. in units)}}{Q} = \frac{F+P}{S-V} \qquad \text{... (iii)}$$

S = Sales price
V = Variable cost
F = Fixed cost
P = Profit

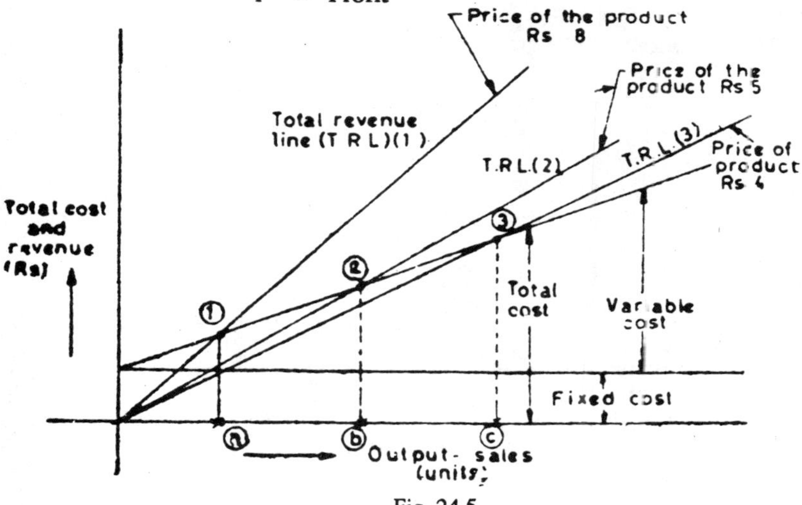

Fig. 24.5

As price changes equation (iii) changes

$$\underset{\text{(New B.E.P. in units)}}{Q_1} = \frac{F+X}{S_n-V}$$

S_n = New sales price
R_1 = New B.E.P. in units

4. Effect of change in costs

The change in costs can be grouped as change in the variable costs and change in the fixed costs.

Variable cost change

An increase in variable cost leads to reduction in the contribution margin. Now immediate question in mind is what should be the sales volume to maintain our present profit without change in the price or what should be the new price to maintain the present profit without any change in the sales volume.

$$Q = \frac{F + T}{S - V}$$

$$Q_1 = \frac{F + T}{S - V_n}$$

Q_1 = New break even points

V_n = New variable cost

The new selling price will be

$$S_n = S + (V_n - V)$$

These relations can be graphically shown as follows:

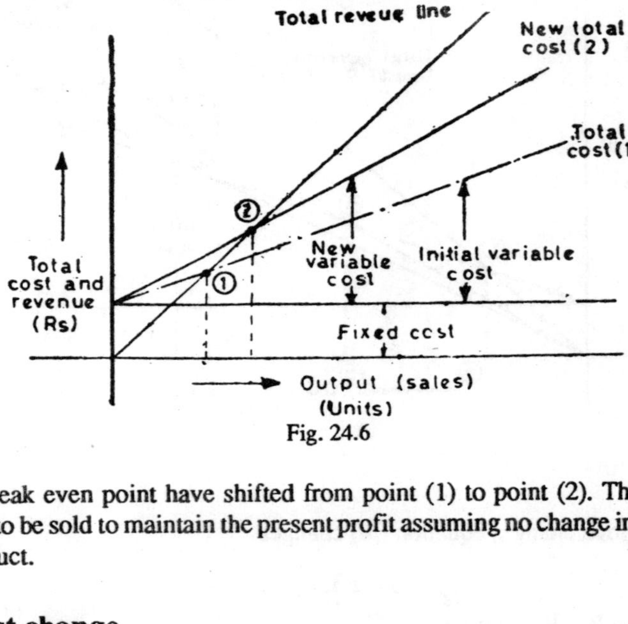

Fig. 24.6

The break even point have shifted from point (1) to point (2). Thus higher quantity is to be sold to maintain the present profit assuming no change in the price of the product.

Fixed cost change

An increase in the fixed costs a company may be due to change of the external environments in which the company is operating. The fixed cost change may be due to increase in executive salaries, property taxes etc. An increase in fixed cost will bring a change in Break even point assuming no change in the price of the product.

$$Q = \frac{F + P}{S - V} \qquad \text{(iv)}$$

$$Q_n \frac{F_n - P}{S - V} \quad \text{(v)}$$

Solving (iv) and (v)

$$Q_n - Q = \frac{F_n - P}{S - V} \quad \text{(vi)}$$

$$S_n = S + \frac{F_n - F}{Q} \quad \text{(vii)}$$

Q_n—New Break Even Point.
F_n—New Fixed Cost.
S_n—New Selling Price.

This can be represented graphically as shown below:

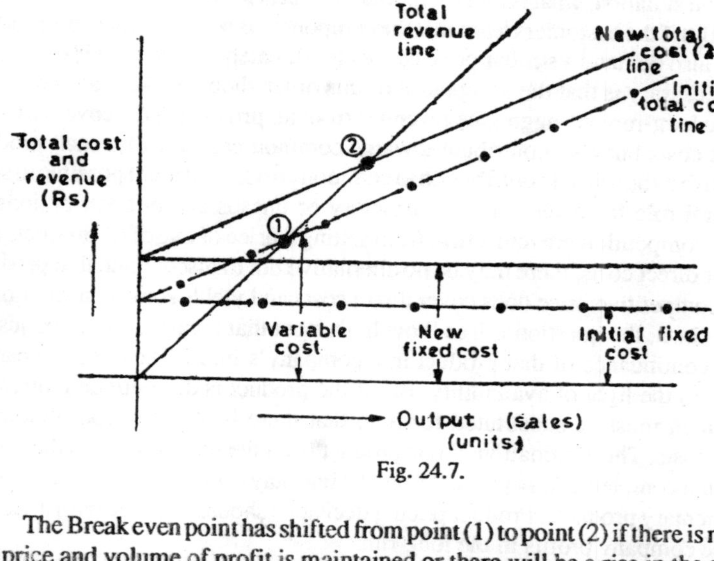

Fig. 24.7.

The Break even point has shifted from point (1) to point (2) if there is not change in price and volume of profit is maintained or there will be a rise in the sales price if there is no change in the sales volume provided profit is maintained.

5. To accept an order or not

Quite often the management is faced with an alternative to accept an order at a price with less than the selling price if extra capacity to produce a product is available. Company can accept an order which meets not only the direct cost but also contribute towards common cost.

A company manufacturing a certain component was operating at 50 per cent of the capacity. A foreign importer offered to purchase 5,000 units of the component at Rs. 5 per unit (The average cost of the product is Rs. 6.00). The question was whether the order should be accepted. The cost data were as follows:

Total capacity	20,000	components
Actual output	10,000	"
Direct material	Rs. 10,000	"
Direct labour	Rs. 10,000	"
Fixed expenses	Rs. 40,000	"
Total cost	Rs. 60,000	"
Average cost	Rs. 6 per unit.	

If we look into the problem deeply, we find that the additional cost of producing 5,000 units would be only Rs. 10,000 (Rs. 5,000 for materials and Rs. 5,000 for labour). The incremental revenue would be Rs. 25,000 and the firm would gain Rs. 15,000 by accepting this order. In fact, it would be profitable for the firm to accept anything more than Rs. 2.00 which is the direct cost per unit. Thus for highly competitive situation, what is more important is that at least the direct costs must be covered. But if the customers learn that the component is being sold at a lower price, they may also demand a similar price cut or else threaten to cancel their orders. So what is necessary is that the acceptance of this order should be kept a secret.

In the long-run, the aggregate revenues from all products must cover not only the direct costs but also contribute towards common cost. Ideally, each product should make a significant contribution to common costs, but it is not possible to state any general rule for determining satisfactory or unsatisfactory contributions. If factors of competition prevent a firm from setting a price of one of its products that will cover direct costs, there may be no alternative but to discontinue that product.

If a competitive price does cover direct costs and yields some contribution to common costs, the question arises 'how high must that contribution to be justify long-run continuance of that product in a company's line'? The question can be answered in the light of availability. But if the product is discontinued, there are others which must be substituted for it so that there is a higher contribution to common costs. The elimination of one product from the line may cause the loss of sale of other complementary product from the line may cause the loss of sale of other complementary products. Product pricing decisions should be made with a view to maximise company profits in the long-run.

6. Whether to add or drop a product Line

Any executive in a business organisation will be confronted with following problems when he decides among the two alternatives of add or drop a product line:

1. Should a new product be added in view of the estimated revenue and cost?

2. If the product is dropped from the product line, what would be the consequent effects on revenues and costs. The break even analysis is quite helpful in deciding the question of product planning.

In a medium size industry the following datas are given:

Product	Price Rs.	Variable Cost Rs.	% Sales Units
A	6	4	30
B	10	6	20
C	20	12	50

Fixed cost per year = Rs. 7,500

Total sales of the three products = 2,50,00 units

It was decided by the management to drop the Product B and introduce the product D. To find out whether it is worth while to drop product B and introduce product D.

Product	Price Rs.	Variable Cost Rs.	% Sales Units
A	6	4	50
D	16	6	10
C	20	12	40

Total fixed cost per year = Rs. 7,500

Sales for the current year = Rs. 26,000

Solution

Production *A* contribution is Rs. (6 – 4) = Rs. 2. WE have the sales price of Rs. 6 or in other words for the selling price of Rs. 6 we get a contribution of Rs. 2. The contribution for 33% sales of product *A* shall be

$$\frac{6-4}{6} \times 30\% = 1/3 \times 30\% = 0.10$$

Similarly for Product *B*,

$$\frac{10-6}{10} \times 20\% = 0.08$$

For Product, *C*,

$$\frac{20-12}{20} \times 50\% = 0.20$$

Thus the contribution ratio for product *A*, *B* and *C* is 0.38.

= (0.10 – 0.08 – 0.20) = 0.38

Total sales in Rs. = 25,000

= 25,000 × 0.38

$= 9{,}500$

Profit $= 9{,}500 - 7{,}500$

$= 2{,}000$ profit

Similarly the profit or contribution on new product line of products, *A, D* and *C*.

$$= \frac{6-4}{6} \times 50\% = 0.17$$

$$= \frac{16-6}{16} \times 10\% = 0.06$$

$$= \frac{20-12}{20} - 40\% = 0.16$$

Thus contribution ratio is 0.39

Total sales

$26{,}000 = 0.39$

$= 10{,}140$

Profit $= 10{,}140 - 7{,}500$

$=$ Rs. 2,640

Hence the proposed change is worth taking.

7. Make or Buy

Break even analysis helps us to a greater extent in resolving the decision of Make or Buy. Make or Buy decisions are vertical integration decisions. Make or buy is specific. It is used to decide whether to utilise the production facilities or not.

Example

A Car manufacturer buys a component at Rs. 10 each. If he decides to make it himself his fixed and variable cost will be Rs. 10,000 and Rs. 5 per component respectively. To decide whether to make or buy the component.

$$\text{B.E.P. (Quantity)} = \frac{\text{Fixed Cost}}{\text{Purchase Price} - \text{Variable cost}}$$

$$= \frac{10{,}000}{10-5} = 2000 \text{ components.}$$

Now interpretation is that if the car manufacturer wants more than 2,000 components it should be manufactured in the plant and for more than 2,000 components should buy from the same supplier.

Scope

Break even analysis can be most helpful in detecting the effect of gradual changes that may have crept into the operating relationship, checking the proposals, soundness, budget planning and evaluating new alternatives.

Budget Planning

The detection of creep can be accelerated by applying break even analysis in budget planning, and the overall soundness of a new budget can be tested as well. The approach under these circumstances would be through a break even chart, comparing the break even point determined from flexible budget figures with the break even point of past operations, and comparing budget figures with the break even point of past operations, and comparing budgeted profit with the profit that should be earned at the budgeted volume according to the break even chart.

Evaluating New Proposals and Alternatives

Proposals to add or drop a product line, changes in selling prices, changes in a manufacturing process, makes a part instead of purchasing it, or take similar courses of action should first be evaluated in terms of the effect on profits at expected operating levels. A secondary consideration however, should be effected on the "cushion" between expected operating levels and the break even point. Knowledge that a change will drastically reduce the cushion should receive careful consideration in determining whether such reduction is too great a price to pay for anticipated benefits.

The Break even analysis is useful in the area of managerial planning and review, including detection of unplanned change, overall review of budget planning, and evaluation of new proposals and alternative actions. The technical problems of break-even analysis, we know that no consideration has been given to such matters as changes in production mix, price-level changes, allocation of fixed costs between plants or products, or non-linear cost factors. These factors are, however, of major importance and must be given due consideration in break even point determinations.

Limitations

The static break even Analysis has serious limitations which we normally ignored. The limitations are:

(1) Errors of estimating the true static cost-function.

(2) Over simplification of static revenue function. The dynamic forces shift and modify the static functioning and managerial adoption to altered environment.

(3) Profits are residuals, the profit function gets the full impact of these inaccuracies.

(4) The correlation between output and selling does not mean a stable relation. Because the salesmen's commissions may be function of sales. Similarly advertising appropriation is determined by certain percentage of expected sales. Thus correlation between output and selling is not a true functional relationship. The output may depart from forecasts which are causing changes in advertising plan.

(5) Plotting Company's past cost and revenue, is plotting its migration path, this has little validity for current profit forecasting.

(6) The other drawback of break even chart is the wage and materials price increase causing trouble because they are nonreversible.

(7) The lines drawn between cost and income are straight lines but these lines should be wary line. We know that if production goes beyond a certain point we have to give overtime, may have to put second shift and add more supervisors and resulting much higher cost at once. The straight line assumptions may also be fallacious on the extreme right side of our charts because of our capacity limitations.

(8) The lines on break even chart should be bands or zones extending across the chart and not these lines only.

(9) Output indices used in most break even analysis are not very satisfactory.

(10) The break even chart is based on the past data and information which are not adjusted for changes in wages, changes in price of raw materials. These adjustments are quite cumbersome. We should use analytical techniques to avoid these adjustments.

(11) The chart assume that the price of the output are given. The assumption of horizontal demand curve holds true only for a perfect competition only.

(12) Break even charts are based on arbitrary assumptions as to the relative importance of different products in multi-product firms.

(13) The simple break even chart makes no provision for corporate income tax. If company suffers loss every alternative year then the adjustment for taxes is quite difficult. One final note of caution is needed for the use of break even analysis. The results of break even analysis are no more reliable than the accuracy of the data used in the analysis. Since the cost information available to most people outside the supplier's firm does not include meaningful details of its origin. It should not be considered as a precision pricing tool, but rather, a general guide in determining buying and negotiating strategy.

Non profit Organisations Pricing

Price Charged for Services Rendered

In a profit oriented company, the amount of revenue is a good measure of output. For the company as a whole, revenue is measured by the prices charged for goods and services sold in the market place. In individual profit centres, revenue is measured both by market-prices and by transfer price. Non profit organisations that provide service to individual clients usually can devise similar monetary measures of output. Other organizations must rely on non monetary measures.

Although prices charged for services rendered are an important considerations in the management control structure, many non profit organisations have given inadequate attention to their pricing policies. To the extent that pricing of services is feasible, the following benefits can be achieved:

1. Charging clients for services rendered makes them more aware of the value of the service and encourages them to consider whether the services actually worth as much to them as their cost.
2. If services are sold the responsibility centre that sells them can become a profit centre.
3. If services are sold at prices that approximate full cost, it helps the management to measure either efficiency or effectiveness.

Full Cost Pricing

Prices should be equal to full cost. A non profit organisation has a monopoly position. It should not set prices that exceed its cost, for to do so would be taking unjustifiable advantage of its monopoly status. Further more, the organisation does not need to charge prices that are higher than costs. If it does so, it generates a profit, and by definition us person can benefit from such a profit. Neither should a non profit organisation price below full cost because that would be providing services to clients at less than the services are presumably worth, this can lead to misallocation of resources in the economy. A full cost pricing policy should normally apply to services that are directly related to organisation's principal objectives, and to services that clients ordinarily take as a necessary concomitant to organisation's principal objectives; but it does not necessarily apply to peripheral activities. For example in a hospital, prices for hospital care, surgical procedures, laboratory procedures, X-rays and meals come within the general rule, but prices in gift shop in the hospital should be market based. Although the pricing strategy should normally be to recover full cost for the organisation as a whole, it may be desirable to price specific services above or below full cost. The relevant considerations are essentially the same as those that profit-oriented companies consider when they depart from full-cost pricing.

Economic Consideration In Price Making

In fact very little is known about precisely how businessmen go about setting prices mainly because, they want to keep their methods secret from competitors. Businessmen would have an important strategic advantage over competitors, if they knew how their prices are determined. Some of the methods about setting prices are:

(i) Cost Approach
(ii) Administering Pricing
(iii) Market Approach

Cost Approach

There are two basic approaches to price making, the first might be described as the cost approach and second as the market approach to price making. The cost approach seems to be the more popular of the two. The central idea of this method is very simple, the price maker adds together the individual cost items as determined by cost-accounting methods. There unit costs would include such items as raw material, direct labour, indirect labour, machine time, factory overhead, warehousing, males advertising, transportation costs, the price maker adds an amount representing his desired profit, and this figure represents his price. At times the cost approach to pricing is reduced to a formula. However one should keep in mind that cost relationships change overtime, and an uncritical adherence to formula pricing may ultimately lead to non competitive pricing. Although the cost method of pricing is extremely popular, there is reason to question its economic soundness. It is obviously true that in the long run the prices a company receives for its products must equal or exceed company costs. If the price is less than cost, the company will gradually go bankrupt. However, the mere fact that the buyers will not pay a price equal to full average costs does not necessarily mean that a company should hold out for that price or quit producing. In many situations a seller will be better off to sell for a time at less than his full average cost in order to carry a part of his overhead then to refuse to sell at less than cost. Thus, although the cost approach to pricing is popular and can be justified under certain circumstances. A price based on cost can not succeed for long in a competitive market if it is out of line with value, since competitors will force the price down to the value level.

Administered Pricing

This is a term that was first used by some economists during the world wide depression of the year 1930, to explain why prices of certain basic materials did not drop enough to stimulate the demand for greater volume and thereby initiate recovery from the depression. The issue of administered pricing has been revived because of the government attempt to hold down prices in the face of rising inflation.

Market Approach

It consists essentially of putting a price on the product that the market is willing to pay. This method of determining the price will vary. It may be done on the basis of market research designed to reveal through questionnaire or market test what volume can be sold at various possible prices. The technique is more commonly applied to consumer goods than to industrial goods because the experimental approach might be upsetting to narrow industrial market.

Psychological Considerations In Price Making

The fundamental psychological factors bearing on price is the prediction of future supply-demand relationships. A particular supply-demand relationship coupled with confidence about the future may result in advancing prices, whereas the same supply-demand relationship in on atmosphere of uncertainty may bring about declining prices. This attitude about the future can not be measured, either quantitatively or qualitatively. Although it is true that a general attitude about the future can not be measured, a purchasing agent can do much toward verifying his personal appraisal by talking with other purchasing agents or with purchasing association.

Another psychological factor deals with knowing how far to press a bargaining advantage that a purchasing agent may have from a supplier. It the seller's alternative to taking the order would be to reduce his operations substantially, he might find it advantageous to sell at a price that contributed nothing toward his overhead costs. Another psychological factor in price making is the process of haggling over price. The technique of price determination have almost disappeared from the consumer goods field. If the price can be changed by bargaining, it tends to prolong the selling. Another psychological factor appear "after the sale is made", it leaves the buyer with the uneasy feeling that he might have obtained a still better price if the buyer had bargained harder. However although "haggling" often created suspicion rather than goodwill. This is likely to be so because price is a more important element in an industrial sale, since the industrial buyer must resell a product made from purchased goods at a competitive price. Therefore a buyer must develop good trading and bargaining skills. The final psychological consideration in setting on a price has to do with non business consideration such as cultivating a friendly feelings between buyer and seller. At other times non business considerations may express themselves in terms of entertainment and gift etc.

Discounts

The price determination revolves around the discounts that are available or can be secured on a given purchase. The buyer must not only be familiar with the discounts available from his suppliers but most have a sound understanding of the various types of discounts commonly used in commercial practice.

Cash Discounts: The cash discount is usually described as the payment of interest to the buyer in return for the buyer's prompt payment for goods that he has bought. Some cash discount is granted by almost every seller of goods in the industrial market. The decision to take or not to take the discount is a fiscal matter rather than one of purchasing policy. However it is the responsibility of the purchasing department to make certain that the incoming shipment and all the paper work associated with it are cleared as promptly as possible, so as not to jeopardize the discount by delays in handling.

Trade Discounts: A trade discount represents the compensation of the buyer who assumes certain distribution functions for the seller. Trade discounts are usually granted for the purpose of protecting a certain channel of distribution. The buyer who buys directly from the manufacturer may expect a discount from list price that nets him a lower price than he would get if he bought through a whole seller, but, the buyer should not expect a discount as great as that granted to the wholeseller who performs many additional distribution functions for the producer of the goods. Trade discounts are usually granted for the purpose if protecting a certain channel of distribution. Channels that are efficient and perform a needed function should be preserved.

Quantity Discounts

The seller usually justifies such discounts on the basis of savings that he realises when he sells in large quantities. The seller saves on his marketing expenses because marketing costs do not increase in proportion to an increase in the size of an order. When quantity discounts are judiciously taken, they effectively lower the price. Therefore the buyer should inform himself of the availability of all quantity discounts and take them whenever indicated.

Chapter 25

PRICE—COST ANALYSIS

Introduction

The price to be paid for purchased materials may be routine as in the case of buying from catalogs or it may involve detailed analysis and direct or indirect negotiations between the buyer and seller. The analysis of all the factors that enter into price, and the attempt to ensure that the final price is a reasonable one in terms of the use to which the material is to be put and the competitive situation faced by the buying and selling firms is called "price cost analysis". Price-cost analysis has a number of economic benefits to firms that engage in it. There is obvious possibility of a reduction of the price that will be paid for materials and supplies. The information developed in such analysis can be shared with the supplier to the mutual benefit of both the organisations in matters relating to production methods, and materials used.

Price

Price is the value expressed in terms of money. The relating of price to value is the primary responsibility to purchasing agent. In order to know that the price being quoted is right formula, a purchasing agent must know, what quality is suitable. The purchasing agent must familiarise himself with the prices being asked by acceptable suppliers. It should be recognised that a price quoted by the vendor reflects more than costs and profits. Costs furnish a floor for price making, but they do not determine the price. The buyer must acquire knowledge of the sellers, productive capacity, the degree to which that capacity is being utilised and his own company's needs and plans. The buyer attempts through price-cost analysis to establish the proper level of costs for the various components of total cost. It is possible that through such analysis the buyer may detect means of lowering costs that had not occurred to the seller. The seller in turn can use this information on all of his production, not just that sold to this buyer.

Costs

Costs are composed of different classes viz direct and indirect costs. The direct costs are those that can be attributed to specific units of production, such as direct material and labour cost. The indirect cost are costs that can not be directly attributed to specific units of production such as executive salaries, machinery depreciation etc. The earning curve concept has direct application to many of the cost elements.

Learning Curve

Learning curve is the realisation that per unit cost of production of a new item decreases as additional units of that product are manufactured. The cost should decline with each succeeding unit produced, as the supplier becomes more skilled or learns how to make the product. Learning curve concept was developed in connection with new products. Out it has its application for products in which a company has a long history. A series of synonyms for the learning curve have been developed, including improvement curves, progress curves, cost curves, experience curves, time reduction curves, production functions and efficiency curves. In adopting the learning curve concept to an analysis of costs, one must first identify the factors that bring about lowering of costs. The factors commonly found in such analysis are improvement in production control; type of work and methods in use; Product; the ratio of assembly hours to machine hours; tooling quality and co-ordination. The learning curves are applied to the manufacture of production-line goods. It has been observed that anyone with an average knowledge of mathematics can comnute learning curve idea.

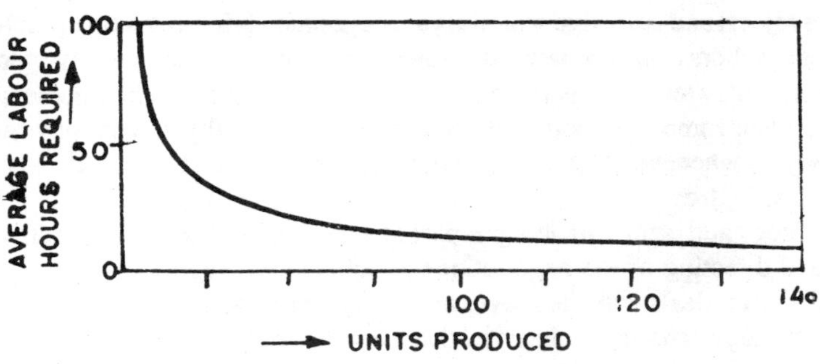

Fig 25.1 Learning Curve

Negotiations

In established concerns sources of supply have been developed over the years which have proved satisfactory in quality, service and price. When the usual source is found to be higher in price or to offer delivery terms that are not so good as those offered by a competitor, the buyer will frequently negotiate with the regular source for better price or delivery terms. Negotiations are most frequently employed with respect to non standard items that have to be produced by the buyer's specifications. Negotiations permit a more personalised approach to the problems of getting together on the terms of the sale than the formal bid-invitation method. Negotiations are useful when ever compromises are likely to be necessary in arriving at any of the terms of contract. With open negotiation it is possible to call on any of the departments of the buying and selling companies to bring about a complete understanding and agreement on all factors involved in the transaction. The time spent in negotiations is time spent in ironing out details that might otherwise have led to trouble at the time of delivery. Not all purchase-sales transaction involve negotiations. Branded items that are part of the shelf stock of the supplier and are catalog-priced are seldom subject to negotiations. As a rule, negotiations should be limited to cases where there are one or more elements in transaction which must be discussed and on which compromise or change is possible.

Certainly the buyer should negotiate any time he suspects that the prices quoted under one of the other means of determining prices yields a price that does not seem to be reasonable.

What to Negotiate

Negotiations involve discussions between the buyer and seller, on any element of the transaction on which discussion is needed and where alternative choices exist is an appropriate issue for negotiations. Thus any aspect of cost and, to a lesser extent profit is negotiable. The quality of material, change in dimensions of a raw material, a change in composition of a chemical; change in method of packing a material are negotiable. Similarly, the service aspects of a transaction are negotiable. The handling of rejects and defective materials are negotiated prior to making purchase commitment. Sellers may also negotiate lower prices by lowering quality specifications. Sellers may legally depart from the prices that are charged in order to keep customers, when forced in good faith by competition. Finally sellers may quote prices to buyers whenever cost savings on the transaction can be proved.

Strategy and Tactics

The strategy and tactics are integral part of negotiations. Strategy concerns the planning and directing of the negotiations to achieve the negotiator's goals and objectives. Tactics deals with the moves and maneuvering techniques employed to implement strategy. It has been observed that the seller has limited strategic strength when the product under consideration is a product readily available from many sources or when the selling industry is composed of sellers or when sellers are financially weaker than the buyers; or when it is easy to enter the field by new firms. The vendor can resist downward pressure when the product is unique or available from limited sources or industry is dominated by a few large sellers or when sellers are financially sound when it is not easy to enter the field because of huge infrastructure requirement or capital intensive industry or specialised technical skills are required in the manufacturing of the product.

Tactics is more than haggling. Tactics is based on developing as complete knowledge as possible of all elements that are to be discussed between the parties. Tactics requires knowledge of one's own needs, knowledge of vendor's capability, an understanding of the relationship among cost, value and price, and an understanding of the economic and institutional environment within which both negotiating parties must operate.

Successful Negotiation

The team should consist on both sides of members with adequate knowledge of job and skill for negotiations and also should have the full authority to speak on behalf of their respective sides as well as make decisions. A correct understanding of the main issues and an intimate knowledge of operations, working conditions and in addition must also possess balanced views, temperament, analytical mind and objective outlook. The management team especially should consist of those executive who can authoritatively speak on both personnel and production matters.

Make a Good Beginning

Well begin is half done applies to Collective Bargaining. It will be well to stress the end of mutual co-operation before starting the negotiation with a proper climate of mutual understanding and a common desire to reach agreement by objective assessment of facts, the process of negotiations has all the changes to have success.

Maintain Continuity of Talks

During the negotiations there are always chances of emotional outbursts. The important thing is to develop side issues and keep talks continuing. When the main issue gets confused sometimes it is better to come to the fundamentals aspects. Sometimes it is always advisable to leave the controversial points and leap over to the next issue.

Develop a Problem Solving Attitude

Negotiations will be easier if it is recognised and appreciated on both sides. It should be understood that the object of negotiation is not to win a victory over the other but to solve the practical problems of industrial life created through the interaction of various forces and various interests and also to lay the foundation for better understanding, better performance and increased prosperity in future for the benefit of all concerned.

Encouraging Leadership

It is much easier and much more practical to deal with a few representatives of a strong and organised body then with a heterogeneous mass of divided individuals.

A few points to consider in this respect include, in the first place, nothing must be done to aggravate the situation and for this tempers must be carefully controlled. The second important thing is to try to localise the conflict and not allow it to spread. Thirdly, to continue negotiations in spite of all disagreement and differences of view point. It should also be mutually agreed that the *status quo* must be maintained in the meantime and nothing done from either side to precipitate a crisis.

Principles of Negotiations.

An interesting statement of principles and policies to be followed in negotiation has been suggested by Arnold F. Campo. He describes some rules for guidance of both the parties as follows:

(i) Be friendly in negotiation. Introduce every body.

(ii) Be willing to listen.
(iii) Give every one an opportunity to state his position.
(iv) Always keep in mind the right and fair thing to do.
(v) Don't try to guide the discussion along a straight line directed to solve problem.
(vi) Define each issue clearly and discuss in the light of all available facts.
(vii) At all times search only for correct and real solution.
(viii) Consideration should be given to fatigue and mental attitude in determining the length of session.
(ix) Both parties should respect the rights of public at all times.

Chapter 26

LEGAL ASPECTS OF PURCHASING

Introduction

The materials manager commits a good deal of corporate finance when he places purchase orders. It is imperative that materials manager understands the legal aspects that are relevant to his profession. The primary interest of a purchasing agents in legal matters is to use a knowledge of basic principles of law in such a way as to avoid litigation. Litigation is both costly and of uncertain outcome and should therefore be avoided except as a last resort. On effective way in which a purchasing agent can minimise litigation is by investigating new suppliers as to their ability to perform, their financial responsibility, and their record of performance with other concerns. The rules of law and their exceptions can perhaps be better understood and applied to purchasing routine if it is recognised that they are basically the outgrowth of a long term effort of the courts to establish the intention of the parties. The best assurance that purchasing agent has of avoiding or minimising legal difficulties is through dealing with suppliers that he has carefully investigated, a knowledge and understanding of the basic laws that govern purchasing activities and a willingness to utilise legal counsel advisor whenever questions arise on which trained legal skill is required. But just as a lawyer is expected to exhibit sill in entanglements, so a purchasing executing is expected to exhibit still in avoiding legal controversies. A purchasing executive must understand basic legal concepts well enough to detect potential problems before they become realities. At the same time, the most powerful too he can utilise to avoid legal problems is his skill in selecting sound, co-operative, and reliable vendors. Vigilance in this area of his responsibility minimises his need for legal assistance.

A purchasing executive should never attempt to be his own lawyer. His responsibility is to protect his firm against legal entanglements by recongnising and correcting potential difficulties and by carefully selecting suppliers whose performance is not likely to lead to litigation. Therefore to protect his firm against ensuing legal problems, the purchasing officer should ensure that the contract is satisfactorily drawn and that it is legally binding on the vendor.

Contract

A legally enforceable purchase contract must contain four elements: (a) Agreement resulting from a offer an an acceptance (b) Mutual obligation (c) Competent parties and (d) a lawful purpose. Agreement, then is the heart of contractual liability. Since the human memory is fallible, and misunderstandings are inevitable if contracts are not recorded. There are at least two legal reason why a writer record of the purchase transaction is necessary: for proof of contract; and statute of trends, which operates to deny legal enforceability to oral agreements in certain cases. There is a general agreement that contracts for purchase and sale of goods are not enforceable unless some writing "sufficient to indicate that contract has been made between the parties" is signed "by the party against whom enforcement is sought or by his authorised agent or broker. Even a scratch pad memorandum may be sufficient under this requirement, provided that it (a) Names a seller and buyer (b) Is signed, initialed, or otherwise authenticated by (or on behalf of) at least on party (c) specifies a quantity of goods, and (d) In same manner indicates that it is memorandum of sale. Of course, such a memorandum would ordinarily be building only upon the party who prepared it, since it would not contain a signature of the other party.

Elements of Legal Claim

There are three basic elements in every legal claim:

(i) A factual relationship of the parties by which each party is entitled to have the other act or refrain from acting in certain way. This is called the right duty relationship.
(ii) Conduct of one or both parties that violates the right duty relationship. This is called the "breach".
(iii) Injury or damage to one or both parties resulting from the breach.

Legal Rights and Duties

Legal rights and duties are classified according to the relationships from which they spring. The two basic relationships are public and private. Public relationships give rise to rights of government. In the first group, there are two major sub-classes:

(i) Criminal laws and public regulatory laws
(ii) Tax Laws.

Constitutional and political guarantees are of fundamental importance among the laws defining the rights of citizens against their government, however, a host of other rights of the citizen, ranging from police protecting to social security, are also included.

Agency

A purchasing agent does not ordinarily buy for his own account, nor does a selling agent ordinarily sell for his own account. Therefore before examining the specific rights and duties that arise out of the typical purchase transaction, therefore we should appreciate the basic rules by which an agent can effectively bind his principal. In order for an agent to operate effectively in building a principal, two things are necessary the agent's authority must have been broad enough to cover the transaction and, the agent must have exercised that authority in negotiating the particular transaction. Authority to act in the name or on behalf of a principal most commonly arises by express authorisation. Every express authorisation gives rise to a number of implied authorisation which empower the agent to do those things that are reasonably necessary or customary to carry out the expressly assigned job. No implied authority can arise, however it direct contradiction of an express limitation of the agents authority. Both express and implied authority are legally classified as forms of actual authorisation. Their basic weakness, in everyday practice, lies in the fact that a person dealing with such an agent has no way, other than by direct inquiry of the principal, of knowing just how far his actual authority extends. Multiplicity of Business transaction enjoins upon a businessman to depend upon the service of others. In legal parlance, normally such persons who provide services is called Agents. The law pertaining to the relationship between the Agent and the principal is defined in the law of agency.

Definition of Agent

An agent is a person employed to act on behalf of another called the Principal, for the purpose of bringing the Principal into contractual relationship with a third person. A contract of Agency may be made verbally or in writing. When it is in writing, it is in the form of Power of Attorney.

Essentials of Relationship of Agency

The two essentials of relationship of Agency are Agreement between the Principal and Agent and intention of Agent to act on behalf of the Principal.

Agreement

Agency depends on agreement but not necessarily on contract. No consideration is necessary to creation agency. The relationship of Principal and agent may be created by the express agreement and by implied agreement.

Agency by Express Agreement: A contract of agency may be created by an express agreement. The usual form of a written contract of agency is the power of Attorney of a stamped paper.

Agency by Implied Agreement: Agency is not necessarily contractual in nature. The existence of agency may be in certain case be implied when it is to be inferred from the circumstances of the case.

Law of Contracts—Expressed and Implied

Claims sounding in contract. They arise because one party has either not done something that he agreed to do or has done something that he agreed not to do. Implied in the concept is the idea that, beside from his agreement, he was under no legal duty to the claimant to act or not to act in that particular way. The agreement then, is the heart of contractual liability. It is its source, its definition and its limitation. However, one must be careful not to exaggerate the coverage of the contract itself, so as to suppose that, unless the agreement specifically and expressly calls for a given detail of performance, the performance is not required. To determine what terms, condition and speculations will be implied with an agreement in this way, we must consider all the circumstances under which the agreement was made; including (a) the terms of express agreement (b) the terms that are standard or customary (c) legal rules of interpretation that may have been established by statute or judicial; decision to govern questions of that kind. An agreement for transport by rail, road or air implies a stipulation that all applicable regulatory rules will be observed, including those requiring licenses and permits, and further implies that the rates are in accordance with approved tariff schedules.

From the materials mangers' point of view the Law of Contract is an important branch of commercial Law, because all commercial transactions start from an agreement between two or more people. The object of law of contract is to introduce definiteness in commercial and other transactions. It may be said that the purpose of Law of Contract is to ensure the realisation of reasonable expectations of the parties who enter into a contract. The Law of Contract may be defined as that branch of law which determines the circumstances in which a promise shall be legally building on persons making it. The Indian Contract Act of 1872 (Act IX of 1872) lays down certain general rules regarding contract provides that "An agreement enforceable by law is a contract. The Law of contracts differs from other branches of Law in an important respect. It does not lay down a number of rights and duties which Law will enforce; the parties to the contract make the law for themselves. A contract has been defined as "an agreement enforceable by law'; or in other words, ' a legally building agreement between two or more persons by which rights are acquired by one or more to act or for because on the part of the other or others. To conclude contract Agreement & Enforceability at law. All contracts, therefore are agreements, but all agreements are not contracts. A contract in order to be enforceable by law, must have following elements:

(i) Offer and Acceptance.
(ii) Legal Relationship.
(iii) Lawful consideration.
(iv) Competency of Parties.
(v) Free and genuine consent
(vi) Agreement not declared void.
(vii) Legal formalities.

Stipulations implied in law consists of those terms and agreement that the law itself imposes on all contracts because without them, the agreement for transport, by rail, road or air, implies that all applicable regulatory rules will be observed, including those requiring licenses and permits, and further implies that the rates are in accordance with approved tariff schedules.

Warranties

When a purchased item breaks prematurely and fail to fulfill its purpose, some one must stand the resulting loss. Such loss is not necessarily limited to the cost of repair or replacement of the item itself. The claim can return (as a breach of warranty, misrepresentation, negligence, or strict liability) from the damaged consumer. Express warranties are generally preferable to implied ones. This is true because express warranties can be phrased in more detailed terms than ordinarily possible by implication. Express warranties, as a matter of practice, tend to be filed or noted with the papers relating to the particular transaction. Consequently, they are more easily proved and more reliable. The main difficulty with express warranties is that they take time, effort, and skill to formulate and negotiate. vendors frequently make express warranties for their products in sales and technical literature. Such warranties typical refer to the products' capacity, performance characteristics, and so on. If a buyer has no way of determining the facts of the matter and consequently relies on such warranties, the vendor is usually held liable for them. The buyer should also realise that an express warranty nullifies an implied warranty to the extent that it conflicts with the implied warranty.

In most of the cases, the purchaser will use the goods in an ordinary and conventional way for their ordinary and conventional purpose. In some cases however, a distinction must be observed between a warranty that goods are fit for ordinary purposes and warranty that they are fit for a particular buyer's special use. In such cases, the implied warranty arises only if the seller at the time of contracting has reason to know (a) the particular purpose for which the goods are required and (b) that the buyer is relying on seller's skill or judgement to select or furnish suitable goods.

Inspection, Acceptance, Rejection, Returns

Except in rare cases, a purchaser is entitled to inspect goods before paying for them to determine whether they conform to contract specifications. If the contract includes terms prescribing the method, place or time of inspection, such terms control. If a purchaser has not previously inspected the material purchased to ensure that it conforms with the terms of the contract, the law gives him a reasonable period of time to inspect the material after it is received. If purchaser raises no objection to the material within a reasonable period of time, he is deemed to have accepted it. Non conforming good may be rejected in toto, accepted subject to correction or price adjustment or accepted in part or rejected in part. To whatever extent a shipment is rejected for non conformity, the purchaser must (a) Notify the seller of rejection within a reasonable period of time. (b) Hold the goods for seller's dispositions, and (c) Follow the seller's reasonable instructions with respect to disposition or return. An accepted shipment cannot always be rejected on subsequent discovery of defects. Furthermore, a purchaser has only a reasonable time to reject a shipment or he will be presumed to have accepted by his silence. This is not to suggest that a purchaser who accepts a shipment has no recourse for subsequently discovered nonconformity. If the defect or deficiency of the goods is one that is not reasonably discoverable by ordinary commercial inspection, the purchaser is entitled to claim damages if he notifies the seller of the problem promptly upon its discovery. Some of today's purchases are made "an approval" "sale or return" or "consignment". On approval arrangements permit the purchaser to return even conforming goods if, after a reasonable period of trial, he decides not to accept. Both shipment and return of such goods are, in absence of a different arrangement, at the seller's risk and cost. Purchases on a sale-or-return or on consignment basis are usually purchases for resale. Broker lots are not subject to return under these arrangements, the return is ordinarily at the buyer's expense, and the buyer is responsible for the goods if they are not returned.

Order Cancellation and Breach of Contract

If a vendor fails to deliver an order by the delivery date committed upon in the contract, or if he fails to perform in accordance with contract conditions, legally he has breached the contract. The breach usually gives the purchaser the right to cancel the order. In addition the purchaser can sue for damages if he wishes. Nevertheless, under the law, a buyer may be able to recover damages if he actually suffers injury as a result of a breaks of contract. In the case of delivery failure, if the buyer subsequently purchases the material elsewhere, damages are generally limited to difference between the contract price and price paid from the new vendor. Many situations arise that compel a buyer to cancel an order before the vendor is obligated to supply the material. In making such a cancelation, the buyer breaches the purchase contract. This act is legally termed anticipatory breach, and it makes the purchaser liable for any resulting injury to the vendor. On the other hand, if the cancellation leaves the vendor with semi finished goods or in process material which is salable, the purchaser is usually held liable for the difference between the prorated contract value and the market value of the inprocess material. If the material is not salable, the purchaser's liability usually covers the vendor's costs prior to termination plus a reasonable profit on the contract.

A termination or liquidated damages provision represents prior agreement by both parties on the ground rules to be followed incase of a breach of contract.

Patent Infringement

When a buyer issues a purchases contract—he may be innocently violating some law, infringing upon some one else's rights, or otherwise subjecting his company to possible lawsuits say patent infringement. A patent gives the inventor a legal monopoly for 17 years. If someone manufactures, sells, or uses a patented device during this period without permission, the patent owner may sue and collect damages for infringements Purchasers may innocently buy an item made by a supplier who is in fringing upon the inventor's patent and still be liable for damages because they used the patented device. To protect against such unintentional violations, most organisations include a protective clause in their purchase orders which states that the seller will indemnify the purchaser for all expenses and damages resulting from patent infringement. Infringement suits are rare in the normal course of business activities. However, one area where most manufacturing firms frequently encounter potential infringement problems is the maintenance of productive equipment.

Chapter 27

SURPLUS AND OBSOLETE MATERIALS

Introduction

The efficient redistribution and reuse of surplus and obsolete materials has a significant bearing upon the profitability of firms and the economic strength of the nation. The generation of surplus material, is at least partially, a price paid because of the changing nature of the business. The production innovations involving technological advances almost always result in obsoleting former equipment and materials. In short, surplus is one of the prices of progress. The surpluses can also be, the result of human errors such as an overly optimistic market projection and the resulting production. Schedule that proves to be excessive resulting in excessive inventories which then may deteriorate. In many ways, scarp and surpluses are a paradox. No firm wants to produce surplus, yet they are materials constantly produced. They are virtually the only resources that are never depleted but constantly replenish themselves and, with proper processing and redistribution, are a perpetual source of some raw materials vital to the continued existence of our industrial society.

Surplus

Duplication of inventory always leads to surplus. Every company has surplus inventory that should be weeded out and disposed off. Materials management is responsible not only for identifying the surplus but also for getting rid of it. Surplus indicate all classes of scrap, spoiled material, or obsolete material that still have economic worth.

How Surplus Develop

If a company buys only what it needs, one might wonder why surplus stock is such a problem. One reason is that even if an item can clearly be identified as surplus, there is a natural tendency to save it. The example is that a particular bearing is used on just one machine and finally the machine itself replace. The bearings may just lie on the shelf for years and years. The only way such inventory can be disposed of is for a company to make periodic cheeks to determine whether there has been any "activity" for each item carried in inventory. The materials manager then sets rules usually quite arbitrary—that material that has not been active for a period of perhaps 2 years is automatically disposed of. A policy like this is quite easy to carry out in companies that use electronic data processing for inventory control. The computer can be programmed to automatically print out a list of inventory items on which there has been no activity for some predetermined period of time. These items are then investigated and anything that is obsolete is sold for the best price the company can get.

Categories of Disposable Materials

The disposable materials commonly comprehended under the broad term "Scrap" are given as under:

Spoilage: The items of production that are found to be defective during the manufacturing process.

Scrap: It consists of the residue of process materials left during a manufacturing process. This might include spores and flash form the foundry, Iron. Chips from Lathe machines; Shapers; Planners, paper cutting from Book Bindery. Worn-out equipment and parts are also included in this category.

Disposable Goods: Disposable goods are equipments, materials and supplies that have became obsolete.

Reasons for Generation And Accumulation of Surplus

Following are the reasons for the generation and accumulation of obsolete, surplus and scrap items:

(i) Changes in Product Design: This may lead to some items getting invalid so far as the final product is concerned. Hence the entire stock of such items becomes obsolete.

(ii) Rationalisation: Raw materials are rationalised so as to minimise variety. The rationalisation process renders some items as surplus or obsolete.

(iii) Faulty Planning: Any materials planning has to be based on sales forecast and this could result in surplus items.

Faulty Purchase Practices

Buying in bulk to take care of discounts and transportation economy without taking into account factors such as shelf life, storage space requirements and technological change one again to lead to the accumulation of surplus and obsolete stocks.

Management of Surplus Disposal

The management of surplus gets a stepchild treatment. The main concern of any company is the production of its finished product. The surpluses originating as a by product of this process are often regarded as necessary nuisance to be handled as quickly and simply as possible. They are not simply as possible. They are not usually thought of as a source of supplementary income. Their value seldom, if ever, is shown as a separate item on a company balance sheet. The responsibility for disposal of surplus materials s assigned to the purchasing department, the treasurer, the controller or the production department. The disposal of scrap when handled is an imaginative manner can result in handsome returns to the organisation. An effective disposal requires a compact disposal organisation reporting to the materials manager, continuous market survey on the prices of various categories of scarp generated in the plant and constant touch with the industries which generate similar scrap and with end users. many methods are used for disposal but two methods which are most commonly used are "Action" and "Tender" method. The parties in both the cases are normally required to inspect the scrap in the scarp yard and deposit earnest money. Some companies insist on a basic price depending upon the category of scarp. Disposal section works in this aspect in close co-ordination with the finance department. In many cases the disposal section may try to enter into a long term contract with end users such as steel plants.

Most often it is made the responsibility of the purchasing department for the disposal of surplus materials. The financial and accounting officers are sometime brought into the activity because surplus is a source of revenue and because record keeping is involved. The production department incurs its responsibility because most of the scrap is generated in that department and its employees must classify, handle and store the scarp.

Salvage Department

Large companies may find that the amount of scrap and surplus generated in their operations is so substantial that it justifies the establishment of a separate scrap and surplus department. Following are some of the procedure for the establishment of a separate salvage department:

(i) The salvage executive should be in a position to tabulate the direct cost and return of all his operations to demonstrate profitability by the ratio of scrap return on sales.

(ii) Salvage department should always sell direct to the end user of exotic materials to get the greatest possible return.

(iii) Treat salvage operations the same as production operations. Waste and inefficiency should not be tolerated any more in the salvage department than in production.

(iv) Care should be taken to eliminate material handling in scrap department and should prevent the mixing of high and low scarp value.

In brief scarp industry is characterised by a market that is in many respect unique. Scarp is said to be bought rather than sold and demand for scarp can not be created. The scrap demand is a derived demand completely dependent on the sale of trial products and the derived need for the raw materials. The selling of scrap takes place in a market that resembles perfect competition on the selling side, which means the profit margins often are low.

Chapter 28

ANCILLARY INDUSTRY DEVELOPMENT

Introduction

Ancillary industry is a secondary line of industrial development. It supports major industries components parts, sub assemblies and intermediates for the manufacture of main products. Ancillaries may also supply specialities like tooling bearings, instruments and maintenance requirements and auxiliary supplies and services to any industry. Ancillary supplies may also be made direct to any replacement market.

Ancillary industries occupy a very significant and important position in the industrial economy of our country. There industries offer many advantages which, to name a few, include higher industrial mobility better utilisation of resources, production at low cost decentralisation of industrial growth etc. Ancillarisation is also a very powerful tool for the purpose of generating employment. Ancillarisation is one of the powerful tools for achieving generation of employment, removal of poverty, reduction of disparities of income and wealth and correcting the regional imbalances.

Why are the Ancillary Industries Necessary

Following are some of the important reasons for ancillarisation:

(i) To effect the growth of a low cost economy through reduction in cost brought about by appropriate technology followed by the ancillary units.

(ii) To develop a single or multi-discipline expertise in different fields in tune with the smaller volume required of engineering goods.

(iii) To strike a balance with the available capital in the country.

(iv) To provide and accelerate employment opportunities to the educated unemployed in various fields in the different parts of the country. The ancillarisation can help as to reduce the soaring costs within the factory.

Growth of Ancillary Industries

In the present day world of industrialisation interdependence among large, medium and small industries is increasingly evident and is essential. There is a growing trend towards specialisation in every field and consequently it is much better for the large units to sepcialise in production of items which require use of sophisticated technology and expertise and leave it to the small units to meet the needs of the various parts and components not requiring that much of a sophisticated technology and expertise. As a result of this,the cost is minimised and substantial investments are saved, beside opening a vast scope for employment opportunities. Moreover extension of the ancillary units to backward areas helps in arresting the trend in shift of population from backward areas to urban areas reducing the regional imbalances and improving the economic condition of rural and backward sections of our society.

Since independence, Government has been giving considerable importance to the small scale sector. In the Industrial Policy Resolution 1956 a lot of stress has been given on the growth of this sector. Similarly in the new policy statement announced in 1977, emphasis was given to the development of cottage and small units for meeting the basic minimum needs of the people living in rural areas and small towns. Over the years, Government have examined and modified the definition of ancillary units more than once with a view to develop this sector. The definition of ancillary industries as it stands today is as under:

Undertakings having investments in fixed assets in plant and machinery not exceeding rupees 15 lakhs engaged in:

(a) the manufacture of parts, components, subassemblies, tooling or intermediates, or

(b) the rendering of services and supplying or rendering or proposing to supply or render 50% of their production or the total services as the case may be to other units for production of other articles, provided that no such undertaking shall be a subsidiary or, or owned or controlled, by another undertaking.

Apart from the increase in the investments ceiling the new definition for ancillary involves changes in the following important aspects:

(a) Units producing intermediates will now be recognised as ancillaries.

(b) Units providing servicing facilities viz sandblasting; Machining; Pressure cleaning; Grinding etc. will be recognized as ancillary;

(c) the concept of "parent" unit will now include small industries also.

(d) A unit to be recognised as ancillary should supply or propose to supply as 50% of its production to one or more parent units.

Organisational Framework

The small scale Industries Board appointed a Standing Committee on Ancillary Development. This committee has met a number of times and has made useful recommendations on ancillary development and monitoring systems. Based upon their recommendations, the Bureau of Public Enterprises issued comprehensive guidelines to the public sector units to undertake on continuous basis, techno-economic assessment for ancillary and auxiliary supplies. Some of the recommendations are:

(a) Public enterprises should commit to a programme of development of ancillaries.
(b) Management should appoint an Ancillary Development officer who would primarily be responsible for development of ancillary industries.
(c) To earmark particular lines of production of items of manufacture for ancillary units.
(d) To give price preference upto 15% over the landed cost for a period of 3 years.

There has been a feeling that a few public enterprises have not been able to take adequate steps to implement the guidelines and they may, therefore by entrusted with a specific responsibility to provide the much needed support to ancillaries. It has been observed that if the desired objectives in the growth of ancillaries have to be achieved, the programme should be undertaken, not as a closed door affair of the management of the public enterprises, but a coordinated institutional effort involving the public enterprises themselves, SISI'S, State Directorate of industries, Financial Institutions and last, but not least, the entrepreneurs themselves. Unless a suitable and regular mechanism is developed at the plant level and the result are monitored and discussed at regular periods, the outcome will continue to be below expectation.

Some Experiences of Ancillary Development

Ancillary development in Indian Telephone Industries (ITI) started with first Ancillary Mahila Udyoga Sahakara Sangha employing female dependent of ITI employees. Even earlier to this, the company had started farming out simple sub assemblies to co-operatives run by women to assemble from pieceparts supplied by ITI. Besides, ITI encourages several social co-operatives under the social welfare Scheme for carrying out labour contracts. Serving the Bangalore complex of ITI, there are number of Socially organised Units, including the Mahila Udyoga Sahakara Sangha and the Dooravani Udyoga Sahakara Sangh which primarily employ female dependents of ITI employees.

ITI's support to the Ancillary Units is comprehensive and includes:

(a) Suggestion and guidance in the preparation of Project Reports and Selection of Plant and Machinery.
(b) Transfer of complete technical know how by providing component drawing, design, details, specification of raw materials, process layout tools, costing methods etc.
(c) Assistance in the methods and process of manufacture.
(d) Provision of inspection instruments, tools and gauges on loan basis free of charge.
(e) Supply of imported and scare raw materials.
(f) Help in procurement of critical items of raw materials and components. By

and large, the ITI has been able to achieve the objectives visualized by the Government while initiating the polices and guidelines for ancillarisation by Public Sector Undertakings.

Ancillary Industry Around Steel Plants

The endeavour of the steel plants has always been to encourage the development and growth of small scale/ancillary industries, as has been the case in the past. However to enable this sector to play a significant role towards meeting the requirements of steel plants, it would be essential to plan the developments of these industries in a proper and selective manner so as to avoid a mushroom type of growth with its connected problems. The integrated steel plants recover various valuable chemical products from the coke-oven gas in their by product plant. Apart from this, certain miscellaneous products are also available which can be profitably utilised by small scale industries. Similarly, steel products and pig iron emanating from steel plants create a conducive atmosphere for development of small scale/ancillary or auxiliary industries. Products like skelp sheets, pars rods and billets etc. be further processed and fabricated giving added value to these items. As a part of policy to develop small scale ancillary industries around the steel plants, endeavour is made to encourage growth of industry utilizing by products and waste materials etc. The development of small scale ancillaries around steel plants is a conscious corporate policy decision. In keeping with its above policy, SAIL is presently associated with more than 1000 small scale and ancillary industries which are located around various steel plants.

Chapter 29

TRANSPORTATION AND TRAFFIC MANAGEMENT

Introduction

Physical Distribution is concerned with getting goods from the manufacturer to customer. While physical distribution usually involves substantial expenditures for warehousing and internal materials handling, the biggest element in the process is usually "Transportation". Efficient handling of the transportation of materials is of major importance to industry and consumers, who must ultimately pay for the charges involved. In the typical manufacturing company transportation services are the third greatest expenditure, only purchased materials and labour are more important.

Transportation is of particular importance to purchasing personnel for several reasons. The companies organised under the materials management concept often include transportation as a function of that department. However, complex regulations make transportation purchasing sufficiently different from conventional purchasing activities so that in large companies it is usually not carried on in the purchasing department but in a separate traffic department. Because of the complexities traffic management is often placed in a separate department. This department's responsibility include; incoming fright; outgoing fright and internal plant transportation. The traffic matters of greatest concern to purchasing include; Ascertaining rates; Selecting Carriers and routing; Auditing freight charges and preparing claims; Tracing Lost or overdue shipments; Determining cost reduction possibilities by consolidation of shipments and Determining Cost reduction possibilities by consolidation of shipments and many special arrangements available from shipping concerns. The important aspects in traffic and transportation management are choice of mode of transport, route selection, rate verification and auditing, management of claims as well as application of linear programming to minimise transportation costs. Let us consider the various transport avenues that are open to the materials managers viz Shipping; Rail. Road and others.

Transport by Shipping

This is generally resorted to in case of imports. At times method is used for movement of materials from one part to another within the country. Shipping transport is used for carrying such vital commodities as foodgrains, oil; etc. The increased use of shipping calls for more birthing facilities at our ports viz Ports of

Bombay; Calcutta; and Madras. The materials handling facilities at ports also require improvement as at present unloading process is slow due to inferior handling device and labour problems at ports.

Rail Transport

The Railway network is Asia's largest and the world's fourth largest system. There has been a continuous modernising of the track locomotives, signalling equipment and other devices for monitoring and control. However, over the years the percentage of freight traffic handled by road has steadily increased. Railways are ideally suited for long distance over 800 kilometer freight transportation with in the country. Quick Transport Service has been introduced to overcome the consumers' apprehension about undue delay in the transport of goods by introducing a guaranteed Quick Transit Service on payment of a small surcharge which is refundable in case of consignments do not reach destination within the target time. In order to compete with the door-to-door service of road transport, the Railways introduced a scheme of road—cum—rail transport in containers of five tonnes capacity ensuring door to door delivery as catered for by road transport. Recently the Railways have introduced Parcel service for collection of small parcel from specified points through Mobile Booking Service. The introduction of an increased number of parcel expresses for quicker transport of perishable and other consignments at low freight rates in coaching vans is receiving the attention of the Railways.

Road Transport

This is an important mode of transportation of material. There are a large number of transport organisations in the country having a fleet of trucks. They are suited for transporting freight of the other of 5 to 10 tonnes usually over distances of 300 to 500 kms. There are many constraints to the movement of freight through road. Some of them are octroi, interstate permits, check posts. There are other areas of movement of materials viz through inland waterways, pipelines and air etc. Shippers of bulky relatively inexpensive raw materials try to ship by water or pipeline when ever possible in order to keep transportation, costs at a minimum. In fact, chemical, aluminum, steel and power plants often are intentionally located at deep water ports or on inland waterways in order to reduce the cost of inbound raw materials. Water-shipment is slow but the rates always are low.

Routing and Delays

Once the carrier is selected, the traffic manager's job would seem to be complete but it rarely is. The carrier does not necessarily carry out its part of the bargain. Trucking companies do not always have tracks immediately available and, if they are busy, do not maintain their committed schedules.

Tracing

The supplier's traffic department may trace shipments for its customers. The buyers follow up with the supplier's sales department. The sales department may give the appropriate bill of lading or way bill number to the buyer so that his own traffic department could trace the shipment or it might do the tracing for the customer.

Transportation Rates

The basic principles on which freight rates are predicted are quite simple. The rail roads are still a starting point in rate making today. Implicit in this approach is an assumption regarding the price elasticity of demand for the service. If demand is inelastic, rate can be set high without a significant loss in total revenue to the carriers. If demand is elastic, the reverse is true. In fact, charging what the market will bear is only sound a procedure for setting the upper limit on rate determinations. Follow are some of the factors responsible for setting the transportation rates:

(i) **The Value of the Product:** More valuable the product the higher the rate can be.

(ii) **The cost of hauling:** Product density is related to the ability of a carrier to obtain complete loads. Similarly the factors such as Experience of past claims on the commodity; Space required (More the space required higher the rates); Packaging Geographic factors (traffic density at the origin and destination; volume of traffic moved (Quantity discount); Distances of goods must be transported; Special facilities required (such as stopover facility).

(iii) Competitions of the transporters viz. intermodal competitions; Intra-industry competition (Number of truckiines).

(iv) Government Policies and regulations regulating transportation.

Like other prices, tariffs charged by common carriers all influenced by supply, demand and cost of production. They also are influenced by peculiar variables of their own. Like most other sellers of goods and the services, common carriers are not free to set their own rates nor can they operate whenever and wherever they please.

Cost-Reduction Opportunities

As the rate structure is very complex, there are many opportunities for traffic experts to make tremendous savings in buying transportation. Every well managed company audits its freight bill and make enormous savings as a result. The rate structure is so complex that errors are inevitable. Even after freight bills have been audited once, it is still possible for a skilled auditor to detect errors. For this reason every large size company sends bills that its own auditors have checked to an independent auditing firm for second review.

Variations within Established Rate Structures

In addition to differentials existing between carriers, there are also rate variations which can be classified as (1) class and commodity rates, (2) Rates related to specific shipping practices and (3) Rates relating to commodity descriptions.

Commodity Rates

The result of this process, a freight classification is an alphabetical list of articles, together with each commodity's "rating". The rating is the class into which the article is placed for rate purposes. The use of this classification system greatly reduces the number of freight traffics in which rates are published. Tariff is the term used for schedules that contain rates and charges, as well as the conditions governing the movement of products or persons by commercial means.

Rates related to Shipping Practices

Quantity Discounts: A commodity will have a lower transportation rate if the quantity shopped meets truck load weight. The minimum rates vary with the cubic densities of the commodities and the specific modes of shipping.

Rates related to Commodity Description

It has been observed that material changes, description changes or regrouping of commodities can result in transportation economies. When various materials or components are included in a shipment the highest commodity rate will apply for the entire shipment. Lower rates can after be obtained by careful separation of materials.

Carrier Alternatives

There are three types of carriers, common carriers, contract carriers and private carriers. The private carrier provides transportation for his own commodities in company owned or leased equipment while common carriers and contract carriers are regulated by government regulations. However the regulations pertaining be contract carriers are less stringent than those pertaining to the common carriers.

Free-On-Board Terms

The designation of F.O.B. indicates the point of origin from which freight charges are calculated. The routing of shipments has economic and legal significance to buyers, carriers, and shippers. In general, the designated F.O.B. point determines who pays the freight charges and also who has legal titles to the merchandise while it is in the hands of the carriers. If no qualifying phase is added the teem F.O.B. is generally understood to be at the point of origin of the shipment. It is at the F.O.B. point where title changes hands and form which freight charges accrue to either buyer or skipper. For a shipment made F.O.B. destination there responsibilities fall on the seller. As indicated, freight rates are subject to varying degrees of flexibility, depending on many variables. It is imperatives that skippers know enough transportation and traffic management to understand that rate economies can be achieved through careful classification goods.

Packaging and Materials Handing

It is often practical to equip or company trucks with special racks or other materials handling devices to cut packaging and materials handling cots. Since carriers are responsible for damage to goods in transit, they naturally insist that shipments be securely packaged. In some cases, it is possible to ship in lighter, cheaper containers with little increase in damage. Experience has shown that damage losses can be cut by so percent if merchandise is handled more gently in company—operated trucks.

Damage Claims

Common carriers are forced to pay huge amount in damage claims. Even if the skipper is reimbursed in full, damaged shipments cause production delays, and the processing of claims is a huge burden on the typical firm's traffic department. Not all claims are the carrier's fault rather carrier's maintain that most of the claims occur as a result of inadequate packaging. The exact cause of damage is not clear cut in many cases. The shipment would certainly not have been damaged it it had been handled with sufficient care and merchandise been packed more carefully in costlier containers. Traffic departments spend a great deal of time investigating damaged shipments and making claims against carriers. Similarly the traffic department work with company's other departments such as packaging engineers etc. to reduce damages. The procedure for claiming damages is fairly straight forward, where the skipper presents the carrier with claim. Skipper gives him his bill of lading, the paid freight bill and a copy of supplier's invoice or other evidence that establishes the value of the damaged merchandise. The claimant may include photographs of the damage to serve as a basis for the development of ways to prevent future damage. The carriers must include an allowance for damage claims in their tariffs and it is to everyone's interest to help minimise such claims.

Demurrage Charges

Demurrage charges are penalties assessed by carriers on vessels held by or for a consignor or consignee beyond a stipulated free time provided for loading or unloading. Most business concerns operate under what is known as an "average agreement" with respect to demurrage charges. The gist of such an agreement is that a receiver is given a credit for each vessel released before the expiration of the first 24 hours or 48 hours as the case may be as free time. This credit can be used to off set a debit of one or two day's demurrage.

Insurance Buying

The materials manager has to arrange insurance of materials in transit and in stores scientifically, so that the possibility of catastrophic and profit shattering loses either to the organisation or to those dealing with the organisation or to those dealing with the organisation like the suppliers and purchasers is avoided. The responsibility for decision making and management of insurance is handled by an insurance department headed by a specialist in insurance.

Insurance Management

This aspects of insurance management that affect materials management are: (a) Arranging an adequate insurance cover for materials in transit and storage (b) Claims management; and (c) reduction of insurance costs.

Marine Insurance

The insurance department deals with insurance of Transit of incoming material; storage;and transit of outgoing materials including finished goods. Insurance of transit of materials is known as marine insurance and the same holds true for air consignment and inland transit by road or rail or other means of transport. The marine policy for covering ocean voyage is issued in a standard form and the terms and conditions of the standard policy are modified by a set of clauses known as Institute Cargo clauses which have also been standardised by the Institute of London Underwriters. The marine policy is a valued policy; that is the sum at which cargo is to be valued is left at the discretion of the insured. The cardinal principle of insurance law is that a contract of insurance is a contract of indemnity and so the law does not permit the insured to make a profit out of an insurance claim but in case of marine policy, it is possible for insurance to be taken for the invoice value of the cargo plus the amount of import duty and a reasonable amount of profit and incident expenses. All marine policies are issued subject to the transit clause which is part of all Institute cargo clauses. The various clauses impose the following limitation.

(a) The insurance cover cease as soon as the goods are delivered to the consignee or place of storage at the destination named in the policy.

The cover ceases on expiry of 60 days after completion of discharge of goods from the over seas vessel at the final port of discharge. Some of the important considerations are:

(i) The sum insured take care of invoice value, duty, incidental expenses and reasonable profits.

(ii) The scope of the cover should be clearly defined.

(iii) Where the value of the container is high, it is better to be clear as to whether the cost of the container has to be paid or not even when the contents are not damaged.

(iv) Where importing is a continuous process it is advantages to take a floating policy or an open policy instead of a specific policy for each consignment.

Inland Transit

The same policy form is used for covering internal transit but the clause attached to the policy are different and the scope of the cover is also different. The term of the cover should be as wide as an "all risks" policy or as restricted as "road risks or rail risks policy".

The nature of packing, the mode of transport and to extent of care exercised in materials movement have a bearing on the probability of losses occurring and on the quantum of such losses. A systematic and periodic, preferably an annual review of the existing insurance arrangement of the organisation, the cost benefits should be undertaken. The insurance cover designed with care today may not remain a perfect fit for the future ever after 2 years.

Chapter 30

THE MODIFIED VALUE ADDED TAX (MODVAT)

Introduction

The modified value added tax was introduced in India from 1st March 1986. It has its origin in the system of Value Added Tax (VAT) which is in vogue in many Western countries. The VAT in western countries, in its comprehensive form extends from the mining and manufacturing stages to the retail stage. It can replace all other forms of internal indirect taxes. Thereby, the maximum benefit can be derived from VAT.

The Indirect Taxation Enquiry Committee set up in 1976 under the chairmanship of Shri L.K. Jha went in to the question of long-term reform in the indirect tax structure in sufficient details. The committee went in to the question of adopting the VAT system in India. The committee however, recommended that serious consideration be given for moving over to a VAT system at the manufacturing level—the so called "MANVAT" and in the committee's view "in the ultimate analysis, a satisfactory revolution to the various distortions and problems that arise from an extended system of excise taxation lies in the adoption of MANVAT. The committee observed that theoretically VAT can be applied in two ways—either a given weight of tax can be applied to a base which is equal to the value of output minus cost of inputs, or the producer may be allowed to deduct from the tax paid on inputs. This method would ensure that the actual rate of tax paid on a final product would be equal to the nominal rate of tax on it. Moreover this method would enable us to tax value added at stages before the manufacturing stage where "MANVAT" may not be made applicable for some reasons. The committee, however, sounded a note of caution by stating that an attempt should not be made to apply MANVAT to all the industries, and that it would be prudent to make a start with 3 or 4 industries which produce final products in respect of which cascading and all other ill effects arising from widespread input taxation are pronounced. Such a cautions approach of starting with a pilot project was, according to the committee, quite essential "because in the interest of safe guarding, revenue it is necessary to establish its workability before a widespread application of the system is contemplated. If the system of MANVAT were to be adopted according to the committee the sales taxation on inputs were also to be eliminated, substantial benefits would accrue to economy. The saving will still be sizeable even if VAT were to replace the existing excises alone. Additionally, a considerable amount of scarce working capital which is locked up as the tax component in inventories would be released for productive purposes.

In applying the "MANVAT" system, some practical problems may have to be faced. A point often made is that the system would mean maintaining detailed books of account, as a result, a much heavier burden of tax compliance on the small and medium scale of manufacturers at present. A more important problem to be faced in extending the system of MANVAT would be on account of the fact that as indicated by the study, several inputs even by bigger manufacturers are brought through the medium of deals who are not subjected to central excise.

Recommendations of Technical Study Group

The technical Study Group on Central Excise Tariff, 1985, also went into the question of measures to mitigate the cascading effect on indirect taxes. After considering the merit and demerits vis-a-vis the "MANVAT" procedure suggested by the Jha Committee, the Technical Study Group felt hesitant to recommend the MANVAT system on a full scale in Indian conditions. Instead, they suggested certain improvements in the existing performa credit procedure itself, and partial implementation of the "MANVAT" scheme. Government announced a Long Term Fiscal Policy in December 1985 introducing the concept of "MODVAT"

MODVAT

Taxation of inputs (Raw Materials, Components etc) generally distorts the production structure, results in cascading of taxes and makes it very difficult to assess the distribution of the tax burden across different sections of society.

MODVAT is intended to greatly expand the scope of the provisions for set offs for excise and countervailing duties paid on inputs, with a view to coming as close to the generalised set off for excise, taxation of inputs as is administratively feasible. The basic approach is to move towards an extension of the present system of performa credit to all excisable commodities with the exception of a few like petroleum, tobacco and textile products.

Introduction of "MODVAT" is to decrease the cost of final product considerably through the availability of instant credit of the duties paid on the inputs and consequentially reduction of interest cost. MODVAT scheme avoids the payment of duties on earlier duties paid. The payment of duty drawback will be swifter as the element of excise duty will be transparent. "MODVAT" benefits both the consumers and exporters. MODVAT Scheme has come in force from 1st March 1986. MODVAT Scheme enhance the scope of concessions available to the small scale sector. Under the scheme, the full exemption is available up to clearance of Rs. 7.5 lakh in a year which account for nearly 85 per cent of the small scale units in the country.

MODVAT is basically a duty collecting procedure which at the same time allowing relief to a manufacturer on the duty element borne by him in respect of the raw materials used by the manufacturer. Under the MODVAT scheme the excise levy in vogue earlier, the input first suffered duty, and duty so paid become part of the cost of the final product, and the final product again suffered duty with the result that duty was paid on duty. MODVAT is an improvement over this earlier scheme, in the sense that duty becomes payable on the value added at each stage of production, instead of on the gross value including the duty paid in the earlier stages of Production.

Review of MODVAT Scheme

Government of India has set up a working Group for Review of MODVAT Scheme under the Chairmanship of Shri. S. Venkataraman Iyer, the Group has submitted the report and according to the report all sections of the trade and industry have welcomed the introduction of MODVAT in the excise system and want it to continue. Though there are several areas of dispute and procedural problems even now, the benefits of the scheme have been appreciated by the tax payers especially its alleviating effect on cascading. A study of the National Institute of Public Finance and Policy came to the conclusion that it has reduced the cascading effect of excise duties appreciably in a number of cases. This has had a perceptible restraining influence on prices. The growth in excise revenue after introduction of the Scheme as compared to previous years clearly shows that the Scheme had not led to any overall revenue loss. It has strengthened the revenue structure by inducing many units in the small scale sector to work within the ambit of the excise tax net work so as to avail the benefits of the scheme.

The collectors of central Excise as well as the Industry Associations have expressed several difficulties in regard to the interpretation of the scope of the term inputs in the MODVAT rules. It has been stated that a large number of disputes between the Department and assesses relates to this point. Industry wants a liberal approach to be adopted. The term should be redefined to permit MODVAT credit on goods used in the manufacturing process and forming a part of the final product and also to such goods as are cleared with the final product and whose value is included in the assessable value of the final product. The rules should be amended to give power to the Government to notify specifically such other items which are essentially for the manufacturing process but which may not form a part of the final product. Some of the other observations of study group are:

(i) At present the Department allows MODVAT credit of duty paid on packaging materials but not in respect of duty paid on inputs for the manufacturing of packaging materials. The definition of the term packaging materials should be amended so that all packaging inputs get the benefit of MODVAT benefit.

(ii) It has also been observed that in case of some commodities, the MODVAT credit of duty paid on the inputs exceeds the duty payable on the final product leading to misutilisation of credit clearing other goods or accumulation of credit. The Government should identify such areas and suitably adjust the rates of duties.

(iii) At present manufacturers can opt for or opt out of the MODVAT Scheme at any time of their choice. The rules do not however stipulate the procedure to be followed and precautions to be observed to avoid loss of revenue or misuse of the facility. There is need to regulate the exercise of option for working under the MODVAT Scheme.

(iv) The statute should be amended so as to permit MODVAT credit not later than six months from the date of clearance of the inputs from the factory of manufacture.

(v) The Government should notify a uniform procedure for accounting of MODVAT Credit when a manufacturer uses the same inputs to produce exempted as well as non exempted final products.

(vi) The MODVAT Scheme has created an additional work for the Central Excise Department. There are also certain types of abuses/malpractices of the scheme which have to be tackled without adequate supervision, malpractices and loss of revenue are likely. The Group recommends urgent action regarding staff augmentation and computerisation.

(vii) The MODVAT rules should be amended to provide for reversal credit taken in the case of rejected inputs which are returned to the factory where the inputs have been manufactured.

(viii) Uniform instructions for verification of gate passes should be issued by the Central Excise Department.

Chapter 31

WAREHOUSE MANAGEMENT

Receiving And Storage

Introduction

Receiving and storage activities constitute the final link in the materials supply chain. The receiving activity is responsible for expeditious receipt and general inspection of all in coming materials. It also completes the communication activity by promptly notifying all interested parties of the receipt and condition of incoming materials. The stores organisation is responsible for the physical identification and safe storage of materials. The way in which receiving and stores activities are conducted directly influence inventory carrying costs and, to some extent, the direct labour costs of production. A sound stores operation does a thorough job of current and future planning for the storage methods, layout and equipment it employs. The planning process can produce benefits such as: Ready accessibility of major materials; A high degree of flexibility of arrangement; a reduced need for materials handling equipment; Minimum of material pilferage, easy physical counting and efficient utilisation so storming space. Since the materials management department is responsible for materials up to the point where they are ready for production use materials personnel should have interest in the receiving and stores operations. If the stores department is independent of the purchasing department, the relationship between the two should be closer and more continuous than those between any other two departments. On all stock items the stores department initiates the purchase requests on which the buyer acts. The buyer's decision concerning a purchase is based on such factors as rate of use, number of defective parts, and trends in the rate of use. The buyer must keep the stores department informed on minimum stocks and reorder points so that the stores department can deep its inventories at proper levels.

The system of store keeping and stores inventory control is very important. If inaccurate stores keeping exist in an organisation, it will result in greater opportunity for their; waste; over or under ordering wastage of space and labour and excessive inventory investment. The poor store keeping results in a larger investment in inventory, the firm's working capital will be less liquid and effectively less adequate in amount than would otherwise be the case. Given poor control and bad store keeping, there may also be a problem of product quality deterioration.

Definition of Stores Management

Stores management has acquired greater importance in today's business organisations. In this age of cut throat competition and multiple products no industry can maintain favourable position if the cost of production is not maintained at a competitive level. The present concept of storekeeping has been given stature because of changing tastes, technical complications, attitude of buyers, increasing specialisation in industries. One can define storekeeping as air and water of modern industry. Store keeping refers to the safe custody of all materials stocked in stores for which the store keeper acts as a trustee. It simply means that the materials are to be stored in stores in such a manner that there is least possibility of theft, fire, damage and they may be easily located and issued whenever required for use.

Storage of material, spares, goods and equipments is an integral parts of the process by which the materials management department of an organisation maintains a continuous flow of these items form the point of their origin outside the organisation to their point of use inside the organisation. It will thus be clear that stores cannot be treated as a dumping ground but an active organ of the Business concern. Store keeping embraces all the activities right from the receipt of supplies of raw materials, spare parts, equipments, their proper storage and issue to used department. This also includes the storage of finished product before despatch to dealers. These activities involve maintenance of proper records of all the transactions.

Aims of Stores Management

Minimisation of cost of production: The main aim of storekeeping function is to minimise the various costs involved, while providing efficient and effective storekeeping service. Over and above the costs of materials as required for product are the costs of storage itself. These include the cost of capital investment in materials and supplies, the cost of preservation and handling of stores, the cost of record keeping, cost of use of storage equipment, and store building, and expenss for arranging light, heat, ventilation and paying taxes, insurance, losses due to spoilage and improper location of stores. Since these costs directly and indirectly influence the production cost the objective of store-keeping is to make efforts in the direction of reducing them to their minimum so as to minimise the cost of production.

The primary aims of storekeeping are to provide service to the organisation by:

(a) Making available a balanced flow of raw materials, equipment, tools and other components to the product line within the least possible time, and that too of right quality and quantity.

(b) Providing spare parts, general stores, and other materials required by the production and proper functioning.

(c) Receiving from production unit and issuing to the sales unit the finished products.

(d) Accepting and storing the scarp and other discarded materials and making arrangement for their disposal, in consultation with the appropriate departments and authorities.

Coordination with other departments: The stores department for its very existence has to establish coordination with the materials control department. But it does not mean that it can ignore other department of the organisation. The following departments are closely linked to the stores department. The smooth and efficient functioning of the stores department cannot be thought of without the active co-operation of each of the following departments:

★ Production Department,
★ Inspection Department,
★ Design and Engineering Department,
★ Finance and Accounts Department,
★ Purchase Department
★ Sales Department, and
★ Transport Department

The stores department is dependent on each of them for its day-to-day operations. It may not be out of place to mention here that without proper functioning of any one of thee departments, the smooth functioning of either the stores department or any other department will come to a standstill, hence the need for a positive correlation between various departments has lately been recognised by stores managers as one of the objectives of the stores department.

Functions of store-keeping

The following are the important functions of store keeping:

(i) Receipt of materials into store
(ii) Storage and preservation
(iii) Record-keeping, and
(iv) Issue of materials.

(i) **Receipt of materials into store.** The raw materials, tools, equipment and supplies which come from outside are delivered to the receiving section where they are inspected and then moved into appropriate storage areas.

(ii) **Storage and preservation.** Storage means custody of materials in a scientific way so as to help in the maintenance of regular flow of materials in and out of the store-house for the smooth and efficient running of the entire organisation with which that storehouse is connected. For proper storage, a storehouse should be well laid out and equipped with bins, racks, boxes and other in order to facilitate access, identification and storage for each item of stock. On the other hand, preservation refers to the safe custody of the materials so as to help the maintenance of its value and quality. Reservation helps in making available the materials in perfect serviceable condition. Proper preservation of stores over a period of time able condition. Proper preservation f stores over a period of time may entail elaborate measures, depending upon the nature of the material, the length of time in storage and the rate of deterioration.

(iii) **Record keeping.** Maintenance of records of goods carried in and out of the store is one of the most important functions which storekeeping has to perform. Proper maintenance of records helps the management in minimising the cost both of storage and production. This in turn assists in planning the future course of production and purchasing. Records also extend a helping had to the Costing Department.

(iv) **Issue of Materials.** Ultimately the materials received, stored and preserved are to be issued to various departments on proper authorisation and requisition as and when demanded. This is one of the most important functions of storekeeping because the materials are supplied to the stores department by the suppliers on the purchase orders of the purchase department for their issue.

Factors Contributing to Successful Functioning of Stores

The following factors lay down the foundation of the successful functioning of a stores department:

Location of the Store: On the location of the store depends the successful performance of storekeeping functions. If the storeroom is centrally situated, it may be easily accessible to other departments resulting in better coordination, greater facilities for the receipt and issue of materials, and making the storage more economical.

Layout of the Store: The layout of a store offers an opportunity to the storekeeper for an efficient store keeping. To ensure free movement of materials, timely inspection and day-to-day verification of the receipts and issues, it is desirable that store should be free from congestion. Proper grouping, classification and coding of stores, proper arrangement of storeroom equipments, proper indexing for easy accessibility, maximum possible utilization of available space, and proper placement of receipt, issue, record and inspection counters are the essential of a good layout of a storeroom. If the layout is good, it will go a long way in making the storekeeping functions a success.

Records. Proper, up-to-date and complete records results in reduction or elimination of wastage and misappropriation in the stores department. It also acts as a check on dishonest workers in the store and removes the possibility of theft and pilferage. Efficiency and economy, protection from all kinds of damages, settlement of disputes with creditors, debtors, insurance companies and government, checks against overstocking and under-stocking, are some of the advantages of store records which make storekeeping more successful and efficient than it would be in the absence of records.

Preservation. The underlying idea of storekeeping function is to protect the stores from all kinds of damage so that the materials carried in the store may not lose their quality and value for a long time to come. This requires a bright, airy, fire-proof and well-ventilated storeroom in which materials can be kept in safe custody. Proper arrangement for keeping the materials safe is also required. If the materials are preserved properly, naturally it will make the storekeeping function successful and efficient.

Verification. There should be a constant check on the movement of materials and on the balances of materials in bins.The physical verification of stores makes storekeeping successful since timely detection of fraud, mismanagement, misappropriation, and laziness on the part of storekeeper helps in prompt action. The verification, that too perpetual, may prove to be a boon for successful storekeeping.

Management. There cannot be two opinions if it is said that the success or failure of an action is largely dependent on its management. The storekeeping functions cannot, therefore, be an exception. The internal management, the policy level management the distribution of different functions of storekeeping among main store, sub store and different classes of officials can définitely make a success of failure of it.

From the foregoing discussion it is clear that factors underlying successful store-keeping are to be always kept in mind if the stores department is to secure more and more advantages from its day-to-day operations.

Benefits of Good Storekeeping

The success of storekeeping will be judged by smooth running of production department. Following are the advantages that accrue from a successful and efficient storekeeping:

(a) Location of materials in the storeroom becomes easier, thereby avoiding unnecessary delay and confusion.

(b) Smooth running of the production department is ensured because of regular and timely supply of materials to the department.

(c) Blocking of capital by avoiding overstocking becomes out of question.

(d) Hold ups and delays in factories are avoided by ensuring against understocking and its resultant disadvantages.

(e) Physical verification becomes the order of the day and renders all its subsequent advantages to the stores department.

(f) Accounting of all the materials is facilitated.

(g) Minimisation of wastage of time, labour and money due to leakage, theft, pilferage, damage, etc., is achieved.

(h) Availability of statistical information and proper recording makes the data more reliable.

(i) Ascertaining of cost of storage and cost of production comes within reach which in turn equips the sales department for better performance. This also helps in correct costing and market study.

Types of Storehouse

The store depots according to their functions and utility may be divided into the following broad categories:

(a) Main or Central Stores Depot.
(b) Sectional or Branch Stores Depot.
(c) Tool Stores Depot.

Central Stores Depot

The functions of the main or central stores depot are:

(1) to receive all the materials, tools, equipments, etc.
(2) to issue the materials to sectional or branch stores depots, tools to the tool stores depots and equipments to the various departments (generally production department) as and when required by them.
(3) to take steps for the replenishment of stock. The main stores depot should be under the charge of Stores Officer. Of course, the actual handling of stores would be done by the storekeeper and his assistants. Thus the central store is a wholesale supplier to other departments, and sub-store depots, who operate on a retail basis and are engaged in issuing goods directly to the users of the materials. The following are the advantages of centralised storage system.

Advantages

★ Minimum possible stock of spares, equipments, tools and fixtures are to be kept, thus avoiding unnecessary blockade of money.
★ Range of goods becomes wider so as to benefit the users more than can be possible under smaller stores depots.
★ Scientific and better method of stock control becomes possible.
★ Storage cost can be reduced, since bulk stores always take less space.
★ Efficient and successful organisation of inspection and verification can become possible.
★ Standardisation becomes easier.
★ Deterioration in stores can be minimised through more regular turnover of stocks.
★ Coordination between the central store and the different departments can be improved.

Disadvantages

However, central store system also has its own disadvantage which are enumerated below:

★ Because of duplication of work, handling and transport costs are increased.
★ More staff may be required to handle huge stocks.
★ Recurrent shortages at the point of usage may occur, if the organisation is not efficient.
★ A tendency towards rise in the stock investment prevails, if the sub-stores are not rigidly controlled.

★ Increased documentation work may involve extra cost.

★. Risk of deterioration, fire, pilferage and left in increased mainfold.

Branch Stores Depot

The sectional or branch stores depot is located in each section, unit, department or branch from where the material are drawn by the letter group. This depot, in turn, draws its requirements from the Main or Central Stores Depot to which it places its requirements form time to time. The main stores depots issues the materials to the sectional stores depots for a certain period say, a fortnight or a month. These sub-stores order to facilitate the different production centers with issues of materials different in specification and qualities, and in time. The following are the main advantages of a sectional stores depot.

(a) Prompt and efficient execution of demand requisitioned by the department becomes a possibility,

(b) If regular supplies are received, unnecessary hold ups and delays in work are avoided.

(c) In fact the advantages received from a sectional store are the disadvantage faced by the central stores depot.

Tool Stores Depot

Tool stores depot, even if there is a centralisation of storage facility, is generally maintained as a separate depot in large industrial enterprises. This store is responsible for issuing tools, spare part and other accessories to different sections (department) in general and production department, in particular. The tools are drawn from the main store once and then they are issued by the stores depots as and when required by the departments. The main advantage of such store is to relieve the main stores depot from the head of executing the retail requisitions of the departments. In this way it helps in smooth and efficient running of all the departments without any stoppage of, or delay in work. Another advantage is that proper and uptodate records of tools, which are issued on loan basis temporarily, can be easily maintained than would be done in the case of central stores.

Warehouses

Warehouses are the godowns which take the responsibility for keeping and storing goods and provide ancillary service in order to help the small and medium sized traders and manufacturers who, due to technical and economic reasons, may not like to have their own storehouse. These warehouses, undertake to preserve the goods in a scientific and systematic manner so as to maintain their original value, quality and usefulness, in exchange of which they charge certain prescribed rent at a fixed rate in advance. Thus, we may say that a warehouse is a store depot not in the strict sense of the term but in a broader sense. Its functions are:

(a) To keep the goods in safe custody till these are not claimed back by their owners.

(b) To preserve the goods so that they do not lose their value, quality and usefulness.

(c) To undertake these duties against agreed charges, known as rent, paid by the owners of the goods.

(d) To work as an agent of the owner (trader and/or manufacturer) by—
   (i) undertaking the job of loading and unloading the merchandise on the form ships, railways, etc.
   (ii) arranging carriage for transporting the merchandise.
   (iii) classifying packaging, packing, dealing with purchasers under instructions of the owner, and
   (iv) providing other facilities in export and import trade as and when required by the owner.

(e) To function is bankers of the owner of goods stored in the warehouse by:
   (i) Advancing loan on the security of the goods carried in the warehouse,
   (ii) getting clearance from customs authorities on behalf of the owner,
   (iii) keeping the sale proceeds (if authorised) till it is not claimed by the owner, and
   (iv) honouring hundis, bills, etc., on the security of goods warehoused.

Importance of Warehouse

Warehouses enjoys importance of their own. The traders and manufactures have started realising the role which warehouse can play in the advancement of their business. The services of warehouses are being utilized advantageously bu import and export houses, and they have not to bother for the complicated procedures for clearing off the materials. The trader has only to instruct the latter. Thus he saves his time, energy and money, without caring for the arrival of goods at the dock, and can devote his full attention to his business which no doubt brings him increased profits, and does a good service to the community by supplying the materials without any break. Likewise in export business the trader is relieved of the botheration of loading, taking care of customs authorities, arranging and waiting for ships, etc. leaving t entirely to the care of the warehouses.

Those traders who are interested in taking advantage of the price fluctuations, if the trend is bullish, and those who are interested in avoiding the current market trend because of its bearish tendency, find warehouses as the great refuge under such circumstances. Manufactures who have produced in anticipation of demand have no alternative but to wait for the favourable market for them, the warehouses are the source of great solace. The merchants or manufactures (generally monopolists), who want to influence the price curve in the market by their action, take the help of warehousing facilities. Warehouses also offer facilities of packaging, grading, packing, etc., which naturally are the added advantages of warehousing system, that too economic ones, in the sense that these facilities make the goods more acceptable to general public. The warehouses can broadly be divided into two categories.

1. Ordinary warehouse, and
2. Bonded warehouse.

Bonded Warehouse

Ordinary warehouse takes the responsibility of keeping, storing and preserving the goods against certain fixed charges. The bonded warehouse is licensed and authorised by the customs authorities for storing the goods till the import duty due on it is paid. The bonded warehouses may be either Government owned or privately owned. The following are that advantages and privileges which a bonded warehouse as compared to the ordinary one, enjoy and offers to its customers.

(a) The goods which are kept in bonded warehouse can be inspected, handled, sampled, packed, packaged and blended by the owners.
(b) The goods in bond can be shown to the buyers and sold out to them from the warehouses itself.
(c) The customs authorities may supervise and inspect the good in bond, i.e., on which the duty is still not paid.
(d) The owner is offered the facility of removing the goods in bond in instalments and duty is payable on the removed part of the goods.
(e) The customs authorities can specially permit delaying in the goods on which duty is still unpaid.

Layout of Stores

The stores is not a dumping ground, but part of the economy of the business and one of the resources of production. The stores should be designed for quick and simple operation and for economic use of space. It should be situated when deliveries can conveniently be made bot by suppliers to the stores and by the stores to its customers. It equipment and layout should be such that incoming goods can be off-loaded, checked and put to stores and out going goods collected and issued without any delays. Before detailing the dimensions of the storage area, the methods of storage will have to be worked out. The materials may be piled up, stacked, placed in bins, racks or shelves, depending upon the size and nature of the individual item.

For achieving that aims of a good layout first of all the storeroom should be divided into rows and columns or bays with proper numbers allotted to them so as to make easy the location of materials in the storeroom. Further, storeroom should be divided into sections according to the stature of classification of materials like chemicals, tools, paints, iron and steel, stationery, machinery, etc., Articles of like nature should be grouped together. Small items, such as nails, screw, bolts, nuts, etc., should be stored in small but closed bins, whereas for the storage of lengthy and bulky goods, open or wide space should be utlitized. The best of storing these things are the containers in which they have been received from the suppliers. The use of unit load containers is recommended.

There should be proper arrangements for receipts and issue counters, and a place should be provided for record-keepers and personnel of the inspection department. It is advisable to provide separate counters, rooms, endorsers for receipt, issue, inspection and records. Adequate space in between two rows for the movement of men and materials is a must for ensuring prompt execution of orders of the production department. Adequate provision for expansion should also be made. Proper placement of fire extinguishers sand bags, buckets, etc., is also one of essential requirements of a good layout of a storeroom. Entry of unauthorised persons into the storeroom should be strictly watched.

Environment Conditions Effecting Stores Functioning

Stores play a vital role in the operations of a company. Stores is often equated directly with money as money is locked up in stores. It is important that stores are constructed with a futuristic orientation, so that sufficient flexibility for expansion needs is inbuilt. The activities of receiving the goods, stocking in appropriate locations, material handling and issues must be done swiftly and economically. Comfortable working conditions must be provided to the stores personnel to get maximum efficiency and morale. Some of the environment conditions such as Noise; Improper lighting; and Extreme Heat; Coal and Dust have direct impact on the working of stores.

The improvement in these conditions contribute the fatigue alleviation which results into higher morale, low accident r ate and less absenteeism. The conditions which affect fatigue and are responsible for effective working atmosphere are:

(i) Noise Industrial Music.
(ii) Illumination.
(iii) Temperature
(iv) Humidity
(v) Ventilation
(vi) Safety

(i) Noise. Noise is unwanted sound and it increases fatigue. If the noise is too much and continues for a along time it might cause deafness, for example, boiler maker deafness, sheet iron worker and blacksmith deafness. The effect of noise depends on the kind of noise and kind of work. Mental work is affected more than manual work by noise. The effect of noise is greater when it is irregular. Sounds of either very high or low tone qualities are more irritating than those in middle zone. In a study of mental arithmetic metabolism was mush higher during the first noisy period but reduces with adjustment.

The noise of moderate intensity serves as a psychological inducement to work. One study of the reduction of noise concludes that it is an investment which under ordinary conditions will increase productivity by 10 to 15 per cent. But if the individuals who are exposed to very high pitch noise such as boiler makers and aeroplane pilots they suffer permanent deafness.

(ii) Industrial Music. Music in factories and stores has become fairly common and therefore, requires an evaluation. some of the studies made in England where researchers found the initial interest for dealing with monotony. The effects of musical programmes on simple assembly operations showed production increase up to 6 per cent, when production on days with music was compared to that on days without music. In a radio-tube assembly factory in which music was customarily played, the effectiveness of fast, slow and mixed programmes was studied. The scrap rate was found to be less when either fast or slow music was played than when there was non music or when fast and slow musical programmes were alternated. Musical programmes also had a beneficial effect on employee morale.

The increase in output varies considerably with the job and the shift. Simple repetitive jobs that can be performed well while talking seem to benefit most by music. The research findings indicate that music seems to benefit most by music. The research findings indicate that music seems to encourage young, inexperienced workers to increase production on routine jobs. No significant effects were found for the older skilled workers. The general finding is that employees like music. At least 75 per cent strongly favour it and only 1 to 2 per cent oppose it. Slow music seems more desirable than first music, variety is essential to keep young and older employees satisfied with the programmes. Vocal music may be distracting for some employees, and music with storing beats may disturb or help depending on how it fits into the movement rhythms of a job.Spaced programmes seem to be favoured. At present, it appears that the music should be on about 12 per cent of the time for the day shift and as much as 50 per cent of the time for the night shift. Most favourable effect of music its influence on boredom. It takes the mind from the work as well as frees the brain of the obligation of initiating the activity.

(iii) Illumination. Many industrial undertakings take this advantage of natural light during the day time. But it should be remembered that the illumination of the work place by means of artificial modern lights is far better than taking the natural day light in carrying out any work efficiently. Any natural light which the industry uses should be carefully utilized in the working conditions. North light is commonly used in industries because the variation of light is not much during the day time in a factory. Engineers are utilizing modern techniques in the plant layout to avoid such changes of illumination during the day in the workshop either by putting the transparent shades on the top of the factory or cutting down lights from all directions except from the north. Some jobs need special light which needs more illumination. Because of the uniform light in the work pace, the workers do not find any visual difficulty while coming out from a specific work situation which is illuminated brightly.

The entire work area should be uniformly illuminated. Areas outside the immediate focus of observation, wall surfaces, for example, if unevenly illuminated cause continual adjustment changes and consequently higher visual fatigue. Since the pupil of the eye must adjust itself when focusing on a bright spot and then on a dark spot, expansion and contraction of the pupil sets up an increased strain and fatigue in the worker.

Indirect lighting in the best method of producing uniforming. Eye muscles tend to pull towards areas of high illumination. Where the high point of light is not in the work area, a tug-of-war exists between the muscles that are concentrated on the work area and those that veer to the higher illumination. The human eye adjusts so readily to changes in illumination that the effects of poor lighting are usually not immediately observable to the untrained eye. Errors in judgement are often found when people's reports on brightness are checked against readings on light meters. Poor illumination causes fatigue and irritability and is a source of errors and industrial accidents. Money spent to correct improper lighting will be more than repaid in higher output per worker, lower production costs, and a generally happier, healthier and probably safest work force.

The colour of surrounding objects and surfaces is related to lighting. The use of white or light pastes improves illumination by reflecting high percentage of light, while deeper tones have a considerably lower reflective value. The occurrence of glare should however, be avoided. Several studies made on the use of coloured light show that people prefer the light of daylight colour. The use of this so-called while light is said to assist materially in visual efficiency.

(i) Various jobs requires different intensity of light above 50 foot candles.

(ii) The severe and prolonged visual tasks, such as fine engraving, and discrimination or inspection of time details of two contrast requires 50 to 60 foot candles.

(iii) The prolonged critical visual task such as drawing, fine assembling, fine machine work, and proof reading, require 50 to 60 foot candles.

(iv) The visual tasks such as skilled bench work, require 19 t 20 foot candles.

(iii) Temperature. Indian are accustomed to working in a temperature which will be considered as high. At several places like Calcutta, Madras, Bombay etc. where the employees work in a moderate climate throughout the year, there the temperature does not rise or drop to the extremes. The efficiently goes down during the extreme temperature conditions.

(iv) Humidity. Variation in humidity play very important role in industry. Rise of humidity in low temperature to a moderate extent gives relief to workers from severe dry cold, whereas, rise in humidity adds further discomfort to the rise of temperature. It is more discomfortable to withstand wet heat and dry cold.

Low temperatures can also affect productivity. Ability to make precise movements with the hands and fingers decreases. discomfort has been within a room, that is, cool air at floor level and warm air at head level.Furthermore, where sizable temperature differences existed within a building and the nature of the work required worker's movement from the area to area, discomfort was noted.

(vi) Ventilation. Temperature and humidity can be controlled to a great extent if adequate ventilation by the circulation of fresh air is arranged in the factories. The circulation of fresh air is generally done by fans, ventilations, the blowers. Artificial arrangements are also made in chemical industries to avoid pollution of air, through gases and fumes. In cement factory where the stones are crushed the operation crates lot of dust. Similarly in the spray shop the spray particles pollute the air. In such cases, exhaust fans are not adequate enough to supply fresh air and so gas marks are provided to workers to avoid fumes and dust during work. Dust and fumes are constant health hazards in the Indian industries.

1. During winter the temperature for light work should be 65°F, for active yet light work 60 to 65°F. For work involving more muscular exertion, 55°F to 60°F.
2. During summer the temperature should be kept below 68°F.
3. The introduction of fresh air should not be less than 1,000 cubic.feet per person per hour.
4. In summer adequate air circulation should be arranged. The efficiently increases if the air movement is moderately high.
5. During summer the relative humidity should be 70 per cent at least.

(vii) Safety. This factor is perhaps the most important aspect. In stores a large number of goods are handled every day. Accidents considerably reduces the morale and effectiveness of the system. Following are some of the measures necessary if accident are to be checked:

(a) Safety appliances such as goggles etc. should be provided and their use must be encouraged.
(b) Good house keeping is essential. Stocking must lie in appropriate locations so that handling is minimum.
(c) All stores equipment must be kept in good order.
(d) Safe actions should be stimulating by installing "safety awards".
(e) Provisions of fire fighting facilities is necessary especially where inflammable materials are stored and handled.

Chapter 32

STORES SYSTEMS AND STORES ORGANISATION

Introduction

There are two basic systems for controlling stores materials : (a) Closed stores system and (b) An open stores system. A company normally employs both systems. The application of each system depends upon the nature of the production operation and the way in which materials are used in production.

Close System

Closed stores system is one in which all materials are physically stored in a closed or controlled area. Whenever possible, the general practice is to maintain physical control by locking the storage area. This system is designed to afford maximum physical security and to ensure tight accounting control of inventory material.

Open System

Open system represents the second major type of stores system. It finds its widest use in highly repetitive types of operations. In plants, using the open stores system, no storeroom as such exists. Each material is stored as close to the point of use as is physically possible. Materials are stored in bins, on shelves, in racks, on pallets and so on. However the storage configuration at each work station is arranged to fit the available space. The open system is designed to expedite production activities. It places little emphasis on the physical security of materials. The open system also places less emphasis on the accounting control of materials. No perpetual inventory records are kept in an open system and the accounting charges are determined indirectly rather than directly. As a result the system provides control over material usage only if it is used in conjunction with an accounting system employing standard cost technique.

The open system is must applicable in situations where a repetitive production operation produces standardised products. Materials handled in an open system should not be subject to pilferage, nor should they be easily damaged. If production requires delicate or pilferable item, they should be controlled in a closed store room.

Stores Classification; Identification

In any factory storeroom the problem is of properly locating the various materials with in the store room. A proper storing arrangement requires: A method for classifying and identifying the items stored; A workable system for identifying and working storage spaces; and a system for assigning the actual location for materials to the stored in the store rooms. Once all locations in the store room have identifying symbols and all materials and other stored items also have identifying symbols or numbers, all that is needed is a set of index cards showing which materials are put where in store room.

Identification

In normal way of identifying an article in the storehouse is by its simple description, but this is neither satisfactory for stores purposes nor this will help in doing the operation speedily and effectively. The description is sometimes vague and may be confusing. Accurate identifications of an article, sometimes, demands lengthy descriptions which may generally be complicated and thus adding to the confusion in understanding, A "chair" if said as such is not the identification. An arm chair, plastic caned back, revolving, steel frame, foam cushioned and so on may be the accurate description of the chair in question.

In order to identify correctly and on a logical basis and to avoid multiplication of items several times and to save time and labour, to facilitate easy location and proper functioning of the storehouse, a proper codification is needed. The importance of classification can be explained by taking library as an example, considering a well organised library where books are classified, numbered, and properly stocked. One can find any book he wants easily and also can find out whether the book is in the library or not. A sense of orderliness is introduced with the result the functioning and management of library is greatly simplified and effective control could be established.

Need of Classification and Codification

The need for classification and codification is even greater in an industry. Classification is the operation of bringing alike things together and coding is the allocation of a symbol (alphabetical and/or numerical) which **uniquely defines an article or a subject and places it in its correct classification. The cost accountant needs a logical code reference to each part and of each process and each piece of plant and equipment. The material controller must be given the basic information upon which all his controls are built in a code form which is complete and systematic. The major areas where classification and coding could be applied are:**

(i) Materials in stores.
(ii) Parts, subassemblies and assemblies.
(iii) Equipment, dies and tools.
(iv) Drawings and other design reports.
(v) Process and operations.

(vi) Identification of standards and other documents.

Principles of Classification

(i) **Comprehensive Principle:**
The system of classification must cover the entire range of items for which it is devised and at the same time allow reasonable scope for extension.

(ii) **Mutual exclusiveness:**
There must be only one place for anyone thing. As the user progresses in his search from main class to sub-class, from sub-class to group, and so on through consecutive classification, he is able to discard vast information and is able to restrict his search to a very narrowing range.

(iii) The appropriate order of complexity must be maintained in the arrangement of classification criteria i.e. from cheap to expensive, from soft to hard, single to complex.

Codification of Materials

One of the most important factors in dealing with the materials is the human element, which cannot be ignored or by passed in devising any method of identifying or codifying the materials. Hence any stores management has to keep into the problem considering 'human being' as one of the important elements. Though the normal way of identifying an article in the storehouse is by its simple description but this is neither satisfactory for stores purposes nor this will help in doing the operation speedily and effectively. The description is sometimes vague and may be confusing. The 'dust bin' may be known as 'refuse container' 'rubbish box' etc. This may result in confusion and out of which duplicate ordering or overstocking may become the order of the day. In England, an electrical firm had as many as 12 names of an items depending upon its function in various using departments. Will this not results in utter confusion, inefficiency to the storehouse as a whole? Accurate identification of an article, sometimes, demands lengthy description which may generally be complicated and thus adding to the confusion in understanding. A 'Chair' if said as such is not the identification. An arm chair, plastic caned back revolving steel-frame, foam cushioned and so on may be the accurate description of the chair in question. The whole story of the article is to be told if accurate identification is needed.

Merits of Codification

In order to identify correctly and on a logical basis to avoid multiplication of items several tines, to save time and labour, to facilitate easy location and proper functioning of the storehouse, a proper codification is to be evolved so as to obtain the following benefits to: avoid the long and unwieldy description; have accurate and logical identification; prevent duplication; standardise the items,; reduce the varieties; have efficient purchasing department; have efficient recording and accounting; simplify and facilitate the mechanical recording; simplify and facilitate the pricing and costing; have proper system of location and indexing; assure correct and efficient inspection and assure production as planned and as required.

Long and Unwieldy Description. There is no denying the fact that if there is no logical system codification then for identification as store one has naturally to depend on the description of the material which has to be in greater detail. If one is interested in properly and correctly identifying the materials carried into the store. It is, but obvious that these descriptions will be lengthy enough, which will naturally become unwieldy. Unfortunately, they will not bear fruit. Instead that may further complicate the situation. A scientific codification system, thus, will avoid all these and make the storehouse more efficiently and effective operating organisation.

Accurate sand Logical Identification. A separate code is allotted to each of the items available in the storehouse indicating different sizes, quality, price, usability special characteristics, specification, etc., of the item concerned. This distinguishes, one item from the other, even if nomenclature is the same. This obviously help in accurate identification, which is logical in the sense that cannot override each other. If it does, it will result in the defeat of the very purpose of codification.

Prevention of Duplication. All items are separately codified and are arranged in certain logical order. Similar materials are grouped together such as stationery item, and is given a code, e.g., 07. Once a code is allotted to a particular group in no case the code number is changed. This prevents duplication. Neither duplicate ordering is possible nor because of having different nomenclature materials pile up in the storehouse due to different places, bins and nomenclature. As in any codification system it is not the name given to an item is taken into account but the code is considered and action taken accordingly. Thus, duplication at all stages is prevented with the help of proper and scientific system of codification.

Standardisation and Reduction in Varieties. Standardisation is the order of the day and codification's main and important aim is to achieve standardisation. For codification grouping of similar identical item is a must. This enables the store authorities to examine the entire range of stores. This facilitates in eliminating those varieties in place of which other varieties of the like quality and use can profitably be used by adhering to lesser varieties, thus, reducing the number of varieties to the minimum. By this process standardisation can be achieved and investment in items can also be reduced to a greater extent thereby administering economy in purchasing. Inventory carrying cost may also be prepared to examine the range from details and length points of view. If it is found on examination that it is again detailed enough and there is a further scope of reduction, then an examination may be carried out for further reducing the range making it more standardised and less cumbersome.

Efficient Purchasing Department. The filling up of purchase requisition particularly the specification column is a task in itself in the absence of a code which may easily indicate the materials required. Buying instructions to the suppliers become easy and quick. Items are grouped for facilitating the allotment of codes and in turn section wise organisation of purchase department based on the code groups becomes a possibility, which in centralised purchasing serves well in dealing with the purchase orders and in taking the advantages of bulk purchasing.

Efficient Recording and Accounting. The codes improve chances of effective stock control efficiency recording and result yielding accounting. Since due to codes everything is clear and numerical codes, if used make the store-room operation efficient, accounting become up-to-date, scientific and perfect. Chance of mistake in minimised. Presence of codes minimises the fraud, takes less time and energy in recording detect the defects with quick and ease, pricing and valuation become more accurate and reliable.

Facility in Mechanical Recording. Mechanical Recording has come to stay in today's accounting process and since it is neat and clean, free of mistakes, less time consuming and less fraudulent, people have started more in believing mechanical records then in pen kept records. It is also less costlier. But the mechanical recording would have been a distinct possibility in the absence of codes. Keyboard, purchase cards, computers, etc., would stop working if no codes are there. The use of machines is limited so far as the long description is concerned, because that will be more time consuming and hence costlier thereby defeating the very purpose of mechanical recording. But codes solve the problem.

Facility in Pricing and Costing. Long description of prices is a cumbersome job and fails to satisfy the need of indexing and easy referencing. Referencing also becomes slow in a long descriptive price list. In order to make it easy and more reliable codes are introduced. Costing in a manufacturing units, is to be done in a manner which may make it more reliable and simplified. The codes can do it. As per the requirement the cost may be calculated job wise, for which different cost headings are to be provided. Codes become helpful here, thus, facilitating the costing.

Facility in Locating and Indexing. Again long descriptions are not of much help in locating and indexing the material in the storehouse. The materials in the storehouse have to be kept n an order which may facilities their placement and location. Also Indexing in logical order facilitates the easy operation in the storehouse. For making it less time and energy consuming, items may be arranged according to the codes allotted to the materials. This may, thus facilitates the location and indexing of the materials in the storehouse.

Efficient Inspection. Inspection is checking of the quality and utility of the materials as per the purchase order and requirement of the production unit. This has to be efficient, as on correct and proper inspection of the material depends the standardised and qualitative production, which in turn helps in maintaining the goodwill of the product in the market and ensuring at least the previous margin of profit. Codes and not lengthy description clearly indicate the correct quality of the material assisting in efficiency inspection.

Planned Production. From the above discussion it is evident that codification helps in avoiding lengthy and unwieldy descriptions resulting in accurate identification, achieves standardisation, reduces the varieties, facilitates mechanical recording, simplifies costing and pricing ensures efficiency inspection, takes less time and energy in store-room operation. All these, naturally, help in planned production ; in preparing the production schedule and strict adherence to, it comes within easy reach because of the codification of materials.

Systems of Codification

There are different systems of codification for nationalised storekeeping. But the best system is that, which also gives The history and sizes of materials along with standard form. Codification should also avoid calling the material by its function or its used name. It should give an objective name which should be versatile in nature. The system is more commendable for adoption where large number of items having large variety are in storage however the following systems for codification are generally used in the modern industrial concern:

- ★ Arbitrary
- ★ Alphabetical
- ★ Numerical
- ★ Alphanumerical
- ★ Mnemonic
- ★ Decimal.

Arbitrary System

Arbitrary system as the word 'arbitrary' denotes; is a system arising from accident rather than from rule. It is based on the serial number under which a material is received in an industry and the same is allotted a code number. This system often adopted in the initial stage of an industry. In this system either one has to follow the arbitrary number allotted to a material upon its receipt or the vocabing department gives the arbitrary number. For example, if vocabing department has so far standardized 9100 items and if now it wants to standardize a lathe machine which has been received, then 9101 code number will be allotted to the lathe machine.

This system has the primary advantage that there is no fixed limit for codifying any number of items. But the disadvantages are that there are changes of duplication of items and one cannot know the history of materials or any specific description of the material but for each item will have to refer to the key which become cumbersome. This is the reason why this system is not popular.

Alphabetical System

Under this system of codification 'alphabets' are the basis and each material is allotted a certain letter from the alphabet which has no relation with number. The first alphabet of the name of the material is invariably the staring point of codification in this system, Subsequently, sub-alphabet is also used depending upon its other characteristics. The following illustration may make the system more clear.

Acid	A
Brass	B
Iron Ore	IN—O
Iron Pig	IN—P
Iron Steel	IN—S
Iron Sheets	IN—ST
Iron Bars	IN—BA

The alphabetical system is not easy to remember and it is not possible to expand it to the desired level because of the limited availability of alphabets. It is difficult to select proper alphabet for each of the items in the store. That is why this system is not so popular and is out-dated. Small concern which have a very limited stock can adopt this system.

Numerical System

This system is based on numbers. The materials are codified with the aid of numbers making provisions for further expansion as well. For instance, number I may be allotted to iron and number 2 to stainless steel and so on. The numerical system like the alphabetical suits only to small stores. Though, this is a simple system, but there are chances of duplication. This system is also very old and not so popular. Hence, it is not so much used in the modern industries.

Mnemonic System

Mnemonic system as the word 'mnemonic' denotes, is a system of assisting memory. Under this system the material is codified by giving letters and figures as codes. It may be decimal or arbitrary. Letters are assigned to different materials according to the sound of the names. For example:

PM	Packing Materials
BS	Brass Screws
SS	Steel Screws.

Under this system one can easily know what a particular item is meant for by just looking the code number. The system is adopted in small concerns where the number of items is not much because it has limitation as one will have to accommodate the code out of 26 alphabets for copying all the items. An ideal system may be to use letters to represent the names of materials and number to represent the size and shape and other specifications of the material. For example:

SS—Represents Steel Screws.

20—The first two numbers, viz., 20 represent the length of the screws in mm.
= 20 mm.

08—The 3rd and 4th numbers, viz. 08 represent the diameter of the screw in mm.
= 8 mm.

Hence SS2008 means steel screw 20 mm long and 8 mm in diameter. This system is also most common in numbering the vehicles, e.g., DHS—4965. Here DH stands for Delhi, S for scooter and 4965 is the arbitrary registration number.

Alpha-numerical System

This system is same as Mnemonic System. Rather we can say that other name of mnemonic system is alpha-numerical system because in this system the material is codified by giving alphabets and numbers both as codes.

Decimal System

Decimal system of codification is the universal method of codification. It is simple and easy to codify large stores. Under this system items up to 5,00,000 can easily be codified and at the same time each symbol will give the history size, specification and complete picture of the item. To follow this system one has to categorize stores in classes, groups, sub-groups, types and last three digits can be left for sizes or sub-types. Decimal system works from 0 to 9 figures and on adopting 7 to 11 digits. Each digit indicates something or the other. For example:

Ist digit	Section
2nd digit	Class
3rd digit	Group
4th and 5th digit	Type of materials
The onwards	Size, part No., specification or any other detail required.

Let us consider that stores of a particular industry can be divided into the following main sections and allotted numeral as shown below:

0	Raw Materials
1	Plants and Machinery
2	Machine and Hard Tools
3	Construction Materials
4	Maintenance, Repair and Operation Materials
5	Spare Parts
6	General Stores
7	Fixtures
8	Paints, Oil and Lubricants
9	Finished Products.

Mild steel bar would be raw material and as such fall under section (0). This raw material could be further sub-divided into classes as follows:

0	Timber	5	Paper
1	Rubber	6	Glass
2	Metals	7	Leather
3	Textile	8	Chemicals
4	Plastics	9	Miscellaneous

Therefore code number of metal would be 02.

Raw Materials

The classification of raw material—metal could again be divided into the following group:

0	Aluminium	5	Brass
1	Zinc	6	Mild Steel
2	Lead	7	Stainless Steel
3	Nickel	8	Alloy Steel
4	Copper	9	Other Metals

Similarly the fourth number could show any of the following type:

0	Ingot	3	Wire
1	Plate	4	Mesh
2	Sheet	5	Bar

Again the fifth digit to indicate the following classification of shape:

0	Square	3	Round
1	Flat	4	Hexagonal
2	Angle		

The sixth, seventh and eight digit could show size—say in millimeters. Thus a round mild steel bar of 25 diameter could be shown as—02653025.

These digits show :

0	2	6	5	3	025
Raw Material	Metal	Mild Steel	Bar	Round	25 mm dia.

With a fully significant coding arrangement like this, the code No. 02553100 would mean 100 mm round brass bar in the raw material stores.

Stores Vocabulary

When all the items of stores are codified according to standard Material Code, these should be compiled in the form of a book in the chronological order. This compiled from of codification will be known as Stores Vocabulary or Stores Catalogue. Stores Vocabulary should be circulated among all the departments concerned for their use. Catalogue should be prepared when there are sufficient items in the stores. However, as and when fresh items are received, these should be codified accordingly and amendment slips should be issued.

Marking of Stores

For identification of materials, marking of stores is another method. These are two types:

★ Colour Marking.
★ Secret Marking.

Colour Marking

Colour marking of materials is often used to distinguish different grades of steel or copper or brass. Alloy steel costs several times more than the mild steel but looks alike to the naked eye. Hence for storekeeper to identify the different sheets and other materials it is necessary to adopt a suitable identification code. Normally, colour bands of three or four colours are adopted and painted at the end of bars, sheet etc. If metals are to be coloured marked the following colour code may be assigned to different metals:

Aluminium	Black	Steel	Blue
Copper	Red	Zinc	White
Iron	Green		

Secret Marking

In order to minimise the risk of pilferage, it is sometimes advisable to mark stock items with the secret code or initials of the firm so that, if anything is stolen, it may subsequently be traced and the mark will serve to prove that the article is the firm's property. Discretion should be exercised in this matter e.g., forging, casting, heavy steel, etc., are not worth the trouble of marking but articles suitable for domestic use, such as hand tolls, soap, towels, clothing, electric lamps etc. will usually repay some attention.

Thus secret marking is a moral check on the staff and theft and pilferage of costly items must be avoided to a greater extent due to secret marking.

Demerits of Codification

The above merits of codification do not lead us to a safe conclusion that it suffers with no disadvantage. There are certain demerits of codification which are enumerated as under:

1. **Mistake in Coding.** The success of codification depends on 'a check-up' line for verification of codes allotted from time to time, place to place and position to position. In normal circumstances this checkup line may not succeed in verifying the codes at all times, in all places and positions. The coding mistake, thus, may crop up and avoidance of which may not be possible, howsoever alert the store management may be. A busy or a new assistant may err somewhere unknowingly and unconsciously, the incidence of which may bring disaster to nay of the department affected by his error.

While filling up a stores requisition slip, an assistant of the production department, if he has wrongly entered the code number, may get the wrong quality of materials from the stores department, resulting in production of higher substandard or high-standard product. Both may be bad from the goodwill point of view. A substandard item may lose the goodwill in the market. In the same way a high standard product may have more cost of production but will not yield the same high price as the product is to be sold out at the same price at which other products of the like standard are being business in the market as a correction will, in future, be made and the same high standard material which came into the market because of error in coding may not come up and the customer might be expecting the same high standard. They may be disappointed and may be desert you by switching their linking for your competitors product out of annoyance and dissatisfaction.

Likewise, a coding mistake in the purchase requisition by the stores department to the purchase department may result in wrong placement of orders to the supplier, consequently wrong supply of materials to the stores department by the supplier. This may be rejected by the inspection department, though the inspection department may be in an awkward position as the materials supplied are conforming to the purchase order but are not confirming to the production plan. They have no moral and legal support for rejection, but they have no moral grounds to accept either. However, if they accept, it may result either in overstocking or may at a later date be declared as obsolete. In both the cases there is a loss, which is due to mistake in coding.

A grave situation may arise when in a certain accounting statement a mistake in coding has crept in. This may lead to wrong decisions, wrong formulation of policies, wrong course of action which may sometimes disturb the business routine.

Though the mistake in coding might have crept in because of mechanical defects, bad handwriting, careless writing, negligence or carelessness, etc., it is enough to say that it may be disastrous, but is unavoidable as human element is involved in the entire store-room. The only things which may be suggested here is that whenever applying codes we have to be cautious and alert.

2. **Detection of Coding Mistake.** It involves long time and labour to find out the mistake which has been committed. Finding out of exact code against a wrong code, is a strenuous task, then, he has to go from page to page. It is, thus, a costlier job with sometimes is not worth undertaking.

Stores Organisation

The stores and receiving jobs are closely related. Therefore, the receiving activity is often placed under Jurisdiction of the storekeeper and stores personnel reporting to materials management department. The following are the two strong views for this organisational arrangement.

(a) Stores activity is a materials-oriented activity, therefore, it should report to a department whose primary interest likewise lies in materials and supply operations.

(b) Receiving is the last step in material acquisition process and stores is the last step in materials supply process.

Under this kind of system the relationship between stores, inventory control and purchasing will receive proper attention. In some companies the stores activity are under the Chief of Production. The reason for this set up is as follows:

(a) Production management is responsible for running the production operation smoothly and for meeting product delivery dates. The production department therefore have to control the material supply to ensure smooth delivery of material to the production work stations.

(b) Receiving and stores should not be supervised by the department that buys and authorities payment for the materials they receive and disburse.

Both the above systems of Stores reporting are of equal importance to management. The final decision, therefore, will probably be based on other factors in a particular firm's organisational and operational pattern. A final factor which conditions the decision is the location of the inventory control responsibility. While there is no requirement that stores and inventory management should report to the same department. But if the two departments report to the same department head many mutual control problems can be solved quickly at a lower level before they become serious. In all cases however, the decision should be based on an attempt to fulfill the following objectives as completely and realistically as possible: To keep materials in good condition and to have then immediately available; To develop and order filling and delivery system which satisfies production requirement, and to achieve the activities at a minimum cost.

Chapter 33

STORES PLANNING AND STORAGE EQUIPMENTS

Location of Storeroom

Store room location is one aspect of the plant layout problem. In production plants the process is laid out for a straight line, forward moving flow of materials through the process. Materials move one operation at a time. Space is thus utilised to the fullest degree possible, handling costs are minimised, and writing of production orders standardised. This helps in manufacturing cost. Other factors determining store room location include temperature and humidity control needs; types of handling equipment in store room, and the bulk, weight and value of the items stored. The space allocated to a store room in a factory must be sufficient for warehousing the maximum stores inventory in the busiest season of the production year. It must be large enough also for efficient receiving and issuing operations. The store room should be adjacent to the production floor for fast, easy delivery of materials to first users. The location of store depends to a greater extent on the location of plant which is discussed here. A good plant location will help in providing loading platforms, siding, Truck trailor access; parking facilities and storage area. The factors responsible for plant location are also responsible for the location various other departments such as Production Block; Store Houses, Administrative and Marketing Departments etc. Similarly the centralisation of storage facilities also yields significant benefits. The major advantage of centralisation is that it facilitates control of the total stores operations viz materials, space utilisation and equipment and manpower. Up to a certain point, the larger the storage area, the more efficiently space and equipment can be used. A company normally attempts to use both centralised and decentralised locations in its total stores operation. The objective is to secure the major advantage of both approaches to the extent possible in a particular situation.

An appropriate slogan for well located storeroom is "A place for everything and everything in its place. A "place for everything" can be planned. Keeping "everything in its place" though is not always an easy job. The development of a good storage location address system provides assistance to those who try to keep everything in place.

Plant Location

A new business is always faced with the problem of where to locate. The problem of plant location in established industry receives more attention. A number of conditions can lead to the consideration of the plant location problem. These conditions are: (1) expansion, (2) decentralization, and (3) economic factors, such as a shift of the markets or an inadequate labour supply. Expansion is the most frequent cause for considering the problem of plant location. Established industries often expand when (1) their facilities become obsolete, (2) market demand grows beyond a capacity of the plant site and facilities, or (3) inadequate services are available to the customer.

The decentralization of industry in this country is increasing at a rapid pace. Many of the industrial giants that historically grew in one location have found that decentralization pays off in a number of respects. The company benefits by the availability of new sources of labour supply, the improved labour relations of a smaller plant, a lower absentee rate, and the greater interest in their work shown by citizens of small communities. The worker benefits from the lower cost of living in uncongested town, the elimination of expensive and annoying buying off. The increased opportunities for advancement and better opportunities to utilize his spare time is available in bigger towns.

Objective of Location

The objective of any location is to able to deliver the products to the customer at a cost equal to or less than the competition within the product field. The cost of goods delivered to the customer depends upon

(a) The cost of gathering the material;
(b) The cost of fabricating the material;
(c) The cost of distributing the finished product to the consumer.

Keeping the above cost breakdown in mind it is possible for any manufacturing facility to make a list of those location factors which will tend to effect one or all of the above three costs. The list will vary depending upon the product and production characteristics, the objective and the sizes of the particular installation. There are a number of factors, however, which tend to have an effect on plant location viz nearness to market and raw material; availability of power and water; climate, availability of capital, labour; transportation facilities; site availability etc.

Definition

Plant location can be defined as the determination of that location which when considered will provide minimum cost delivered to the customer. Amongst the different problems relating to the management of the production system is that of location of industrial plant. The plant must be located in a place which influences the cost of production. It can be imagined that manufacturing and distribution costs may vary to an extent of 10 percent simply by virtue of the choice of plant location.

Location Problem

Two levels of problems must be considered when considering plant location viz. (1) the selection of the general territory, and (2) the selection of the community and plant site. The continuous treat of disruption of trade along the borders automatically prevent any concentration of industry near these areas. Such major factors are generally considered to eliminate (or alternatively, narrow down) the choice of the general territory after which the selection of the community and plant site follows.

Territory Selection

When a making the selection of a general territory, obtaining specific information about a given community can be a waste of time. Territory selection calls for information of a more general nature. Location information of a general nature may be obtained from the following sources:

- ★ Ministry of Industrial Development and Internal Trade.
- ★ Institute of Public Opinion.
- ★ Techno-economic surveys conducted by State Governments.
- ★ National Control of Applied Economic Research.
- ★ Indian Federation of Chambers of Commerce.
- ★ State Chambers of Commerce.
- ★ Department of Industry in State Governments.
- ★ Survey of India maps.

Community and Site Selection

Once the general territory for location has been selected, it becomes necessary to choose a community and a site. This choice is based upon consideration of the factors discussed in the next section. It should be noted that some of these location factors must be considered at the community and site level as well as when making the selection of the general territory. An early decision must be made regarding the size of the community in which the plant is to be located. The alternative choices can be classified as: City; Suburban; and Country locations.

City *versus* Suburban *versus* Country

Wide open spaces and freedom to expand are probably two of the biggest inducements for industrial rush to the country.

The type of manufacturing process may decide the site selection. For example, a country location is desirable for a plant producing explosives. Some of the general conditions leading to the selection of an appropriate type of community might be listed as follows:

Conditions suggesting urban location

(a) Large skilled labour force required.
(b) Processes heavily dependent upon availability of city utilities.
(c) Multi-floor building desirable.
(d) Close contact with suppliers demanded
(e) Rapid public transportation available.

(f) Technical and Research discussion needed.

Condition suggesting a rural location

(a) Semi-skilled or female labour force required.
(b) Avoidance of heavy city taxes and insurance desired.
(c) Labour force residing close to plant.
(d) Plant expansion easier than in city.
(e) Community close to but not in large population centre.

Conditions suggesting a country location

(a) Large site required for either present demands or expansion.
(b) Lowest property taxes available desired.
(c) Unskilled labour force required.
(d) Low wages required to meet competition.
(e) Morale of working force improved by country location.
(f) Manufacturing process is dangerous or objectionable.
(g) Processes causing environmental pollution.

One rule of thumb regarding the size of a site is that it should not be less than five times the actual size of the plant itself. *This is considered a minimum in order to allow for loading platforms, siding, tractor trailer access, parking facilities, and storage area. Wherever possible, open land is desirable on two or more sides to allow future expansion.* Unfortunately favourable offers of a fine site or attractive tax promises frequently influence plant location decisions. Objective data is essential to good plant location. In order to select a site, a list of following general specification should be prepared as follows:

(a) Description of building to be constructed (including sketch).
(b) Size of plot.
(c) Necessary railway, highway and waterway facilities.
(d) Minimum size of water mains, gas line, and power line.
(e) Volume of ground water to be utilized.
(f) Sewerage and effluent disposal requirements.
(g) Safety area for offensive odors, noise, smoke etc.
(h) Provisions for sprinkler pressure (gravity tank or local waterman).

The maps published by the Geological Survey of India are very useful in selecting a good plant site. These maps show land elevations, water features and works of as such as roads, dams, buildings, railways, but not power lines.

Factors Influencing the plant location

Following factors must be kept in mind before final selection of plant location is made:

Market: Proximity to market is one of the important factors affecting the choice of plant location because both promptness and cost of service to customers depends upon proximity to the market. Depending upon the product, market may be concentrated or widely dispersed. When a market is concentrated, the market factor would tend to influence the entrepreneur to choose close to this concentration.

Labour: The business can never bring fruits unless it can obtain and maintain a productive labour force. Not only must the labour force be available in adequate number but also it must contain the skill required in a given manufacturing process. There may be any development in modern machinery, which in many instances reduces the importance of skilled labour, the key to success in any business or organisation is the human factor. Wage levels must of course be considered. In general wage and skill are lower in south than in the west or east. Therefore industries requiring many unskilled workers, which traditionally pay low wages are attractive to the south.

Transportation Facilities: The problem of transportation is of great importance specially when raw materials are bulky and low value. The more rent of material can consume a very high percentage of the final cost to the customer. An industry tends to be localized at places which have developed means of transport.

(i) Railways. Indian Railways have very large net work of traffic system. According to the type of the product, Railway carriages are designed for better transportation. This is one of the cheapest mode of transport also.
(ii) Roadways. Many transport organisations are existing in India. For hill station and to haul heavy machinery, Road transportation quite good and Rail transportation may not be suitable for this purpose.
(iii) Waterways. This mode of transportation is mainly for international transits. Bulk and non perishable materials can be transported to far of places with low charges. But the transportation time is very high. Port Trust of India, and some Shipping Corporations of India are playing very vital role in this method of transport.

Availability of Power and Fuel: In the last century the industries were located near the coal mines or the locations where coal could be taken cheaply and conveniently. But today all industries require electric power of some sort. There are certain processes, that require usually large amounts of electric power. For example heavy water plants or chemical processes of hydrolysis nature are all located in areas where large sources of cheap power are available. In India we have three types of power sources: (i) Thermal power (ii) Hydro electric power (iii) Nuclear power. For any industry the availability of power should be cheap, continuous and regular. Technologist are exploring the possibility of obtaining power from wind and sea waves.

Availability of Raw Materials: The location of raw materials is influential in the location problem. Some industries by nature of their manufacturing process are forced to locate near raw material sources. The iron and steel industries have been located close to coal fields since it uses coal in large quantities.

Climate and Atmospheric Conditions: Climate greatly influences the process in several industrial such as textile industry where atmospheric high humidity is essential. Clean and dust free atmosphere for pharmaceutical industry. In modern days, air conditioning has helped to a great extent in solving the climate and atmospheric conditions.

Availability of Water: This is another important factor for the selection of plant location. Chemical process plants especially require huge quantities of soft and pure water. The temperature of water may also be a influencing factor for plant to location. For example selecting the site of Antibiotics Plant at Virbhadra is due to low temperature and less bacteriological load and plenty of Ganges water to reduce the refrigeration loads.

Laws and Taxation: State and local laws should be studied when considering various locations. Labour laws and employment regulations vary widely from one location to another. Some of the aspects of industrial operations regulated by laws are hours of work, minimum age and wages of workers and working conditions for woman employees.

Special and Recreational Facilities: As social and recreational facilities are the necessities of one's life after the plant hours and on holidays, the employees need the same. Therefore it is essential that Government should provide suitable parks, cooperative stores, community halls, cinemas and education facilities for the employees.

Waste Disposal: Pollution control act is in force now. The effluents and work disposal of a plant should not harm to the public. So proper effluents treatment and water disposal methods should be available.

Storage Equipments

There are following types of equipments commonly used in Storing materials.

(a) Skids
(b) Pallets
(c) Open type Shelving
(d) Closed Shelving
(e) Cabinets
(f) Bins
(g) Staking Boxes
(h) Special Storage Racks
(i) Various Outdoor Storage Platforms and racks.

Prior to World War II, most industrial storehouses were equipped with wooden shelving and storage facilities. Wooden facilities still offer several advantages. Wood being softer than metal and provides safer storage for delicate items which might be dropped or scuffed in the bin. Wooden facilities can also be built to special configurations and can generally be installed quickly and inexpensively. The steel equipments are more expensive initially, its long-run advantages usually outweigh the additional cost. The steel equipments have the additional advantages of strength and fire resistance. The steel equipments are easy to keep clean because of its smooth surface.

Open type shelving. This type of shelves are most suitable for small boxes of components, screws, ball bearings, types of paints, files, drills, conisters or boxes of cleaning materials.

Closed types of shelves. This can accommodate a very wide range of stock. It is just as convenient for packaged goods as open shelves (but more expensive) and it is most suitable for loose items such as nuts and bolts, hand tools, pipe fittings, machinery spares, small components etc. This types of shelves can be provided with proper segregation and lockable doors for security and protection of open dirt etc.

Arrangement for stocks. Individual bays of shelving can be bolted together to form a single sided stack as large as is required and a saving of material is made by using common-sheet sides between each bay. In a similar bay, two ranges of bins be set up back to back with the main frames bolted together to form a very strong and rigid structure.

Multi binning. Any storage fixture above 2.2 mm height will require the use of steps or ladders to reach the materials in the top compartments. This slows down the process of binning on receipt and selection for issue, and the steps are always an impediments in narrow gang ways. It is, however, possible to make the best use of the available spare by having two or more tiers of bins, one on top of the other. This can be arranged quite economically because, within limits, the lower tiers of the bins will support floors above ground level. In a multi-tier binning arrangement, the gang ways for the upper tiers can be provided by the use of chequer plate or metal gratings supported also on the underneath bins.

Pallets. A pallet is a piece of equipment especially designed to facilitate mechanical handling by fork-lift trucks, and may be used for both storage and transportation purposes. The flexibility and economy of this method of dealing with unit loads has great attractions and the employment of pallets in recent years has been steadily increasing. There are different types of pallets like the two way entry , four-way entry, box and pest pallet depending upon their functional utility and the way a forklift truck can handle them.

Racks. A rack is any kind of store fixture which cannot be classified shelving or binning. Racks for the accommodation of palletised stores, tubes bars, sheets, plates, tyres, cables and drums are the commonest types encountered in store houses, but there are many racks designed for special purpose *e.g* shovels, V-belts chain and avoid variety of heavy stores.

Portable receptacles or Tote Boxes. Tote boxes are usually made of sheet metal, they are arranged to hold a standard quantity of materials or components and often have special internal fittings. They vary in size and shape to match the particular materials and handling methods in use, and can be attached on top of each other fully or empty. The use of tote-boxes in store houses is very frequently associated with the standardisation of this equipment throughout the whole of the production shops.

Protection of Stores. The protection of stores from fire, rust an corrosive, dust, theft, weather, heat, cold and moisture is an important aspect of the store-keeping function. Each kind of material such as textiles, rubber goods, leather goods and metal chemical requires its own kind of care. The following points should be kept in view in this regard:

(i) **Protection against fire.** It is essential to store them in fine proof buildings and bins with adequate automatic sprinkler provision. Adequate fire fighting equipment such as high pressure water lines, modern sprinkler system, suitable chemical extinguisher, fire pail, sand etc. should be provided.

For certain classes of goods such as oils etc., foamite sprinklers should be supplied. Gasoline and fuel oil should be stored in under ground tanks. Explosives such as blasting power and dynamite should be stored at a distance from all other buildings in store houses used for no other purpose.

(ii) **Protection of goods from damage by dust.** Storage should be in boxes or in closed cabinets. In city areas, where there is considerable dust in the atmosphere air conditioned storage areas may prove advisable for such materials. Writing paper and finished textiles goods are examples of goods requiring special protection from dust.

(iii) **Protection against weather conditions.** Materials whose bulk and nature require that they be stored out of doors can be protected by open sheds or by textiles or by plastic coverings.

(iv) **Protection against deterioration.** Some materials deteriorate with age. Such material should not be over-stocked and first in first out storage system should be adopted. Another form of deterioration in the damage which may result from improper materials handling. The adoption of the most suitable container, handling equipment and methods can do much to reduce this source of damage.

(v) **Protection against theft.** Protection against theft can be ensured by locking the store room and excluding all persons not directly concerned in the receipt and issue of stores. Stores should be issued only on the authority of proper signed requisitions.

Protective Measures

(i) **Cement.** Cement solidifies if it gets wet. Materials of this nature should be stored in a dry and heated buildings. The stores floor should be stored, because even in warm hours, there will be a certain amount of condensation at times on concrete floors.

(ii) **Textile.** Textiles are subject to damage by moth and rat. This can be overcome by treating them by moth-proofing chemicals and wrapping bales in air-tight packages. Food grains can also be stored by this way.

(iii) **Machines and Equipment.** If there is a need to hold machine on expensive equipment for a period of years, to keep them in good condition they are completely enveloped in an air light covering or a suitable plastic material.

Storekeepers Role of Restocking

In this complex and competitive industrial and commercial set-up the store-keeper is well aware of his role of restocking his stores in order to ensure the steady and efficient functioning of his department. Without stocks a business, whether manufacturing or commercial, could not be run efficiently. The stock-keeper cannot afford to depend on trial and error policy in the matter as it may prove to be a costly affair. This will take into account the probabilities of running out of stock with different stock levels and by balancing the cost of being out of stock with that of stock to be held in particular period. This will obviously be the most economical level at which to operate. In a nutshell, this is the crux of the problem of restocking a store which we have to analyse and study in the following pages.

The materials are received by the storekeeper. They are stored, preserved and issued on demand. This implies that a point of stock will reach when the storekeeper will be alarmed and would like to move the purchase department for having the stock replenished in order to honour the future requisition. Suppose a stage comes when the storekeeper refuses to honour the requisition. Suppose a stage comes when the storekeeper refuses to honour the requisitions. The whole of industry will be at standstill. The business will stop operating, the organisation will start incurring wasteful expenditure and the whole economic activity will come to a stop. Thus a 'Sero Level 'has not to be reached in a proper functioning of a storekeeper. Materials in a store move in and out automatically and hence the issued stock has to be replaced by fresh arrivals for achieving the desired aim of the organisation. This is termed as Replenishment of stock which denotes taking steps for the fresh purchase of those stocks which have exhausted and for which requisitions are to be honoured in future. For acting judiciously, systematically and scientifically on this score the store-keeper first of all fixes different levels (points).

1. Maximum level
2. Minimum level
3. Order level
4. Danger level.

. **Maximum level.** Maximum level represents the label above which the stock in hand is not allowed to exceed. This is because:

(i) If exceeds this level it will (a) involve more investment (b) require more space, (c) amount to more wastage because of more handling, chances of more damage, spoilage, obsolescence, and (d) involve more carrying cost.

(ii) Excess stock will devoid the capital in its diversion to other gainful use and thus not making it available for more profitable use.

(iii) Excess stock will increase the cost of storage thereby increasing production/selling cost defeating the very purpose of efficient store keeping.

(iv) Stock in excess will devoid the management of taking advantage of price fluctuations and favourable market conditions. The fixation of maximum level depends on the following factors:

- ★ Rate of consumption of the materials.
- ★ Time necessary to obtain the deliveries.
- ★ Amount of money available.
- ★ Storage space available.
- ★ Possibility of loss due to evaporation deterioration, etc.
- ★ Market condition, seasonal and price fluctuation.
- ★ Economic order in quantity.
- ★ Government restrictions as in the case of explosive materials etc.
- ★ Staff and other facilities available for the maintenance of stores and the maintenance cost involved.
- ★ Need of buffer stock (safety stock) in relation to active stock.

Minimum Level. Minimum level points to the level below which the stock in hand shall not be allowed to fall. This limit is fixed in order to avoid the possibility of suspension of production due to shortage of materials. It is necessary that the stock on hand shall always be kept a little above this level to be on the safe side but never to fall below this level. This is usually fixed taking into account two important factors among others, namely the time required to obtain fresh stock i.e. lead time and the rate of consumption of materials. Minimum level gives as element of safety in production as materials can always be kept in reserve for emergencies. This is why sometimes the stock at this level is known as Emergency Reserve Stock. The level in any case is not allowed to touch the zero level.

Order level. This is the quantity of stock(level) fixed between the maximum and minimum levels of stock at which it becomes the duty of the stores incharge to initiate the purchase so as to replenish the stock within reasonable time. This level is usually a little higher to that of the minimum so as to cover such emergencies as abnormal usage of materials, unexpected delays in delivery of new supplies etc. while fixing this level we ordinarily take the following points into consideration:

(a) Time required for obtaining fresh supplies.

(b) Quantity required to be ensured to a certain level of production at a given time.

(c) Possible unexpected requirement which cannot be avoided.

(d) Possible unexpected delays in getting the fresh supplies because of rains, political situation, war, labour trouble, transport inadequacy, etc.

The objective of fixing up the order level is to re-stock the materials at the lowest cost ensuring at the same time the uninterrupted operation of the manufacturing until/business organisation. It ,ay, however, be pointed out that the order quantity is determined by taking into account the supplier's discount, rate of consumption, price of the material, storage cost, danger of deterioration and obsolescence besides the availability of funds, space available for storage and preservation facilities. Again the loss due to interruption of operation will also have to be examined. These taken together will determine the order quantity which in its turn affects the point at which the order level has to be fixed. It is necessary because the supplier has also to be given sufficient time for making arrangements of the supply. The larger is the consignment, the greater will be the time taken by the supplier. Thus order quantity has its own say in fixing the points of order (or recorder) level.

Danger level. This level is below the minimum level and represents the stage at which emergency and immediate steps have to be taken for getting the stock replenished. It is fixed taking into account the time required to get the materials by the quickest possible means of transport, i.e. the minimum time required for obtaining supplies form any any possible source. Danger level of any item in the store gives red signal to the stores incharge that the materials have touched the lowest point and if no emergency steps are taken to restock them, they will completely be exhausted i.e. closure of operation is in the offing.

The job of the stores incharge is not over with the fixing up of these levels. These levels are subject to change. Hence they should be reviewed from time to time. This is important because these levels are fixed on the basis of two assumptions, i.e. the procurement time and the rate of consumption. Since these are themselves not static the different levels can also not remain static. Hence a periodic review makes them more realistic and reliable.

Receipt of Materials

In a storehouse materials are received from:

(a) The supplier

(b) The Production Department—the finished goods, the semi-finished goods, the unused materials and the scrap; and

(c) The other departments—the scrap, the goods issued in excess and repaired ones.

The Receipt Procedure

The receipt procedure in all the above cases in one and the same, but with a slight difference from one organization to another. The requisitions for the stores are submitted to the Purchase Department for placing orders with the suppliers. The order is placed by the Purchase Department a copy of which is sent to the Materials Control Department a copy of which is sent to the Materials Control Department and Store Department's Receipt Section in which time of delivery is generally mentioned.

The supplier delivers the materials to the receipt section of the stores department along with a supplier's advice note. The note is supplied to the Receipt Section either by post or through the driver of the carrier. The goods, if purchased from outstation, will be carried by some transport agency which will give a carrier's consignment note to the suppler who will send it to the purchaser for taking the delivery of the consignment from the transport agency. Supplier may send a supplier's packing note to the purchaser detailing the packages and their contents. This facilitates the verification of the goods purchased with the help of the purchase order. As soon as materials are received at the receipts section of the stores department, the receipts clerk signs the delivery challan in testimony to the fact that he has received the materials recorded in the document. The receipt clerk, then, records the receipts in materials receipt book. After recording the receipts in Materials Receipt Book, the next step is to prepare the Daily Receipt Voucher/or Materials receipt note. The daily receipt voucher is generally prepared in triplicate along with four notes, namely:

(1) Damage Report (2) Storage Report (3) Excess Report and (4) Package Slips.

Immediately after the receipt of the materials and after making necessary entries in the Materials Receipt Book and Daily Receipt Voucher, the storekeeper proceeds to check the quantity of the materials with the help of the copy of the purchase order and with the documents which have been supplied to him along with the materials by the supplier. Any discrepancy detected is reported through the above mentioned notes with an intimation to the purchase department for necessary action at its end. In some organisation a separate department, known as claims department, functions in addition to the purchase department which deals with such matters.

When the packages/goods are received by the receipt section in damaged condition, a damage report is prepared in four copies; one of which is sent to the supplier, the second to the Purchase/Claims Department, the third one to the Transport Agency/Carrier's Driver and the last is retained as the office copy of record. Likewise, shortage and excess reports are also prepared in case the materials have been received short or in excess. These are also prepared in four copies. In order to reduce of damage, shortage and excess reports are combined and only one proforma is prescribed. After completing the process of the preparation of the reports mentioned above the receipt incharge proceeds to open the different packages received. Then after the DRV is prepared and the goods are sent to the inspection department for inspection along with the voucher for reporting back the suitability/non-suitability and recommending the acceptance/rejection of the materials. In the meantime the Receipt Section prepares and Package slip.

Packages

Packages in which goods are received may be of the following categories:

1. Non-returnable. The packages which are not to be returned to the suppliers are classed as such. for such category of packages a documentation is required. They are generally sent to scarp section for necessary disposal or sometimes (if can be used further), they are used in despatch section for wrapping the consignment or used for preserving the materials in the store.

2. Non-returnable but charged. The packages which are not to be returned to the suppliers, but the suppliers, includes the price of such packages in the price of the consignment since they are costly enough and as per agreement packing is not free. In such cases also the package slip is prepared and after filling up necessary columns of the slip it is sent to the suppliers as well as to the Accounts Department for necessary action, i.e., for adjusting the price charged for the packages, etc.

3. Returnable and Price adjusted. In case of packages to be returned to the supplier, the supplier charges the packing cost and includes the same in the invoice. When the packages are returned to the supplier, the purchaser recovers the price so charged by the supplier by making price adjustment. Here too, the Package Slip is prepared and after filling up the necessary columns it is sent to the supplier as well as to the Accounts Department and Claims Section of the Purchase Department for necessary action.

4. Charges Realisable afterwards. The packages are free at the time of supply but the packing charges are realised by the supplier if within reasonable time the packages are not returned back to the supplier. In such cases also the Package Slip is to be filled in and a copy is sent to the Supplier and Despatch Section of the Store Department for necessary action.

The receipts section, after completing its own process receiving the materials will send the same for inspection to the Inspection Department. The inspection department may either accept the materials and recommend their use or reject the materials and recommend their use or reject the materials and recommend either their return or keeping them in suspense for want of necessary instruction from the Production/Purchase Department. In case the goods have been rejected the inspection department will send a rejection note to the receipts section.

It is just possible that at the inspection stage certain defects of the materials might not have been detected and the goods accepted, binned and stock ledger posted. In such cases too a rejection note might be prepared and stock ledger might be credited by the figure involved. Though the Inspection Officer is responsible for such a lapse yet the possibility of such occurrences cannot be ruled out.

Stock Ledger. As soon as the materials are received back from the Inspection Department necessary entries are made in the Stock Ledger.

The modern trend is against keeping the voluminous stock ledger. Instead Stock Cards are being used in order to have the following advantages:

(a) The advantage of Kardex System in which cards are kept in a cabinet in horizontal.
(b) The advantage of quick and easy review of stock levels.
(c) The advantage of easy indexing system.
(d) The advantage of signalling system for correct and prompt replacement of stock.

The Stock Record Card may show the placement and position of purchase order through insertion slip at the bottom of the card, which is the latest advantage of Kardex System and which avoids not only duplication of work but correct and easy position at any time could be ascertained by making the use of signalling system.

Despatch. Where the Centralised Storing System is being adopted and the Branch/Sub-Departmental Stores are not authorised to make their own purchases and are dependent on the Central Store for their supply, a separate despatch section is established and attached to the Stores Department which is responsible for making supply of the materials to different Branch Stores, etc., as per their requisitions. In such cases, the despatch section at the time of despatching the consignment to different branch stores, etc., prepares a Store Advice Note giving all details of such despatch.

Binding, Placing and Indexing

After goods are received from the Inspection Department and necessary records are completed in respect of Stock Ledger or Stock Record Cards, they are moved to bins for placement and storage. simultaneously (with the placement of the materials in appropriate bins) index is prepared for facilitation of location and bin card is filled in. It is prepared for each and every item moved into the store and is either attached to the bin itself or is kept separately. Separate keeping of bin cards is done either in cabinets (library type cabinets) or in folders. This avoids exhaustive indexing for location of materials and at the same time safety of cards is assured to a larger extent. A bin card which is said to be a ready reference of the item stored in the bin indicating the latest position of the item, is a must for an efficiency storekeeping, which is helpful in locating the materials, preparing the index, acquiring the knowledge of the movement of materials in and out of the store and in replenishing the stock.

And this completes the procedure of the receipt of material from the supplier. The same procedure is followed when the goods are received from the production department returns from the department returns from the department, sub-store, surplus, scraps, obsolete materials, etc. In all these cases the procedure is the same of course, at times, slight modifications are to be made in the proforma used in different cases. For example, if the finished goods have been received from the production department it is first to be recorded in a separate book. Goods Inwards Book (Production Units,) and in a place of DRV Doily Received Note (Production Unit) may be prepared which may be sent to the Inspection (or Quality Control) Department (Marketing Division) for getting the goods passed as 'Marketable' after thorough inspection.

Chapter 34

RESPONSIBILITIES OF STORE KEEPER

Introduction

A store keeper is an employes who takes case of the stores lying under his control. A storekeeper is taken as a person who executes the retail orders of production supervisor just like a shop assistant serves the customer at the counter. Store keeper is an important member of the organisation because of the advancement of technology and scientific knowledge in the area of industry; trade and commerce. A more apt description of the storekeeper would be an "individual who cares the stores and keeps a watchful eye on the movement of both men and materials with a view to keep the whole organisation moving." This covers the enlarged functions of the storekeeper.

Qualifications

The type of persons required to operate a storekeeper system varies from one store to another depending upon the nature, size and composition of the stores department. Typical storeroom personnel would consist of a Chief Storekeeper, Assistant Storekeepers, and one or more store clerks if store records are kept in the storeroom. They work under the direction of a Store Officer who is the overall incharge of the Stores Department. The person incharge of actual handling of stores is known as assistant storekeeper where there is Chief Storekeeper senior to him. However, a 'Storekeeper' as he is known in most of the companies, is the most important of all. Some of the qualifications that this storekeeper should possess are:

(i) A hard working and painstaking individual.

(ii) An individual of extra-ordinarily honest habits, pleasing personality, and sweet temperament.

(iii) He should have some knowledge of account.

(iv) He should have some managerial qualities so as to create confidence in his collegues and exercise control over his subordinates.

(v) He should be fully conversant with the materials carried in the store so as to enable him to preserve them rightly and properly.

(vi) Lastly, he must possess basic academic qualifications, which will vary from one store to another. For example, a storekeeper of an engineering storehouse should be at least a graduate in Science or Engineering. A storekeeper required to handle general stores or stores not much of technical nature, may have Higher-Secondary of Matriculation qualification with training in the art of storekeeping.

Duties and Responsibilities

Duty denotes moral or legal obligation, i.e. what one is ought to do whereas responsibility refers to an act of doing a thing without detailed guidance but for which one may be morally accountable. Thus duty comes first which is followed by the responsibility which always clusters to duty. Hence the duty and responsibility is to be dealt under separate heads, although responsibilities and functions are more or less identical terms.

Duties

The following are the duties of a storekeeper:

* To receive the materials.
* To keep materials in the right place and in the manner prescribed.
* To issue the stores on proper authorisation and to proper persons following the correct procedure and, of course, within least possible time.
* To maintain complete, uptodate and correct store records.
* To preserve the materials for maintaining their original value and quality.
* To replenish the stock.
* To advice the management on day-to-day affairs of the stores department, particularly regarding obsolete, unserviceable and slow moving items.

Responsibilities

To the above duties following responsibilities of a storekeeper may be added:

(i) The storekeeper is responsible for the materials which he receives. Hence he should receive them on proper authorisation and should satisfy himself regarding the quality, quantity and value of the materials and check them with specifications given in the order form. He is also responsible for getting them inspected by the experts and obtaining the necessary certificate.

(ii) The storekeeper is also responsible for keeping the materials at the right place and according to the prescribed manner. To do this he has to classify the material received according to its nature, code and classification and place them at an appropriate place after giving each of them the correct code-number etc.

(iii) Issue of stores is the most important duty of the storekeeper which involves comparatively more responsibility on the part of the storekeeper. Since in some of the storehouses some of the parts are quite similar, the storekeeper must ensure that only the right type of part s issued, after comparing the code number and correct nomenclature of the part, otherwise it can create enormous difficulties to the production department. The issues should also be made without any loss of time, making sure that the materials received first in the store are issued first, and, of course, on proper written authorisation

(iv) The storekeeper is responsible for every theft, pilferage, damage and spoilage in the store. Proper recording, preservation, help the storekeeper in discharging his duties with full responsibility.

(v) It is the responsibility of the storekeeper to keep coordination with all the departments in the interest of smooth functioning of the organisation. Coordination with production, purchase, materials control, stores accounting and sales departments helps him in his day to day working.

(vi) Again it is the responsibility of the storekeeper to act in close cooperation with the purchase department in indenting the materials and suggesting the possible names of the suppliers quality and quantity to be purchased and the time by which it is required. In this way, he automatically becomes responsible to the production department.

(vii) For the purpose of valuation, stores verification is a must. The storekeeper is responsible for offering facilities to the stock verifies and for any irregularity detected by them.

From the above, it is clear that the job of the storekeeper is difficult at every step and for every action whether small or big, he is held responsible. Though his duties are simple, his responsibilities are full of obligations—both moral and legal.

Inspection of Material

The Inspection has acquired a new meaning with a development of new products and the quality improvement of old products which is the result of increasing precision capabilities in measurement and manufacturing techniques. The quality and cost of materials are so inter-related in the modern manufacturing world that they demand complete and wholesome inspection of materials purchased. The main aim of inspection is to prevent the production of nonstandard items. No one likes to waste his money for products which are non-standards or less in quantity or not according to his taste and liking. In industries where huge amounts of stores are purchased for production, the inspection is of utmost importance and done both for quality and quantity:

Objectives

The objective of inspection are:

(i) To maintain standard of quality of the product by accepting only materials of prescribed specifications as per purchase order.

(ii) To receive only the right quantity of materials.

(iii) To let the supplier always be careful in supplying the right quality and quantity of materials.

(iv) To utilise the money rightly.

(v) To let the purchase and store staff always be on guard against any irregularity.

Advantages of Inspection

If goods are inspected properly the following advantages are expected to accrue from such inspection.

(i) Standard of living will be maintained and a steady development will be expected due to qualitative use of the materials, which is assured because of inspection.
(ii) The goodwill in the market will be enhanced because of qualitative production, that too, completely at a lower cost since inspection will assure the quality of materials which will go to the production department.
(iii) The depreciation cost will go down because of less wear and tear and thus less repairs and renewals cost, due to standardised items put forth in the production department.
(iv) Standardisation of goods is achieved.
(v) Saving is achieved because of lower cost curve.
(vi) These will result in more margin of profit resulting in large scale production and its economies, thereby opening new employment opportunities. This will increase the Social Income resulting in the increase of per capita income and consequently all round national economic prosperity will be the result of proper and scientific inspection.

Goods received in the store must be inspected for quality. This maintains the production standard and helps in better utilization of money. Whether goods are ordered on formal specifications or by any other means of quality description the inspection of deliveries including the application of appropriate tests in some cases is essential to ensure that the quality of the delivery is in conformity with the purchase order and as per the requirement. This does not mean that there is any lack of confidence in the supplier but it is a routine precaution which every buyer takes. Once of the main reasons of inspection is to assure that no improper materials goes into production. It is, at the same item a check on the purchasing department for the responsibility of procuring materials of right quality and quantity. A provision for inspection and tests is made the routine or receiving procedure and custody of materials. The very fact that inspection is to be done makes the supplier careful while making supply of the materials to the stores department.

Inspecting Officer

Qualifications, duties and responsibilities: Inspection is done by authorized and qualified persons, who can do the job of inspection thoroughly and honestly. An Inspection Officer may be the storekeeper, foreman, mechanical engineer or an engineer deputed by him paint manager of any person authorized by the management, depending upon the nature and amount involved and importance of the materials received. There is no hard and fast rules. The designation of Inspection Officers differs from organization to organization. While the inspection of deliveries may have been done by the Purchase Department as a part of its duty, the final inspection at the time of receipt of materials at the store is very important.

Security Measures for Storehouses

Security measures for storehouses and stores can be discussed under the following heads:

- ★ Security of Building and Stockyards.
- ★ Custody of Keys.
- ★ Movement of Men, Staff and Visitors.
- ★ Marking the Stores.
- ★ Statutory Regulations.
- ★ Inspection by Supervisors.
- ★ Fire Precautions.

Security of Building and Stockyards. The building housing the stores should be of reasonable substantial construction. There should be restricted number of doors, fitted with adequate locks. All windows and skylights should be capable of being securely fastened and also fitted with bars and iron mesh, where they overlook a public highway. While designing the internal layout of the store-care should be taken to provide an issue counter segregated from the main storage area. Stockyards should be surrounded by an adequate fence with locking gates with the number of gates being the minimum.

Custody of Keys. Typical precautions are necessary for the custody of keys. The keys must be numbered, registered and kept under the control of a responsible person near the entrance gate. Written instructions should be issued regarding handling of the keys by nominated persons, particularly during off-duty hours. A key movement register should be maintained and every one collecting and depositing a key should be required to sign it on each occasion. All duplicate keys should be kept in the safe custody of a senior officer. The number of duplicate keys should be kept minimum. Whenever a key is lost, stolen or misplaced, the lock should be replaced by a new one, and the erring official adequately penalized.

Movement of Men. In the interest of security, access to the storehouse must be strictly regulated. Since the storekeeper is responsible for the safe custody of the materials, he has the full authority to supervise not only his own staff but all other persons who have the occasion to visit the store for any purpose whatsoever. For the staff identification cards or passes bearing their passport size-photograph are generally issued which the storekeeper can always check at the time of issue of stores etc. For casual visitors the use of Daily Visitor Slip should be made, and no one without she slip should be allowed entry into the storehouse. The Daily Visitor Slip should mention the name of the visitor, date, time and purpose of his visit and bear his signatures. It is preferable to mention also the name of the officer/official whom the visitor wishes to meet. The storekeeper should ensure that all those who have come to receive store are kept on the 'Public' side of the issue counter and are not normally admitted into the storage area. The same principle should apply to those whom come to deliver the goods. Movement of employees inside the store should be watched carefully particularly of those who do not belong to the section in which they are moving. During closed hours, a watchman should be provided to look after the stores building properly.

Fire Precautions. Fire is likely to break out easily in storehouse where all kinds of stores are kept, and unless adequate-measures are taken to prevent fires, huge losses will occur. The extent of fire risk depends upon three factors:

(i) Construction of the building,

(ii) Nature of the stock held, and

(iii) Arrangement of goods in the store.

Construction of the building should be such as may render it fire proof. It is, therefore, wise to avoid the use of timber in construction work, particularly doors, windows, etc. Asbestos sheets are supposed to be the safest material for roofing the storehouse. While constructing the building, suitable places for locating the fire-extinguishers and keeping the sand bags and buckets should be provided. Water mains with an adequate supply and sufficient hydrants should be provided at a suitable position. Where the fire-risk is great and the stocks are of high value, it is advisable to construct wide access roads and the main gangways to accommodate local fire engines, in case of need. It is also desirable to keep a mobile pump in the premises, and there should be adequate provision of standpipes, hoses, chemical extinguishers and water and sand buckets. An overhead sprinkling system can also be installed to check fire instantly. The local authority and the insurance company naturally have some interest in the fire risk. Their views and regulations should be taken into account while planning for fire precautions.

The stock held, its nature and arrangement in store also play an important role in the havocs of fire. Due precautions have, therefore, to be taken to guard against fires to stocks of inflammable nature, and preserving those items in such a way as would not permit any change of fire. Internal setting of store room can also be responsible for fire in many cases. The staff working in the store and factories should be trained in fire fighting procedures. Practice for them at regular intervals will prove very useful. Necessary information by way of instructions should be given publicity regarding the steps to the taken in case of fire. Information such as telephone numbers of nearest fire bridges, police stations, hospitals and the local fire officer should be available and kept handy and up to date.

Chapter 35

INDUSTRIAL SAFETY AND GOOD HOUSE KEEPING

Introduction

Industrial accidents are mainly due to human failure—somewhere in the claim of circumstances which lead to injury, we find the human factor. Specialist sections of management—engineers, electricians, designers, work study offices—are often lacking in an appreciation of the need to apply the principles of accident prevention to their work. "Unsafe" method accounts for a very high proportion of accidents. Therefore safty must be an integral part of any industrial undertaking, it must be built in at the design stage, in production planning and in operator training. The challenge of true of mind by efficient and regular safty training for all levels of management and worker. The aim must be to make every individual in industry have more regard not only for his own personal safty, but also for the safty of others.

Features of a Safty Organisation

Many persons influence safty directly. The chief executive, production managers, maintenance personnel or industrial relations employees, the plant physician the supervisor and production employee can affect safty qualitatively. Factors that govern plant safty effectiveness include choice of equipment, procedures and materials; budgets, the selection of personnel, the kind of leadership provided, and the work habits of the individual. When a safety specialist is employed to direct the plant safety programme his function usually is to assist line managers to control the safety of their operations. Ordinarily he does not assure any management prerogative but, develops information and materials which enable managers to optimise their authority is the pursuit of safty. Some of the features of safty organisation is the chemical Industry are:

A Management participation in safty programme.(Declaration of company safty policy).

B Supervisory responsibility for employee safety. (Each member of the supervisory staff is held responsible for safety).

C Assignment of staff function to safety personnel.

- (a) Safety department, safety safety engineer or other designated personnel given recognition and responsibility.
- (b) Duties include correlation of accident-prevention activities, promoting the safety programme.

D Provision for safe working conditions, building and equipment.
- (a) Establishment of engineering standards.
- (b) Review of plans for new processes or equipment from safety and fire-protection engineering point of view.
- (c) Industrial hygiene surveys to evaluate potential chemical exposure hazards.

E Safety education and safety training.
- (a) Education of supervisory personnel to assist them in carrying out their assigned safety responsibilities.
- (b) Employee education (New employee safety induction programmes).
- (c) Development of safety consciousness in all employees (use of bulletins, posters, films, and other visual aids).

Safety department should have a reasonable "Central Location" near the dispensary if possible, and with sufficient space available to provide for group meetings. Facilities must be available for strong and displaying samples of safty equipment, posters, safe-practice references, equipment catalogs and for the necessary records, files ad charts of the department.

Safety committees. A safety committee or group of plant committees is common to many plant safety organisations.They are subject to the usual problems of committee operation. When safety committees are established they require executive initiative. The committee size should be kept small for effective work but large enough to include all involved in plant's operation. Co-ordination of the committee activities, encouragement of their effectiveness, and provision of assistance in their studies are leading functions of chief executive of safety.

Accident Prevention Programme

Basic steps in safety Programme

In industries, many plants, some of them far reaching, have been formulated for the prevention of accidents. Some of the useful plans are based on fundamental principles which start with simple steps undertaken usually in the following order:

- (i) **Obtain co-operation of plant manager:** The manager's desire for safety achievement must be clearly visible through his action to achieve it.
- (ii) **Obtain co-operation of other Heads of Departments.** The other heads of departments must make safety an integral part of the operating organisation.
- (iii) **Analyse Accident records:** Accident reports for the past year or two should be analysed to earn, if possible, the how, who, where, when, and why of each accident.
- (iv) **Hold meetings of Operating Executives:** All supervisors, sectional heads and operating heads should then be summoned to a general meeting presided by chief of safety.

(v) **Organise Educational Work:** Formulate a programme to maintain interest and supply infomation on safety to management supervisors and workers.

Role of Safety Director. On man must be responsible for development and codification of safety information, counselling managerson safety implementation methods, and developing progress measurement data in every plant regardless of its size or the type of safety organisation. He may be called safety engineer, safety specialist, safety inspector, safety manager or safety director. The chief operating executive in effect directs the plant safety effort. A safety director's actual position in the plant organisation varies with the general organisation of the individual plant. The following are general functions performed by the safety director whether he is a line executive or head of a seprate department:

(i) Responsible for formulating and administering the safety programme.
(ii) Advice management on all safety matters.
(iii) Maintain accident records.
(iv) Supervise or advise on safety training.
(v) Personal plant inspection.
(vi) Co-ordinate with medical department.
(vii) Consult with other agencies on safety problems.

Good House-Keeping

It is essential wherever chemicals are stored or handled. Chemical burns caused by workers tripping or slipping while handling containers can after be avoided if floc.rs are kept in good repair and free from rigid system of orderliness in the plant and in the operations of the workers is essential to reduce the frequency of injuries. Labels, warning tags and clear instructions can prevent improper handling and storage of dangerous materials.

Controlling Atmosphere Hazards

Following are some of the factors reducing the dangers associated with atmospheric cartaininants.

(i) Substitute less hazardous compounds.
(ii) Revise process or operation.
(iii) Segregate hazardous process.
(iv) Provide local exhaust systems.
(v) Design, after, and maintain building and equipment to achieve better control.
(vi) Require personal protective equipment.
(vii) Educate employees to use established safe working methods.

For good housekeeping accumulations of dirt and refuse must be removed daily from floors and storage equipments. The cleaning policies turn around two be used.

How to clean might start or contract cleaners. The advantages of using contract cleaners appear to be; They have cleaning expertise; They can purchase cleaning materials more cheaply etc.

Housekeeping Check list

It may be useful to have a check list which covers all factors associated with health, safety and house keeping.

Cleaning

★ Do we accumulate dirt and waste for excessive periods before it is removed?
★ What cleaning policy?
★ Is it effective?

Ventilation

★ Is there appropriate ventilation? Does the ventilation provide sufficient are changes?

Lighting

★ Is the lighting sufficient for the tasks being performed?
★ Is the quality of lights appropriate?

Toilets and Washing facilities

★ Are sufficient provided per the factories Act?
★ Safety clothing and equipment
★ Do we provide adequate safety equipment for:
★ Welding
★ Use of abrasive wheels
★ Power presses
★ Use of toxic fluids.

Fire and safe access

★ Is the fire certificate up to date and in line with current factory layouts?
★ Do we have regular fire drill with the fire alarm sounded at least every three months?
★ Is fire fighting equipment supplied and well maintained?
★ Are employees instructed in how to fight a fire?

Welfare

★ Do we provide adequate:
★ Toilets and washing facilities
★ Dressing and drawing rooms
★ Water drinking facilities?

Chapter 36

STORES CONTROL FORMS AND STORES ACCOUNTING

Introduction

The mechanised materials control systems are frequently used because of the volume of transactions and number of items involved in industries. The three methods of punched card Materials Control system commonly used are:

(i) Balance-Forward Method

(ii) Unit record Method

(iii) Batch Method

Balance-Forward Method

A card is created for each classification of stock, say for 5000 items; 5000 cards would be required. Information carried on the cards will be; Item; Date; Opening Balance; Minimum Inventory; Re-order Paint; Receipts; Issues; Inventory On hand; On Order; Available. Prepunched cards can be employed to reduce the amount of punching required. The system must be maintained. Stock adjustment due to rotating counts or physical inventory can be made as they are identified. Also discrepancies in counts on issues; receipts etc. can be corrected as they are discovered. Periodic Reports such as shown in fig (36.1) can be generated by the balance-forward cards.

Unit Method

This method requires that a card be punched for each item in stock.

The Batch Method

The batch method permits the most complete machine processing. As issues or sales are made a copy of the issue slip or sales order is processed through key punch. The following information is contained relative to each issue:

(i) Customer Code

(ii) Quantity

(iii) Unit selling or Transfer price.

A Balance-Forward card is created by Batch rather than individually as in Balance-Forward Method described earlier.

Repeating Purchase Requisitions

Some companies have developed a repeating purchase requisition for stock material and parts which are ordered on a repetitive basis. This saves making out an individual requisition every time material is required. The heading is typed only when card is originally made up and lists all information regarding that particular part. Alternate Vendors, Price and Price breaks are shown in fig (36.3).

Receipt-and Inspection

In many companies receiving is a function of material control, although sometimes material control takes over after the materials are accepted. The basic receiving functions are unloadings and unpacking materials, checking materials against the purchase order and invoice, having any necessary inspection done, making out receiving and inspection reports, putting materials into standard containers and delivery the materials to store room. One copy of the receiving and inspection report is kept in receiving department and other go to the purchasing department and store room. Fig (36.4) is a typical receiving report.

The Fig (5) shows the most important forms used during the physical inventory viz Inventory tags and Inventory sheet. The tag method is considered as the best way of inventory materials since it provides a visible check of material which has been inventoried and is a convenient way to work to summary sheets and company records. The summary that form shown in fig (36.6) is suitable for all classes of materials when the tags are returned they should be checked in on the summary sheet and any missing tags posted to a sheet such as fig (36.7) so that a search can be made for the missing tags. Tags for work in process materials should clearly indicate the stage of completion or progression of that material.

Stores Requisitions. The important information on any materials or store requisition include the following:

(i) Description of item wanted.
(ii) Quantity wanted and unit of issue.
(iii) Point to which material should be delivered.
(iv) Date wanted.
(v) Charge or order number
(vi) Signature of person making out or authorizing requisition.
(vii) Date of signing
(viii) Initials or signature of person receiving material.
(ix) Initials of store keeper.

Simpler forms carry the above data, but often additional entires are needed. Fig (36.8) for example has space also for stores location new balance on the bin tag, amount issued, cost data, initials of store record clerk who may apportion material in advances of issue. Forms like there are used most frequently when the items come under different cost charge classifications and items are in different store rooms. But when the bill of material is required for a complete order, it can be conveniently arranged to serve as a group stores issue, as in case of an assembly order, a form similar to fig (36.9). This form is prepared as a master form which can be duplicated.

Reorder Schedule No						
Part No.	Description	In Stock	On Order	Total Available	Required For Schedule	Place Orders For

Fig 36.1 Periodic re-ordering schedule

Summary Stock Status Report

To .... Date ....

Item Code	Description	Opening Balance	Actual Transactions			Future Transactions		
			Recd	Issued	On Hand	On Order	Req'd	Not Committed

Fig 36.2 Summary Stock Status Report

Purchase Requisition

To .... REQ. NO. ....

Date ....

Please purchase the following items

Quantity	Description		

Ship to .... Date Required ....

Via ....

Signed .... Approved ....

Fig 36.3. Purchase Requisition

Receiving Report		No	
Received from:		Date .... P.O. No.	
Quantity	Description	Weight	Dept. Charged
Condition of Shipment: Order Complete			Partial ....
Delivered By Freight Charge			Reed By .... Checked By ....

Fig. 36.4. Recieving Report

INVENTORY 4059

Material Symbol ....

....

4059

Material Symbol ....

Description ....

....

Operations ....

Performed ....

Quantity .... Unit ....

Location ....

Counter By ....

Remarks ....

Date	Received After Count	issued After Count

Fig. 36.5 Inventory Tag

Date ....
Supervisor ....

Issued	Group & Location	Issued			Ret'd Used			Ret'd Unused		
		From	By	To	From	By	To	From	By	To

Fig. 36.6 Issues And Receipts of Inventory Tags.

Date ....
Supervisor ....

When Corrected, Cross out and initial in **Red** and post to Form 'A'

Ticket No.	Entry By	Store and Group	Tissue To	Remarks	Block of Tickets Returned	Checked

Fig. 36.7. Record of Missing Tag.

<table>
<tr><td colspan="4">Material Issue
CREDIT OR TRANSFER</td><td>Order No.
..............................</td></tr>
<tr><td>Deliver To</td><td>Shop Symbol</td><td>Name of Shop</td><td>Location</td><td>Credit
....
Date written
..............................</td></tr>
<tr><td colspan="4">Description (Units/Barrels/Coils) etc.</td><td>Date wanted
..............................</td></tr>
<tr><td colspan="4"></td><td>Unit wanted
..............................</td></tr>
<tr><td colspan="4"></td><td>Quantity wanted
..............................</td></tr>
<tr><td colspan="4"></td><td>Approved by
..............................</td></tr>
</table>

<table>
<tr><td rowspan="2">New Bal. Bin Tag</td><td colspan="2">Issued</td><td rowspan="2">Price</td><td rowspan="2">Stores Values</td><td rowspan="2">Handling</td><td rowspan="2">Total Cost</td></tr>
<tr><td>Quantity</td><td>Unit</td></tr>
<tr><td></td><td></td><td></td><td></td><td></td><td></td><td></td></tr>
</table>

Apportioned	Storekeeper	Balance Clerk	Cost Clerk	Material Received By

Fig. 36.8. Material Issue, Credit or Transfer Slip

Sheet No.	Bill of Material	Quantity	Assembly No
Assembly Name			

Part No.	Description	Req'd.	Del. to Deptt.	O.K.	Inventory code No.	Balance in stock	
						Cost	Amount

Remarks	Total This Sheet	
	Total Brought Forward	
	Total Material	
	Authorised by	Date ....
	Filled by	Date ....

Fig. 36.9 Assembly Bill of Materials for group Stores issue requisitioning

Stores Accounting

Materials costing is important in terms of the valuation of the cost of materials consumed by the production departments as well as in terms of the estimation of the value of materials help in stock.

Costing of the Receipt of Materials

Costing means classifying, recording and allocating the appropriate expenditure for determining the cost of product or services and the presentation of the suitable arranged data for the purpose of control and guidance of management. The factors that are to be included in the building up of the cost of the materials received are material price; freight charges, insurance and taxes. Price usually refers to the price quoted and accepted in the purchase orders. The freight costs incurred in transporting the goods are usually collected under a separate head. Goods in transit are mostly covered by insurance. All such insurance expenses must be calculated and added to the base coast and transportation cost. Under the miscellaneous head, we need to classify costs incurred by way of custom duties, taxes and packages. In brief, we can say that the coast of the materials received is equal to the price quoted less discount, plus fright, insurance, duties, taxes and packing charges.

Statistical determination of Costs

The process of budget preparation takes into account only one cost-variation factor: Level of operations. Other factors, however, can be of great significance also. Consider the impact on operations and manufacturing cost of introduction of one or more new products into processing during a given month or quarter. Similarly, consider the impact of such factors as the following; changes in size of production orders; changes in rate of labour turnover; Changes in quality of raw materials used, changes in machine process. All these factors reinforce or detract from the cost impact of the current level of operations. The management can improve its forecasts of future coasts and profits by such statistical determination of costs. Its budget will be more accurate and will conform more closely to actual results if operating conditions actually prevailing were correctly anticipated. It has been observed that management's increased cost knowledge will enable it better (i) To evaluate proposals for cost reduction, and (ii) to point out where it should make all efforts for cost reduction.

Costing of the Issues to Production Department

Some of the methods of costing are : First in First Out; Last in First out: Standard cost; Basket stock method; Market price at the time of issue; latest purchase price; Replacement or current cost are some of the methods used in costing the issues to production.

(i) **FIFO:** The assumption made in First-in First-out costing method is that the oldest stock is depleted first. Therefore the time of issues, the rate pertaining to that will be applied. This is logical in the case of items which deteriorate with time. In FIFO process, the value of the stocks held on hand is the money that has been paid for that amount of stock at latest price levels and hence can straightaway be used in balance sheet reflecting the true value.

(ii) **LIFO:** The assumption made in Last in First out is that the most recent receipts are issued first, we can apply LIFO system in a period of rising price. The latest prices are charged to the issues thereby leading to lower reported profits and hence saving in taxes. However the LIFO systems have the same disadvantages as that of the FIFO systems.

Average Cost Method

In this method, the issues to the production department are split into equal batches from each shipment at stock. It is a realistic method reflecting the price levels and stabilizing the cost figures. As more purchases are made, new average is computed and this average is applied to the subsequent issues.

Market Value Method

This method is also known as replacement rate costing. Here the materials that are issued are costed at the market rate prevailing at the time of issue. This method requires continuous monitoring of the market rates for all materials and hence it is unwieldy.

Standard Costs

In this method a standard rate is determined based on detailed analysis of market price and trends. Efficient use of materials is truly reflected by adopting this method as the accounting is divorced from fluctuations in rates. In this method the standard rate is kept fixed for a definite period of six month or more.

Costing the Closing Stock

In this method the guide line used here is that either the market price or stock at cost, is to be used, which ever is less. The factors which determine the cost of closing stock are price levels, obsolescence and deterioration. While evaluating the closing stock costs, some stock items, such as machinery spares, tools etc. tend to become obsolete earlier than others. In evaluating the cost of stocks, at the close, a provision therefore should be made to account for obsolesence.

Chapter 37

ORGANISATION OF MATERIALS CONTROL

Introduction

Providing raw materials and parts in proper quantities and when they are needed is one the major concerns of any manufacturing business. Unless this is done properly people will be idle and delivery promises will not be met. Therefore, it is virtually important to provide proper delineation of authority and responsibility for this function and to place in company's organisation structure that it will function most effectively. It is for this reason that the entire production planning and inventory control function is becoming systematised and in large companies computerised. The Fig (37.1) shows the inventory control module of the production planning control system in large size organisation. In this company order are entered or received and shipment follows from the available field stock. The orders are received centrally and through communication system the proper field warehousing is advised to ship the order. Data are kept on the following:

(i) Orders shipped complete
(ii) Orders shipped on time
(iii) Items not shipped or out of stock
(iv) How long items were out of stock.

Monitoring, Evaluation And Control

Monitoring is like a "watch dog" function which involves keeping a constant watch on any operation and giving a warning signal regarding any thing unexpected happens. The purpose of this warning is to enable the concerned executive agency to take corrective action either to remove the deviations or meet the situation caused by these deviation. **Monitoring therefore, can be defined as the process of watching during the implementation or execution** of a project, policy operation, activity etc.. the actual progress against what was planned, identifying deviations if any and informing the concerned agencies regarding there deviations with the object of evaluating them to know when action is required. It is generally advisable to entraust Monitoring and evaluation to a seprate unit distinct form the executive unit to ensure:

(i) The bias of execution unit should not come in objectivity of the system.
(ii) In the priority of line function the monitoring and evaluation functions should not get lost or neglected.

Customer Service Inventory Policy

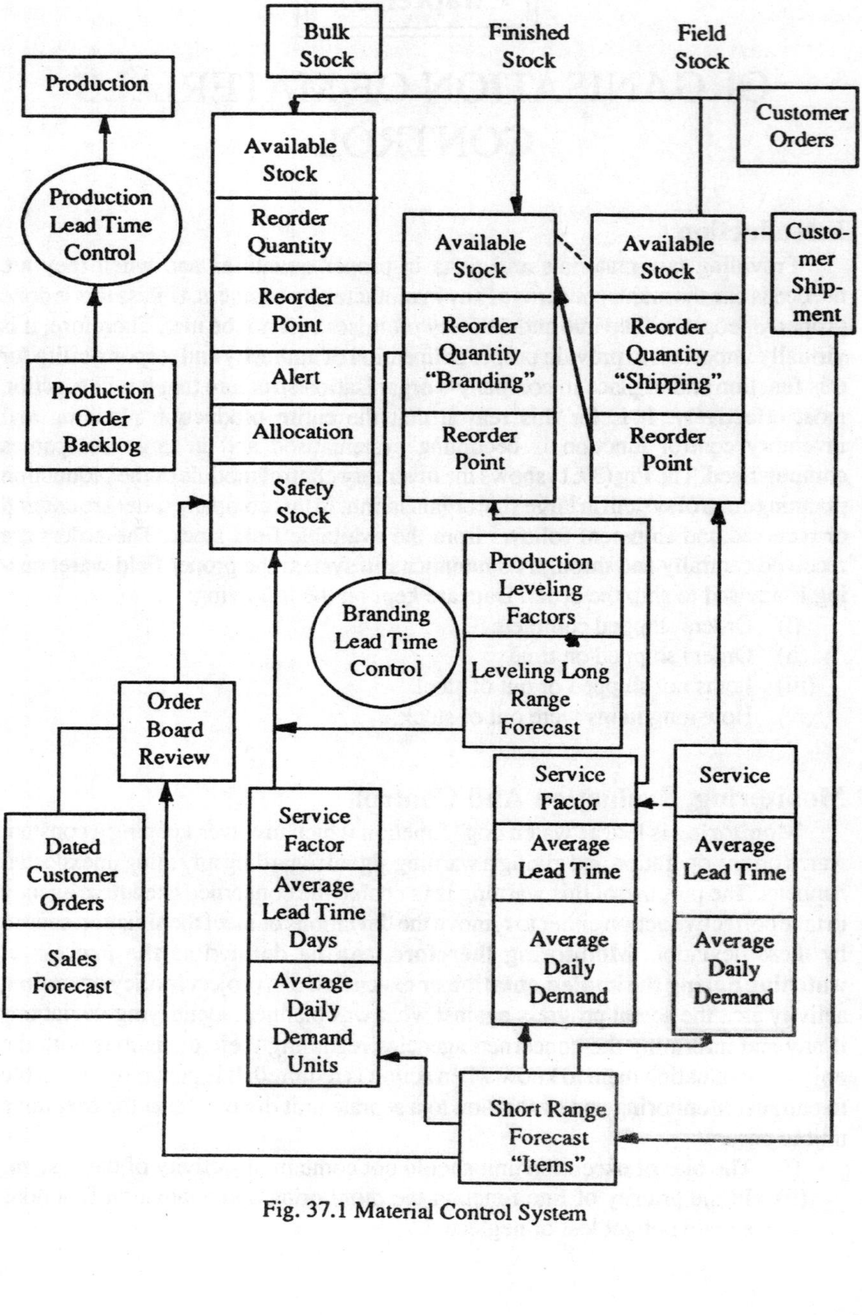

Fig. 37.1 Material Control System

(iii) The professional expertise and skills necessary for monitoring and evaluation should be inducted into the organisation.

Essentials Steps In Monitoring; Evaluation and Control

Monitoring should follow the following steps.

(i) Availability of a plan of action.
(ii) Continuous feed back on actual performance.
(iii) Comparison of actual performance with planned course of action.
(iv) Identifying on deviations
(v) Giving information an deviations.

Evaluation should follow the following steps:

(i) Analysis of deviations, the plans of action and performance.
(ii) Identifying alternative course of corrective action and applying judgement to evaluate them.
(iii) Suggesting the corrective action to the executive agencies.

Control should follow the following procedure

(i) Taking corrective action to overcome deviations and bring the performance back to the planned course of action.
(ii) Where necessary revise the plan and replan for the future.

Monitoring, evaluation and control are the senses of an organisation system which observe and act to keep the organisation on the track. Without an effective monitoring, evaluation and control organisation may slip from the desired or planned course, therefore for achieving the organisational goals and mission we must work out monitoring, evaluation and control system.

Management Control

It is the process by which managers assure that resource are obtained and used effectively and efficiently in the accomplishment of the organisation's goals. Management control system consists of a process and structure. The process is the set of actions that take place, and the structure is the organisational arrangements and information constructs that facilitate this process. Since managers are human beings, psychological considerations are dominant in management control. Activities such as communicating, persuading, exhorting, inspiring and criticising are important part of the process. Management control is the control that managers exercise over other managers.

Strategic Planning

It is the process of deciding on the goals of the organistion, on changes in these goals, on the resources used to attain these goals, and on the policies that are to govern the acquisition, use and disposition of these resources. The word strategy is used here in its usual sense of deciding on how to combine and employ resources. Thus, strategic planning is a process having to do with the formulation of long range strategic, policy type plans that change the character or direction of the organisation. Strategic planning is essentially irregular and usually relates to some part of the organisation. In strategic planning management works now on one problem, then on another, according to the needs and opportunities of the moment. Strategic planning relies heavily on external information viz on data collected from outside the company such as market analyses, estimates of costs and other factors involved in building a plant is a new locality, technological departments etc.

In the management control process the communication objectives, policies, guidelines, decisions and results throughout the organisation is extreemly applicable to economics, where as management control involves both economics and social psychology.

Operational Control

Operational control is the process of assuring that specific tasks are carried out effectively and efficiently. The focus of operational control is on individual tasks or transactions, scheduling and controlling individual jobs through a shop as contrasted with measuring the performance of the shop as a whole. As an example of an activity to which operational control is applicable, consider the inventory area as a whole, specific personnel action, as compared with personnel management and so on. If the demand for an item, the cost of storing it, its production cost and production time, and the loss involved is not filling an order are known, then optimum inventory level and optimum production or procurement schedule can be calculated. Even if there factors can not be known with certainty, sound estimates can be made, inventory levels and production or procurement schedules based on these estimates can be calculated and reasonable men will agree with the results of these calculations. As inventory control system using rules derived form such calculations is an example of operational control. By contrast, the legal department of a company provide the legal service which can not be measured in quality or even the quantity and no formula can show the amount of costs that should be incurred. Impressions as to the "right" amount of service, the "right" amount of cost and the "right" relationships between the service actually rendered and the cost actually incurred are strictly subjective. Yet the legal department as a part of the whole organisation must be controlled; the chief counsel must operate within the framework of policies prescribed by the management. The type of control in this situation is management control. The control of the whole accounting department is management control, even though operational control is appropriate for certain aspects of the work such as posting and cheque writing. The operational control uses exact data where as management control only needs approximations. The formal management control system is only a part of the management control process, actually a relatively unimportant past. The system can help to motivate the manager to make decisions that are in the best interest of the orgnisation that aids the manager in making these decisions, but many other stimuli are involved in motivating the manager and good information does not automatically produce good decision.

Management Control System

Management control process involves informal communication and interaction. In addition to the informal activities most of the organisations have a formal management control system. It consist of some or all of the following phases:

1. Programming
2. Budgeting
3. Operating and Accounting
4. Reporting and Analysis.

1. Programming: It is a process of deciding on the programs that the company will undertake and approximate amount of resources that are to be allocated to each programme. Programmes are the principal activities that the organisation has decided in order to implement thee strategies that it has decided upon.

2. Budgeting: A budget is a plan expressed in quantitative, usually monetary terms that covers a specified period of time usually one year. In addition to the monetary statements of plans, the plan for the year also includes a statement of objectives that are to be accomplished during the year. There objectives are usually expressed in non monetary terms. It prices regularly fluctuate around same mean, it is possible to beat the market with budgeting buying. The materials manager budgets regular amount to be spent for the material, regardless of its selling price. As a result the company automatically bus more when prices are low and less when they are high. A budgeted programme is successful only when materials manager can predict the average price that will prevail with reasonable accuracy. Despite its short comings, budgeted buying is a useful technique for certain commodities, especially when the materials manager is reasonably certain that the overall price trend will be.

3. The Materials Budget. Price performance is most directly related to overall company objectives when actual costs are compared with materials budget. The professionally managed organisations try to budget sales and costs at least a year ahead. Such projections help management evaluate over all performance in reaching profit and sales goals. The finance department works out the standard unit material costs for each product. The materials budget is then calculated by multiplying these standard costs by proposed production volume for each product. The performance is measured from the difference between actual costs and budgeted costs, (variance cost). Variance can arise both because the unit cost of material was different from the plan or because usage (or scarp) varied. The former is the materials manager's responsibility; the latter is the manufacturing manager's the management measure the materials departments performance based on the materials budget. However the materials budget has serious short comings for performance measurement. These include:

(i) **The materials budget includes only direct materials.** Most of the organisations spend substantial amount for indirect materials, which should not be overlooked in cost reduction programms.

(ii) **Actual costs show up in Variance Only after they are incurred.** It is due to the lag between the materials is ordered and the time it is finally used after having been in inventory.

(iii) **Variance does not indicate why Price changed.** IN the ogranisations, usually the price increases and decreases are balanced against on another and are not segregated. The costing department data is also not organised for item-by-item analysis. Yet this procedure is essential for good materials management.

Control of operating Costs

Management measure the performances of materials department and materials manager from how effectively they control operating costs for years. The assumption is that the materials department is a service activity and should be interested primarily in providing its service at the lowest possible cost. In some oganisations the assumption is materials department is a clerical activity and its performance should be measured in terms of how much it costs to process each purchase order. The finance department calculate the materials department's costs and divide them by number of forms its process. However it is a false concept. Control of operating costs is just one objective of materials department and not the most important one by any means. Nevertheless, control of operating cost is still a fairly important objective. Were there no control, costs would soon get out of hand. Operating costs should be budgeted as part of the overall materials plan. Performance can be measured in two ways.

(i) Measurement of productivity of the person employed in the materials department with either absolute or relative standards.

(ii) Measurement of success in controlling direct materilas department expenses by comparing actual costs with budgeting costs.

The materials manager rarely has any problem controlling his biggest operating expense: Wages and salaries. The materials manager gets his personnel budget approved and allows for salary adjustments. His performance will inevitably be satisfactory so long as he does not grant salary increases or increase his staff in excess of the budget. The other expenss are order to control. Travel and telephone expenses can easily get out of hand in a materials department, particularly if there are many unexpected quality and delivery problems with suppliers. A budget for each should be included in the overall purchase plan. For example, both telephone calls and travel expenses would tend to vary with rupee volume of purchases, the number of supplier and number of employees in the department. Similarly other expenses can be controlled in similar fashion.

3. Operating And Accounting

During the period of actual operations, records are kept of resources actually consumed and of revenues actually earned. Data classified according to programmes and by responsibility control and used as basis for future programming and to measure the performance of responsibility center managers.

4. Reporting And Analysis

The management control system serves as a communication device. This information keeps managers informed as to what is going on and helps to ensure that the work done by the seprate responsibility centers is co-ordinated. Based on the formal reports and also on information received through informal communication channels, managers decide what, if any action should be taken. They may decide to change the plan as set forth in the budget and this leads to a new planning process.